Principles of Economics

MICRO

Willis L. Peterson
Morse Distinguished Teaching Professor
Department of Applied Economics
University of Minnesota
St. Paul, MN 55108

Tenth Edition

Hobar Publications
3943 Meadowbrook Road
Minneapolis, MN 55426

ISBN 1-885079-01-X

Suggestions for Study

The social science called economics is commonly divided into two major parts: micro and macro. Microeconomics, the topic of this book, deals mainly with the spending decisions of households, the production decisions of business firms, and how prices and wages are determined in the product and input markets. In addition, some special topics—including the cost and returns of a college education, and how to allocate time efficiently—are covered toward the end of the book.

Macroeconomics, in a companion Macro text, is concerned largely with the problems of unemployment and inflation: what causes these economic problems and what can be done to mitigate or avoid them.

The general objective of this Micro text is to introduce you to the most important concepts in microeconomics, and to help you develop your skills in using these concepts to answer economic questions or to make economic decisions. In other words, major emphasis is on concepts and their applications, as opposed to factual or descriptive material.

To gain a good understanding of the material and to do well in the course, the following procedure is recommended. First read the assigned chapter thoroughly. Don't try to speed-read as you would a magazine or a novel. The chapters are rather compact; most are designed to be read in 45 minutes to an hour. But each is packed with ideas or concepts. So take your time. After reading each chapter, refer back to the "key concepts" at the beginning of the chapter to help draw out the main points. Then try your hand at the self-test, answering the questions as you would on an ordinary exam without looking back at the material. After completing the self-test, you may want to refer back to the material to see if you made any mistakes. Also you can further your understanding of the material by answering the end-of-chapter discussion questions. Good luck and enjoy your exploration into economics.

Willis L. Peterson

CONTENTS

PART VI ■ MARKET TOPICS

Part I

Introduction

_____

Chapters 1-3

Chapter 1

Economic Decisions and Questions

Key Concepts

Micro and macro economics

Scarcity

Economic decisions

Theory

The three economic questions

Market economy

Private sector

Public sector

Centrally planned economy

This is a get-acquainted chapter. After a brief introduction of what economics is and why we study it, there is a short discussion on the nature of economic decisions and the usefulness of theory. The second half of the chapter provides an overview of how resources are allocated in a market economy and in a centrally planned (Communist) society.

WHAT IS ECONOMICS?

Economics has been defined as "what economists do." While this is not a very helpful definition, it does show that economics encompasses an array of human activities, and it is not possible to adequately define the field with a single sentence.

In general terms, economics is a social science that deals with the behavior of people. The aim of economics is to help people obtain the greatest possible satisfaction or utility out of the resources at their disposal—to do the best they can with what they have. Economics also is concerned with increasing the amount of resources available to people—economic growth—and with how income is distributed.

As economics developed into a discipline, two major areas of study emerged: micro and macro. Microeconomics is concerned mainly with the economic activities of individual consumers and producers, or groups of consumers and producers known as markets. In the area of consumer behavior, major emphasis is given to the question of how consumers can maximize their utility or satisfaction, given their tastes and income levels. Consumer behavior also is related to the concept of demand for goods and services. Producers or business firms represent the supply side of the economy. Here we will see how producers can minimize costs for a given level of output and how they determine the level of output that will maximize their profits. Producer behavior is then translated into the supply of goods and services. Markets consist of buyers and sellers. The interaction of buyers and sellers in markets establishes the prices of goods and services, as well as of productive resources such as labor and capital. In microeconomics, considerable emphasis is given to price determination in both the product and resource markets—how prices are established and why they change.

Macroeconomics, on the other hand, is concerned with economic aggregates, or the economy as a whole. The two major problem areas of macroeconomics are unemployment and inflation. These areas are of great concern to individuals, but they are also problems over which the individual has relatively little control. Both the causes and the solutions to these problems tend to lie in the realm of government action, which affects the entire economy.

It would be a mistake, however, to conclude that the micro and macro areas are distinct or unrelated fields of study; there is a certain amount of overlap. For example, we will see in later chapters that much of what the government does in enacting laws or levying taxes directly affects individuals and markets, and these effects can be analyzed with the tools of microeconomics. However, the actions of large groups of individuals. such as the increased desire to save on the part of many people, are analyzed with macroeconomic concepts.

Because it is impossible to completely separate the micro from the macro, some economists argue that more appropriate labels would be *price theory* instead of microeconomics and *monetary and income and employment theory* rather than macroeconomics. In more advanced courses, particularly at the graduate level, microeconomic principles are generally referred to as price theory, mainly because the material deals with the determination of prices and their effect on the output and input mix in the economy.

THE PROBLEM OF SCARCITY

In studying economics, as in any other activity, we like to have some reason for exerting effort. We attend the theater or go to a ball game because it is enjoyable. We attend school to learn or to make it possible to have a job and earn a living. But why study economics?

There may be a few people who would be willing to study economics purely for the enjoyment it brings. For most, however, learning economics is not 100 percent entertainment. Mastering a subject provides a certain amount of intellectual satisfaction, but it is hard to justify economics on only this basis. Crossword puzzles or chess might do as well or better on this score. The social science of economics must rest on a different foundation. I have posed this question to my students and so far all have been too kind (or too smart) to say that we study economics because it is a required subject. Why is it required?

The answer can be simplified to a single word—*scarcity*. Human wants are greater than the resources available to satisfy them. In fact, economists traditionally have argued that human wants are unlimited or insatiable. At first you may find this hard to believe. Surely there is some level of income or standard of living where one would be completely satiated. But if you spend a few minutes making a list of the goods and services that you wouldn't mind having, chances are that their purchase would put a billionaire in a financial bind. Of course, you need not limit your list to the familiar private-sector goods and services, such as housing, cars, or vacation trips. You might want to include cleaner air and water, or a comfortable and convenient public transportation system.

Suppose by some stroke of magic that all the items on your list were supplied. Would you be completely satisfied or satiated? Probably not—especially if everyone else also were granted his or her fondest wishes. Human nature being what it is, we always seem to be just a little dissatisfied with what we have. A new compact car may satisfy for a time, but eventually we give admiring glances to a Mercedes or a BMW. In addition, we must remember that entirely new goods and services, many of which do not even exist in our imagination, will be developed and come on the market in the future. A dream list prepared by your great-grandparents would not have contained most of the items on your list because they were not imagined at that time.

It is less difficult to envision the scarcity of resources at our disposal. In recent years, attention has been drawn to the day when our nonrenewable natural resources, especially fossil fuels, will be exhausted. Although less newsworthy, it is important to realize that most resources, including land area, labor, and physical capital such as buildings and machines, are in limited supply. Being finite, these resources can produce only a finite amount of goods and services.

Since human wants are greater than the resources to satisfy these wants, people must decide what they will produce and what they will forgo. In other words, we are forced to make economic decisions.

ECONOMIC DECISIONS

We must make these decisions (or, if you wish, economize) from the time we are aware of the world around us. This harsh reality becomes apparent the first time a child stands in front of a candy counter, clutching a quarter. The coin might buy a candy bar, a package of gum, or a roll of Life-Savers, but not all three. An economic decision must be made.

It would be misleading, though, to conclude that economic decisions all involve money. Probably the best example of a nonmonetary economic decision is how we allocate our time—a scarce resource that seems to become scarcer as we become older. The student must decide if he or she will spend the evening studying mathematics or history, or even more fundamentally, whether to devote time to study or leisure. Allocating time to its best use is one of the most important economic decisions we make. It is one of the more important experiences gained in college.

More traditional types of economic decisions involve the operations of households and firms. For the household, a continuing array of economic decisions must be made on how to allocate the weekly or semimonthly paycheck. How much money goes to housing, food, clothing, transportation, entertainment, and so forth? Managing a modest income for a family requires thousands of economic decisions each year.

Considering the complexity of a household's economic decisions, we can appreciate the decisions that must be made in managing a business. What items should the firm produce? Should it specialize or diversify? Should it produce a large volume and sell at a low price or produce less and charge more? How do the decisions of rival firms affect each business? Should the firm employ more labor and save on machines, or should it substitute machines for labor? These are some examples of economic decisions each manager must make. How well these decisions are made largely determines the success or failure of the firm.

The need to make economic decisions does not stop at the level of the household or the firm. Economic decisions must be made at all government levels, ranging from local governments, such as townships and municipalities, to the states and to the federal government. Perhaps the most basic of these economic decisions concerns how much of the total production of society is provided through the public sector and how much is provided through the private sector. In a democracy, government decisions tend to reflect the broad wishes of society, but they cannot please everyone. People of a more conservative philosophy tend to desire a greater share of production in the private sector, while persons of a more liberal bent stress the need for more public goods and services.

Once society settles on a mix between public and private goods, it must decide what kinds of public goods and services should be produced. For example, what is the appropriate mix between military and nonmilitary public goods? Should we have fewer weapons and greater public expenditures for slum clearance, public parks, pollution control, and so forth? Economic decisions involving governments or nations have this in common with the decision made by the child at the candy counter: Both require making a choice among alternatives involving as little as a quarter or as much as billions of dollars.

THE USEFULNESS OF THEORY

Economic theory has suffered from a bad press for many years, and not entirely without justification. Students tend to be turned off by theory because they visualize dry, abstract material that has little relevance to their world. But theory does not have to be dry or irrelevant. In fact, little is to be gained by theory if it cannot help in making day-to-day economic decisions or in resolving economic problems.

A theory is an abstraction or simplification of the real world. It encompasses only the important information bearing on a decision, question, or problem. The main value of theory is that it provides a framework for thinking. We need such a framework because the world is too complex to account for every bit of information that affects a decision or problem, and we have to sort out important from unimportant knowledge. But information does not come in neat categories labeled "important" and "unimportant," nor is it always obvious which is which.

For example, some goods and services increase in price during their peak seasons, such as Christmas cards and hotel rooms on Miami Beach. Other products decrease in price during the time of year they are most actively bought and sold—such as fresh fruits and vegetables in the northern states. For some commodities, price rises when the quantity exchanged increases; for others, it declines when the quantity increases. To the person untrained in economics, there may appear to be little order in markets. But, after gaining an understanding of the theories of demand and supply (by the end of Chapter 12), you will be able to explain such phenomena and even predict future changes in price and the quantity of goods and services. In the latter sense, theory serves as a sort of crystal ball.

Theory has come to be known by a number of names. One synonym is *principle*, as in the title of this book. A theory is also sometimes referred to as a *model*, probably because theory represents and predicts reality without necessarily duplicating it exactly or in detail.

In the use of economic theory, it is common to see the phrases *other things equal* or *other things constant*. To simplify reality, it is useful to consider the effect of one factor at a time—holding everything else constant. This practice allows us to focus our attention on a specific point, pushing into the background other factors or bits of information, even though they may also be an important part of the theory. In the real world there may be a number of important factors operating simultaneously. But if we tried to incorporate all of them at once into the analysis, it soon would become too complex to be useful. Thus, *the other things equal* phrase is not an attempt to distort the real world but an attempt to better understand and predict the world's events by making the theory more manageable and more powerful.

THREE ECONOMIC QUESTIONS

Regardless of its economic organization—capitalism or communism, rich or poor, large or small—every society must answer three basic economic questions:
1. What and how much of each good should be produced?
2. How should each good be produced?
3. For whom?

A major share of this book deals with these three economic questions. In the rest of this chapter, we will introduce how these three questions are answered in three different economic settings: (1) the private sector of a market economy, (2) the public sector of a market economy, and (3) a Communist or centrally planned economy.

THE MARKET ECONOMY

A. The Private Sector

In the private sector of a market economy, the three basic economic questions are answered by markets. Markets consist of two groups of people: buyers and-sellers. Buyers represent the demand side of a market, and sellers the supply side.

All markets have a demand and a supply. The interaction of demand and supply establishes a price for every good and service. In this kind of economic setting, there are thousands of markets, establishing thousands of prices for the thousands of goods and services bought and sold.

To see how markets answer the three basic economic questions, let us consider a simple economy having just two goods: bread and circuses. The production of these goods is carried on using three inputs or resources: land, labor, and capital (machines).

If we cut in at a point in time, the amount of each item produced and sold per year depends on several factors. Perhaps most basic is the number of people who reside in this simple economy. The greater the number of people, the greater the demand for each. Of course, most people are producers or suppliers as well as demanders. Thus, the greater the population the greater the supply of each good.

Another important factor determining the quantity of each good exchanged in the market is its price. Buyers or users like low prices, whereas sellers or suppliers like high prices, at least for the items they sell. Markets establish prices that are a compromise between the wishes of buyers and sellers.

Returning to the simple bread and circuses society, consider what happens when there is a change in the demand for one of the goods. Suppose people decide they are consuming too many calories but not enough excitement. As a consequence they decide to buy less bread and more circuses. The decrease in the demand for bread, causes a decrease in its price, and bread becomes less profitable to produce. Conversely, tickets to the circus come into greater demand and become more expensive.

This change in the relative prices of bread and circuses precipitates further changes. Farming and baking become less profitable. Sons and daughters of farmers and bakers run off to join the circus where their services are now in greater demand and enjoy higher prices. Gradually the amount of bread produced in the economy decreases and the number of circuses increases. This is how the private sector of a market economy answers the "what" and "how much" question.

The second, or "how" question is answered in much the same way. Suppose the bread and circuses society prospers such that the price of labor increases relative to the price of capital (machines). This is what has happened to the world's more highly developed countries over the past couple of centuries. The higher price of labor provides an incentive for producers to save on the high-priced labor by utilizing more machines. Farmers buy more and larger machines to produce the wheat, and bakers install automatic ovens and bread- wrapping devices. The economy is transformed from a labor-intensive to a capital-intensive means of production. This answers the "how" question. Notice that prices play an important role in answering both the first and second questions.

Regarding the "for whom" question, everyone in the bread and circuses society is free to buy as much or as little of the two goods as they wish. How much each buys depends on several factors. Income is an important one. People with high incomes can claim a larger share of society's output than their poor relations. If a society does not think the poor are able to purchase the basic necessities of life, it may try to transfer income from the rich and middle class to the poor. In our simple society, the poor may receive bread stamps paid for by taxes on those with higher incomes. Circus stamps are less likely.

B. The Public Sector

In the United States, about one-third of the total output is purchased and distributed by various agencies of the federal, state, and local governments. Thus, it is important to consider each of our three economic questions from the standpoint of the so-called public sector. The goods and services purchased and distributed by the public sector tend to be those that do not lend themselves to individual purchase and use. *Public goods* are goods and services produced and/or distributed by government for society's use. They are so called because they don't lend themselves to private purchase or use. The major public goods include the military, police and fire protection, streets and highways, waste and water treatment, the postal service, and public parks. The government also provides regulatory services such as law enforcement, labeling, keeping harmful products off the market, and reducing pollution, with the aim of improving the working of the market economy. In addition, the government plays an important role in subsidizing the purchase of certain goods and services such as education, and in transferring income to certain people through the various welfare programs and the social security program.

In a democracy, the short-run decisions of what and how much of each public good is to be produced are made by elected officeholders and their appointed officials. Of course, over the long run the general public has the final say because in a democracy elected officeholders serve at the discretion of the electorate. Different people have different ideas regarding the proper kinds and amounts of public goods. People with a conservative political philosophy tend to prefer fewer public goods (with the possible exception of the military) and less government influence over private decisions than do their more liberal counterparts. Thus, the actual kinds and amounts of public goods produced tend to be a compromise between different wants.

The preference for public goods also is likely to be influenced by the incidence of benefits and costs. People who perceive the benefits of public goods to be small relative to the taxes they pay will likely favor a reduction in the production of such goods, or at least a slowing down of their growth. On the other hand, people who benefit from government spending more than in proportion to the taxes they pay are more likely to favor increased government spending, or at least no reduction in such spending.

In the United States and most other market economies, the actual production of most public goods is carried out by private firms under contract to the government. For example, aircraft companies produce the nation's military aircraft, and construction companies build the highways and dams. However, in the case of services, most people providing services—such as military personnel, teachers, postal workers, and regulatory personnel—are employed by government agencies.

There is a class of goods and services that falls somewhere between the public and private goods categories. These are called *public utilities;* examples include local power and light or telephone companies. Goods and services provided by these companies generally are purchased by individuals in the marketplace, so in this sense they resemble private goods. But for reasons that will become clear in a moment, society has decided that the normal production of these goods by many firms in each area would not be desirable. Thus, the government regulates their production, and in this sense public utilities resemble public goods.

The main reason for having public utilities is to avoid a costly duplication of facilities and services. Suppose, for example, there were several electric power companies serving a given locality. If each company owned its own power lines, the duplication would increase costs over what would exist if just one set of lines served each street. The same is true for each local telephone company. Natural gas also is commonly supplied by privately owned public utilities. For other goods and services, such as the postal service and city water and sewers, ownership is vested in governmental agencies.

In recent years, there has been increasing pressure to inject more competition among public utilities and publicly owned enterprises. The breakup of AT&T reflects this trend. The U.S. Postal Service is under increasing pressure to allow private firms to compete for the first-class mail business. Private firms are delivering an increasing share of packages and third-class mail. Electronic mail and fax machines add an additional element of competition for the postal service.

By giving a business exclusive rights to operate, the government makes a public utility a virtual monopoly, free from the competitive forces in the market. To guard against excessive prices or inferior service to the public, the government also regulates these firms by setting the prices they charge and establishing standards of performance.

THE CENTRALLY PLANNED ECONOMY

When Communist governments ruled the former Soviet Union and its satellites in Eastern Europe, their economic system was described as central planning. Under this system the three economic questions were answered by the government instead of markets. In the former Communist countries, resources were owned and controlled by the government and people were employed by the government. The governnment, really the central planning committe, an agency of the government, decided what and how much of each good and service was to be produced. The government issued annual quotas to factories and farms, instructing them how much production was expected during each year.

Prices of goods and services and resources were also set by the government rather than by markets. The ability to set price was a powerful force in the hands of government. By manipulating prices, the authorities were able to entice people to change their behavior in line with the wishes of the government. For example, if the government wanted people to eat more bread and less meat, they lowered bread prices and raised meat prices.

Price manipulation did not eliminate all problems, however. If the price of a good did not correspond to the price people wished to pay for the quantity produced, either a shortage or a surplus was created. If the price was set lower than would have existed in a free market, a shortage was created; people had to wait in line to purchase a limited amount, and black market activities and bribery emerged. Conversely if price was set higher than would have existed in a free market, unsold stocks accumulated.

The question of how goods and services were to be produced also was answered by the central planning committee. By setting quotas for the production of machines or capital, the planners implicitly determined the capital-labor mix in the economy. However, the actual use of capital fell short of its potential due to the problem of spare parts. Some machines had to be cannibalized for parts in order to keep others running. For some reason, the production of spare parts did not rank high on the agenda of the planners. Perhaps parts were less visible than machines, and once the machines were produced they became someone else's problem.

The "for whom" question received high priority in the central planning economies, and provided much of the motivation for the adoption of this system in the first place. The communist system resulted in a more equal distribution of income than a capitalist or market economy. Because individuals did not own capital such as land, buildings, and machines, there was no income from property, a source of income inequality. Also these governments set wages in a narrower range than typically exist in a free labor market. In the Soviet Union, tractor drivers earned more than medical doctors, but neither earned a high salary by western standards. In addition, these governments subsidized the prices of some basic necessities including housing, food, and medical care. The government derived its income from the ownership of capital and paying workers less than what they produced.

Achieving greater equality of income and wealth came at a high cost, however. These were both economic and noneconomic. The economic cost was due in part to the loss of efficiency inherent in the centralized planning process. A small group of central planners no matter how intelligent cannot know the billions of bits of information that bear on the billions of economic decisions made each year. Kiev mathematicians once calculated that to plan in detail just one year's production in the Ukraine would require the entire world's population for 10,0000 years! In other words, it cannot be done. Colossal waste and misallocation of resources resulted from the system including the waste of human talent and creativity. Granted, decision makers in capitalist economies also make mistakes. But being closer to the point where decisions have their impact, both physically and intellectually, increases the accuracy and availability of information, thereby reducing the possibility of major mistakes.

Lack of incentives in centrally planned economies was another economic problem. Few people outside of the higher echelons of government harbored any illusions of ever getting rich. Perhaps more important, there was no room in the Communist system for entrepreneurship. As a result, these societies did not receive full benefit from those citizens who had the talent for creating new and better products, or devising innovative and less costly ways of carrying on production.

In the realm of noneconomic costs, the loss of personal freedom must rank highest, at least by those who value freedom. Restrictions on religion, choice of occupation, travel, place of residence, political dissent, as well as the lack of consumer goods and housing were sources of both fear and anger among people living in Communist countries. These governments held power only through the use of brute force exercised by the military and the secret police.

The transition from a centrally planned to a market economy has created even more hardship for the people of the former Soviet Union and Eastern Europe. Because such a transition has never before been done, there is no clear idea of how it should proceed. Some people believe it should be done quickly, discard the old institutions, and let markets take over the task of allocating resources to their most productive uses. Others would prefer a longer term adjustment process allowing time for markets and new institutions to evolve before the old institutions are abandoned completely. Whichever approach is taken one should expect a chaotic situation to exist for years to come. Initially, real per capita income will decline for many. In the long run, however, as markets evolve, private property is established, and incentives created, economic growth should far exceed what would have taken place under the old system. The wide difference of per capita incomes between West and East Germany when the two countries united illustrates the failure of central planning to achieve sustained economic growth.

Equally important is the disappearance of the fear factor, so prevalent in Communist societies. In a democratic, market oriented system, people do not have a fear of the midnight knock on the door by the secret police, and death or imprisonment for expressing their political views. It is not easy to put a price on freedom but the fact that many people were willing to risk their lives and leave behind friends and family, and all their material possessions in an attempt to flee Communism suggests that people value freedom highly. Freedom is not measured by per capita income.

QUESTIONS

1. What is an economic decision and why is it necessary for everyone to make economic decisions?
2. Of what use is economic theory in making economic decisions?
3. What are the three economic questions that must be answered by every society?
4. a. What role do market prices play in answering the first two of the three economic questions?
   b. What determines how much of the output of the private sector a person can claim?
5. Suppose there is a sudden cutoff of oil from the Middle East, as occurred in the 1970s. Trace the effects of this disruption in a market economy.
6. a. What is the main argument used to justify a centrally planned economy?
   b. What are the main problems of this economy?
7. Suppose your instructor announces during the first class that everyone, regardless of performance on exams, will receive a C in the course. How would you react? Now compare the analogy to the entire economy.
8. What factors contributed to the collapse of communism in Eastern Europe?

SELF-TEST

1. Which of the following topics is (are) included in the study of microeconomics?
   a. how consumers maximize utility
   b. how producers maximize profits
   c. how prices are established
   d. all of the above
2. Economics exists:
   a. to provide employment for economists.
   b. to provide intellectual stimulus for students and teachers.
   c. because human wants exceed the resources available to satisfy these wants.
   d. because the ability to produce exceeds the ability to purchase, thereby causing employment.
3. Which of the following involve making an economic decision?
   a. how to allocate one's income across a variety of alternatives
   b. the allocation of study time between economics and other courses
   c. deciding whether to attend a basketball game or go to a movie
   d. all of the above
4. Economic theory is like a movie or stage play because:
   a. it draws attention to the important information bearing on making a decision or solving a problem.
   b. it provides entertainment for both students and teachers.
   c. it is a mystery to most people.
   d. it has little economic value to society.
5. Which of the following is not one of the three economic questions that every society must answer?
   a. What and how much of each good should be produced?
   b. How much employment and inflation to have?
   c. How should each good be produced?
   d. For whom should the output be produced?
6. In the private sector of a market economy, which of the following provides the information and the incentives to act on it in

regard to what and how much of each good should be produced?

a. the government

b. prices

c. farmers

d. bakers

7. In the private sector of a market economy, prices are established by:

a. the government.

b. markets.

c. sellers.

d. the central planning committee.

8. Markets are made up of:

a. buyers.

b. sellers.

c. members of the U.S. central planning committee.

d. a and b.

9. In the simple bread-and-circuses economy, the desire on the part of consumers to buy more entertainment and less calories was made known by the _____ in the price of circus tickets and by the _____ in the price of bread.

a. increase; decrease

b. decrease; increase

c. increase, increase

d. decrease; decrease.

10. The change in the relative prices of bread and circuses described in question 9 made farming and baking _____ profitable and the circus business _____ profitable.

a. more; less

b. less; more

c. more; more

d. less; less

11. The change in the profitability of farming and baking and the circus business described in question 10 resulted in a(n) _____ in bread production and a(n) _____ in the number of circuses.

a. increase; decrease

b. decrease; increase

c. increase; increase

d. decrease; decrease

12. As the simple bread-and-circuses economy prospered, the price of labor (wage rate) _____ relative to the price of machines. This change in the relative prices of labor and machines (capital) resulted in more _____ intensive production techniques for both bread and circuses.

a. increased; labor

b. decreased; labor

c. increased; capital

d. decreased; capital

13. The developed countries utilize _____ intensive production techniques because in these countries capital is _____ relative to labor in comparison to the less developed countries.

a. capital; cheap

b. labor; cheap

c. capital; expensive

d. labor; expensive

14. In a market economy, goods and services are produced for those people who have:

a. the greatest political influence

b. the money to purchase them.

c. the greatest need.

d. ration coupons.

15. In the private sector of a market economy, _____ determines how much of each good a person can consume. Most societies have enacted policies or programs enabling their low-income people to increase their consumption of _____

a. the government; necessities

b. income; necessities

c. the government; luxuries

d. income; luxuries

16. Which of the following is not a public good?

a. military

b. food

c. streets and highways

d. police and fire protection

17. Public utilities:
    a. sell public goods.
    b. are firms owned by the government.
    c. are given exclusive right to operate in a market to avoid duplication of facilities.
    d. are publicly owned firms that provide competition for those that are privately owned.

18. In centrally planned economies, resources were allocated to alternate uses by _____. This system has turned out to be _____ efficient than the process employed by market economies.
    a. relative prices; more
    b. the government; more
    c. relative prices; less
    d. the government; less

19. Centrally planned (Communist or Socialist) economies have fallen out of favor throughout the world because of:
    a. restriction on personal freedom.
    b. inability to achieve acceptable economic growth.
    c. high-level corruption among members of the ruling class (the government bureaucracy).
    d. all of the above.

Chapter 2

How to Read Graphs

Key Concepts

Positive relationships

Negative relationships

Linear

Curvilinear

Graphing numbers

Slope of a line

In studying economics, graphs are frequently used to convey concepts or ideas. In a way, a graph is a picture of an idea. While the cliché "a picture is worth a thousand words" may exaggerate a bit, a graph provides a precise means of expressing an idea.

All graphs presented in this book are of two dimensions; they express a relationship between two variables. Therefore, each graph has two axes—vertical and horizontal. When drawing or viewing a graph, it is important to specify or ascertain what each axis represents.

A graph can convey either a positive or a negative relationship between the two variables. A positive relationship exists when both variables move in the same direction. Both either increase or decrease, as illustrated by panels A through C of Figure 2–1. Positive relationships are graphed with upward-sloping lines. There is a negative relationship when the two variables move in opposite directions—one increases and the other decreases as illustrated by panels A through C of Figure 2–2. These graphs have downward-sloping lines.

POSITIVE RELATIONSHIPS

A. Linear

Figure 2–1A illustrates a *linear positive relationship* between the two variables—nickels and dimes. The line represents the number of nickels and dimes that have equal value: one dime equals two nickels, and so on. In this graph, the upward-sloping line comes out of the origin. It is possible for such lines to begin at a point on either the vertical or horizontal axis.

B. Curvilinear

Panels B and C of Figure 2–1 represent a curvilinear positive relationship between the two variables—points obtained on an examination and the number of study hours used to prepare for the exam. In panel B, hours are on the vertical axis and points are on the horizontal axis. The graph shows that 10 points out of a maximum 100 are obtained with zero study; 5 hours yields 80 points, and a perfect score (100 points) is obtained with 10 hours of study. Also note that it takes more and more time to obtain each additional point the closer the student gets to a perfect score. In the first few hours of study, the easy material is learned, but a perfect score requires the mastery of the more difficult material that takes more time to grasp. While a graph cannot prove that this relationship holds true in all cases, it is reasonable to believe that it usually exists. Notice that in panel B the line increases at an increasing rate. When it reaches 100 on the horizontal axis, it becomes vertical. After 10 hours of study, more study time will not increase points because 100 is the maximum.

Figure 2–1 Positive Relationships

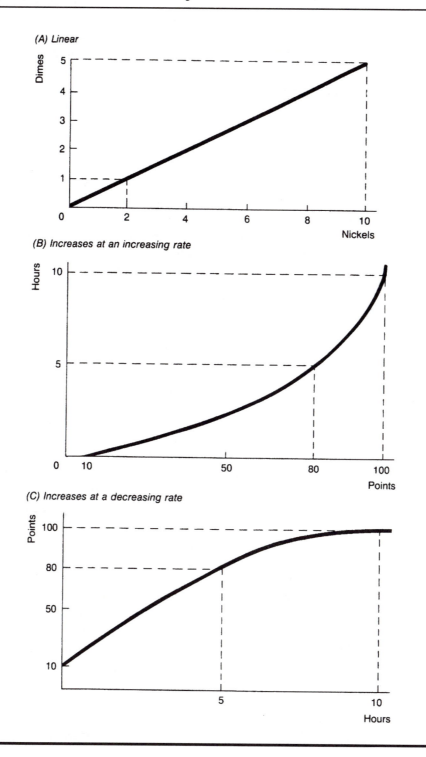

Panel C graphs the same two variables except the variable represented on each axis is switched—hours of study now are on the horizontal axis and points on the vertical axis. This line increases at a decreasing rate. After 10 hours and 100 points, the line becomes horizontal. Notice also that the same two variables can yield differently shaped graphs simply by changing the label on each axis.

NEGATIVE RELATIONSHIPS

A. Linear

A *linear negative relationship* is illustrated between the two variables in panel A of Figure 2–2. The number of hours a person is awake each day is graphed against the number of sleep hours obtained. The two must add up to 24. At the point where the line intersects the vertical axis, the person is sleeping 24 hours and awake zero hours. The converse is true at the intersection of the horizontal axis. It is hard to imagine either extreme. Therefore, it is not necessary for a downward-sloping line to intersect the two axes. The relevant area may be only a portion in the middle of the line—say between 4 and 10 hours of sleep and 20 and 14 hours of awake time.

B. Curvilinear

Curvilinear negative relationships are illustrated by panels B and C of Figure 2–2. Panel B represents the relationship between points on an economics exam and points on a math exam. Let's say that both tests are given on the same day and that only 10 hours of study are available for the two. To have the graph intersect the two axes, assume that with zero hours of study, zero points are earned on each exam. Therefore, at the point of intersection on the vertical axis, 100 points are earned on the econ test and zero points on the math quiz. As the student takes a little time away from economics and devotes it to math, the math score rises by a larger amount than the econ score decreases. This is consistent with the example in panels B and C of Figure 2–1 where it took more time to learn the hardest material than the easiest. Therefore, if only one or two hours are taken away from econ and given to math, only a few points of the relatively hard econ material is given up but more points are earned on the math quiz because the easiest material is learned first. At the other extreme, the last few hours taken from econ causes a large loss of points compared to what is gained in math. A graph that bends out and away from the origin is called concave to the origin. Such a line decreases at an increasing rate.

Panel C of Figure 2–2 decreases at a decreasing rate. Such a line, which bends in toward the origin, is called convex to the origin. This line might represent a ski jumper coming off a ski jump. At the point where the line intersects the ver-

Figure 2–2 Negative Relationships

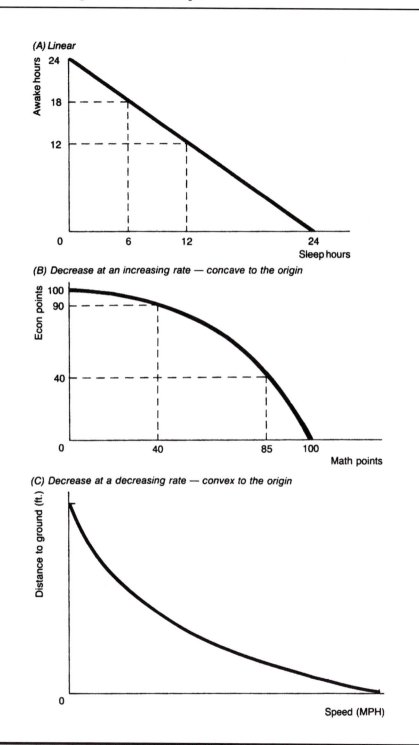

(A) Linear

(B) Decrease at an increasing rate — concave to the origin

(C) Decrease at a decreasing rate — convex to the origin

tical axis, the ski jumper is ready to push off. Distance to the ground is at a maximum and speed is zero. Coming down the slide, distance to the ground decreases rapidly at first, and then decreases at a decreasing rate. At the point where the skier first touches the ground, speed is at a maximum. It is not necessary for the graph of a line convex to the origin to intersect either or both axes, although in this example, it does.

Graphs may or may not imply a cause-and-effect relationship between the two variables. In panels B and C of Figure 2–1, and panel B of Figure 2–2, it was implied that the amount of study time influences the grades on examinations. In other words, study is a cause and grades are an effect. The other panels show a relationship between two variables. Most of the graphs used in economics imply some kind of cause-and-effect relationship.

GRAPHING NUMBERS

The preceding sections illustrated how specific values of the variables represented on the two axes can be determined from a graph or diagram. It should be stated, however, that the graphs are determined from numbers rather than the other way around. That is, one must obtain or be given specific values of the two variables before a graph can be drawn. In this section the numerical relationships that give rise to the various graphs discussed above are presented.

A. Positive Relationships

1. Linear. An example of numbers that yield a linear positive relationship is given below.

Vertical axis	0	2	4	6	8
Horizontal axis	0	4	8	12	16

The preceding numbers would graph an upward-sloping line starting at the origin. (It is not necessary that all such lines start at the origin.) Notice that both variables move in the same direction—both go up or both go down. Because the difference between the numbers on both axes remains constant over the array, the graph will be a straight line. The vertical axis variable changes by two units each step, and the variable shown on the horizontal axis changes by four units. Both variables do not have to change by the same number of units each step, but the change of each variable must remain constant in each step over the array.

2. Slopes Up at an Increasing Rate.

Vertical axis	2	4	7	11	16
Horizontal axis	0	4	8	12	16

In this example, the vertical axis variable increases by larger and larger increments each successive step, while the horizontal axis variable increases by a constant amount. Hence the line slopes up, or rises, at an increasing rate.

3. Slopes Up at a Decreasing Rate.

Vertical axis	1	6	10	13	15
Horizontal axis	0	4	8	12	16

In this example, the vertical axis variable increases by successively smaller increments each step, while the variable on the horizontal axis increases by a constant amount. Therefore the line slopes up at a decreasing rate.

A. Negative Relationships

1. Linear. Recall that a negative relationship exists when the two variables move in opposite directions—one up, the other down. The relationship is linear (straight line) if both change by constant amounts as shown below.

Vertical axis	20	15	10	5	0
Horizontal axis	0	4	8	12	16

2. Slopes Down at an Increasing Rate.

Vertical axis	20	18	14	8	0
Horizontal axis	0	4	8	12	16

In this example, the vertical axis variable decreases by larger and larger increments each step while the variable represented on the horizontal azis increases by a constant four units. Therefore, the line slopes down, or decreases, at an increasing rate.

3. Slopes Down at a Decreasing Rate.

Vertical axis	20	12	6	2	0
Horizontal axis	0	4	8	12	16

Notice in this case, the vertical axis variable decreases by smaller and smaller increments, while the horizontal axis variable continues to increase by a constant four units. Consequently, the line decreases at a decreasing rate.

To summarize, there are two general classes of relationships—positive and negative. And within each of these there are three subclasses: linear, increasing rate, and decreasing rate.

SLOPE OF A LINE

The slope of a line is obtained by dividing a given change along the vertical axis by the corresponding change along the horizontal axis as shown in Figure 2–3. Change along the vertical axis is ΔV and change along the horizontal axis is denoted by ΔH. An easy way to remember the numerator and denominator is to think of ΔV as the rise of the line and ΔH as the run. Thus, slope is rise over run. Upward-sloping lines have a positive slope, and downward-sloping lines have a negative slope.

The slope of a straight line, linear positive or linear negative, remains constant at all points along the line. The slope of a curved line changes at different points along the line. The slope of an upward-sloping line that increases at an increasing rate becomes larger and larger at points higher on the line. If the line should become vertical, the slope becomes infinite. Conversely, the slope becomes successively smaller at points higher on an upward-sloping line that increases at a decreasing rate. If the line should become horizontal, the slope becomes zero.

Figure 2–3 Slope of a Line

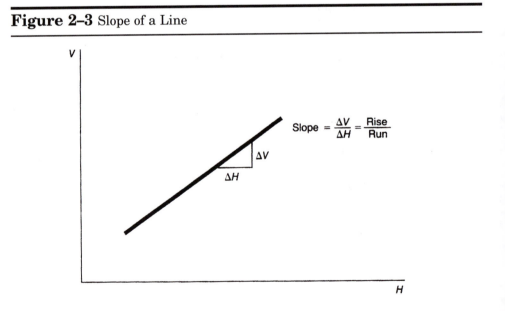

As mentioned, the slope of a downward-sloping line is negative. The change from a larger to a smaller number is a negative change. When dividing a negative number by a positive value, or vice versa, the answer is always negative. Hence, the slope of a downward-sloping line is negative.

QUESTIONS

1   On a graph, show the likely relationship between hours of study and points on an exam. Show points on the vertical axis and hours of study on the horizontal. Would the line be different for an average student than for a brilliant student? Explain.

2. Graph the relationship between earnings per week from part-time employment and average scores on exams during the term, using the numbers in the following table:

Earnings	Points
$300	0
200	50
100	75
0	80

   a. Graph points on the vertical axis and earnings on the horizontal.

   b. Connect the points. What are the ways of describing the shape of this line?

   c. What is the meaning of the line?

3.   a. Draw an upward-sloping line that first increases at an increasing rate and then increases at a decreasing rate.

   b. Draw a downward-sloping line that first decreases at an increasing rate and then decreases at a decreasing rate.

4. Which of the two graphs in question 3 most accurately describes the relationship between hours of study per week on economics and average points on the examinations? Let points be on the vertical axis and hours of study on the horizontal.

5.   a. What is the meaning of a vertical line that intersects the horizontal axis?

   b. What is the meaning of a horizontal line that intersects the vertical axis?

6.   a. What is the slope of the line in panel A of Figure 2–1? What would be its slope if nickels were graphed along the vertical axis and dimes on the horizontal?

   b. Does the slope of an upward-sloping, straight line change at different points along the line? Explain. What about a downward-sloping, straight line?

   c. How does the slope of a line that is concave to the origin change as you move from points high on the curve to lower points?

   d. What are the slopes of the lines referred to in questions 5a and 5b?

SELF-TEST

1. A two-dimensional graph expresses the relationship between____variables.
   a. two
   b. three
   c. one or more
   d. an unlimited number of

2. A positive relationship between two variables exists when the variables move in:
   a. all directions.
   b. opposite directions.
   c. the same direction.
   d. a circular motion.

3. Two variables that exhibit a positive relationship are graphed by____line.
   a. an upward-sloping
   b. a downward-sloping
   c. a straight
   d. a curvilinear

4. A negative relationship between two variables exists when the variables move in:
   a. all directions.
   b. opposite directions.
   c. the same direction.
   d. a circular motion.

5. Two variables that exhibit a negative relationship are graphed by____line.
   a. an upward-sloping
   b. a downward-sloping

c. a straight

d. a curvilinear

6. A linear positive relationship is graphed by a _____ line.

   a. straight downward-sloping

   b. straight upward-sloping

   c. curvilinear upward-sloping

   d. curvilinear downward-sloping

7. A line that slopes up at an increasing rate expresses a _____ relationship between two variables.

   a. curvilinear positive

   b. curvilinear negative

   c. linear positive

   d. linear negative

8. A line that slopes down at an increasing rate expresses a _____ relationship between two variables.

   a. curvilinear positive

   b. curvilinear negative

   c. linear positive

   d. linear negative

9. A graph of the two variables shown below yields a line that slopes_____at a(n) _____ rate.

Vertical axis	2	4	6	8	10
Horizontal axis	4	8	12	16	20

   a. upward; increasing

   b. upward; constant

   c. downward; increasing

   d. downward; constant

10. A graph of the two variables shown below yields a line that slopes_____at a(n)_____ rate.

Vertical axis	5	4	3	2	1
Horizontal axis	1	2	3	4	5

   a. upward; constant

   b. upward; increasing

   c. downward; constant

   d. downward; decreasing

11. A graph of the two variables shown below yields a line that slopes_____at a(n)_____ rate.

Vertical axis	100	95	80	50	0
Horizontal axis	0	20	40	60	80

   a. downward; decreasing

   b. downward; increasing

   c. upward; decreasing

   d. upward; increasing

12. A graph of the two variables shown below yields a line that slopes_____at a(n)_____ rate.

Vertical axis	100	60	30	10	0
Horizontal axis	0	20	40	60	80

   a. downward; decreasing

   b. downward; increasing

   c. upward; decreasing

   d. upward; increasing

13. The slope of a line is obtained by dividing:

   a. the vertical axis by the horizontal axis.

   b. the change in the vertical axis by the change in the horizontal axis.

   c. the horizontal axis by the vertical axis.

   d. the change in the horizontal axis by the change in the vertical axis.

14. What is the slope of the line in question 12 of the segment extending from 100 to 60 on the vertical axis and 0 to 20 on the horizontal axis?

   a. -2

   b. 2

   c. -1/2

   d. 1/2

15. What is the slope of the line in question 12 of the segment extending from 10 to 0 on the vertical axis and 60 to 80 on the horizontal axis?

   a. -2

   b. 2

   c. -1/2

   d. 1/2

Chapter 3

Opportunity Cost

Key Concepts

Opportunity cost
Production possibilities schedule
Production possibilities curve
Increasing opportunity cost
Transferability of resources
Efficiency and full employment
Economic growth

Once upon a time a wise king instructed the most learned person in his kingdom to teach him the most important lesson in economics. The only condition was that the lesson had to consist of ten words or less. The king was a very busy man. After months of deliberation the sage apporached the king and was heard to say, "There is no such thing as a free lunch."

It is clear that the sage had something more profound in mind than someone always picks up the tab for a restaurant meal. More likely the sage had in mind, opportunity cost.

OPPORTUNITY COST DEFINED

Opportunity cost is defined as what has to be given up to obtain more of something else. Opportunity cost exists because resources are scarce. We cannot produce everything we want or would like. Thus, if we want more of something, we must be willing to settle for less of something else. Opportunity cost can be measured in either monetary or nonmonetary units. In either case, opportunity cost is the next best alternative to whatever is chosen.

The idea of opportunity cost was already introduced in Chapter 2, Figure 2-2 panel B, without calling it such. Recall that 10 hours were available to study for two exams—economics and mathematics. In that case, time was the scarce resource. Twenty hours of study could have yielded a perfect score in both. But only 10 hours could be spared from other courses or activities. Thus, to obtain more points in one exam, a lower score must be accepted on the other.

PRODUCTION POSSIBILITIES SCHEDULE

The exact relationship between the two exam scores can be more easily seen with a production possibilities schedule. This is a table showing alternative combinations of two goods (exam scores) that can be produced from a given amount of resources (10 hours of study time).

Possibility	Economics Points	Mathematics Points
I	100 (A)	0 (F)
II	90 (A)	50 (C)
III	50 (C)	85 (B)
IV	0 (F)	100 (A)

From this table, it is possible to compute how much of one good must be given up to obtain an additional unit of the other good. Let us begin with possibility I and move to II. A useful formula to calculate the cost of each additional math point obtained is:

$$\text{Give up/Get} = 10/50 = 1/5 = .20$$

The ratio of two numbers gives the units of the top number per unit of the bottom number. Therefore, moving from I to II, each additional math point obtained costs .20 of an econ point. The opportunity costs of moving down the table among the other combinations are given below:

Possibility	Econ Points Given Up for Each Math Point Obtained
I—II	.20
II—III	1.14
III—IV	3.30

One could also begin with possibility IV and move up the table. In that case, more econ points are obtained by giving up math points.

Possibility	Math Points Given Up for Each Econ Point Obtained
IV—III	.30
III—II	.88
II—I	5.00

Notice the increase in the size of the above numbers moving from one extreme to the other. At first, just a fraction of an econ point must be given up to obtain one more math point. This figure becomes successively larger in the next two steps. The same is true moving to higher econ scores. This example represents increasing opportunity cost. The cost of each additional unit of whatever is being increased becomes larger and larger as one approaches the maximum output of that item. Increasing opportunity cost occurred in this case because it became more time-consuming to add points the closer one came to the maximum 100; the hard material took longer to learn than the easy material.

Before leaving this example, you might ask, which combination of econ and math points (or grade letters) would the student choose? The two extremes where an F is obtained on one or the other exam most likely would be avoided. Aside from that, it is hard to tell. If the student wished to maximize grade points, possibility II is the best—as grade of A in econ and a C in math. However, if the student were a math major and wished to avoid a C in math, possibility III might be chosen—C in econ and a B in math. It is important to remember that when moving from one possibility to another, move only if what you get is worth more than what you give up.

PRODUCTION POSSIBILITIES CURVE

Plotting the numbers from a production possibilities schedule yields a *pro-*

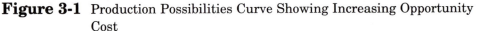

Figure 3-1 Production Possibilities Curve Showing Increasing Opportunity
Cost

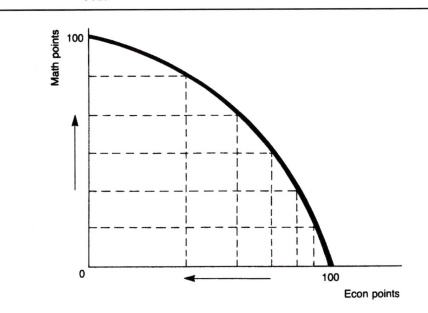

duction possibilities curve, as illustrated in Figure 3–1. This is a line showing various combinations of two goods that can be produced from a given amount of resources.

Increasing opportunity cost always yields production possibility curves that are concave to the origin—they bend out. This can be seen by starting at the zero math/100 econ point combination and move up by equal increments along the math axis. The first block of math points obtained requires giving up only a small number of econ points. Notice, however, that each additional step up the math axis requires giving up a larger and larger number of econ points. This is increasing opportunity cost. The same holds true if one begins at the 100 math/zero econ combination and moves out by equal increments along the econ axis. You might try this with a diagram of your own.

It is virtually impossible to come up with realistic examples of *constant opportunity cost* where the cost of adding a unit of one good in terms of another good given up does not change over the entire range of observations. If such an example did exist, it would be characterized by a straight, downward-sloping production possibilities curve such as in Figure 3–2.

SOCIAL CHOICES

The production possibility curve is a useful device for illustrating choices that must be made by every society. Three important choices are: (1) the share of

Figure 3-2 Production Possibilities Curve Showing Constant Opportunity
Cost

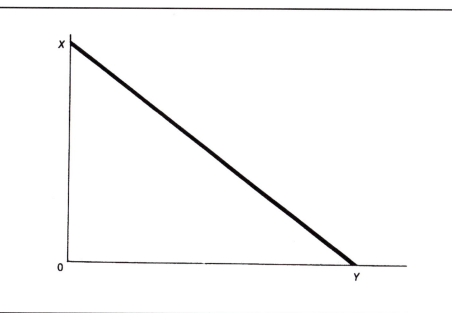

resources devoted to military goods versus nonmilitary production, often called
"guns and butter," (2) public versus private goods, and (3) consumption versus
investment.

A. Guns versus Butter

A nation that needed to maintain a large military establishment or went to
war with another nation would be located at point B on its production possibilities curve, as opposed to point A in Figure 3–3. The opportunity cost of the military is the nonmilitary goods and services given up. War also destroys
resources—people and property. In countries ravaged by war, the production
possibilities curve also shifts inward because of the loss of resources, as illustrated by the lower line in Figure 3–3.

B. Public versus Private Goods

Public goods are goods produced and/or distributed by government. In contrast to private goods, which are consumed by the individuals or families that
purchase them, public goods are consumed by the society-at-large. Examples
include public parks, streets and highways, the military, and police and fire protection. Governments also may subsidize certain kinds of private goods such as
education, housing, food, and medical care, with the objective of helping low-

---

Figure 3-3 War and Peace

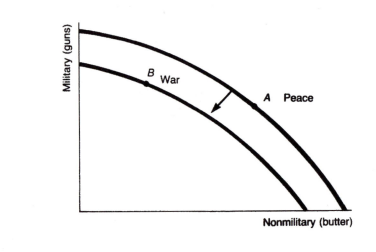

income people attain the basic necessities of life.

The amount of public goods available to a **society depends** on its willingness to levy taxes to pay for these goods, and the wealth or total resources owned by a nation. Figure 3–4 illustrates the case where people living in a rich nation enjoy more of both public and private goods than the inhabitants of a poor nation. But given the wealth of a nation, the decision to produce more public goods must cause a reduction in private goods, and vice versa.

C. Consumption versus Investment.

A third way to divide up the output of a society is between consumption and investment. Investment goods are capital such as buildings and machines that increase the total resources of a society. In turn, these resources increase society's output in the future. The greater the share of a nation's resources devoted to the production of investment goods, the smaller the share devoted to consumer goods production. However, the absolute amount of consumer goods will increase over time due to the increase in the nation's capital resources. The investment versus consumer goods trade-off can be illustrated with a diagram similar to Figure 3–4.

TRANSFERABILITY OF RESOURCES

Virtually all production possibilities curves drawn to illustrate social choices are concave to the origin. Recall that this implies increasing opportunity cost. This phenomenon is thought to exist for every society because resources are not

Figure 3-4 Public versus Private Good

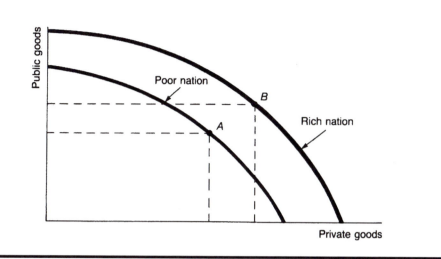

equally productive in all uses. As a nation moves toward the extremes—the intersection of the curve with either axis—resources must be pressed into tasks for which they are not well-suited. Or, perhaps they cannot be used at all. For example, as a nation moved up and to the left past point B in Figure 3–5, farmland and machinery would become redundant. Thus, a small increase in non-food output causes a large reduction in food production.

Figure 3-5 Production Possibilities or Transformation Curve

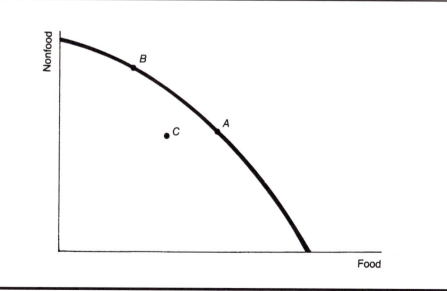

The production possibilities curve is also known as the transformation curve. As a nation moves along the curve, it transforms one kind of output into another. Moving from point A to point B in Figure 3–5 transforms food into other goods.

When a nation moves in small increments somewhere in the middle of the curve, increasing opportunity cost is not so evident. In this region, the resources that are suited to just one kind of production can be utilized in that area. The smaller incidence of increasing opportunity cost is especially true when time is allowed for resources to adjust to their new uses. For example, time allows farm people to acquire skills that are necessary for other occupations.

EFFICIENCY AND FULL EMPLOYMENT

When drawing a production possibilities or transformation curve, two implicit assumptions must be made: (1) resources are used efficiently, and (2) resources are fully employed. Much of the material in microeconomics deals with the attainment of maximum efficiency in resource use, and reducing unemployment is an important issue in macroeconomics. If these assumptions are not met, the nation will be at a point below the surface of the curve—such as point C in Figure 3–5. By reducing unemployment or increasing efficiency, the nation can increase the output of both goods and improve its standard of living.

Figure 3-6 Production Possibilities or Curve Illustrating Economic Growth

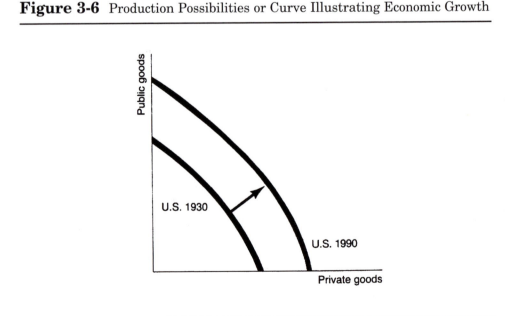

ECONOMIC GROWTH

An increase in the output of goods and services over time is known as economic growth. Sustained economic growth is attained only by an increase in a nation's resources. In recent history, nations have increased their resources mainly by producing more capital—both nonhuman and human. Nonhuman capital includes machines, tools, computers, buildings, roads, communications facilities, and so on. Human capital is the increase in knowledge made possible by research and education. Both forms of capital enhance the productivity of labor—thereby increasing society's per capita output.

Economic growth is illustrated by an outward shift of a nation's production possibilities curve, as in Figure 3–6. The increase in total resources increases the nation's ability to produce. The curve drawn in Figure 3–6 refers to total output of society. While an increase in total output is an acceptable definition of economic growth, standard of living will increase only if total output increases at a faster rate than population.

QUESTIONS

1. Consider the following production possibilities schedule:

Points on Econ Quiz	Points on Math Quiz
0	200
25	180
50	140
75	80
100	0

a. What is the opportunity cost of increasing econ points from 25 to 50? From 75 to 100? (Present your answer in terms of each econ point obtained.)

b. What is the opportunity cost of increasing math points from 80 to 140? From 180 to 200? (Present your answer in terms of each math point obtained.)

c. Does this example represent constant or increasing opportunity cost? Explain.

d. Represent this production possibilities schedule by a production possibilities curve.

2. Suppose that later in the day you have an hour available for anything you wish to do. What factors should you consider in deciding how to spend that hour?

3. a. What is the opportunity cost to you of this economics course?

b. What can be inferred from your decision to take this course rather than doing something else with your time and money?

4. Why is increasing opportunity cost a normally expected phenomenon in the economy?

5. Is it possible for a nation to increase the production of both goods represented on a transformation curve without adding to its stock of resources? Explain and illustrate.

6. Using a production possibilities curve, illustrate the following:
   a. A nation goes to war.
   b. A drought reduces food production.
   c. Economic growth.
   d. Unemployment.

SELF-TEST

1. Opportunity cost is:
   a. the cost of producing opportunities.
   b. $4.98.
   c. what has to be given up to obtain more of something else.
   d. what is obtained when a unit of something else is given up.

2. A production possibilities schedule is a table showing various possible combinations of two:
   a. goods that can be produced by a fixed quantity of resources.
   b. goods that yield a given level of satisfaction.
   c. resources that can produce a given level of output.
   d. resources that cost a given amount of money.

Answer questions 3-7 from the following production possibilities schedule.

Possibility	Dollars Earned per Week on a Part-Time Job	Grade Points
I	0	60
II	100	50
III	200	30

3. The opportunity cost of increasing earnings from 0 to $100 is_____grade point(s) per dollar.
   a. 50
   b. 60
   c. 10
   d. .1

4. The opportunity cost of increasing earnings from $100 to $200 is____grade point(s) per dollar.
   a. 50
   b. 30
   c. 20
   d. .2

5. The opportunity cost of increasing grade points from 30 to 50 is____dollars per grade point.
   a. 5
   b. 100
   c. 2
   d. 20

6. The opportunity cost of increasing grade points from 50 to 60 is____dollars per grade point.
   a. 100
   b. 10
   c. 5
   d. 1

7. This example depicts____opportunity cost.
   a. constant
   b. increasing
   c. decreasing
   d. zero

8. A production possibilities curve is a line showing various possible combinations of two:
   a. resources that will produce a given output.
   b. goods that cost a given amount.
   c. goods that can be produced from a given quantity of resources.
   d. resources that cost a given amount.

9. A production possibilities curve representing increasing opportunity cost is:
   a. convex to the origin.
   b. concave to the origin.
   c. a straight downward-sloping line.
   d. a straight upward-sloping line.

10. The two axes of a production possibilities curve represent:
    a. resources or inputs.
    b. dollars of resources or inputs.
    c. goods or outputs.
    d. dollars of goods or output.

11. When moving from one possibility to another, a person should make the move only if:
    a. what is obtained is worth more than what is given up.
    b. what is given up is worth more than what is obtained.
    c. nothing has to be given up.
    d. forced to do so.

12. When a country goes to war the point at which the country is located on its production possibilities curve moves____if ``guns'' are represented on the vertical axis and ``butter'' on the horizontal. If the country also is ravaged by a war the entire curve shifts____.
    a. up; out
    c. up; in
    b. down; out
    d. down; in

13. Virtually all production possibilities curves are drawn____to the origin which represents____opportunity cost. This situation is expected to prevail because resources____equally productive in all uses.
    a. convex; increasing; are not
    b. convex; decreasing; are
    c. concave; increasing; are not
    d. concave decreasing; are

14. To be on the surface of its production possibilities curve a nation must:
    a. utilize its resources efficiently.
    b. have full employment.
    c. have stable prices.
    d. a and b.

15. Unemployment can be represented by a_____of the production possibilities curve.

    a. point inside
    b. shift inward
    c. point outside
    d. shift outward

16. Economic growth is made possible by_____and is represented by_____of the production possibilities curve.

    a. investment; a point outside
    b. investment; an outward shift
    c. consumption; a point outside
    d. consumption; an outward shift

Part II

Consumer Choice

Chapters 4-7

Chapter 4

Utility Maximization

Key Concepts

Consumer Sovereignty

Utility

Marginal unit

Marginal utility

Law of diminishing marginal utility

Marginal utility per dollar

Utility maximizing rule

Interdependence of utilities

Price of present consumption

The main objective of this chapter is to develop the utility-maximizing rule. By following this rule, consumers obtain the greatest possible utility or satisfaction from a given expenditure. In conjunction with the utility-maximizing rule, the law of diminishing marginal utility is presented. The law of diminishing marginal utility and utility maximization form the foundation of all economic theory relating to consumer behavior and demand.

CONSUMER SOVEREIGNTY

It is fitting to begin with the individual consumer, because without consumption there would be no justification for production. The ultimate aim of all production is to satisfy the wants of consumers. In some instances, the producer also is a consumer. The artist, musician, or craftsperson who receives satisfaction from a job well done is in effect "consuming" part of the product even though the product may be purchased by a second party. In cases where a person produces for home consumption, production and consumption are embodied in the same person or family.

In the U.S. economy and in all other free-market economies, the consumer is king (or queen). It is in the interest of producers to cater to the wishes of consumers because if they produce what is most highly demanded, they are rewarded by higher profits and a better standard of living for themselves and their families. Economists refer to an economic system where production is carried on to satisfy the wishes of consumers as one characterized by consumer sovereignty.

Society has found it necessary to restrict the sovereignty of the individual consumer somewhat, however. If consumption of a good is seen as harmful to either the consumer or to others, society may pass a law against it. The use of habit-forming drugs is one example. Drug addicts, as well as harming their health, may also harm others if they drive an automobile under the influence of drugs or turn to crime rather than employment to obtain money for their purchase. Laws regulating the consumption of alcoholic beverages are another example of restricting consumer sovereignty to a certain degree. Although society might prefer that consumers have cornflakes for breakfast rather than bourbon, in general, consumers are free to choose what they most desire, and producers respond to their wants.

In recent years, however, some people have begun to question whether the idea of consumer sovereignty accurately depicts our current economic system. They argue that today's giant corporations, with their multimillion-dollar annual advertising budgets, are able to persuade consumers to buy what the corporations want to produce, and this is not necessarily the same as what consumers would buy in the absence of such advertising. If the basic wants of consumers are altered or determined by the advertising campaigns of corporations, it might be more accurate to refer to "producer sovereignty" rather than consumer sovereignty.

Probably the most compelling argument in favor of consumer rather than producer sovereignty is that it would be unprofitable and, hence, irrational for corporations to spend millions of dollars to change the basic wants of consumers. Rather, it is more profitable for producers to discover the basic consumer wants, cater to these wants, and then advertise to expand the sales of their particular product brand.

The increase in demand by consumers for smaller automobiles that gave better gas mileage during and after the Arab oil embargo, and the consequent scramble by the auto manufacturers to satisfy this demand, is a case in point. When the abrupt increase in the price of gasoline prompted consumers to switch to smaller cars, the auto manufacturers did not mount a large advertising campaign in an attempt to convince consumers to continue buying large cars, while continuing to produce them in the same numbers as before. Instead, the companies invested millions of dollars to retool some of their factories to increase their production of small cars. Then, each company began to advertise in an attempt to convince consumers to buy its small cars instead of the small cars produced by competitors.

TASTES

Since consumers are such an important part of our economic system, it will be useful to study them in some detail. No two consumers are exactly the same in likes and dislikes. One may like to spend leisure time watching baseball on television while drinking beer and eating pretzels; another may prefer to attend the opera or a symphony concert or travel to far-off places.

Even though it is generally recognized that tastes differ among people, we have a tendency to forget this when we criticize others for liking things that do not appeal to us or for spending their income on a different mix of goods and services than we do. One person may place an expensive home high on the list of priorities, while another prefers to spend more on travel or an expensive automobile. But who is to say which is the superior taste—the expensive home or the expensive auto? If a person were forced to sell the expensive auto and buy a higher-priced home, his or her total satisfaction might be decreased considerably. For this person, the superior taste is represented by the automobile. The main point to remember about taste is that there is no absolute standard—each person decides what he or she likes best and then tries to satisfy these wants.

UTILITY

Although tastes and satisfaction are familiar ideas, it is difficult to express them in concrete terms. Suppose you had just eaten an apple and a candy bar. Could you tell someone how much satisfaction you received from each of these items? Possibly you could tell which item you liked best, but could you tell how much better you liked one over the other? You might say "quite a bit" or "just a little" or some such vague descriptive term. But how much is "just a little" or "quite a bit"?

We need a more quantitative measure of satisfaction. For this reason, economists have developed the concept of utility. The word utility means the same thing as satisfaction. For illustrative purposes, however, economists have created the concept of a "util," which is a unit of utility. Although it is not possible to measure utils in a quantitative sense, for the purpose of instruction it is useful to assign numbers to levels of utility or satisfaction. This is not as unrealistic as one might think as long as it is agreed that a large number represents greater satisfaction than a small number. Suppose you agreed to arbitrarily assign 100 utils as the satisfaction or utility you received from the apple. If you liked the candy bar less, you would then assign it a number smaller than 100, or if you liked it more, you would give it a number greater than 100. If, for example, you assigned 50 to the candy bar, we could say that you liked the apple about twice as much as the candy bar.

If you wanted to take the time, you could assign utils to all the things you consume or might consume, using one of the items as a reference point. The important thing in assigning utils to each item is not the absolute size of the util measure of each item but its size relative to the other items. Because tastes are an individual matter, utility is not something that can be compared from person to person. An individual might assign numbers to a partial list of the things consumed during one week in the following manner:

Items Consumed per Week	Number of Utils
Two pounds of steak	100
One-fourth pound of coffee	30
Two quarts of milk	60
Shelter of house	300
Repair of auto	200

This example illustrates two important points. First, consumption is measured as an amount per unit of time. In this example, we used one week. It does not make sense to say two pounds of meat were consumed if you do not specify per day, per week, per year, or per lifetime. The time dimension is necessary to know how much is being consumed relatively. The second point is that we consume services as well as goods. In the example, the repair of the automobile is a service. We could list services purchased from a doctor, lawyer, dentist, barber, or beauty shop operator. In economics, a service is treated as if it were a good. For our purposes, they are essentially the same; both yield satisfaction or utility to the buyer.

THE MARGINAL UNIT

A concept that is often used in economics is the marginal unit. Perhaps the easiest way to grasp this idea is to think of marginal as the same as extra or additional. If you have 10 units of something, say 10 pencils, and you acquire one more, then the eleventh one is the marginal pencil. The marginal unit is the one that is added to or subtracted from the top of whatever you have.

The marginal unit is one of the most important and useful concepts employed in economics. This is because most economic decisions involve relatively small (or marginal) changes. For example, you do not decide whether to spend all your income on steak or none on steak. Rather, you decide whether you should buy a little more steak and a little less hamburger or vice versa. Thus, the decisions you make generally involve the extra or marginal unit. It is the unit where economic decisions are made. In understanding this idea, do not confuse the marginal with the average or the total, which may be more familiar measures.

MARGINAL UTILITY

Marginal utility is the extra or additional utility you obtain by consuming one more unit of a good or service per unit of time. It can also be the utility you lose by reducing your consumption by one unit. In a previous utility example, 100 utils were obtained by consuming two pounds of steak per week. Now suppose you increased your steak consumption to three pounds per week and received 140 utils from this amount. The utility received from the third, or marginal, pound of steak in this case would be 40 utils. We could take the same example and subtract one pound of steak from weekly consumption. If, for example, we received 55 utils from one pound, then the marginal utility of the second pound is 45 utils. The following table summarizes what total and marginal utility might be for zero, one, two, and three pounds of steak consumed per week.

You will note that the utility added by the marginal unit—the marginal utility—can be calculated by subtracting the total utility obtained before the marginal unit is added from the total utility obtained including that unit.

Pounds of Steak Consumed per Week	Total Utility (utils)	Marginal Utility (utils)
0	0	—
1	55	55
2	100	45
3	140	40

Another method of calculating marginal utility is to divide the *change* in total utility by the *change* in the number of units consumed:

$$\text{Marginal utility} = \frac{\text{Change in total utility}}{\text{Change in units consumed}}$$

Also note that the total utility of a given quantity is the sum of all the marginal utilities up through and including that quantity.[1]

LAW OF DIMINISHING MARGINAL UTILITY

The preceding example also illustrates the *law of diminishing marginal utility*. This means that as you increase consumption of one good or service, say steak, holding constant the other things you consume, beyond some point the extra or marginal utility you obtain from the last unit will begin to decline. The intuitive appeal of diminishing marginal utility stems largely from our personal experience. If we consume more and more of something, even steak, we soon tire of it and desire more variety.

The idea of diminishing marginal utility also is supported by lack of evidence of "monomania" among people, even among heroin addicts. If diminishing marginal utility did not prevail, there is no reason why some people would not spend all their income on one thing. In that case, you could choose an item that gives you the most satisfaction for the first dollar spent and then devote your entire income to it.

MARGINAL UTILITY AND PRICE

The utility or satisfaction we receive from a good or service is a major reason we buy the things we do. Generally, if we do not like a product, we do not buy it. But it is not quite this simple. For one thing, likes or dislikes are not all-or-nothing concepts. We all have varying degrees of likes and dislikes, as indicated by the diminishing marginal utility concept. Also, there is another problem we all have to face: the problem of price.

When faced with a choice between two or more items that we could buy, we often deliberately choose the item we like the least. Looking over a menu in a restaurant, for example, you may prefer the $15 T-bone steak to the $6 chopped beef, but you choose the latter. Or, when buying a car, you may like the $30,000 sports car better than any car in the showroom, but you buy the $10,000 sedan. Is your behavior irrational or inconsistent with the concept of utility? Not at all. In purchasing decisions, you must consider price and utility.

When you choose an item that is less desirable and less costly, you implicitly decide that the extra cost is not worth the extra satisfaction it brings. You

---

1 In terms of calculus, marginal utility is the first derivative of the total utility function.

decide, for example, that the additional satisfaction from the steak over the hamburger is not worth $9 to you. There are other things you can buy with that $9 that will give you more utility. In deciding what things to spend your money on, you really look at marginal utility per dollar rather than marginal utility alone. Using the steak example, suppose the marginal utility, price, and marginal utility per dollar (marginal utility divided by price) are as follows:

	Marginal Utility (utils)	Price	Marginal Utility per Dollar
Chopped beef	60	$ 6	10
T-bone	90	$15	6

This example illustrates that choosing chopped beef over T-bone steak is a rational choice. The marginal utility per dollar of the cheaper cut exceeds the marginal utility per dollar obtained from the T-bone. This is only an example; we could have easily created an example in which T-bone would have been the best choice by raising its marginal utility or lowering its price. The point is that it is not always best to buy the cheaper item.

UTILITY-MAXIMIZING RULE

So far we have considered choosing between only two items. We know, however, that life is more complex than this. During a normal shopping trip to the supermarket, for example, we have thousands of items to choose from. How do we decide what to buy?

The first thing we must realize is that our budget is limited: We have just so much to spend. Given this constraint, our objective is to maximize our satisfaction or utility. The basic rule is to equalize, as much as possible, the marginal utility per dollar for all the goods and services we buy. Recall that marginal utility per dollar is obtained by dividing marginal utility by price. For example, if the marginal utility (MU) of good A is 30 and its price is $5, then its marginal utility per dollar is 6. The general rule to follow for all goods and services A through Z is:

$$\frac{\text{MU of A}}{\text{Price of A}} = \frac{\text{MU of B}}{\text{Price of B}} = \cdots = \frac{\text{MU of Z}}{\text{Price of Z}}$$

Thus, to maximize utility, we should try to make the marginal utility per dollar of good or service A equal to that of good or service B, and make these equal to all other things we consume.

Why does an equalization of the marginal utility per dollar for all goods we consume result in maximum satisfaction for us? This is perhaps easiest to see if we look at a situation where they are not equal. Suppose the marginal utility per dollar spent on food per month is 50 but the marginal utility per dollar spent on entertainment is 30. Consider what would happen if one less dollar is spent on entertainment and one more dollar on food.

$$
\begin{array}{lr}
\text{One less dollar on entertainment} = \text{lose} & \text{30 utils} \\
\text{One more dollar on food} = \text{gain} & \text{50 utils} \\
\text{Net gain} & \text{20 utils}
\end{array}
$$

After making this switch you gain 20 units of satisfaction without spending an extra cent. Thus, if the marginal utility per dollar is not the same across the entire range of goods and services available to you, it is always possible to rearrange your purchases to increase your total satisfaction or utility. Only when the MU/P ratios are equal is it not possible to rearrange purchases and increase utility.

If a person is not at the utility-maximizing equilibrium, how does the adjustment process reestablish this equilibrium? A person will buy more of the high MU/P items and less of those with low MU/P ratios. Because of the law of diminishing marginal utility, an increase in the purchase of the high-ratio items lowers their marginal utilities which, in turn, lowers their MU/P ratios. Conversely, a decrease in the purchase of the low-ratio items increases their marginal utilities and increases their MU/P ratios. At some point, the high and low ratios will equalize, or come together. No one can tell you how many units of each good or service you should purchase per week or month when you reach equilibrium. This will depend on your tastes and income.

THEORY VERSUS REALITY

Although the preceding rule for maximizing utility cannot be questioned from the standpoint of pure logic, one might question its practical usefulness. Surely, you might argue, no one takes time to think of the utils obtained from consuming an item, much less writing them down and dividing by price. It might come as a surprise to learn that most people implicitly follow such a rule in their daily purchases. Many of us have felt at one time or another that an item was a good buy or that it wasn't worth it. In doing so, we have made an implicit calculation of the item's marginal utility per dollar. If we decide that an item is a good buy, it is an indication that its marginal utility per dollar is large relative to other things we could buy. If an item isn't worth it, its marginal utility per dollar for us is low. We have also purchased items that we could not be sure were good buys; these items provided a marginal utility per dollar that was about equal to that of the other things we buy.

If people do attempt to maximize utility, how can charity and gift-giving be explained? Here, people give without expecting anything in return. But givers do receive something in return—-the good feeling that someone else's utility is increased by the charity or gifts. Thus the practice of gift-giving increases the utility of two people: the giver and the receiver. This is in contrast to items purchased for one's own use where just one person benefits. One might conclude, therefore, that the more generous a society is in terms of gift-giving or helping others, the greater will be its utility, given its income or resources. The Good Samaritan was not necessarily a bad economist.

CHANGES IN THE OPTIMUM MIX

If a person reaches the utility-maximizing optimum, will that mix of goods and services be consumed for all time to come? No. The MU/P ratio of an item will change if either the MU or its price changes. MU can change for several reasons. First, we may grow tired of something that we have consumed for a long while; most of us like some variety in our lives. Thus, the marginal utility of what we consume today depends somewhat on what we consumed yesterday. Second, new products or services may appear on the market that make old ones less desirable. This phenomenon is most evident in products that change in fashion or style. How many times have we admired a certain model of automobile only to have a new model come out that made our former dream car seem ugly and old-fashioned? Third, our tastes or estimates of utility may be changed by advertising. If a popular movie star or athlete uses a product, for example, it might become more appealing to some people.

A second reason to change the mix of goods we consume is because prices are always changing. If the price of one item increases relative to other alternatives, its marginal utility per dollar will decrease relative to other things. We would then want to buy less of it.

INTERDEPENDENCE OF UTILITIES

The marginal utility of each good or service we consume may depend on the other things consumed along with it. Economists call this interdependence of utilities. Interdependence between goods can take the form of either a complementary or a substitute relationship. Two goods are complements to each other if consuming one enhances the marginal utility of the other. Bacon and eggs are a good example. Most people find eggs more appealing at breakfast when accompanied by a strip or two of bacon. Or, take the woman who has purchased a new dress; a new handbag, gloves, and shoes generally will make the dress more desirable, and the dress also complements the accessories. On the other hand, a substitute relationship between goods exists if consuming one good reduces the marginal utility of another. For instance, the marginal utility you obtain from consuming a glass of orange juice at breakfast probably would decline if you also had a glass of grapefruit juice at the same meal.

Because of the many complications that have the effect of changing the marginal utility of each good or service we buy or consider buying, the optimum bundle of goods and services that will maximize utility is constantly changing. Therefore, it is necessary to continually reevaluate purchase decisions if we hope to get the most for our money.

CONSUMPTION VERSUS SAVING

Although we must decide what mix of goods and services will give the most utility for a given expenditure, this does not imply that all income is spent. Most people attempt to save at least a small portion of their current income for various reasons. We may save "for a rainy day" to have something to fall back on in case we cannot work, or for retirement to supplement a pension. Most people save to make a large purchase such as a car or a down payment on a house. Others may wish to leave an estate for their heirs or some institution.

The decisions to save or not to save and what to save for are like the expenditure decisions we have just considered. The marginal utility of saving is the satisfaction we can expect to obtain when we eventually spend that extra dollar, or the satisfaction we now obtain from knowing that someone else will be able to spend it.

The marginal utility obtained from an extra dollar saved varies among individuals. Some people like to spend what they earn relatively quickly and do not place a high value on saving. Economists say that these people have a *high rate of time preference*. They prefer to consume now rather than later. The stereotyped soldier or sailor who epitomizes the eat, drink, and be merry attitude is a good example of someone with a high rate of time preference. The marginal utility of present consumption to this person is high relative to that of future consumption.

Other people, perhaps more patient, are willing to devote a relatively large share of their current income to saving, with the idea of adding to their consumption in the future. These people have a *low rate of time preference*. The miser represents the extreme case of a person with a low rate of time preference, although it is doubtful that most misers ever envision spending the entire amount of their savings at some future date. Even the miser has some degree of time preference. No one can postpone all consumption for the future; if a person tried, there would be no future!

Most of us fall somewhere between the spendthrift and the miser regarding time preference. Persons who have a low rate of time preference tend to obtain more utility from future consumption than their counterparts with a high time preference. Hence, they will be likely to save a larger fraction of their income.

In estimating the marginal utility of future consumption, it is also necessary to account for the interest or dividends received on savings. If the rate of interest received on savings is 10 percent, $1 saved today will be worth $1.10 one year from now. Assuming no increase in prices,[2] the extra dollar saved will buy some-

---

2 A stable price level is assumed to simplify the example. But the rule still holds; the higher the interest rate, the higher the price of present consumption for any given rate of inflation. The effect of inflation on the interest rate is discussed in Chapter 23.

what more in the future than it buys today. Hence, the interest return on savings compensates us for waiting to consume in the future. The higher the interest or dividend returns on our savings, the more each dollar saved at the present will buy in the future. In other words, a higher interest rate increases the price of present consumption compared with future consumption.

THE PRICE OF PRESENT CONSUMPTION

The basic idea that the combination of goods we presently consume depends on both marginal utility and price also applies to decisions to consume now or in the future. The price or opportunity cost of present consumption is what must be given up in the future. The higher the rate of interest, the more $1 saved will buy in the future, and consequently the higher the cost or price of present consumption.

We can therefore consider the price of $1 in present consumption as the dollar plus the interest return. If we specify the marginal utility that an extra dollar of present consumption will provide, we can divide this by price to obtain marginal utility per dollar. As an example, consider two individuals, one a spendthrift and the other a miser. In situation 1, both receive a 10 percent rate of interest on their savings; in situation 2, the rate is 20 percent. The two situations are shown in Table 4–1.

Because the spendthrift in this example enjoys spending money in the present more than the miser, whatever the rate of interest, the marginal utility per dollar of present consumption is higher for the spendthrift. But, at higher rates of interest, the price of present consumption rises, which results in a reduction in marginal utility per dollar of present consumption for both individuals.

The decision to save or to consume at the present, therefore, is similar to the decision on what mix of goods to buy, depending on taste and price. Theoretically a low rate of time preference and a high price (high interest) are associated with a high rate of saving, and vice versa. Empirically, however, economists have found it difficult to measure the relative importance of each of these factors in people's decisions to save or to spend. For one thing, an independent, quantitative measure of time preference is lacking. Although there is general agreement that the rate of time preference affects the proportion of income saved, there is much less agreement on the importance of the rate of interest. The measurement of the impact of the interest rate on saving is complicated by other factors that also are expected to influence saving. These include the level of income, changes in the general price level (mainly inflation), and expectations of future economic conditions. The probable impact of these factors on saving is discussed more thoroughly in the companion macro text.

TABLE 4-1 Price of Present Consumption and Marginal Utility

	Marginal Utility of an Extra Dollar Consumed at Present	Interest Rate	Price of Present Consumption	Marginal Utility per Dollar
Situation 1:				
Spendthrift	20	00.10	$1.10	18.18
Miser	10	00.10	1.10	9.09
Situation 2:				
Spendthrift	20	00.20	1.20	16.67
Miser	10	00.20	1.20	8.33

QUESTIONS

1. Because of the large amount of advertising that currently takes place, some people have argued that consumer sovereignty no longer characterizes the United States and other market economies. Is there any evidence to suggest that consumer sovereignty still exists? Explain.

2. a. What is the marginal unit?
   b. Why is it important in making consumer decisions?

3. a. What is marginal utility?
   b. What is the law of diminishing marginal utility?
   c. What evidence is there to suggest that diminishing marginal utility exists?
   d. Calculate the marginal utilities of additional glasses of orange juice from the following figures:

Number of Glasses	Total Utility
0	0
1	100
2	190
3	200
4	150

4. Suppose you are in the market for a new bicycle. A salesperson shows you a new 10-speed model for $249. You say the bicycle is nice but you cannot afford such an expensive model. What do you really mean?

5. "The more the merrier" contradicts the law of diminishing marginal utility. True or false? Explain.

6. The marginal utility of a steak and a fish dinner for an individual is given below. Under the following prices, is the individual maximizing utility for a given expenditure? Why or why not?

	MU	Price
Steak dinner	100	$10
Fish dinner	75	5

7. Let's say that the combination of food that maximizes your satisfaction for lunch consists of one cheeseburger, one slice of apple pie, and one cup of coffee. According to the marginal-utility-over-price approach to making consumer decisions, you should continue to consume this mix of foods for lunch the rest of your life. True or false? Explain.

8. It is a common practice in restaurants for customers to be given as much coffee as they desire free of charge when they purchase a meal. Under these circumstances, what is the marginal utility of the last cup of coffee; that is, what should be the marginal utility of the last unit consumed of goods received "free?"

9. a. What is the price of present consumption?
   b. How does the rate of interest affect this price?

SELF-TEST

1. Consumer sovereignty describes an economic system whereby:
   a. production is carried on to satisfy the wishes of consumers.
   b. consumption is carried on to satisfy the wishes of producers.
   c. consumers have more political influence on government policy than do producers.
   d. consumers allocate the nation's resources according to their representation in the government.

2. It has been argued that advertising dictates what consumers want to buy. This argument is _____ with the idea of consumer sovereignty. An argument in favor of consumer sovereignty is that business firms find it more profitable to:
   a. consistent; produce what they wish and then advertise to entice consumers to buy what they produce.
   b. in conflict; find out what consumers desire and then produce the items that fill this demand than to change their tastes.
   c. consistent; find out what consumers desire and then produce the items that fill this demand than to change their tastes.
   d. in conflict; produce what they wish and then advertise to entice consumers to buy what they produce.

3. A person who likes to attend the theater and concerts has _____ tastes compared to one who wishes to attend sporting events.
   a. inferior
   b. superior
   c. different
   d. greater

4. Utility means the same thing as:
   a. money.
   b. usefulness.
   c. taste.
   d. satisfaction.

5. In economics the marginal unit refers to the:
   a. unit of lowest quality.
   b. the last unit added or first unit subtracted.
   c. the unit having the highest price.
   d. the unit having the lowest price.

6. Marginal utility is the satisfaction received from the:
   a. last unit of a good or service consumed.
   b. average unit of a good or service consumed.
   c. total units of a good or service consumed.
   d. poorest quality unit consumed.

7. If the law of diminishing marginal utility did not exist we should observe people:
   a. spending the same proportion of their income on each good.
   b. spending the same dollar value of each good.
   c. spending all of their income on one good.
   d. buying the same quantity of each good.

8. The MU/P ratio tells us:
   a. the utils per dollar received from the marginal unit of this good.
   b. the dollars per util spent on this good.
   c. the dollars required to purchase an extra unit of the good.
   d. the income required to maximize satisfaction.

Answer question 9 from the following table:

Units	Total Utility of A	Total Utility of B
0	0	0
1	100	50
2	180	70
3	200	65

9. The marginal utility added by the third unit of good A is _____ and the marginal utility added by the third unit of good B is ____
   a. 200; 65
   b. 20; 65
   c. 200; -5
   d. 20; -5

10. The decision to purchase a more expensive item over one that is less expensive is:
    a. irrational because a wise consumer always buys the lowest-priced item.
    b. irrational because a person's income will go farther if the lowest-priced items are purchased.
    c. rational if the MU/P ratio is higher for the more expensive item.
    d. rational if the MU/P ratio is lower for the more expensive item.

11. In comparing two items, the one having the _____ should be purchased.
    a. highest MU/P
    b. lowest MU/P
    c. highest MU
    d. lowest P

12. The rule for maximizing utility from a given amount of money is to:
    a. equalize the MUs of all items available for consumption.
    b. equalize the MU per dollar of all items available for consumption.
    c. equalize the amount spent on each item available for consumption.
    d. equalize units consumed of each items available for consumption.

Answer questions 13 and 14 from the table preceding question 9.

13. Suppose the price of good A is $20 and the price of good B is $10, and that the consumer is purchasing two units of each per month. From this information we can conclude that the individual:
    a. is maximizing utility for a given level of income.

    b. should buy more of good A and less of good B.
    c. should buy more of good B and less of good A.
    d. is maximizing income for a given level of utility.

14. By spending one more dollar on _____ and one less dollar on _____ the consumer can gain _____ utils with the same expenditure of money.
    a. B; A; 70
    c. A; B; 180
    b. B; A; 2
    d. A; B; 2

15. It is a common practice in restaurants for customers to be given as much coffee a they wish to drink without paying extra after they've ordered a meal. A person who wishes to maximize utility for a given income should drink coffee until the:
    a. restaurant runs out of coffee.
    b. person's money is gone.
    c. MU of the last cup approaches zero.
    d. MU of the last cup is negative.

16. Suppose you are in the market for a new bicycle. A salesperson shows you a nice ten-speed model for $289. You say the bicycle is very nice but you cannot afford such an expensive model. What do you really mean when you say you cannot afford something like this?
    a. The MU per dollar of the item is negative.
    b. The MU per dollar of the item is less than the MU per dollar of cheaper alternatives.
    c. It is impossible to get ahold of $289.
    d. The MU per dollar is greater than the MU per dollar of cheaper alternatives.

17. A "good buy" is an item whose MU per dollar is _____ the MU per dollar of other things we can spend our money on.
    a. greater than
    b. less than
    c. equal to

18. If people really try to maximize utility, given their income, how does one explain gift-giving and charity, where people give without expecting to receive something in return?

    a. People are irrational.

    b. People really do not try to maximize utility.

    c. People receive utility from giving.

    d. People who give have MU/P ratios that equal zero.

19. People change the mix of goods and services they purchase because:

    a. the MU of current purchases depends on past purchases.

    b. new products come on the market.

    c. relative prices change.

    d. all of the above.

20. Spendthrifts have a _____ rate of time preference, causing them to have a _____ MU per dollar of saving compared to a miser.

    a. low; low

    b. high; low

    c. low; high

    d. high; high

21. An increase in the interest rate _____ the price of present consumption, causing people to save _____, other things equal.

    a. increases; more

    b. increases; less

    c. decreases; more

    d. decreases; less

Chapter 5

Substitution Among Products

Key Concepts

Indifference curves
Imperfect substitutes
Perfect substitutes
Perfect complements
Budget line
Maximizing utility
Individual differences

When product prices change relative to one another, consumers have an incentive to substitute the relatively cheaper items for more expensive items. The main objective of this chapter is to provide a framework for classifying substitution possibilities. This framework is known as indifference curves.

INDIFFERENCE CURVES DEFINED

An *indifference curve* is a line showing various combinations of two goods that yield a constant level of satisfaction or utility. The best way to understand indifference curves is to construct one from a specific example. Since we are limited to a two-dimensional diagram, the example is restricted to considering two goods at a time. In this case, let us use the entertainment obtained from viewing football games and theater plays as the two goods. As a starting point, suppose you are given 10 tickets to see your favorite football team and 10 tickets to the theater of your choice. We can represent this combination by point A in Figure 5–1. Ask yourself this question: If 2 football tickets were taken away from me, how many additional theater tickets would I have to be given to remain equally satisfied? Assume there is no chance to sell the tickets, so you cannot exchange the extra theater tickets for football tickets. Also, do not be concerned about the price of the tickets. Assume they are given to you or taken away without charge or compensation.

Figure 5–1 An Indifference Curve

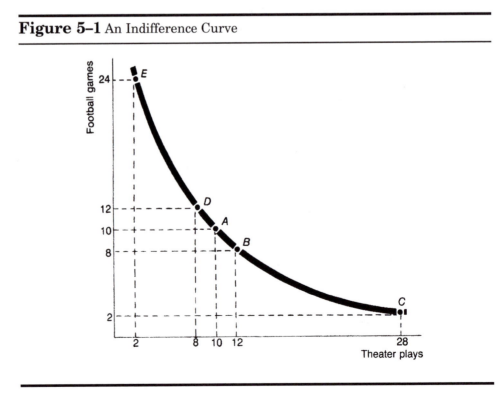

Your answer to this question will depend on how well you like football and the theater. Suppose you decide that 2 additional theater tickets would compensate you for the loss of the 2 football tickets. In other words, you are indifferent between the combination of 10 football and 10 theater tickets and the combination of 8 football and 12 theater tickets. Let this second combination be point B in Figure 5–1.

We might go through the same procedure again, this time taking away a total of 8 football tickets. Now you only have 2 football tickets left. How many theater tickets would you have to be given to remain as satisfied as you were in the original combination of 10 of each kind of tickets?

According to the idea of diminishing marginal utility, additional nights at the theater will provide less and less satisfaction. Moreover, the closer you come to no football tickets, the loss of football tickets will mean giving up increasingly more satisfaction. It is reasonable, therefore, that you will require more than 8 additional theater tickets to compensate for the loss of 8 football tickets. Suppose you want 18 more theater tickets. We could say that you are indifferent to the following combinations:

Combination	Theater	Football
A	10	10
B	12	8
C	28	2

Thus, we are tracing alternative combinations that would make you equally well off. We could also trace out points on the upper part of the curve by taking away theater tickets in exchange for football tickets. For example, you might choose 8 theater and 12 football tickets, or 2 theater and 24 football tickets as additional combinations, labeling these points D and E, respectively.

Assuming that the general relationship holds between the points as on them, we can connect points A through E. We have now constructed what economists call an *indifference curve*. From the standpoint of total satisfaction, you are indifferent at all points along this curve.

Of course, any number of curves can be drawn, as shown in Figure 5–2. We started out with 10 tickets of each, but we might have started with 6. If you prefer more tickets to less, then the smaller combination would be on a lower indifference curve, such as I_0 in Figure 5–2. Similarly, a larger combination, such as 14 of each, would be on a higher curve, say I_2. Economists call many such curves on a single diagram an *indifference map*. The indifference map is a picture of your preferences, much like a contour map is a picture of the landscape. Curves farther from the origin represent higher levels of satisfaction.

Figure 5–2 An Indifference Map

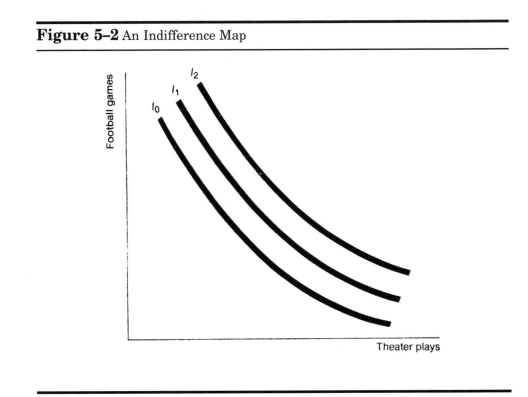

SUBSTITUTION POSSIBILITIES

A. Imperfect Substitutes

The shape of a person's indifference curves tells us the degree of substitution that exists between the two goods represented on the axes of the diagram. In the preceding example, the indifference curves are drawn with a slight curvature, convex to the origin. An indifference curve of this shape implies that the two goods represented on the axes are substitutes for one another but that they are imperfect substitutes. This means that as you move down along the curve, more and more units of the abundant good must be obtained to make you willing to give up each successive unit of the relatively scarce good. This is illustrated by Figure 5–1. Moving from point A to point B, you are willing to give up 2 football tickets if you gain 2 theater tickets. In other words, one theater ticket is enough to compensate you for giving up one football ticket. Now move from point B to point C. By giving up these 6 football tickets, you insist on 16 additional theater tickets. In other words, you now require nearly 3 theater tickets to compensate you for the loss of one football ticket. Under these conditions, we say that the two goods are imperfect substitutes. It is possible to substitute between them but as one moves to the extremes, it takes more of the abundant good being added to substitute for each unit of the scarce item given up.

B. Perfect Substitutes

Two items are defined as perfect substitutes if the amount of one good that is necessary to compensate for giving up each unit of another good remains constant at all possible combinations. For example, under most conditions, a person should be willing to give up one dozen white-shell eggs for one dozen brown-shell eggs of comparable size and quality, regardless of the combination being consumed. Indifference curves depicting perfect substitutes are drawn as straight, downward-sloping lines as illustrated by Figure 5–3. Notice that one brown-shell egg compensates for one white-shell egg regardless of where one is on the curve.

However, the ratio between the two items does not have to be one for one to have perfect substitutes. It may be that a person who had a preference for brown-shell eggs would have to be given two white-shell eggs to compensate for each brown egg given up. Or it could be that the size of the eggs are different. If the brown-shell eggs are large and white eggs are small, the ratio may have to be two white for one brown. The distinguishing characteristic of perfect substitutes is that the ratio remains constant at various combinations, not that the ratio is always one for one.

Figure 5–3 Indifference Curves for Perfect Substitutes

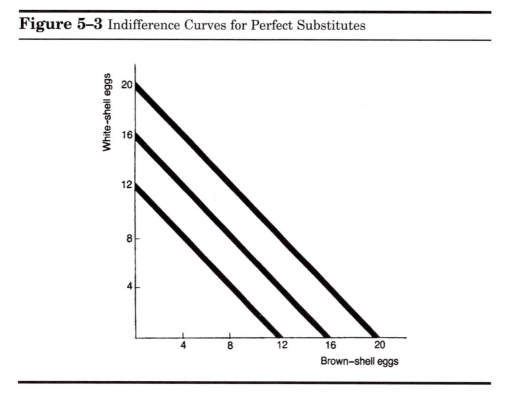

C. Perfect Complements

The third possible kind of substitution relationship that may exist between two items is zero substitutability. These items often are called perfect complements because they always must be used in a certain ratio or proportion to yield any utility. Good examples are right and left shoes. Presumably a two-legged person would not be any better off with one left shoe and two right shoes than with one left shoe and one right shoe. The individual would be on the same indifference curve with the one left and one right shoe combination as with one left and two right shoes. The indifference curve reflecting this situation is L-shaped as illustrated by Figure 5–4.

Remember that a person is on the same level of utility or satisfaction at all points along an indifference curve. Thus, adding more right shoes to the one left shoe does not, in this example, give the person more satisfaction. Moreover, it is not possible to stay on the same level of satisfaction by taking away left shoes and adding right shoes. In other words, two right shoes are not as good as one left and one right. Thus, the indifference curve runs parallel to each axis after the exact combination that makes the two items useful is attained. More units of one or the other good are redundant and add nothing to satisfaction. These goods are perfect complements because they must be used in the fixed ratio to be useful. Again, the ratio does not necessarily have to be one for one, although most pairs of perfect complements seem to occur in this ratio. The main point is that the ratio cannot be altered.

FIGURE 5–4 Indifference Curves for Perfect Complements

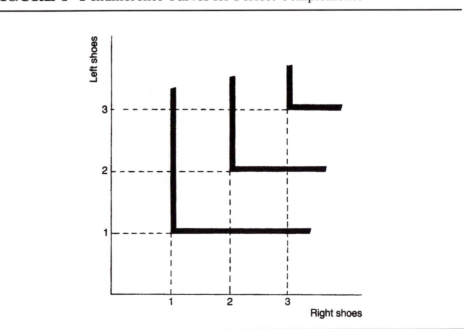

Note in the case of perfect complements that the indifference curves are parallel (Figure 5–4). In the cases of imperfect and perfect substitutes, however, the curves do not have to run parallel to each other. The only restriction is that they do not cross, for if they did, they could not be indifference curves.

In the area of consumer behavior, economists have not been greatly interested in perfect substitutes or perfect complements. For all practical purposes, pairs of perfect substitutes or perfect complements are seen as just one good. For example, white- and brown-shell eggs are considered eggs, or right and left shoes as pairs of shoes. The most interesting case is that of imperfect substitutes, in which various alternative combinations of two goods can provide the same level of satisfaction. Does this mean, therefore, that it doesn't make any difference to the individual which combination is selected? No. We will soon see that only one combination will give the individual the most for his or her money.

THE BUDGET LINE

To determine which of the many possible combinations of imperfect substitutes will give the individual the most for his or her money, it is necessary to add or superimpose a budget line on the indifference curve diagram. A budget line shows various possible combinations of two goods that can be purchased for a given amount of money.

Perhaps the easiest way to gain an understanding of a budget line is to construct one from a simple example. Let us continue to use the football and theater ticket example discussed in the preceding section. In constructing a budget line, two pieces of information are necessary: (1) the person's budget, or how much money he or she can spend on the two items under consideration, and (2) the price of each item. In this example, suppose you decide to spend $60 on football and theater entertainment for the upcoming season. Also suppose that the price of football tickets is $4 while theater seats cost $6.

To construct a budget line, determine where the line intersects the two axes. This can be accomplished by asking a couple of questions. First, how many football tickets could be purchased if you decided to spend your entire $60 entertainment budget on football if the price of each ticket were $4? The answer is 15 tickets. Now pose the same question for theater tickets. How many theater tickets could you purchase if you spent your entire $60 entertainment budget on the theater if the price of theater tickets were $6? In this case, the answer is 10. We now have the two points where the budget line intersects the two axes. It intersects the football axis at 15 tickets and the theater axis at 10 tickets. To complete the budget line, draw a straight line between the two points that have been identified on the axes, as shown by Figure 5–5. The budget line is always a straight line regardless of the degree of substitution that exists between two goods[1]. This is because of the way the budget line is defined. All points on the line represent a given expenditure. At the point where the line intersects the

---

1 This is true as long as the prices of the two items remain constant at all points along the budget line, which is the common situation for consumers.

football axis, $60 is being spent on 15 football tickets. At the 12 football-2 theater combinations, $48 is being spent on football and $12 on the theater. Moving down the line, you spend more on the theater and less on football, but you always spend $60.

MAXIMIZING UTILITY: INDIFFERENCE CURVE-BUDGET LINE APPROACH

We are now ready to combine indifference curves with the budget line to find out what combination of tickets would give you the most satisfaction for your $60. In Figure 5–6, we have imposed an indifference map on the budget line from Figure 5–5. First, let us choose any combination of tickets that totals $60, for example 12 football and 2 theater tickets. Will this combination give you the most satisfaction for your money? This question is answered by looking at Figure 5–6. Note that the highest indifference curve that can be reached with the 12 football-2 theater combination is I_0. But, a higher indifference curve can be reached by moving down the budget line, that is, by choosing a different combination of tickets that will be worth $60 (say, 9 football and 4 theater tickets). As you move down the budget line, you reduce your purchase of football tickets and increase the number of theater tickets you buy.

FIGURE 5–5 A Budget Line

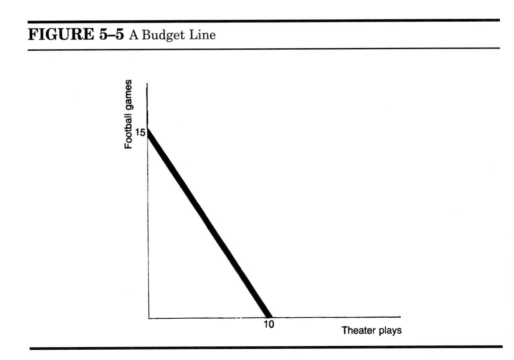

Remember that your overall objective is to reach the highest possible indifference curve within the constraint of the $60 you have to spend. The highest possible indifference curve you can reach is the one just tangent to the budget line, I_1 in Figure 5–6. Indifference curve I_2 could not be reached unless you wanted to spend more than $60. Thus, the general rule is that satisfaction will be maximized when you select that mix of goods on the budget line that enables you to reach the highest possible indifference curve.

In this example, the combination that maximizes your satisfaction is 9 football and 4 theater tickets. The cost of this combination, $60, is the same as any other combination on the budget line, such as 12 football and 2 theater tickets, or 3 football and 8 theater tickets, but your level of satisfaction is the greatest only at the 9 football—4 theater ticket combination.

Thus, even though we can purchase many different combinations of goods and services for a given expenditure, there is only one combination that will maximize our satisfaction. That is the combination that corresponds to the point of tangency between the budget line and the indifference curve.

FIGURE 5–6 Budget Line on Indifference Map

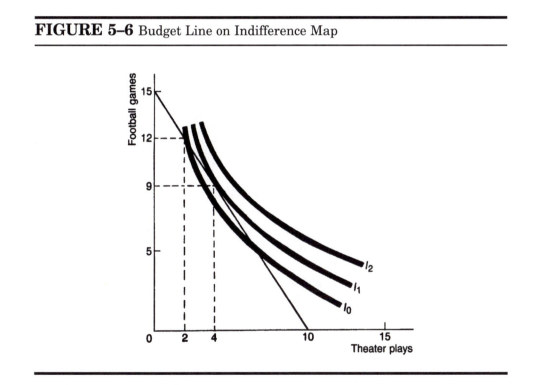

INDIVIDUAL DIFFERENCES

The indifference curves drawn in Figure 5–6 are an arbitrary representation of a person's tastes. The 9 football—4 theater ticket combination that maximizes satisfaction for the $60 resulted from how the indifference curves were drawn.

We could have as easily drawn the curves to illustrate a tangency point at any other combination. For example, an avid football fan who has little time for the theater likely would exhibit a different configuration of indifference curves, causing the tangency point to occur at a combination that weighed more in favor of football,such as the 12 football—2 theater combination illustrated by Figure 5–7A. On the other hand, a theatergoer would exhibit a set of indifference curves that would give rise to a tangency point favoring relatively more theater, such as the 3 football-8 theater ticket combination illustrated by Figure 5–7B. Again, each person has unique tastes and therefore exhibits a unique set of indifference curves between any given pair of goods.

In the preceding examples, we considered only one budget level—$60. The position of the budget line is determined in part by how large the budget is: the larger the budget, the farther to the right the budget line will be. For example, a $120 entertainment budget would cause the budget line to intersect the football and theater axes at 30 and 20 tickets, respectively. As a result, more of both items would be purchased, allowing one to reach a higher indifference curve, that is, a higher level of satisfaction. It will also be shown that changes in the price of each item also influence the position of the budget line and therefore affect the utility-maximizing combination, that is, the tangency point.

Although we have dealt with an example of imperfect substitutes (football and the theater), the same procedure applies to perfect substitutes and perfect complements. In the case of perfect substitutes, the utility-maximizing point will occur at one axis or the other if the slope of the budget line is different than the slope of the indifference curve. This means that the individual would buy only one of the two items, whichever is cheapest. This is reasonable to expect. If one item is as good as the other in satisfying one's tastes, why purchase any of the good that is more expensive? In reality, two goods that are perfect substitutes generally sell for the same price; otherwise no one would buy the good that offered less for the money. We will not be interested in two goods that are perfect substitutes and sell for the same price; essentially they are just one good. In the case of perfect complements, the utility-maximizing combination will occur at the corner of the indifference curve.

To summarize briefly, in this and the previous chapter we considered two approaches to the analysis of consumer behavior: (1) the marginal utility over-price approach and (2) the indifference curve-budget line approach. Both approaches yield the same results. In the first approach, utility is maximized for a given expenditure when the consumption pattern is such that the marginal utility per dollar is equalized across all purchases. In the second approach, utility is maximized when the combination that is consumed corresponds to the tangency point between the budget line and highest possible indifference curve. As shown in the appendix to this chapter, the marginal utilities per dollar of the two goods represented on the indifference curve-budget line diagram are equal for both goods only at the point of tangency.

Both approaches have their place. The marginal-utility-over-price approach is

Figure 5–7 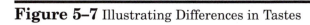 Illustrating Differences in Tastes

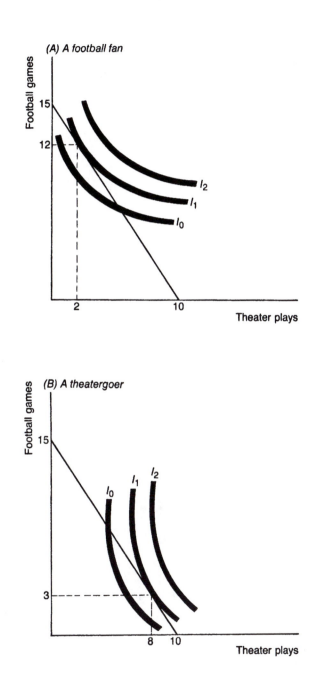

most useful for showing why additional utility can be gained by rearranging purchases until the marginal utilities per dollar of all items are equal The indifference curve-budget line also shows this point, but in addition it is useful for illustrating differences in the degree of substitution between goods, as reflected by the shape of the indifference curves.

Appendix: Proof of the Equivalence of the Utility-Maximizing Rule and the Points of Tangency of the Indifference Curve-Budget Line Approach

This appendix shows that at the point of tangency between a budget line and an indifference curve, the MU/product price ratios for two products (A and B) are equal.

Along a budget line:

$$\Delta TC = P_A \bullet \Delta A + P_B \bullet \Delta B = 0$$

Where: ΔTC is the change in total cost of products A and B along the budget line, P_A and P_B are the prices of A and B, and ΔA and ΔB are the changes in A and B purchased.

$$\text{Or:} \qquad \frac{\Delta A}{\Delta B} = - \frac{P_B}{P_A}$$

Since the slope of the budget line is $\frac{\Delta A}{\Delta B}$, its slope is also equal to $- \frac{P_B}{P_A}$.

Along an indifference curve:

$$\Delta U = MU_A \bullet \Delta A + MU_B \bullet \Delta B = 0$$

$$\text{Or:} \qquad \frac{\Delta A}{\Delta B} = - \frac{MU_B}{MU_A}$$

Since the slope of an indifference curve is $\Delta A / \Delta B$, its slope is also equal to

$$- \frac{MU_B}{MU_A}$$

At the point of tangency between a budget line and an indifference curve the slopes of the two lines must be equal. Therefore, at the point of tangency:

$$\frac{P_B}{P_A} = \frac{MU_B}{MU_A}$$

Rearranging the above expression, we obtain:

$$\frac{MU_A}{P_A} = \frac{MU_B}{P_B}$$

Therefore, at the point of tangency, the MU/P ratios are equal.

QUESTIONS

1. a. What is an indifference curve? An indifference map?
   b. What determines the shape of indifference curves?
2. Draw indifference curves for the following pairs of products and explain why you have drawn them in a certain shape:
   a. Paper and pencils.
   b. Pens and pencils.
   c. Baseball games and movies.
3. a. What is a budget line?
   b. Is a person equally well off at any point along a budget line? Explain.
4. a. Construct a budget line for a consumer who has $24 to spend on meat (beef and pork) for the week. Assume the price of pork is $2 per pound and the price of beef is $3 per pound.
   b. Add some indifference curves to the above diagram to indicate the combination of beef and pork that will maximize the consumer's satisfaction.
5. a. Draw an indifference map for a person who likes olives better than pickles but considers the two items as good substitutes for each other.
   b. Draw an indifference map for a person who likes pickles better than olives and considers the two items as poor substitutes for each other.
6. For many goods and services, the marginal utility of what we consume today depends on what we consumed yesterday. Translate this statement into an indifference curve-budget line diagram.

SELF-TEST

1. An indifference curve is a line showing various combinations of two goods that:
   a. cost a given amount.
   b. can be produced from a given amount of resources.
   c. can be produced from the same resources.
   d. yield a given amount of utility.
2. The shape of an indifference curve:
   a. is determined by how much each item costs.
   b. is the same for all people for a given pair of goods.
   c. is determined by a person's tastes.
   d. is the same for all possible pairs of goods for a given person.
3. For every pair of goods, there are _____ indifference curves.
   a. two
   b. an infinite number of
   c. three
   d. several
4. A higher level of satisfaction is shown by:
   a. points higher up on an indifference curve.
   b. indifference curves closer to the origin.
   c. indifference curves farther away from the origin.
   d. points lower down on an indifference curve.
5. An indifference curve for two goods that are imperfect substitutes will be:
   a. L-shaped.
   b. concave to the origin.
   c. convex to the origin.
   d. a straight downward-sloping line.
6. An indifference curve that is convex to the origin means that:
   a. it takes more and more money to purchase successive units of the abundant good.
   b. it takes less and less money to purchase successive units of the abundant good.

c. it takes more and more units of the abundant good to substitute for each successive unit given up of the scarce good.

d. it takes fewer and fewer units of the abundant good to substitute for each successive unit given up of the scarce good.

7. Goods that are perfect substitutes have _____ indifference curves.

   a. convex-to-the-origin

   b. concave-to-the-origin

   c. L-shaped

   d. straight downward-sloping line

8. The slope of indifference curves that are perfect substitutes:

   a. is -1.

   b. is +1.

   c. is infinite.

   d. depends on the units of measure.

9. Goods that are perfect complements have _____ indifference curves.

   a. convex-to-the-origin

   b. concave-to-the-origin

   c. L-shaped

   d. straight downward-sloping line

10. Most goods of interest are _____ to one another.

    a. perfect complements

    b. imperfect substitutes

    c. perfect substitutes

    d. unrelated

11. Which of the following pairs of goods would most likely exhibit indifference curves which are convex to the origin?

    a. right and left shoes

    b. automobile and bus transportation

    c. brown-shell and white-shell eggs in making an omelet

    d. sugar and salt in baking a cake

12. Which of the following pairs of goods would most likely exhibit L-shaped indifference curves?

    a. apples and bananas in making a fruit salad

    b. beef and pork as the main dish for a meal

    c. sugar and salt in baking a cake

    d. brown-shell and white-shell eggs in making an omelet

13. A budget line is a line showing various combinations of two goods that:

    a. cost a given amount.

    b. can be produced from a given amount of resources.

    c. can be produced from the same resource.

    d. yield a given amount of utility.

14. A budget line for imperfect substitutes is:

    a. convex to the origin.

    b. concave to the origin.

    c. L-shaped.

    d. a straight downward-sloping line.

15. Suppose a person has $100 to spend on goods A and B. Let the price of A be $25 and the price of B $20. The _____ will intersect the A axis at _____ and the B axis at _____ .

    a. budget line; 4 units; 5 units

    b. indifference curve; 4 units; 5 units

    c. budget line; $25; $20

    d. indifference curve; $25; $20

16. To maximize utility for a given budget a consumer must consume that mix of goods which corresponds to the point of tangency between:

    a. the indifference curve and highest possible budget line.

    b. the demand and supply curves.

    c. the budget line and lowest possible indifference curve.

    d. the budget line and highest possible indifference curve.

17. Consider an indifference curve-budget line diagram that has basketball games attended per season on the vertical axis and hockey games attended on the horizontal. If the two forms of entertainment are imperfect substitutes but the person is a basketball

fan, the indifference curve will be tangent
to the budget line at a point:

a. high on the line.

b. at the middle of the line.

c. low on the line.

Chapter 6

Demand

Key Concepts

Demand defined

Marginal utility and demand

Indifference curves and demand

Income and substitution effects

Market demand

Demand shifts

Demand shifters

The material in the previous two chapters is utilized to construct the concept of demand. Demand reflects the idea that consumers buy less of an item when it increases in price and they buy more when an item becomes cheaper. This chapter ends with a discussion of the factors that can increase or decrease quantity demanded at a given price.

DEMAND DEFINED

Demand is a negative *relationship* between price and quantity. The important thing to recognize about demand as used by economists is that it is not a set or fixed quantity but a relationship between price and quantity. To know what quantity a person or group of persons will demand, we must first know what price they will have to pay. For example, if you were asked how many football tickets you planned on purchasing this year, you would probably be reluctant to answer unless you knew what price you had to pay. The number of tickets you buy likely would be quite different if you had to pay $20 per ticket than if the price were $4. This chapter conceptualizes the relationship between the price of an item and the quantity people buy. We will begin by using the football ticket example.

In Figure 6–1, only 2 football tickets are demanded per season if the price is $8 per ticket; at a $4 price, 6 tickets are demanded; and at the bargain price of $2, 9 tickets are demanded per season. By connecting the series of points on the graph, we obtain a curve that is known as a *demand curve*. A demand curve describes a relationship between price and quantity. If we establish a price, the demand curve tells us what quantity will be demanded. Or, if we specify a quantity, the curve tells us what price the person is willing to pay.

It is important to distinguish between demand and quantity demanded. Demand, as we have noted, refers to the relationship between price and quantity. However, quantity demanded refers to a particular quantity or point on the demand curve. Thus, when you wish to stipulate a particular quantity you can avoid confusion by calling it "quantity demanded" rather than "demand."

A second important characteristic about demand is that it reflects *wants,* not *needs.* If you tell me that you need 6 football tickets if the price is $4 per ticket, it would be easy to disagree with your statement. It could be argued that you do not need *any* football tickets because watching football is not necessary to sustain life. Or, you might say you need a new car or a vacation trip to a distant city. Again, neither is necessary to sustain life. On the other hand, if you said you wanted 6 football tickets or a vacation trip, this could not be disputed. Only you can determine what you want, and these wants are partly satisfied by the things you buy.

A third point about a demand curve is that it reflects what people actually would do if faced by certain prices rather than what they would like to do. Your favorite make of automobile may sell for $30,000, and you might like a new one

FIGURE 6–1 The Concept of Demand (football ticket example)

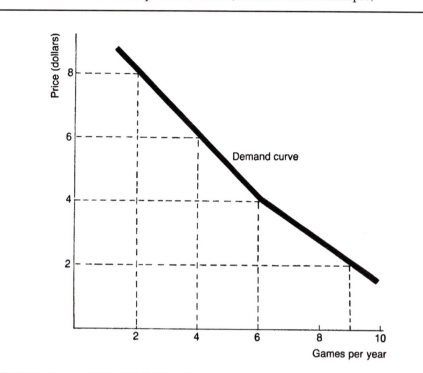

every year, but that does not mean you would actually purchase one of these cars every year or even one in a lifetime. Demand is useful only if it reflects the actions of people, not what they would *like* to do. In other words, demand reflects wants that are translated into action, not mere intention or desire.

A fourth item to note about demand is that quantity is measured as an amount per unit of time. In Figure 6–1, the quantity of football tickets is measured by the number of tickets per year. However, there is no set time period that is always used. We can measure quantity as amount per week, per month, per year, and so forth. The time dimension that is chosen is often the one that is most useful in analyzing the problem at hand. When you change the time period, you also change the scale on the quantity axis.

The demand curve shown in Figure 6–1 is only an example. In this diagram, the demand curve is drawn with a slight curvature. This is not meant to imply that demand curves for all products look this way. Some may be straight, downward-sloping lines; others may have more curvature. For the moment, our main concern is with the downward-sloping characteristic rather than with the curvature of the line, or with how steeply it slopes down.

MARGINAL UTILITY AND DEMAND

Although the downward-sloping nature of a demand curve has an intuitive appeal, we can establish this characteristic more rigorously using what we learned about marginal utility and price in Chapter 4. A consumer maximizes satisfaction when the marginal utilities (MU) per dollar are equal for all the goods and services available. The following expression summarizes this idea:

$$\frac{\text{MU of good A}}{\text{Price of good A}} = \frac{\text{MU of good B}}{\text{Price of good B}} = \ldots = \frac{\text{MU of good Z}}{\text{Price of good Z}}$$

Recall also that marginal utility per dollar depends on both marginal utility and price. For a given marginal utility, the higher the price, the lower the marginal utility per dollar. For example, suppose a consumer is initially maximizing utility, as illustrated in the expression above. Now consider that just one of these goods, good A, changes in price as shown below:

	Initial Situation	Price of A Rises	Price of A Falls
Marginal utility of A	20	20	20
Price of A	$4	$5	$2
Marginal utility per dollar	5	4	10

In the initial situation, all goods consumed by this person yield a marginal utility per dollar of five utils. When the price of good A rises, this good only yields four utils per dollar. In this case, it behooves the consumer to reduce the amount of good A purchased. One dollar less spent on A will reduce the person's satisfaction by four utils, but spending this dollar on something else that has not risen in price will yield close to five utils. Thus, the consumer can gain one util of net satisfaction by spending one dollar less on good A and one dollar more on one or more other goods.

As the consumer continues to reduce consumption of A, the marginal utility of A will increase (increasing the marginal utility per dollar of A). Also, as more other goods are consumed, the marginal utilities of these goods will decrease. Eventually the consumer will reach a new equilibrium where the marginal utilities per dollar are again equal for all goods. Note that as the price of a good rises, marginal utility per dollar declines, and this creates an incentive for the consumer to reduce purchases of the good in question. The end result is consistent with a downward-sloping demand curve, such as the curve in the preceding section, in which a higher price leads to a decreased rate of purchase.

Similar reasoning applies for a decrease in the price of A. Here, marginal utility per dollar increases, which provides an incentive for the consumer to increase purchases of A at the expense of other goods. This also is consistent with the concept of demand.

INDIFFERENCE CURVES AND DEMAND

So far we have shown that the downward-sloping nature of a demand curve is consistent with the marginal-utility-over-price approach of maximizing utility. In this section we will go one step further and derive a demand curve, using the indifference curve-budget line approach. It is necessary first to understand what happens to the budget line when the price of one of the two items changes. Recall from the preceding chapter that the intersection of the budget line with each axis is determined by dividing the dollar value of the budget by the price of each respective good. In terms of the football-theater ticket example, the 15- and 10-unit intersection points were obtained by dividing the $60 entertainment budget by $4 and $6, respectively.

What happens to the budget line if we change the price of theater tickets from $6 to $4? At the $4 theater price, the budget line intersects the theater axis at 15 tickets. If we hold the price of football tickets constant at $4, the budget line continues to intersect the football axis at 15 tickets. By drawing the budget line between the original point on the football axis and the new point on the theater axis, you will notice that a decrease in the price of theater tickets causes the budget line to rotate in a counterclockwise fashion, as illustrated by Figure 6-2. A further reduction in the price of theater tickets to $3 causes the budget line to rotate further, intersecting the horizontal axis at 20 theater tickets.

FIGURE 6–2 Indifference Map and Budget Lines Illustrating Changes in the Price of Theater Tickets

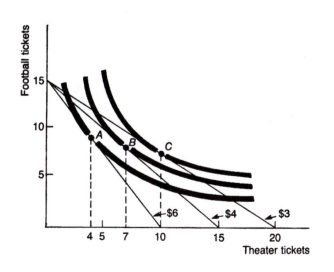

By superimposing the indifference curves that are tangent to these three budget lines, we obtain the utility-maximizing combination for each set of prices, as denoted by points A, B, and C on Figure 6–2. Notice that as the price of theater tickets declines, the optimum number of theater tickets purchased increases. By selecting three different theater ticket prices, we have determined three different quantities of theater tickets that will be purchased, given these indifference curves and the $60 budget. If this relationship between price and quantity looks familiar, it should, because it is none other than the information shown by a demand curve.(Recall that a demand curve is a relationship between price and quantity). By plotting the quantity of theater tickets that goes along with each price, we obtain a demand curve for theater tickets as shown by Figure 6–3. At the $6 price, 4 tickets are demanded; at the $4 price, 7 tickets are demanded; and so on. Thus we have derived a demand curve for theater tickets from the indifference curve-budget line diagram.

This procedure brings out one additional characteristic of a demand curve: Each point on a demand curve corresponds to a point of tangency between an indifference curve and a budget line, meaning that the individual is maximizing utility for a given expenditure. Notice also that this demand curve is drawn for a given income or budget and a given price of the good represented on the vertical axis. We could easily derive a demand curve for football tickets by going through the same procedure. Only now we would hold the theater ticket price

FIGURE 6–3 Demand Curve for Theater Tickets (as derived from Figure 6–2)

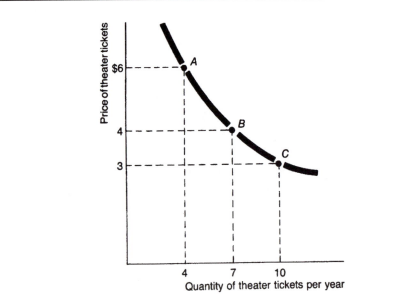

constant while changing the price of the football tickets. Notice that a decrease in the football ticket price causes the budget line to rotate in a clockwise fashion.

INCOME AND SUBSTITUTION EFFECTS

It is somewhat reassuring to see that the downward-sloping nature of the demand curve that we obtained first by appealing to our intuition also is obtained by the somewhat more rigorous procedure we have just used. It will be useful to probe deeper into the relationship between price and quantity in order to more fully understand why people buy more of a product when its price declines, or less when its price increases.

Economists have identified two major factors or effects that help explain why people behave this way: (1) the income effect and (2) the substitution effect. The income effect accounts for the fact that a change in the price of a good you buy changes the purchasing power of your income. It has the same effect as if you had experienced a change in income. For example, as the price of theater tickets declines, your $60 entertainment budget can buy a larger number of tickets. It is as if your income has been increased. The opposite occurs, of course, if the ticket price rises; then the $60 buys fewer tickets, so it is just like a decrease in your budget or income. The substitution effect occurs because when the price of one good changes relative to another, there is the incentive to buy more of the lower-priced good and less of the higher-priced one. In other words, you try to substitute the good that is relatively inexpensive for the one that is relatively more expensive.

The income and substitution effects can be defined in more specific terms by means of the indifference curve-budget line diagram. In Figure 6–4 we illustrate, using the theater ticket example, the effect of a decrease in the price of tickets from $6 to $3. Because of this price decline, the quantity of theater tickets demanded increases from 4 to 10. We will now determine what part of this increase in tickets demanded is due to the income effect and what part is due to the substitution effect.

Probably the most common procedure is to measure the substitution effect first. This is done by drawing a hypothetical budget line parallel to the new budget line but tangent to the original indifference curve. The hypothetical budget line is illustrated by the downward-sloping dashed line in Figure 6–4. It is tangent to the original indifference curve at point B. The horizontal distance between point A and point B (four theater tickets in our example) represents the substitution effect. Because of the lower price of theater tickets, illustrated by the flatter budget line, people substitute theater for football in their entertainment budget. The remaining two additional theater tickets are due to the income effect. This is shown by the movement point from B to C in Figure 6–4. These two additional theater tickets are purchased because the $60 entertainment budget goes further due to the decrease in the theater ticket price. It is

FIGURE 6–4 Illustration of the Income and Substitution Effects

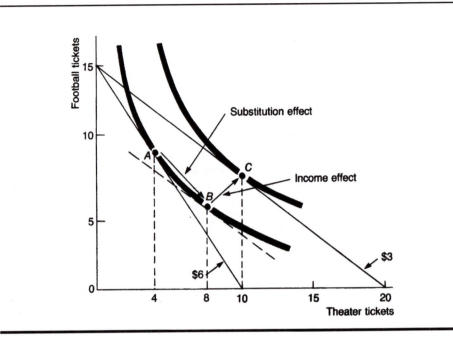

like having an increase in income, hence **the name** *income effect*. The substitution effect is always found by moving **along an indifference curve**, whereas the income effect is determined by moving **from one indifference curve to another.**[1]

MARKET DEMAND

While we have been concerned with the demand curve of an individual consumer, the concept of demand is most useful when applied to a market situation—an entire group of consumers.

It is simple to develop the idea of a market demand from the demand of individual consumers. First, suppose that every consumer has a demand for every product. For some consumers, the demand will be large at a given price; for other consumers, the demand might be zero at the same price. No two consumers necessarily have the same demand for a product. To visualize the idea

---

1 It is possible, and equally correct, to show the substitution effect along the new indifference curve rather than the original curve as explained above. This is accomplished by drawing the hypothetical budget line parallel to the original budget line and tangent to the new indifference curve. In this case the income effect is measured first and the remainder is the substitution effect.

of market demand at each possible price, add up the quantity demanded by all consumers in the market. In other words, we obtain a horizontal summation of the demand curves of individual consumers. Figure 6–5 provides an example of how this is done.

At $6 per ticket, consumer 1 demands 4 tickets per season, whereas at $3 per ticket, this person will buy 10 tickets. Consumer 2 is less of a theater fan. At $6 per ticket, consumer 2 would not attend the theater at all, and at the $3 price this individual will buy 2 tickets. Consumer 3 is a more ardent theatergoer than either consumers 1 or 2. This person demands 5 and 11 tickets at the $6 and $3 prices, respectively.

To keep the example simple, assume that the market consists of these three demanders. The market demand curve is found by adding, at each price, the quantities demanded by all the consumers in the market, as shown in the following table. The market demand curve is plotted in the lower right frame on Figure 6–5.

FIGURE 6–5 Constructing Market Demand from Individual Demand (theater ticket example)

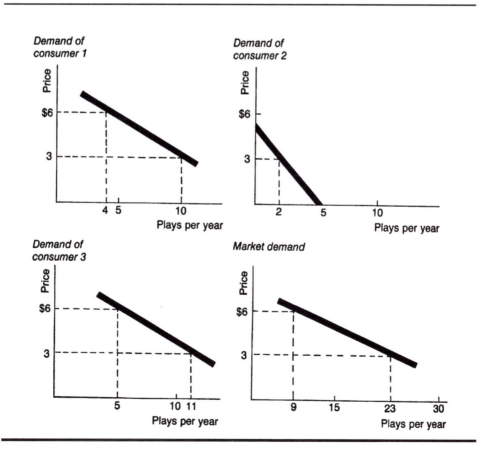

| Price | Quantity Demanded by Consumer: | | | | | | | Market Demand |
	1		2		3			
$6	4	+	0	+	5	=		9
3	10	+	2	+	11	=		23

Notice in the above example that the increase in quantity demanded by the market as price declines comes from two sources: (1) the increase in quantity by the existing demanders in the market, and (2) the entrance into the market of new demanders when the price declines, as illustrated by consumer 2.

DEMAND SHIFTS

When drawing a market demand curve for a good it is necessary to hold constant several factors other than its price that can affect the amount purchased. When one or more of these factors change, the entire demand curve will shift or change to a new position. This is called a change or shift in demand. A shift to the right of the demand curve means that consumers will purchase a greater quantity at a given price. This is referred to as an increase in demand, as illustrated in Figure 6–6. After demand has shifted from D_1 to D_2, consumers increase their purchases from Q_1 to Q_2 at price P_1. The opposite occurs if demand decreases, or shifts to the left. Now consumers purchase a smaller quantity, Q_0 rather than Q_1, at price P_1.

It is important in demand terminology to differentiate between a change in demand and a change in quantity demanded. The former refers to a shift of the entire demand curve, left or right. The latter refers to a movement along a given

FIGURE 6–6 Demand Shifts

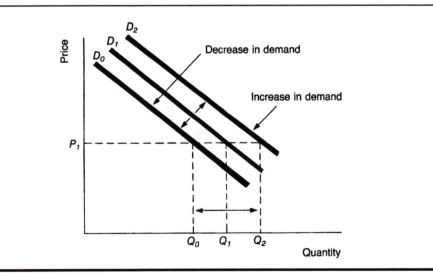

demand curve, up or down. For example, an increase (change) in demand is depicted by a shift to the right of the demand curve. An increase in quantity demanded refers to a movement down along a given demand curve.

DEMAND SHIFTERS

There are five main factors that cause the demand for most goods and services to shift. They are summarized below. A more thorough discussion of these and other demand shifters, and how they affect market price is given in Chapter 12.

1. Changes in Prices of Related Goods or Services. The demand for a good, say Pepsi, will increase if the price of a substitute good, such as Coke, increases. Consumers, in an attempt to avoid buying as much of the higher-priced Coke, increase their purchases of Pepsi, thereby increasing the demand for Pepsi (i.e., shifting its demand to the right). The opposite would hold true if the price of a substitute good declined.

2. Changes in Money Incomes of Consumers. The demand for most goods and services tends to increase or shift to the right as the money income of consumers increases. Again this is reasonable to expect; when we have more money to spend, we are able to increase our purchases of certain items. By the same token, a decrease in consumer incomes, say because of an increase in unemployment, tends to decrease the demand for many items, that is, shift it to the left.

3. Changes in Expectations of Consumers Regarding Future Prices and Incomes. If consumers expect the price of an item to increase in the future, they are likely to attempt to increase their rates of purchase of the item in order to stock up before the price rise. Similarly, if people expect their future incomes to be larger than their present incomes, we can expect them to buy more at the present. The opposite would be true, of course, for expected lower prices or incomes in the future.

4. Changes in Tastes and Preferences. Sometimes people will step up their purchases of an item if they suddenly take a liking to it. For example, the demands for motorcycles and blue jeans have increased in recent years. On the other hand, yo-yos and bobby sox no longer are "in."

5. Changes in Number of Consumers. The total market demand for an item will be greater as the number of consumers in the market increases. Nationwide, the demand for most goods and services has been shifting to the right because of population growth. Of course, in places where population has declined, such as in rural areas and small towns during the 1950s and 1960s, the demand for many goods and services has declined.

These five demand shifters include those that apply to most goods and services. There may be other demand shifters that occur because of special circumstances. For example, if the purchase of a good or service is illegal and subject to a stiff penalty, people may decide the risk is not worth taking and therefore refrain from buying it. The markets for illegal goods and services are discussed in greater detail in Chapter 13.

QUESTIONS

1. a. What two things does a demand curve tell us?
    b. Distinguish between demand and quantity demanded.
2. a. What is implied by the downward-sloping characteristic of a demand curve?
    b. Is a downward demand curve consistent with the utility-maximizing rule? Explain.
3. a. Draw an indifference curve-budget line diagram showing the mix of the two goods represented on the axes that would maximize utility for a given budget. Assume the budget is $100 and the price of the good on the vertical axis is $20 and the price of the good on the horizontal axis is $25. Also assume imperfect substitution between the two goods.
    b. Next show the utility-maximizing quantities, letting the price of the good on the horizontal axis decline to $20, and then to $10.
    c. On a separate diagram plot the demand curve for the good on the horizontal axis for the $25, $20, and $10 prices.
4. Show the substitution and income effects on the indifference curve-budget line diagram drawn in question 3 above, for the $20 to $10 price change.
5. Define in your own words the meaning of the substitution and income effects.
6. a. Using the table below, plot the market demand curve on a diagram.

Price	Quantity Demanded by Consumer:		
	1	2	3
$40	0	5	10
30	5	8	12
20	10	12	20

   b. Would you expect the market demand to exhibit a larger or smaller response to a price change than the demand of an average consumer in the market? Explain.
7. a. Define an increase in demand. A decrease.
    b. Illustrate each on a diagram.
8. a. What factors are held constant when drawing a given demand curve?
    b. What happens when one or more of these factors change?
9. State whether the following changes increase or decrease the current demand for new, American-made cars, and explain why. Also illustrate each on a diagram.
    a. An increase in the price of Japanese cars.
    b. A decrease in money incomes.
    c. Consumers expect lower U.S. car prices in the future

SELF-TEST

1. Demand is:
   a. a negative relationship between price and quantity.
   b. a positive relationship between units consumed and marginal utility.
   c. the number of units purchased per time period.
   d. the number of units that a person would like to purchase per time period.

2. A demand curve is _____ sloping line on a diagram having _____ on the vertical axis and _____ on the horizontal axis.
   a. a downward; quantity; price
   b. a downward; price; quantity
   c. an upward; quantity; price
   d. an upward; price; quantity

3. The utility-maximizing rule is consistent with a downward-sloping demand curve because an increase in the price of a good _____ the MU/P of that good, causing people to purchase _____ of it.
   a. increases; more
   b. increases; less
   c. decreases; more
   d. decreases; less

4. As consumers purchase less of a good in response to an increase in its price, the marginal utility of this good _____ causing its marginal utility per dollar to _____ which reestablishes an equilibrium.
   a. increases; decrease
   b. increases; increase
   c. decreases; decrease
   d. decreases; increase

5. A decrease in the price of the good represented on the horizontal axis of an indifference curve-budget line diagram causes the _____ to rotate in a_____ fashion.
   a. indifference curve; clockwise
   b. budget line; clockwise
   c. indifference curve; counterclockwise
   d. budget line; counterclockwise

6. The effect of the rotation described in question 5 is to _____ the consumption of the good represented on the horizontal axis. (Assume the indifference curves are convex to their origin.) The new point of tangency is located on a _____ indifference curve.
   a. increase; higher
   b. decrease; lower
   c. increase; lower
   d. decrease; higher

7. A demand curve for a good can be derived from an indifference curve-budget line diagram by plotting the:
   a. maximum amount of the good that could be consumed at various levels of income.
   b. maximum amount of the good that could be consumed at various prices of that good.
   c. the utility-maximizing quantities of the good at various possible prices.
   d. the utility-maximizing quantities of the good at various possible incomes.

8. Which of the following statements is/are true of all points on a demand curve?
   a. Marginal utility per dollar is the same for all goods available.
   b. Consumers are at the points of tangency between the budget lines and highest attainable indifference curves.
   c. The marginal utility of all goods is the same.
   d. a and b.

9. When the price of an item declines, the substitution effect occurs because:
   a. each good is unique so that substitution among goods is not possible.
   b. money income is increased.
   c. a given money income can buy more.
   d. its price has declined relative to other goods.

10. When the price of an item declines, the income effect occurs because:
    a. each good is unique so that substitution among goods is not possible.

b. money income is increased.

c. a given money income can buy more.

d. its price has declined relative to other goods.

11. The substitution effect is shown by the movement _____ and the income effect is shown by the movement _____ .

a. between indifference curves; along an indifference curve

b. along an indifference curve; between indifference curves.

c. between indifference curves; along a budget line.

d. along a budget line; between indifference curves.

12. The market demand for a product is obtained by adding the _____ at each _____ .

a. prices paid; quantity

b. prices paid; income level

c. quantities demanded; price

d. quantities demanded; income level

13. An increase in demand means that consumers will purchase a _____ quantity at a given price, or will pay a _____ price for a given quantity.

a. larger; higher

b. larger; lower

c. smaller; higher

d. smaller; lower

14. Japanese cars and U.S. cars are regarded as substitutes. An increase in the price of Japanese cars will cause the demand for U.S.-made cars to _____ thereby _____ the quantity of U.S.-made cars demanded at a given price.

a. decrease; increasing

b. increase; increasing

c. decrease; decreasing

d. increase; decreasing

15. When people suffer a decrease in income because of unemployment, the demand for new cars can be expected to _____ causing a(n) _____ in their quantity demanded at a given price.

a. decrease; increase

b. increase; increase

c. decrease; decrease

d. increase; decrease

16. If people expect the price of single-family homes to increase in the near future because of expected inflation, the current demand for homes will_____, causing a(n) _____ in the number of homes purchased.

a. increase; decrease

b. decrease; decrease

c. increase; increase

d. decrease; increase

17. During the 1980s consumers revealed a preference for vans over station wagons. The result was a(n) _____ in demand for vans and a(n) _____ in demand for station wagons.

a. increase; increase

b. decrease; decrease

c. increase; decrease

d. decrease; increase

18. Many small towns in rural areas lost population during the 1980s. As a result, the demand for housing in these communities _____ , causing a(n) _____ in the construction of new housing.

a. increased; decrease

b. decreased; decrease

c. increased; increase

d. decreased; increase

Chapter 7

Demand Elasticities

Key Concepts

Response to price changes
Price elasticity of demand
Price elasticity and total revenue
Factors affecting price elasticity
Income elasticity of demand
Cross elasticity of demand

This chapter deals mainly with the responsiveness of consumers to price and income changes as measured by elasticities of demand. There are three: price elasticity, income elasticity, and cross elasticity.

RESPONSE TO PRICE CHANGES

Our interest thus far has centered mainly on the downward-sloping nature of the demand curve, meaning that people buy more of an item when its price decrease and less when its price increases. It is necessary, however, that we become somewhat more specific than this. In this section we will consider the *responsiveness* of consumers to price changes. Even if we know that consumers buy more of a good when its price decreases, it is equally important to know whether they buy a lot more or just a little bit more.

The shape of the demand curve can tell us something about the responsiveness of consumers to price changes. A demand curve that is relatively flat, as illustrated by Figure 7–1A, reflects that consumers are relatively responsive to a price change. In this example, the individual increases the quantity of tickets from 12 to 18 when the price declines from $6 to $4. On the other hand, a demand curve that is relatively steep implies that consumers are relatively unresponsive to price changes. This is illustrated in Figure 7–1B, where the consumer buys only one more ticket per year when the price declines from $6 to

FIGURE 7–1 Differences in Response to Price Changes

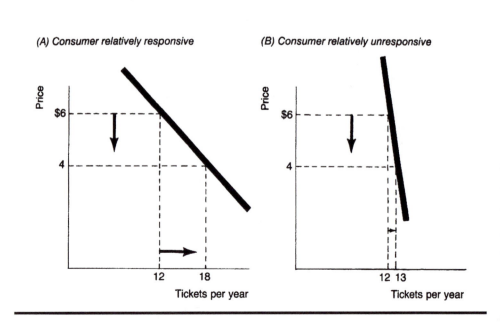

$4.

Gauging the responsiveness of consumers to price changes by the shape or slope of the demand curve can be misleading, however, because it is possible to change the shape of the curve simply by changing the scale along one or both axes. For example, the market demand curve can be made to appear relatively flat by expanding the units of measure on the quantity axis while squeezing together the price axis scale as illustrated by Figure 7–2A. In viewing the demand curve drawn in Figure 7–2A, a person might conclude that consumers are relatively responsive to changes in ticket prices. By the same token it is possible to represent the same price-quantity relationship as a relatively steep demand curve by contracting the scale on the horizontal axis while expanding the price axis scale as shown by Figure 7–2B.

Whenever viewing statistical phenomena presented by a graph or diagram, it is a good idea to be aware that the message conveyed may to a certain extent be influenced by the scale on the two axes. Although economists frequently use a flat demand curve to convey the idea that consumers are relatively responsive to price changes and a steep curve to indicate the opposite tendency, they are aware of this shortcoming and consequently supplement the diagrammatic representation with another measure of price response that is not dependent on the scale used. In fact it does not even require a diagram. This measure is called *price elasticity of demand.*

PRICE ELASTICITY OF DEMAND

Price elasticity of demand is defined as the percent change in quantity

FIGURE 7–2 The Same Response to a Price Change by Different Shaped Demand Curves

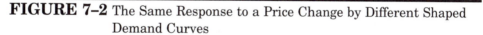

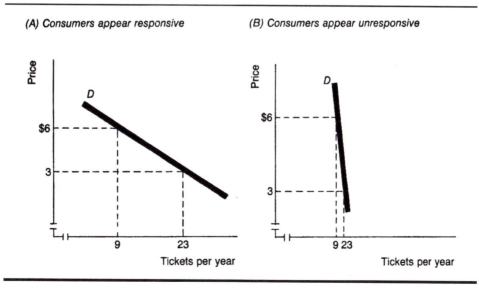

demanded resulting from each percent change in price. The price elasticity of demand formula is:

$$E_d = \frac{\% \, \Delta \, Q}{\% \, \Delta \, P}$$

where E_d is an abbreviation for price elasticity of demand, and the symbol "Δ" means "change in." For computational purposes the above formula is written as:

$$E_d = \frac{\dfrac{Q_0 - Q_1}{Q_0}}{\dfrac{P_0 - P_1}{P_0}}$$

where Q_0 and P_0 are the beginning quantity and price, respectively, and Q_1 and P_1 are the ending quantity and price. In order to become somewhat more familiar with the formula, let us compute the price elasticity of demand for the change shown in Figure 7–1A. In this example the Q_0 is 12, Q_1 is 18, P_0 is \$6, and P_1 is \$4. Thus we have

$$E_d = \frac{\dfrac{12 - 18}{12}}{\dfrac{6 - 4}{6}} = \frac{\dfrac{-6}{12}}{\dfrac{2}{6}} = \frac{-0.50}{0.33} = -1.5$$

In this example, a 1 percent decrease in price is associated with a 1.5 percent increase in quantity. You will note that the price elasticity of demand is a negative number. This occurs because as we move along a demand curve, quantity and price change in opposite directions; when price goes down, quantity goes up, and vice versa.

Although the price elasticity measure is a negative number, when economists refer to a specific elasticity measure they often drop the negative sign and designate the number as an absolute value. For example, a price elasticity measure of –1.5 generally is referred to as 1.5. Once one is aware that the negative sign is implicit in the discussion, it is redundant to keep repeating it.

In order to further facilitate discussion, economists have grouped the price elasticity measure, or coefficient, as it is often called, into three categories. Generally the groupings are made according to the absolute size of the *coefficient* (minus sign dropped). These categories of elasticity coefficients are:

Less than 1 = Inelastic
Equal to 1 = Unitary elastic
Greater than 1 = Elastic

When the demand for a product is inelastic to price, we say that consumers are relatively unresponsive to a price change. In this case the percentage change in quantity is smaller than the corresponding percentage change in price. If demand is elastic, on the other hand, we say that consumers are quite responsive to a price change. Here the percentage change in quantity is greater than the percentage change in price. In the intermediate case of a unitary elastic demand, price and quantity both change in the same proportions.

The smallest possible value of the elasticity coefficient is zero. If E_d is zero, a change in price will not result in any change in quantity whatever. In this case demand is said to be perfectly inelastic. Demand that is perfectly inelastic is represented by a demand curve that is perfectly vertical (Figure 7–3).

FIGURE 7–3 Perfectly Inelastic Demand

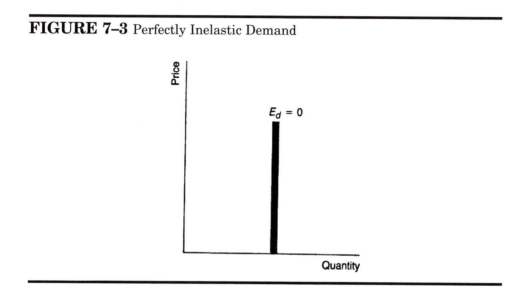

The largest possible value of the elasticity coefficient is infinity. Here a very slight change in price corresponds to an infinitely large change in quantity. In this situation demand is said to be perfectly elastic and is characterized by a demand curve that is perfectly horizontal (Figure 7–4).

Two characteristics of the elasticity coefficient ought to be mentioned at this point. Both stem from the fact that elasticity deals with percentage changes. The first is that the size of the elasticity coefficient becomes larger as we move higher up on a downward-sloping, straight-line demand curve. This phenomenon occurs because the base or beginning values change at different points along the demand curve. At points high on the curve, the beginning price is high. Thus for a given dollar change in price, the percentage change is relatively small. For example, a $1 change in price will be only 10 percent if the beginning price is $10, whereas the same $1 change in price would represent a 100 percent change if the beginning price is only $1. The same reasoning applies to different points along the quantity axis. The beginning or base quantity is small at points high on the demand curve (small quantity demanded), which in turn results in large percentage changes for a given absolute change in quantity. The effect of a change in base values on E_d is illustrated in the following elasticity formulas. Consider the absolute change in quantity $(Q_0 - Q_1)$ and the absolute change in price $(P_0 - P_1)$ to be the same in each case, so that the only things changing are the base values.

Points high on a demand curve:

$$E_d = \cfrac{\dfrac{Q_0 - Q_1}{Q_0} \quad \text{small}}{\dfrac{P_0 - P_1}{P_0} \quad \text{large}} \quad \left| \begin{array}{c} \text{large} \\ \\ \text{small} \end{array} \right| \quad \text{large}$$

FIGURE 7–4 Perfectly Elastic Demand

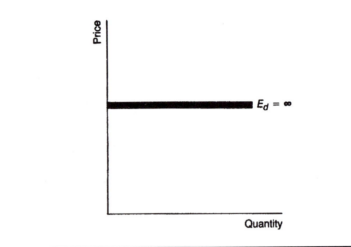

Points low on a demand curve:

$$E_d = \cfrac{\dfrac{Q_0 - Q_1}{Q_0} \quad \text{large}}{\dfrac{P_0 - P_1}{P_0} \quad \text{small}} \quad \left| \begin{array}{c} \text{small} \\ \\ \text{large} \end{array} \right| \quad \text{small}$$

The above discussion is not meant to imply that all demand curves are straight lines. They can also be curved lines. The particular shape depends on how buyer respond to price changes at various possible prices. The nature of their responses may well vary between different points on a given demand curve and between indifferent goods.

A second characteristic of elasticity that occurs because it is measured in percentage terms is that the coefficient depends on the direction of a given absolute change in price and quantity. In the example for computing price elasticity of demand used above, the beginning or base quantity and price were 12 and $6 respectively. But if we had started at the $4 price and moved up along the demand curve, the elasticity coefficient obtained would have been different. This is because the base values would have changed to 18 and $4 for quantity and price. The larger base value for quantity would have made the percentage change in quantity smaller (–33 percent), whereas the percentage change in price would have increased to 50 percent. The overall elasticity coefficient would have declined to 0.66.

Because different answers are obtained for different directions of movement, the elasticity coefficient is accurate only if it is computed over relatively small changes in price and quantity. Economists measuring price elasticity of demand for actual products use statistical tools that measure only very small movements in price and quantity.

For teaching purposes, economists have modified the elasticity formula slightly, using both beginning and ending values of price and quantity for the base in the numerator and denominator. The formula becomes:

$$E_d = \frac{\dfrac{Q_0 - Q_1}{Q_0 + Q_1}}{\dfrac{P_0 - P_1}{P_0 + P_1}}$$

This formula measures the "average" elasticity between two points, and it results in the same answer regardless of the direction of movement.[1] The formula discussed first is sometimes known as the "point elasticity" formula, whereas the second expression has come to be known as the "arc elasticity" formula. Notice that the elasticity coefficient for the example we have been working with is 1.0 using this second formula.

In an effort to master the mechanics of price elasticity, one should not lose sight of its economic meaning. Keep in mind that price elasticity of demand measures the responsiveness of consumers to changes in price. An inelastic demand means that consumers are not very responsive to price, whereas an elastic demand means that they will be quite responsive to price changes. The

---

1 The above formula also can be expressed as

$$\frac{\dfrac{Q_0 - Q_1}{Q_0 + Q_1/2}}{\dfrac{P_0 - P_1}{P_0 + P_1/2}}$$

and referred to as the "midpoints" formula. In this case the base values are taken as halfway between the beginning and ending quantities and prices. However, because the 2s cancel, the same answer is obtained as in the above expression.

elasticity coefficient tells us the percentage change in quantity demanded for each one percent change in price.

PRICE ELASTICITY AND TOTAL REVENUE

One of the most valuable uses of the price elasticity concept is that it enables us to predict what will happen to the total expenditure on a product by consumers, or the total revenue going to the sellers of the product, when its price changes. To understand how elasticity is related to changes in total expenditure or revenue, it is necessary to first understand that a price change has two offsetting effects on total revenue or expenditure.

Consider first a price fall where demand is inelastic. This is illustrated in Figure 7–5. Price declines from $10 to $9 and quantity increases from 95 to 100. Total revenue is price times quantity (P x Q). The increase in quantity pulls total revenue up but this is offset by the decrease in price which pulls total revenue down. If the percent change in quantity is less than the percent change in price(demand is inelastic), total revenue decreases when price decreases. The change in total revenue obtained from the change shown in Figure 7–5 is calculated below. The one dollar decrease in price results in a $50 decrease in total revenue.

FIGURE 7–5 Price Reduction with Inelastic Demand

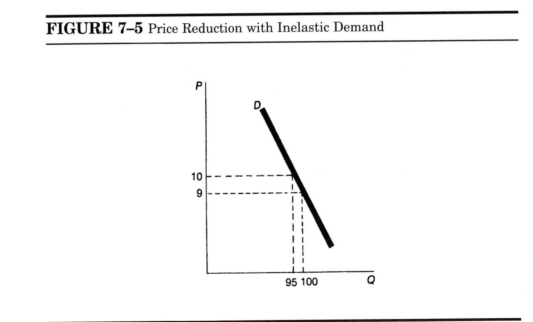

	Price	Quantity	Total Revenue
Start	$10	95	$950
End	9	100	900
Net change			−50

FIGURE 7–6 Price Reduction with Elastic Demand

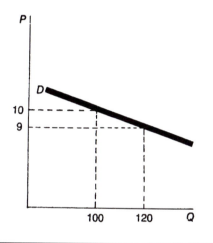

The opposite occurs if demand is elastic. This is illustrated in Figures 7–6 where price declines from $10 to $9 and quantity increases from 100 to 120. Here the percent change in quantity (20 percent) is greater than the percent change in price (10 percent). Therefore total revenue increases when price decreases.

	Price	Quantity	Total Revenue
Start	$10	100	$1000
End	9	120	1080
Net change			+80

In the case of a price increase, the opposite occurs. When demand is inelastic, a price increase causes total revenue to increase. Here the percent decrease in, quantity is less than the percent increase in price. Conversely, total revenue decreases when price increases if demand is elastic. Now the percent decrease in quantity is greater than the percent increase in price.

If the price elasticity of demand is −1, or unitary elastic, a change in price has no effect on total revenue. In this case the percent change in price is the same as the percent change in quantity. Here the two effects cancel out.

A summary of the effects of price changes when demand is elastic, inelastic, or unitary elastic is shown below.

	Change in Total Revenue or Expenditure
Elastic demand	
Price fall	Increase
Price rise	Decrease
Inelastic demand	
Price fall	Decrease
Price rise	Increase
Unitary Elastic	
Price fall	No change
Price rise	No change

Notice that for an elastic demand, price and total revenue or expenditure change in opposite directions, whereas for an inelastic demand they change in the same direction.

PREDICTING QUANTITY CHANGES

Price elasticity of demand also is useful for predicting the change in quantity demanded resulting from a given change in price. For example, suppose the price elasticity of demand of a product is 0.75 and its price increases by 10 percent, other things equal. How much does quantity demanded decrease in this case? The answer can easily be obtained by calling to mind the formula for computing the elasticity coefficient.

$$E_d = \frac{\% \Delta Q}{\% \Delta P}$$

In this case we know E_d is –0.75 and $\% \Delta P$ is +10. Substituting these values into the above formula gives us:

$$-0.75 = \frac{\% \Delta Q}{10}$$

or

$$\% \Delta Q = 10x -0.75 = -7.5$$

Quantity decreases by 7.5 percent because of the 10 percent increase in price. Notice, the larger is the elasticity (in absolute terms) the greater the change in quantity demanded resulting from a given change in price.

ECONOMIC FACTORS AFFECTING PRICE ELASTICITY OF DEMAND

We have seen that price elasticity is affected by the point we happen to choose along a demand curve. But this is strictly an algebraic phenomenon that occurs because of the way we calculate price elasticity. We now want to explore briefly the economic factors that affect the size of a product's price elasticity of demand. The demand for some goods is elastic, and the demand for other goods is inelastic. Why?

The first, and perhaps most important, factor influencing the price elasticity of a good is the degree of substitution between it and other goods. The larger the number and the better the substitutes that exist for a good or service, the more elastic will be that particular good or service.

To understand the economic rationale of this generalization, consider a product that has many substitutes: pork chops, for example. When the price of pork chops goes up, consumers have many other alternative products to choose from other cuts of pork; all other meat, such as beef, poultry, and fish; as well as other protein foods that can be eaten in place of meat, such as cheese or vegetables. A rise in the price of pork chops, then, will provide an incentive for consumers to reduce pork chop consumption and increase their consumption of these alternative products. When pork chop consumption declines, it is an indication that consumers are being responsive to the rising price of pork chops. You will recall that this is the meaning of an elastic demand.

Products that have few or very poor substitutes, on the other hand, tend to have an inelastic demand. Salt is the classic example of such a good. If the price of salt should rise, consumers would still have to buy it in about the same amounts, since there are few satisfactory substitutes. This means that consumers are not very responsive to a change in the price of salt, which is just another way of saying that salt has an inelastic demand.

It is important to recognize as well that the definition of a product influences its elasticity. In general, the more broadly we define a product, the lower will be its price elasticity. This is because there are fewer substitutes for a broadly defined product than for one that is narrowly defined. For example, the price elasticity for all pork would be smaller (less elastic or more inelastic) than it is for only porkchops. The substitutes for pork chops include pork loins and pork roasts, as well as the pork substitutes, whereas the substitutes for all pork include only the other meats or meat substitutes. Similarly, the demand for a particular brand of salt would be more elastic than for all salt, because brand X, for example, has substitutes in the form of the other brands of salt on the market.

The second major factor influencing the elasticity of a product is the proportion of the consumer's budget accounted for by the product. Products that take up every small proportion of the budget tend to be less elastic than those that rank relatively large in the budget. For example, if the price of paper clips doubles, the impact on your budget would be imperceptible; hence there would not be a strong incentive to reduce your use of paper clips. Yet if something like dormitory room rent rises considerably, you might be forced to find an alternative place to stay, such as an apartment or a private home, or you might even have to leave school. Thus we would expect the demand for dormitory rooms to be more elastic than the demand for paper clips.

A summary of the effect of these two factors on the price elasticity of demand is presented in the following table.

Factor	Effect on Price Elasticity
Many good substitutes	Increase
Large item in budget	Increase

It is not unusual to find cases, however, where each of these two factors has an opposite influence on the elasticity of a product. That is, a product may have many good substitutes, making for an elastic demand, but at the same time it maybe a small item in the budget, which makes for an inelastic demand. The resulting price elasticity, therefore, is a summation of these two factors; both must be considered when attempting to assess the elasticity of such a product.

You might have noticed that the two factors named above as influencing the price elasticity of a product closely parallel the two effects, discussed previously in chapter 6, that account for the downward-sloping characteristic of the demand curve—the substitution and income effects. This is not just a coincidence. The first factor, the degree of substitution possible, assesses the strength of the substitution effect; and the second factor, the importance of the item in the budget, assesses the strength of the income effect. The stronger or more significant these two effects are, the more responsive consumers are to a price change, which in turn implies a more elastic demand.

INCOME ELASTICITY OF DEMAND

As noted above, changes in consumers' money incomes are an important demand shifter. To measure the responsiveness of consumers to income changes, economists have developed the concept of income elasticity. *Income elasticity* is defined as the percent change in demand resulting from each 1 percent change in money income. This concept is related to price elasticity of demand. The difference is that price elasticity measures the responsiveness of consumers to price changes as one moves up or down along a given demand curve, while income elasticity measures the responsiveness of consumers to income changes as the demand curve shifts from one position to another as illustrated by Figure 7–7. The increase in demand from D_0 to D_1 is assumed to have been caused by an income increase, I_0 to I_1. The resulting quantity change, Q_0

to Q_1, is measured at a given price, say P_0. The income elasticity formula is:

$$E_I = \frac{\% \, \Delta \, Q}{\% \, \Delta \, I}$$

where E_1 stands for income elasticity. Notice that it is similar to the price elasticity formula except $\% \, \Delta \, I$ is written in the denominator. For computational purposes, the above formula is written as:

$$E_I = \frac{\dfrac{Q_0 - Q_1}{Q_0}}{\dfrac{I_0 - I_1}{I_0}}$$

It may be helpful to insert actual numbers in this formula to illustrate how income elasticity is computed. Suppose a family increases its purchase of beef from 200 to 225 pounds per year as a result of an increase in annual income from \$14,000 to \$15,000. In this formula, Q_0 would be 200, Q_1 225, I_0 \$14,000, and I_1 \$15,000. In this example, income elasticity is 1.76, as shown by the following computations. The 1.76 means that this family increases its beef consumption by 1.76 percent when its income increases by 1 percent, at a given price.

$$E_I = \frac{\dfrac{200 - 225}{200}}{\dfrac{14{,}000 - 15{,}000}{14{,}000}} = \frac{\dfrac{-25}{200}}{\dfrac{-1{,}000}{14{,}000}} = \frac{-0.125}{-0.071} = 1.76$$

FIGURE 7–7 Income Elasticity Illustrated

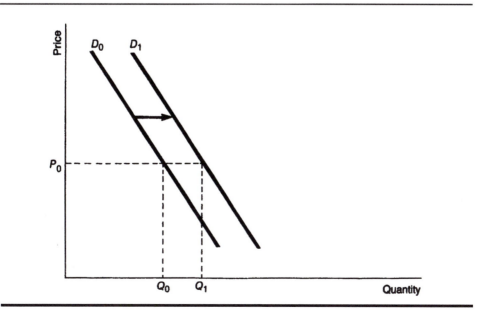

An increase in money income can cause a demand curve to either increase, decrease, or remain constant. If demand increases when income increases as in the above example, income elasticity is a positive number. Such goods are referred to as superior or normal goods. Most items fit this description. However, there are some goods that exhibit a decrease in demand when income increases. In this case, income elasticity is negative. Goods exhibiting a negative income elasticity are called inferior goods. An example is starchy foods; people buy fewer starches as they become more affluent, buying instead more fresh vegetables and meat. It is possible that demand may not shift at all when income increases: Income elasticity is zero. All food, as a composite commodity in a high-income nation, is frequently used as an example of a good with a zero-income elasticity. People can eat just so much; with higher incomes, they usually don't eat more food. In poor countries food is a superior good; people buy more of it when their incomes increase.

The classification of goods by income elasticity is summarized below:

Type of Good	Income Elasticity
Superior or normal	Positive
Inferior	Negative

CROSS ELASTICITY OF DEMAND

Another of the major demand shifters is a change in the price of related goods. There are two kinds of related goods—substitutes and complements. Two goods are substitutes when an increase in the price of one causes an increase in the demand for the other. Beef and poultry are examples of substitutes. When the price of beef increases, for example, people tend to increase their consumption of poultry and eat less of the higher-priced beef. This behavior is represented by an increase in the demand for poultry. The responsiveness of poultry consumption to an increase in the price of the beef is measured by the cross elasticity of poultry demand with respect to a change in the price of beef.

The formula expressing cross elasticity of demand is similar to price and income elasticity formulas:

$$E_{cd} = \frac{\% \Delta Q_i}{\% \Delta P_j}$$

where E_{cd}, the cross elasticity coefficient, is found by dividing the percent change in the quantity of good i by the percent change in the price of good j, i and j being two different goods.

To illustrate how E_{cd} is computed, consider a situation where the price of beef increases to $2.25 per pound from $2 per pound. Suppose this causes a family to increase poultry consumption, say, from 100 pounds to 125 pounds per year.

The cross elasticity of demand for poultry with respect to a change in the price of beef (E_{cd}) is calculated as follows:

$$E_{cd} = \frac{\dfrac{100 - 125}{100}}{\dfrac{\$2.00 - 2.25}{2.00}} = \frac{\dfrac{25}{100}}{\dfrac{0.25}{2.00}} = \frac{-0.25}{-0.125} = 2.0$$

The E_{cd} coefficient of 2.0 means that the quantity demanded of poultry changes by 2 percent for each 1 percent change in the price of beef. The cross-elasticity coefficient for substitutes is a positive number reflecting that when the price of a substitute good increases, consumers will buy more of the good in question and less of the substitute.

The diagram illustrating cross elasticity is essentially the same as in Figure 7–7, which illustrates income elasticity. The only difference is that the increase in demand for poultry is caused by an increase in the price of a substitute (beef) rather than income. Also note that the change in quantity of poultry resulting from the increase in the price of beef is measured at a given price of poultry, such as P_0 in Figure 7–7.

Two goods are complements if an *increase* in the price of one causes a decrease in the demand for the other. Bacon and eggs are complements. If the price of bacon increases, for example, people tend to buy less bacon and, as a result, they may have eggs for breakfast less frequently. Consequently, there is a decrease in the demand for eggs. The calculation of the cross-elasticity coefficient for complements is exactly the same as for substitutes except now the answer is negative.

To summarize the elasticity discussion, there are three elasticities that are commonly used by economists in the general area of demand:

1. Price elasticity of demand.
2. Income elasticity of demand.
3. Cross elasticity of demand.

QUESTIONS

1. a. Using the figures below, plot a demand curve choosing scales along the vertical and horizontal axes such that the resulting demand curve is steeply sloped.
    b. Now plot a demand curve from these figures such that the curve is not as steeply sloped.
    c. If you were unaware that both demand curves came from the same data, what conclusions might you draw regarding the difference in responsiveness of consumers to price changes from each demand curve?

Price	Quantity
$40	100
30	130
20	200
10	250

2. a. How does the slope of the demand curve describe the responsiveness of consumers to changes in price?
    b. How might a person be misled by the slope of the demand curve in gauging the responsiveness of consumers to price changes?

3. a. What is price elasticity of demand?
    b. Define elastic and inelastic demand.
    c. Compute the price elasticity of demand from the following diagram and explain what the coefficient means.

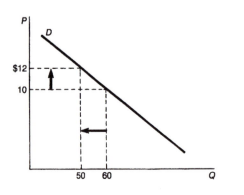

4. a. What are the two economic factors influencing the price elasticity of demand for a good or service?
    b. Explain how each factor has its influence.
    c. How does the price elasticity of demand change in size as one moves down along a straight-line demand curve? Explain why.

5. a. Which would likely be more elastic: the demand for all cars as a group or the demand for Volkswagens? Explain.
    b. Which would likely be more elastic: the demand for coffee at a student coffee shop or at the most exclusive restaurant in town? Explain. (Assume the same number of substitutes are available in each place.)
    c. Which would likely be more elastic: the demand by students for paper clips or the demand for student housing on campus? Explain.

6. a. On most weekdays during the baseball season, professional baseball teams tend to play to less than sellout crowds. Assuming, as is reasonable, that the demand curve for baseball tickets is downward sloping, wouldn't the baseball teams take in more money by lowering their ticket prices in order to fill up their stadiums? Explain.
    b. In view of the answer to part a above, what point on its demand curve should a baseball team try to achieve if it wishes to maximize total revenue from ticket sales. (Assume a linear demand curve.)

7. a. What is income elasticity of demand?
    b. Compute the income elasticity of demand from the information on the accompanying diagram and explain what the coefficient means. (Assume D_0 corresponds to a $20,000 annual income and D_1 to $24,000.)

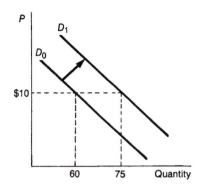

8. During the early 1980s, coinciding with the increase in unemployment and lower incomes, there was a resurgence in demand for old-fashioned washboards. From what you know about income elasticity, was this change in demand expected? Explain.

9. Would you expect the cross elasticity of demand for large American-made cars with respect to the price of gasoline to be positive or negative? In view of your answer, would these cars and gasoline be complements or substitutes?

SELF-TEST

1. A demand curve that is not steeply sloped implies that consumers are relatively _____ to _____ changes.
   a. unresponsive; price
   b. responsive; price
   c. unresponsive; income
   d. responsive; income

2. A demand curve can be made to look more steeply sloped by _____ the scale on the vertical axis and/or _____ the scale on the horizontal axis.
   a. expanding; narrowing
   b. narrowing; expanding
   c. expanding; expanding
   d. narrowing; narrowing

3. Price elasticity of demand is the _____ change in _____ for each ___change in _____.
   a. percent; quantity, one percent; price
   b. percent; price; one percent; quantity
   c. percent; price; one percent; quantity
   d. dollar; price; unit; quantity

4. Calculate the price elasticity of demand from the following figures:

	Price	Quantity
Initial situation	10	100
New situation	15	75

   a. –2
   c. – .25
   b. –.5
   d. –1.5

5. If the price elasticity of demand for a good is –.5, a 50 percent increase in the price of this good will cause consumers to decrease their purchases by:
   a. 50 percent.
   b. 25 percent.
   c. 100 percent.
   d. 50 units.

6. Demand is said to be inelastic if price elasticity of demand is _____ in absolute terms, and elastic if _____.
   a. greater than one; less than one
   b. less than one; greater than one
   c. greater than zero; less than zero
   d. less than zero; greater than zero

7. If consumers are relatively responsive to price changes, demand is said to be _____ .
   a. elastic
   b. inelastic
   c. favorable
   d. unfavorable

8. A demand "curve" that is vertical is said to be _____ while one that is horizontal is _____ .
   a. perfectly elastic; perfectly inelastic
   b. elastic; inelastic
   c. perfectly inelastic; perfectly elastic
   d. inelastic; elastic

9. At points high on a straight-line demand curve the price elasticity of demand will be _____ elastic than at points low on the curve because the base price is _____ and the base quantity is _____ .
   a. more; high; low
   b. less; high; low
   c. more; low; high
   d. less; low; high

10. It is common for sports teams and movie theaters to play to less than sell-out crowds. If the demand for these entertainment services is downward sloping, the owners could increase total revenue from ticket sales by lowering price if price elasticity of demand is _____ . Total revenue from ticket sales will be maximized by setting a price which corresponds to _____ demand.
    a. elastic; unitary elastic
    b. inelastic; elastic
    c. elastic; inelastic
    d. inelastic; unitary elastic

11. The price elasticity of demand for a good will be greater (in absolute value) the _____ the item in the budget and the _____ the number of substitutes.
    a. smaller; greater
    b. larger; greater
    c. smaller; smaller
    d. larger; smaller

12. The more broadly we define a product, the _____ the number of substitutes it will have and the _____ will be its price elasticity of demand (in absolute terms).
    a. larger; smaller
    b. larger; larger
    c. smaller; smaller
    d. smaller; larger

13. Income elasticity of demand is the _____ change in _____ for each _____ change in _____ .
    a. unit; quantity; dollar; income
    b. percent; quantity; one percent; income
    c. dollar; income; dollar; price
    d. percent; income; one percent; price

14. Calculate the income elasticity for good X from the following information.

	Income	Quantity
Initial	$10,000	100
New	15,000	110

    a. 5   c. .25
    b. .2   d. 2.5

15. Superior or normal goods are those whose income elasticity is:
    a. greater than one.
    b. less than one.
    c. greater than zero.
    d. less than zero.

16. Cross elasticity of demand is the _____ change in _____ of one good for each _____ change in _____ of another good.
    a. dollar; price; dollar; price
    b. unit; quantity; dollar; price
    c. percent; price; one percent; quantity
    d. percent; quantity; one percent; price

17. If the demand for cars increases when the price of gasoline decreases the cross elasticity of demand for cars with respect to the price of gasoline will be _____ . From this information we can infer that the two goods are:
    a. negative; complements.
    b. negative; substitutes.
    c. positive; complements.
    d. positive; substitutes.

Part III

Producer Choice

_____

Chapters 8–11

Chapter 8

Cost Minimization

Key Concepts

Production defined

Inputs

Production function

Total physical product

Marginal physical product

Average physical product

Law of diminishing returns

Three stages of production

Cost minimizing rule

In this chapter and the following three chapters, techniques similar to those employed in the preceding four chapters are applied to producers and supply. This chapter presents the cost-minimizing rule—how producers can produce a given level of output at the least possible cost. The law of diminishing returns, an important concept relating to production and supply, also is presented.

INTRODUCTION

We now turn our attention from the consumer to the producer. Just as the theory of consumer behavior is based on the assumption of utility maximization, the cornerstone of production theory is profit maximization. This assumption is not intended to cast the producer as a greedy, self-serving individual interested only in his or her own welfare. Business people are probably no more greedy or self-serving than any other group in society. Consumers try to do the best they can with the knowledge and resources at their disposal; business people have similar aspirations.

For a business to maximize profits, it must first minimize the cost of producing each unit of output. The rule for minimizing costs has much in common with the utility-maximizing rule of Chapter 4. But, before presenting the cost-minimizing rule, it is necessary to lay the groundwork with some basic production relationships. We begin with the concept of production.

PRODUCTION DEFINED

Production is defined as any activity that creates present and/or future utility. This all-inclusive concept of production includes the activities of conventional businesses. The output of the automobile manufacturer yields utility because of the transportation services it provides. The auto dealer provides utility by making the product more accessible to car buyers. If a firm did not produce as much utility as its consumers thought it was worth, it would soon go out of business. Most other activities also involve production as defined above. The dentist who fills a tooth may not create present utility, but the act does create future utility by preventing a toothache. The artist, in painting a picture, creates present utility for himself or herself and future utility for others who view the work. The symphony orchestra and vocalist create utility by the production of harmonious sound. The author creates future utility for others who learn from and/or enjoy reading his or her works. The typist creates utility by making words readable for others.

The activities of homemakers represent a large and important form of production. Utility is created by the preparation of meals, the rearing of children, and the many other activities homemakers perform that enhance their lives and the life of their families. Students take part in a production process by studying and attending classes. The knowledge and experience that are acquired or produced impart both a present and a future utility. Present utility is created by the satisfaction of learning something new or gaining new experiences. Future utility stems from an increased awareness and understanding of the world, as well as from widened economic opportunities made possible by increased earning power. Teachers also perform a production activity by facilitating the assimilation of knowledge by students. Even sleeping creates utility and, as a result, it is a production activity. Production characterizes just about every activity of our lives.

While it is not correct to limit the concept of production to only items we can package, pile up, or count, there are activities that should not be classified as production as far as society is concerned. The arsonist, for example, may derive some satisfaction from burning down a building, but such an activity usually reduces utility for other people. The same is true for the thief. Activities of individuals that destroy property or human beings or forcibly transfer wealth from one person to another by theft or robbery are better described as destructive rather than productive.

INPUTS IN PRODUCTION

In any production activity, there must be inputs that are either transformed or utilized in some way to produce an output. In economics, inputs are also referred to as resources or factors of production. All three names have the same meaning.

In a modern, economically developed economy, most inputs are the product of some other production activity. For example, the steel in automobiles is an output of the steel industry. Even the human input in production has been modified or improved by some past training, whether it be formal schooling or informal knowledge gained from family, workers, or experience. Knowledge also is the output of a production activity, as we will see in Chapter 27.

Most production utilizes several inputs at the same time or in some time sequence. In fact, it is difficult to think of an example where production occurs with just one input. One example that comes close is the production of sound by a vocalist. But even this is not strictly correct, since the singer utilizes energy obtained from food, which should also be considered an input.

For descriptive purposes, inputs can be grouped or classified in several ways. One common classification is that of land, labor, and capital. Land can be seen as the resource provided by nature, including the minerals, petroleum, and water found therein. It is recognized that land is seldom used in its natural state, except perhaps in the production of utility as a wilderness area. Labor is the service provided by human beings. Capital generally is defined as durable, reproducible resources such as buildings, machines, and tools. However, both land and labor also include considerable capital improvements. We will see in Chapter 25 that education involves the production of human capital. Land may have to undergo considerable change, such as clearing, leveling, or draining, before it can be used as an input. In the production of nonagricultural products, land is often treated as a capital input, resulting in two main types of inputs: labor and capital.

It is useful to group inputs into two other categories: fixed and variable inputs. In most production processes, it is possible to identify certain inputs that contribute to production that, for the period under consideration, cannot be increased or decreased to change the level of output. These are called fixed inputs. Variable inputs, as the name implies, can be varied according to the desired level of output. In manufacturing, for example, the building is considered a fixed input because it cannot be readily changed to a different size; and variable inputs include labor, materials, and fuel. Over a long period the building can be changed in size or a new one can be constructed, so eventually even a fixed input can become variable. We will emphasize the distinction between fixed and variable inputs and the importance of time to this classification in the discussion that follows.

PRODUCTION WITH ONE VARIABLE INPUT

In developing basic concepts of production, it is easiest to begin with the simplest case: production with one variable input. It is impossible to visualize a realistic example of production using just one input. But, it is possible to imagine a situation in which one or more fixed inputs such as land or some physical facility are combined with one variable input, such as labor, in the production of an output.

As a specific example of such production, consider a small manufacturing establishment engaged in the production of cookies. Assume there is one variable input—labor—and everything else such as machines, tools, and the building is fixed except the raw materials and energy to manufacture the cookies—which we will assume are available in unlimited quantities. The relationship we are interested in is between the input of labor and the output of cookies.

PRODUCTION FUNCTION

A production function is a physical relationship between inputs and output. If you know the production function and you specify the amount of the input, it tells how much output is forthcoming. It is imperative, therefore, that the owner or manager of a business have a good idea of the firm's production function. Without this information, it is impossible to minimize costs and maximize profits.

TOTAL PHYSICAL PRODUCT

The production function stating the relationship between the labor input and cookie output is given in columns 1 and 2 of Table 8–1. Assume these are weekly figures. As the labor input increases up to the 90th labor day, the output of cookies also increases. The figures in column 2 are called total physical product (TPP). Notice that TPP increases rapidly at first, then continues to increase at a decreasing rate, and finally begins to decline after the 90th day of labor.

The relationship between labor input and TPP is also shown in Figure 8–1. As labor is increased, the TPP curve increases at an increasing rate up to 30 days of labor. Between 30 and 90 days of labor, TPP still increases but at a decreasing rate. TPP reaches a maximum of 90 days and then begins to decline.

This general relationship between labor and output is typical for most production activities. When a small amount of labor is available, it has to do a variety of jobs. Therefore, no person becomes proficient at any one job. Or, people may have to do tasks they are not trained to do. As more labor is added, in this example, up to 30 days per week, greater specialization is possible, and perhaps all the machines are working at least eight hours per day. Thus, output increases more rapidly than labor increases.

TABLE 8–1 Production Function

(1) Labor Input (days)	(2) Cookie Output (TPP)	(3) Marginal Physical Product (MPP)	(4) Average Physical Product (APP)
0	0	—	—
10	100	10	10
20	800	70	40
30	2,000	120	67
40	2,900	90	73
50	3,600	70	72
60	4,200	60	70
70	4,600	40	66
80	4,800	20	60
90	4,800	0	53
100	4,500	–30	45

As more labor is added, holding constant the size of the building and the number of machines, output can still increase but not as rapidly as initially. Crowding occurs. People have to wait to use a piece of equipment or occupy a space. At some point, as more labor is added, people begin to get in each other's way. The crowding problem can become so severe that total output declines. In this example, such a point is reached after 90 labor days per week.

FIGURE 8–1 Physical Product Curves

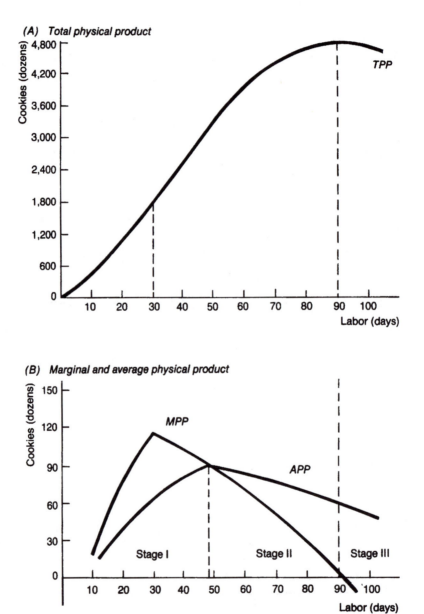

(A) Total physical product

(B) Marginal and average physical product

MARGINAL PHYSICAL PRODUCT

The exact relationship between increases in labor input and output can be measured more precisely by marginal physical product (MPP). MPP of an input is defined as the additional output obtained by adding one more unit of the input holding constant all other inputs. MPP is calculated by the following formula (Δ means change in):

$$MPP = \frac{\Delta \text{ output}}{\Delta \text{ input}}$$

The MPP of labor in the production of cookies in this example is presented in column 3 of Table 8–1. Notice that MPP first increases, reaches a maximum, declines over a wide range of output, becomes zero, and then turns negative when total output declines as more labor is added. MPP describes the rate and direction of change of TPP.[1]

AVERAGE PHYSICAL PRODUCT

Average physical product of an input (APP) is total output (TPP) divided by the total units of the input used up to that point.

$$APP = \frac{\text{output}}{\text{input}}$$

The relationship between APP and MPP is shown in Figure 8–1. When MPP is above APP, APP is increasing. When MPP is below APP, APP decreases. Thus, MPP must intersect APP at the maximum APP.

The easiest way to understand the relationship between MPP and APP is to think of your grade point average (GPA). Say your overall grade point average is 3.0 out of a possible 4.0. If your GPA for the present term turns out to be above 3.0, your overall GPA will be pulled a little over 3.0 after including this term's grades. Conversely, if you earn less than a 3.0 this term, after these grades are factored in, your overall GPA will be pulled a little below 3.0. Thus, the marginal, or last, term pulls your overall GPA up or down, depending on whether the marginal is above or below the overall average. The same relationship is true for APP and MPP.

THE LAW OF DIMINISHING RETURNS

Economists define the law of diminishing returns as follows: As more of a variable input is added, holding constant the quantity of other inputs, beyond some

---

1 In terms of calculus, MPP is the first derivative of TPP.

point the additional output forthcoming from each additional unit of that input will decrease.

This definition refers to a decrease in the MPP of an input. The law of diminishing returns is nothing more than the phenomenon of decreasing MPP.

The law of diminishing returns is to production what diminishing marginal utility is to consumption. These two propositions are the bedrock of all microeconomics—diminishing marginal utility on the consumer and demand side, and diminishing returns on the production and supply side.

Because of the importance of the law of diminishing returns to economics, how can we be sure that it exists? The best proof is the absence of any counter examples. If the law of diminishing returns did not exist, the world's production of cookies could occur in an 8' x 10' room, and the world's supply of wheat could be produced in a flower pot. We do not see such absurd conditions, which is evidence that the law of diminishing returns is a valid proposition.

The Three Stages of Production

Economists classify the levels of input use into three stages of production. As shown in Figure 8–1B, Stage I includes the area of increasing returns and extends to the point where the MPP curve intersects the APP curve. At this point, APP is at a maximum. Notice that Stage I includes a portion of the MPP curve that is declining. The distinguishing characteristic of Stage I is that MPP is greater than APP. As long as the marginal unit is greater than the overall average, the average will always increase.

The distinguishing characteristic of Stage II in Figure 8–1B is that MPP is positive but everywhere less than APP. This results in the continual decline of APP. Stage II ends at the point where MPP becomes negative. Stage III begins where the MPP curve crosses the horizontal axis and extends to the right indefinitely as the negative MPP continues to pull APP down. APP approaches zero but never reaches it because output and input are both positive numbers.

The significance of the three stages of production will be clearer when we relate them to the concept of supply in Chapter 11. For now, we have to settle for an intuitive explanation of their importance. No producer would want to be in Stage III. This is evident from the example in Table 8–1. By adding the 100th day of labor, total output actually declines. A person would be better-off to go fishing or to stay in bed than to put in a day of work that brings negative results.

No producer would want to operate in Stage I either, although the reason why is less clear than for Stage III. Consider the region of increasing returns. If it paid to produce any quantity at all, it would always pay to increase the level of the variable input until the product was past the level of increasing returns. As long as a producer is in the region of increasing returns, each additional unit of input adds more to output. Thus, the more input that is added, the more efficient production becomes, and the cheaper it is to produce the added output. Consequently, it would be foolish to stop adding the variable input when in the region of increasing returns.

We have established that a rational, profit–maximizing producer would add enough of the variable input to go past the region of increasing returns but would stop adding before entering Stage III, the region of negative marginal physical product. Thus, a producer will always produce in the region of diminishing returns. Moreover, if it pays to produce at all, a producer will always avoid Stage I, even though this stage may contain a small region of diminishing returns as shown in Figure 8–lB. For the moment, we will assert this and wait until Chapter 11 to show why it is true. Note that production always occurs in Stage II.

PRODUCTION WITH TWO VARIABLE INPUTS

Although the example of production with one variable is a useful starting point to develop the basic concepts of production, most production activities involve two or more variable inputs. Because our main interest in this chapter is choosing the mix of inputs that yield a given output for the least possible cost, we must expand the original example to focus on this decision. We can retain the cookie example by allowing machines to be a variable input with labor. The building size is still held constant, and we continue to assume that the raw materials and energy to produce the cookies are available in unlimited quantities.

We will also assume that it is possible to use various alternative combinations of labor and machine hours. For example, if few or no machine hours are utilized, a large amount of labor would be needed to produce a given amount of output, whereas with more machine inputs the same output could be obtained with less labor. Having two or more variable inputs that can be used in different proportions brings us face to face with the main question of this chapter. What mix of inputs will produce a given level of output at the least possible cost?

COST-MINIMIZING RULE

To answer this question, we need two pieces of information: (1) the MPP of each input at the various input levels and (2) the price of each input. The MPP of an input is the units of output resulting from the use of one more unit of that input. Because of the law of diminishing returns, the MPP of each input eventually becomes smaller as more of the input is added. In measuring the MPP of an input when there are two or more variable inputs, it is necessary that the quantity of all other inputs is held constant except the one being varied. The MPP of one input will likely be influenced by the level at which the other input is held constant, however. We will return to this point in Chapter 21.

The decision of how much of each input to use to produce a given level of output also depends on the price of each input. Even if an input contributes a lot to output (has a high MPP), it may cost so much that it does not pay to use much of it. Thus, a producer must consider both the MPP of each input and its cost in deciding how much of each to use in producing a given level of output. It makes sense to utilize a relatively large amount of an input that exhibits a high MPP (for a given input and output level) and is relatively cheap. This notion is made more specific when placed in the context of the cost-minimizing rule. To minimize costs at any given level of output, the inputs should be used such that the ratio of the price of each input to its MPP is equal for all inputs, as indicated below:

$$\frac{P_a}{MPP_a} = \frac{P_b}{MPP_b} = \cdots = \frac{P_z}{MPP_z}$$

It is easiest to see why the cost-minimizing rule holds true if we choose a situation where the above equalities are not met. Suppose the P/MPP ratios for labor and machines in the production of cookies are as follows:

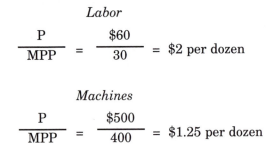

Labor

$$\frac{P}{MPP} = \frac{\$60}{30} = \$2 \text{ per dozen}$$

Machines

$$\frac{P}{MPP} = \frac{\$500}{400} = \$1.25 \text{ per dozen}$$

The labor ratio tells us that another unit (day) of labor costs $60 and that this labor can produce 30 dozen cookies. Thus, the cost of producing one more dozen by adding a little more labor is $2. The P/MPP ratio for machines has the same meaning. Here, the cost of producing another dozen by adding a machine costs $1.25.

Suppose that labor and machines can be varied in small units. Enough machines can be added to produce one more dozen and labor can be reduced slightly to produce one less dozen. Now see what happens:

Produce one less dozen by labor:	saves $2
Produce one more dozen by machine:	adds $1.25

After making this adjustment, the same number of cookies are produced as before, but at a seventy-five cents savings in cost for the last dozen. Therefore, if the P/MPP ratios are not all the same, it is always possible to reduce unit costs of production by using a little more of the low-ratio inputs and a little less of the inputs exhibiting high ratios.

How does this adjustment reestablish a cost-minimizing equilibrium? By using more of the low-ratio input, its MPP declines because of the law of diminishing returns. This, in turn, causes the size of the P/MPP ratio to increase. Conversely, using less of the high-ratio input causes its MPP to increase which, in turn, causes its P/MPP to decline. At some point, the two ratios will converge and costs for a given level of output will be minimized. The cost-minimizing rule does not indicate the specific amount of each input to be used. This decision must be made by management. But the rule brings out the information that is necessary to make the decision.

Notice the similarity between the utility-maximizing rule of Chapter 4 and the cost-minimizing rule just presented. Both require the equality of ratios-MU/P for utility maximization and P/MPP for cost minimization.

QUESTIONS

1. a. What is production?
    b. In each of the following activities, identify what is being produced and the major inputs:
       (1) Baking a cake
       (2) Attending college
       (3) Eating
       (4) Sleeping
2. a. What is marginal physical product (MPP)?
    b. From the figures below, calculate the MPP of labor for each level of labor input:

Labor	Output
0	0
1	100
2	190
3	160

3. In what units is the marginal physical product of labor measured in the production of:
    a. Wheat
    c. Houses
    b. Haircuts
    d. Dental services
4. a. What is the law of diminishing returns?
    b. What evidence is there to suggest that it exists?
5. Delineate the three stages of production, using the MPP and APP curves.
6. Will increasing a variable input in its region of diminishing returns lead to an increase or a decrease in total output? Explain. (Assume the input is in Stage II.)
7. a. What is the cost-minimizing rule?
    b. What is the economic meaning of the input price/MPP ratio?
    c. Why is the cost of producing a given level of output using two or more inputs not at a minimum if the rule is not met?

8. Consider the following information:

	MPP	Input Price
Capital	25	$75
Labor	20	80

a. Is the given level of output being produced at the least possible cost? Why or why not?

b. By what means is the high P/MPP ratio reduced and the low ratio increased when inputs are rearranged to satisfy the cost-minimizing rule?

SELF-TEST

1. Which of the following activities would be characterized as production?
   a. sleeping
   b. eating
   c. studying
   d. all of the above

2. All production utilizes _____ to produce _____ .
   a. money; sales
   b. inputs; sales
   c. money; output
   d. inputs; output

3. Inputs which cannot be varied in quantity to change the level of output are called,_____ whereas those that can be changed in quantity are _____ .
   a. fixed; variable
   b. variable; fixed
   c. monetary; nonmonetary
   d. nonmonetary; monetary

4. A production function shows:
   a. the inputs required to produce a certain output.
   b. the output forthcoming from a given level of inputs.
   c. the amount of profit that can be obtained from a specific level of output.
   d. a and b.

5. Marginal physical product (MPP) is the _____ of output obtained by adding one more _____ of an input.
   a. dollars; dollar
   b. units; unit
   c. dollars; unit
   d. units; dollar

6. If a student's score on an exam increases from 86 to 90 points when the hours of study are increased from 10 to 12, the marginal physical product of study time is _____ .
   a. 2 hours per point
   b. 2 points per hour
   c. 4 hours per point
   d. 4 points per hour

7. The marginal physical product of labor in the production of cookies is given in terms of_____
   a. hours of labor
   b. dollars of labor
   c. number of cookies
   d. dollars of cookies

8. The law of diminishing returns says that as more and more of an input is added in the production process, holding constant all other inputs, after some point the _____ will begin to _____ .
   a. MPP of that input; decrease
   b. MPP of that input; increase
   c. total output; decrease
   d. total output; increase

9. Average physical product (APP) will increase if MPP is:
   a. increasing.
   b. decreasing.
   c. above APP.
   d. a and c.

10. Stage I of the three stages of production ends where:
    a. MPP is at a maximum.
    b. APP is at a maximum.
    c. MPP = APP.
    d. b and d.

11. Stage II of the three stages of production ends where:

    a. APP = 0.

    b. APP is at a minimum.

    c. MPP = 0

    d. MPP is at a minimum.

12. In stage III _____ is negative.

    a. MPP

    b. APP

    c. output

    d. a and b

13. Total output reaches its maximum when MPP:

    a. reaches zero.

    b. reaches its maximum.

    c. reaches it minimum.

    d. is negative.

14. According to the cost-minimizing rule, the cost of producing a given level of output will be minimized when:

    a. the MPPs of all inputs are equal.

    b. the MPPs of all inputs are at a maximum.

    c. the input price/MPP ratios are equal.

    d. the input price/MPP ratios are at a minimum.

15. The input price/MPP ratio of an input tells us:

    a. the price of the output.

    b. the cost of adding one more unit of the input.

    c. the cost of adding one more unit of output, using more of the input.

    d. the total cost of producing a given level of output.

16. If the input price/MPP ratio of input X is $10 and that of input Y is $6, producing one more unit of output by using slightly more of Y and decreasing output one unit by using slightly less of X will yield the same output at a $ _____ savings in cost.

    a. 10

    b. 6

    c. 4

    d. 2

17. The adjustment described in question 16 causes the two ratios to converge because:

    a. the MPP of Y decreases.

    b. the MPP of X increases.

    c. the price of Y decreases and the price of X increases.

    d. a and b.

Chapter 9

Substitution Among Inputs

Key Concepts

Isoquants defined

Imperfect substitutes

Perfect substitutes

Fixed proportions

Isocosts

Least-cost input combination

Changing input prices

When the prices of inputs change relative to one another, producers have an incentive to substitute the cheaper inputs for more expensive ones. This chapter provides a framework for categorizing substitution possibilities among inputs.This framework is called isoquants. It has much in common with indifference curves.

ISOQUANTS DEFINED

An *isoquant* is a line showing the possible combinations of two inputs that can be used to produce a given level of output. Since *iso* means equal, a more literal translation of the term is equal quantity. Returning to the cookie production example, consider the possible ways of producing a given level of output, say 500 dozen cookies. At one extreme, you might utilize a lot of labor and a small amount of machine services. This possibility is illustrated by the 60 labor–1 machine combination in Figure 9–l. Or one could visualize the other extreme of using a large amount of machine services with a relatively small amount of labor, as indicated by the 10 labor–7 machine combination. The first situation would be described as a labor-intensive method of production while the second would be called capital-intensive. Of course, there may well be many other possible combinations of inputs for producing the 500 dozen, such as the 30 labor and 3 machine combination.

In the cookie production example, it is possible to envision a labor-intensive operation where the ingredients are mixed by hand and the cookies are baked and packaged by hand. A middle ground might be where a machine is used to mix the ingredients, form the cookies, and run them through an oven on a conveyor, with the packaging still done by hand. An even more sophisticated machine or machines might do all the tasks. Larger machines could turn out more cookies per hour with the same amount of labor—reducing the labor input per unit of output.

Choosing a higher level of output such as 1,000 dozen would require larger amounts of one or both inputs. As shown by Figure 9–1, 1,000 dozen could be produced by 40 days of labor and 4 1/2 machine days. Whatever the level of output, each isoquant tells us the possible combinations of the two inputs that can be used to produce that output.

SUBSTITUTION POSSIBILITIES

A. Imperfect Substitutes

The particular shape of the isoquant is of interest at this point. Notice in Figure 9–1 that each isoquant is drawn convex to the origin. This implies that the two inputs are *imperfect substitutes* for one another in the production of

FIGURE 9–1 Isoquants of Labor and Machine Inputs (cookie production example)

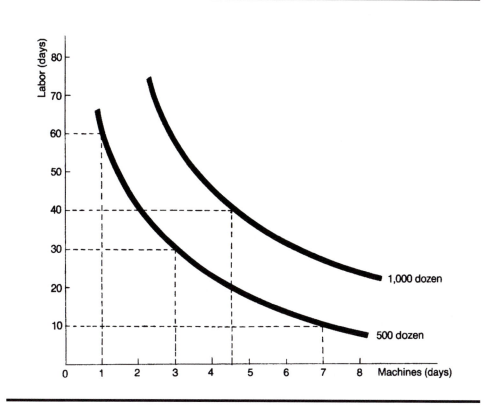

cookies. They are called imperfect substitutes because it takes more of the abundant input to compensate for the loss of each successive unit reduction of the scarce input. As you move down along the labor axis, more machine days are required to compensate for the loss of each unit of labor. Moving from 60 to 50 days of labor requires only about one-half extra machine day to compensate for the loss of 10 days of labor. But moving from 20 to 10 days of labor requires about two and one-half extra machine days. The same relationship is true for increasing labor and decreasing machine time.

The necessity of using more of the abundant input to substitute for the loss of each unit of scarce input has intuitive appeal. The abundant input must be pressed into service on tasks for which it may not be well-suited. Hence, it takes a larger amount of the input to do the job. The distinguishing characteristic of inputs that are imperfect substitutes is the progressively increasing amount of the abundant input required to substitute for the loss of each unit of the scarce input. The isoquant is a close relative of the indifference curve presented in Chapter 5. Also, the meaning of imperfect substitutes is similar. One deals with goods and utility, the other one deals with inputs and output.

Before leaving imperfect substitutes, let's look at how to substitute machines (capital) for labor or vice versa. At first, one might argue that machines and labor have to be used together in a one-to-one ratio because it always takes a person to operate a machine. Although machines require operators, there are two ways that a substitution can occur. First, it is possible to utilize machines for an increasing number of tasks. In manufacturing, one can visualize labor-intensive, hand-crafted operations at one extreme and highly automated facilities where complex machines or robots do the work. A second way to substitute capital for labor is to utilize larger machines to accomplish a given task. Even though larger machines require an operator, the task is completed in a shorter time, which saves labor.

B. Perfect Substitutes

Perfect substitutes exist when the amount of one input required to compensate for a unit reduction of the other remains constant at all possible combinations. The ratio does not have to be one for one—just constant. It is difficult to think of realistic examples of inputs that are perfect substitutes; in practice they would be the same input. If such inputs could be found, the isoquants would be straight, downward-sloping lines such as in Figure 9–2. In this example, natural gas and fuel oil are perfect substitutes as sources of energy for heat in baking cookies, as long as the equipment for using either or both fuels is in place.

C. Fixed Proportions

In this case, inputs cannot be substituted for each other. As the name implies, the inputs must be used together in a fixed ratio or proportion. Probably the most common examples of fixed proportions occur in manufacturing, where products require certain materials or ingredients. For example, a cotton shirt of a given size requires a certain amount of material, a certain number of buttons, etc. In a broader context, one can visualize substitution between different types of material, different buttons, and so on. The fixed-proportion case generally applies to inputs that are narrowly defined or in relatively short-run situations where it may not be possible or economically feasible to substitute one input for another.

Inputs that must be used in fixed proportions are represented by isoquants that are L-shaped, such as in Figure 9–3. This means that when more of one input is added, the other input cannot be decreased if the same level of output is to be maintained. Unless the other input also is increased, the input that is added is simply not used in the production process. Sugar and salt, shown in Figure 9–3, are examples of two inputs that are used in fixed proportions in cookie production. Fixed proportions is analogous to perfect complements in Chapter 5.

FIGURE 9–2 Isoquants Illustrating Perfect Substitutes

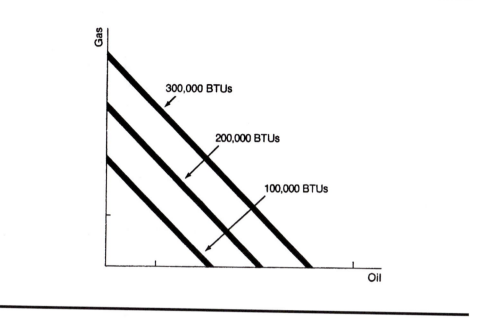

Perfect substitutes and fixed proportions are the extreme or limiting cases of general imperfect substitutes. In the more general case, isoquants can vary in shape from a gentle curvature to a sharp curve. The less curvature of the isoquant, the closer it comes to the limiting case of perfect substitutes. Thus, an isoquant that exhibits a small amount of curvature represents the case of two inputs that can be readily substituted for each other. On the other hand, a sharply curved isoquant comes close to the case of fixed proportions, meaning that the possibility for substitution is limited.

ISOCOSTS

Although the isoquant is a useful device for representing the degree of substitution that exists between two inputs, it is also used to demonstrate the cost-minimizing rule. To do so, however, requires that we first construct the isocost line. An isocost line shows various combinations of two inputs that can be purchased for a given amount of money. As the name implies, it is a line showing equal costs.

To construct an isocost line, two pieces of information are required: (1) the price of each input and (2) the total amount of money to be spent on the inputs. If the total amount of money to be spent and the prices of the two inputs are

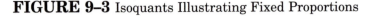

FIGURE 9–3 Isoquants Illustrating Fixed Proportions

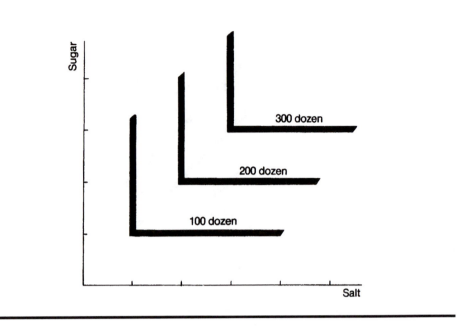

known, the points of intersection between the isocost line and the two axes are easily determined. Consider a $1,000 sum of money. Also assume labor costs $50 per day, and machines cost $100 per day. If the entire $1,000 was spent on labor, 20 labor days could be purchased, $1,000/$50 = 20. If all the money was spent on machines, 10 machine days could be obtained, $1,000/100 = 10. The isocost line is always a downward-sloping straight line. Once the two end points are identified, the line can be drawn as shown in Figure 9–4. Larger and smaller costs are shown by higher and lower isocost lines, respectively.

LEAST-COST INPUT COMBINATION

The 500-dozen isoquant is superimposed on Figure 9–4. Compare this to the three isocost lines. The $600 isocost line does not come up to the 500-dozen isoquant. This means that it is not possible to produce 500 dozen with $600 worth of machines and labor. Next, consider the $1,200 isocost. For $1,200, it is possible to produce 500 dozen with various combinations of machines and labor ranging from the 9.9-machine 4.2-labor combination to the 3.9-machine 16.2-labor mix. But, it would be foolish to do so; the 500 dozen can be obtained in a cheaper way. The cheapest way to produce this level of output is determined by the point of tangency between the 500-dozen isoquant and the lowest possible iso-

FIGURE 9–4 Isocosts and Isoquants Showing Least-Cost Input Combination

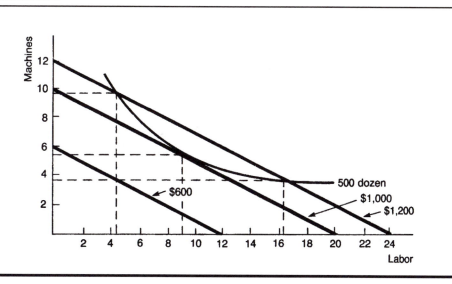

cost line, which is $1,000. The method entails the use of 5.4 machine days and 9.2 labor days. This combination costs $1,000.

In the preceding chapter, the cost-minimizing rule was presented using the P/MPP ratios. This rule is consistent with the point of tangency rule. Their equivalence is proven in the appendix to this chapter; the P/MPP ratios of labor and machines are equal only at the point of tangency. Therefore, we have shown the same concept with two techniques. The advantage of the isoquant-isocost technique is that it allows more precision regarding the degree of substitution and exact input combination that minimizes the cost of a given level of output.

CHANGING INPUT PRICES

Another use of the isoquant-isocost technique is to show what happens to the least-cost input combination when the price of one input changes relative to the other input. In the example of Figure 9–4, suppose the price of labor increases to $100 per day, keeping the price of machines the same. This will cause the $1,000 isocost line to rotate in a clockwise fashion, intersecting the horizontal axis at a point closer to the origin. At the $100 price, $1,000 will purchase only 10 days of labor. The $1,000 isocost line still intersects the machine axis at 10 units because of the assumption that the machine price remains constant. The change in position of the $1,000 isocost line due to the increase in the price of labor is illustrated in Figure 9–5.

The increase in the labor price causes a steeper isocost line than the original

FIGURE 9–5 An Increase in the Price of Labor

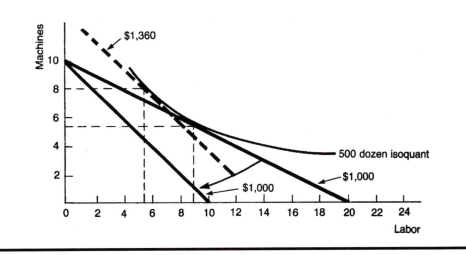

and it is positioned down and to the left. Now, $1,000 will not be sufficient to produce 500 dozen cookies. The lowest possible isocost line that just touches or is tangent to the 500 unit isoquant is shown by the dashed line in Figure 9–5. It represents a higher cost: $1,360 now (8 x $100 + 5.6 x $100 = $1,360).

Also notice that the least-cost input combination changes. Because of the increase in the price of labor, the least-cost combination now entails using more capital and less labor to produce a given output level. The previous combination that used to produce 500 units before the labor price increase now would cost $1,460 (5.4 x $100 + 9.2 x $100 = $1,460). Thus, $100 is saved in the production of the 500 dozen by substituting machines for labor.

It should not be inferred from this example that the same level of output would continue to be produced when input prices change. The intention is to show how a change in input prices alters the cost-minimizing mix of inputs for a given level of output. In the next two chapters, we consider the profit-maximizing level of output and how this level changes when output and input prices change.

Notice the similarity between the material in Chapters 4 and 5 and 8 and 9. The consumer maximizes utility for a given budget by arranging his or her purchases such that the MU/P ratios are equalized, or the combination of goods consumed corresponds to the tangency point between the budget line and the highest possible indifference curve. The producer minimizes cost for a given level of output by utilizing inputs such that the P/MPP ratios are equalized, or the combination of inputs corresponds to the point of tangency between a given isoquant (given level of output) and the lowest possible isocost line. The two sets of decisions are similar.

Appendix: Proof of the Equivalence of the cost-Minimizing Rule and Isoquant-Isocost Points of Tangency

The purpose of this appendix is to show that at the point of tangency between an isocost line and an isoquant, the input price/MPP ratios for the two inputs (X_1 and X_2) are equal.

Along an isocost line:

$$\Delta TC = P_{x_1} \bullet \Delta X_1 + P_{x_2} \bullet \Delta X_1 = 0$$

Where: ΔTC is the change in total cost, P_{x_1}, and P_{x_2} are the prices of inputs X_1 and X_2, and ΔX_1 and ΔX_2 are the changes in inputs X_1 and X_2.

Or:

$$\frac{\Delta X_1}{\Delta X_2} = \frac{PX_1}{PX_2}$$

Since the slope of the isocost line is $\dfrac{\Delta X_1}{\Delta X_2}$, its slope is equal to $-\dfrac{P_{x_2}}{P_{x_1}}$

Along an isoquant:

$$\Delta Q = MPP_{x1} \bullet \Delta X_1 + MPP_{x2} \bullet \Delta X_2 = 0$$

Or:

$$\frac{\Delta X_1}{\Delta X_2} = -\frac{MPP_{x_1}}{MPP_{x_2}}$$

Since the slope of an isoquant line is $\dfrac{\Delta X_1}{\Delta X_2}$, its slope is also equal to $-\dfrac{MPP_{x_1}}{MPP_{x_2}}$

At the point of tangency between an isoquant and isocost line, the slopes of the two lines must be equal. Therefore, at the point of tangency:

$$\frac{P_{x_2}}{P_{x_1}} = \frac{MPP_{x_2}}{MPP_{x_1}}$$

Rearranging this expression, we obtain:

$$\frac{P_{x_1}}{MPP_{x_1}} = \frac{P_{x_2}}{MPP_{x_2}}$$

Therefore, at the point of tangency, the input price/MPP ratios are equal.

QUESTIONS

1. a. What is an isoquant?
    b. What determines the shape of an iso-
       quant?
    c. How is it possible to substitute capital
       for labor, and vice versa, if each
       machine must have an operator?

2. Draw isoquants for the following pairs of
    inputs in the production of automobiles,
    and explain why you have drawn them in
    a given shape.
    a. Capital and labor.
    b. Wheels and tires.
    c. Steel and aluminum.

3. a. What is an isocost line?
    b. Draw a $100 isocost line for two
       inputs, assuming the price of input 1 is
       $10 and the price of input 2 is $25.

4. Using an isocost-isoquant diagram, illus-
    trate the cost-minimizing mix of inputs
    for a given level of output.

5. a. What happens to the slope of an isocost
       line if the input represented on the
       horizontal axis increases in price?
    b. What happens to the cost of producing
       a given level of output when the price
       of an input increases?
    c. What happens to the cost-minimizing
       mix of inputs when the price of the
       input on the horizontal axis increases
       in price?

6. Production in the world's less-developed
    countries (LDCs) is more labor intensive
    than in the developed nations. From what
    you know about isoquants and isocost
    lines, is this to be expected? Explain.

SELF-TEST

1. An isoquant is a line showing various pos-
    sible combinations of two:
    a. inputs that can be used to produce a
       given level of output.
    b. inputs that cost a given amount.
    c. outputs that cost a given amount.
    d. outputs that yield a given amount of
       utility.

2. Isoquants illustrate the _____ between
    two _____ .
    a. degree of substitution; outputs
    b. degree of substitution; inputs
    c. difference in cost; outputs
    d. difference in cost; inputs

3. Two inputs which are imperfect substi-
    tutes will have isoquants which are:
    a. convex to the origin.
    b. concave to the origin.
    c. straight downward-sloping lines.
    d. L-shaped.

4. Isoquants which are straight downward-
    sloping lines:
    a. do not exist.
    b. represent imperfect substitutes.
    c. represent perfect substitutes.
    d. represent fixed proportions.

5. Inputs which must be used in fixed pro-
    portions are represented by isoquants
    which are:
    a. convex to the origin.
    b. concave to the origin.
    c. straight downward-sloping lines.
    d. L-shaped.

6. Isoquants are similar to _____ in the
    area of consumer behavior.
    a. demand
    b. budget lines
    c. indifference curves
    d. isobars

7. Which of the production processes cited
    below would exhibit isoquants convex to
    the origin?
    a. labor and capital in producing automo-
       biles
    b. sugar and salt in producing cookies
    c. family and hired labor in producing
       wheat
    d. wheels and tires in producing automo-
       biles

8. Which of the following production processes cited below would exhibit L-shaped isoquants?
   a. labor and capital in mowing a lawn
   b. sugar and salt in producing breakfast cereal
   c. white-shell and brown-shell eggs in producing an omelet
   d. family and hired labor in producing grapes

9. An isocost line shows various possible combinations of two:
   a. products that cost a given amount.
   b. inputs that can produce a given level of output.
   c. products that can be produced from a given level of inputs.
   d. inputs that cost a given amount.

10. The isocost lines of inputs that are imperfect substitutes are:
    a. concave to the origin.
    b. convex to the origin.
    c. straight downward-sloping lines.
    d. L-shaped.

11. The isocost lines of inputs that must be used in fixed proportions are:
    a. concave to the origin.
    b. convex to the origin.
    c. straight downward-sloping lines.
    d. L-shaped.

12. The point of tangency between an isoquant and an isocost line shows the combination of inputs that:
    a. will produce a given output at the least possible cost.
    b. will produce the largest possible output for a given input cost.
    c. will produce the output which will maximize profits.
    d. a and b.

13. At the point of tangency between an isoquant and isocost line, the _____ are equal.
    a. input quantities

b. MPPs
c. input prices
d. input price/MPP ratios

14. If the input represented on the horizontal axis of an isoquant-isocost diagram increases in price, the _____ will rotate in a _____ direction.
    a. isoquant; clockwise
    b. isocost; clockwise
    c. isoquant; counterclockwise
    d. isocost; counterclockwise

15. An increase in the price of an input increases the cost of producing a given level of output:
    a. only if the inputs must be used in fixed proportions.
    b. only if the inputs are imperfect substitutes.
    c. only if the inputs are perfect substitutes.
    d. regardless of the degree of substitution that exists between the inputs.

16. Assuming imperfect substitutes, an increase in the price of the input represented on the horizontal axis of an isoquant-isocost diagram causes the least-cost input combination to produce a given amount of output to:
    a. move away from the input on the horizontal axis toward the input on the vertical axis.
    b. move away from the input of the vertical axis toward the input on the horizontal axis.
    c. move away from both inputs.
    d. move towards greater use of both inputs.

17. If capital is represented on the vertical axis and labor on the horizontal, an increase in the price of labor causes the production process to move toward a more _____ intensive method.
    a. labor
    b. capital
    c. goods
    d. service

18. If two inputs exhibit L-shaped isoquants, an increase in the price of the input on the horizontal axis:

    a. has no effect on the relative amount of each used to produce the product.

    b. has no effect on the cost of producing a given level of output.

    c. moves the least-cost input combination away from the input on the vertical axis toward the one on the horizontal axis.

    d. a and b.

19. In comparison to inputs that must be used in fixed proportions, an increase in the price of an input that is an imperfect substitute will cause the cost of producing a given level of output to:

    a. increase more .

    b. increase less.

    c. decrease more.

    d. decrease less.

Chapter 10

Profit Maximization

Key Concepts

Explicit versus implicit costs

Fixed versus variable costs

Normal versus pure profits

Marginal cost

Relationship between marginal cost and marginal
   physical product

Relationship between average cost and average
   physical product

Relationship between marginal and average costs

Profit maximizing rule

In the last two chapters, the main question was how to produce a given level of output at the least possible cost. This chapter presents the profit-maximizing rule—how much output a firm should produce to maximize its total profits. To accomplish this objective, one must understand the various kinds of costs and profits. Hence, these concepts are discussed at the outset.

THE CLASSIFICATION OF COSTS

A. Explicit and Implicit

For descriptive purposes, production costs are commonly grouped into two categories: explicit and implicit. Explicit costs include all cash or out-of-pocket expenses incurred in production. Some examples of explicit costs are wages paid to hired labor, interest paid on borrowed money, rent on buildings, and the cost of supplies and raw materials purchased.

Implicit costs are the charge that should be made to the resources, mainly capital and labor, provided by the owner(s) of the firm. This charge can be measured by how much the resources could earn in the next best alternative use, that is, by their opportunity cost. Implicit costs are especially important for small owner-operated enterprises where the owner provides much or all of the labor and a good share of the capital. Implicit costs also are important for corporations. In these firms, the stockholders are the owners. The total cost to the firm should include the return that the money tied up in the firm's stock could earn in the next best alternative uses.

B. Fixed and Variable

Costs can also be classified according to whether they are fixed or variable. As mentioned in Chapter 8, inputs are commonly grouped according to these two categories. Since the purchase of inputs (including one's own time or facilities) is what gives rise to costs, it is reasonable to also classify costs by the same categories. Fixed costs are costs that do not change at various levels of output. Examples of fixed costs include depreciation on capital that occurs regardless of whether it is used; rent on property that must be paid regardless of use; and real estate taxes. Variable costs are costs that vary with the level of output. Examples include the cost of raw materials, fuel, and hired labor.

The items included in each category depend on the time period allowed for adjustment. In the short run, a greater proportion of all costs will fall in the fixed category than in the long run, where agreements and contracts expire, and the decision to purchase the inputs can be made anew. In the long run, all inputs become variable and all costs are variable.

PROFITS

Profits is a word that is used loosely and often means different things to different people. Because profits play an important role in production and supply, it is necessary to define what is meant by profits. In accounting, profits are defined as income minus expenses. (Depreciation on buildings and machines is included in expenses.) Most people think of profits in this way. Economists, however, define profits in a different manner. They begin by dividing profits into two categories:(1) normal profits and (2) pure profits.

A. Normal Profits

Normal profits are defined as the minimum return to the labor, capital, or other inputs contributed by the owner(s) of the firm needed to keep the inputs in a given production activity. By and large, normal profits are the same as implicit costs. They are exactly the same if resource owners are indifferent to where their resources are employed. However, owner-operators of small firms may like what they're doing or prefer to be their own bosses. In this case, they may be willing to accept a lower return from their own firms than they would earn as employees or stockholders of other firms. In this case, normal profits are less than implicit costs.

B. Pure Profits

Pure profits are defined as the return above all costs (explicit plus implicit). Pure profits exist because no one has perfect knowledge or knows the future with certainty. If knowledge was perfect and the future was certain, resources would gravitate to where they could earn the highest returns. As resources moved into the areas where returns were highest, the increase in production would cause output prices to decline along with the returns to resources. Conversely, as resources moved out of low-return activities, the decrease in output would cause output price to increase along with the compensation to resources. When the earnings of each resource became equal in all activities, every resource would earn what it could in the next best alternative. Hence, there would be no pure profits.

Because knowledge is imperfect and the future uncertain, the possibility of pure profits provides the incentive for entrepreneurs and investors to take risks. Whenever there is risk, the possibility of loss as well as gain exists. If there were no possibility of gain (pure profits), there would be no incentive to risk a possible loss. Pure profits also provide a source of funds to invest for increased output when an endeavor is successful. In such cases, it pays producers to increase output. As a source of investment funds, pure profits benefit society by making it possible to increase the output of goods and services that are most highly demanded.

Although pure profits have suffered from a bad press over the years, they play a beneficial role in society by providing an incentive to bear risk and as a source of investment funds. This is not to say that entrepreneurs and investors should be relieved of paying their share of taxes out of pure as well as normal profits. But, it generally is not in the best interest of society to regard pure profits as unnecessary or undesirable.

In the discussion on firms in Chapters 14 through 18, normal profits will be included in production costs unless otherwise stated. When we refer to profits in these chapters, we refer to pure profits—any earnings in excess of explicit plus implicit costs.

PROFIT RATES OF U.S. CORPORATIONS

There are two common methods of measuring and presenting profits. One is to divide the firm's annual accounting profits by its net worth (equity capital) to derive a rate of return on equity capital. This figure has the same interpretation as the rate of return on a savings account or money market fund. For example, a 10 percent return on equity capital means that each dollar invested in the firm by its owners earns 10 cents per year on the average after expenses. The second way is to divide accounting profits by the firm's sales. The resulting figure (multiplied by100) indicates how many cents profit are earned on each dollar of sales. The after-tax profit rates of U.S. manufacturing corporations computed under both methods are presented in Table 10–1. Remember that these figures are accounting profits.

TABLE 10–1 Profit Rates of U.S. Manufacturing Corporations after Income Taxes, 1949–1995

Year	Profits per Dollar of Sales (cents)	Rate of Return on Equity Capital (percent)
1949	5.8	11.6
1954	4.5	9.9
1959	4.8	10.4
1964	5.2	11.6
1969	4.8	11.5
1974	5.5	14.9
1979	5.7	16.4
1984	4.6	12.5
1989	5.0	13.6
1995*	6.1	17.5
Average 1949–95	4.7	11.6

* First three quarters.
Source: Economic Report of The President, 1996, p. 383.

From 1949 to 1995, manufacturing firms earned on the average about 5 cents per dollar of sales. This figure varies among different kinds of firms, particularly at the retail level. Those that have a quick turnover of merchandise, such as the large supermarkets or discount stores, earn less per dollar of sales than do the stores having a slow turnover such as jewelry stores or furniture establishments.

The rate of return on equity capital, after income taxes, earned by U.S.manufacturing firms averaged 11.6 percent during the 1949–95 period. However not all profits are paid out as dividends to stockholders. Some are retained by the firms to finance new investment. From 1949 to 1995, more than half the funds used for new investment came from internal sources. Such funds are called retained earnings.

The figures shown in Table 10–1 are overall averages for the country. In any given year, the rates of return vary considerably between industries. During the 1990–93 recession, several industries, including steel and motor vehicles, experienced negative rates of return on equity capital. One should not conclude that such differences will persist year after year. Demand and cost conditions change, which change profit rates. Even if these market conditions did not change, profit rates would begin to equalize because capital would move out of low-profit industries and into industries that offer more attractive returns. As capital moved out of low-return industries, profit rates would increase because of the decrease in output and the resulting price increase. Similarly, as capital moved into the high-return industries, their output would increase causing price and profit rates to decline.

MARGINAL COST

Marginal cost is defined as the additional cost incurred by producing one more unit of output; or it is the amount saved by reducing output by one unit. The information required to calculate marginal cost is obtained from the firm's production function. The first two columns of Table 10–2 reproduce the cookie production function presented in the first two columns of Table 8–1.

Since output is rarely increased by just one unit at a time, marginal cost (MC) requires a computational formula:

$$MC = \frac{\Delta TC}{\Delta Q} = \frac{\Delta TVC}{\Delta Q}$$

where TC is total cost (fixed plus variable) and Q is total output. Because MC is derived from changes in cost, fixed costs do not influence its level. The same answers are obtained using the change in total cost (ΔTC) or the change in total variable cost (ΔTVC) in the numerator. In this example, labor is priced at $100 per day, and fixed costs are assumed to be $1,000.

RELATIONSHIP BETWEEN MARGINAL COST AND MARGINAL PHYSICAL PRODUCT

Notice that marginal cost (MC) begins at a high figure, declines rapidly, reaches a minimum, and then increases. This behavior is due to the law of diminishing returns (diminishing MPP). In the early stages of production, output increases more rapidly than inputs. This means that MPP is increasing. The rapid increase in efficiency causes production costs (MC) to decline. After production enters the regions of diminishing returns and MPP begins to decline, the cost of producing each additional unit of output (MC) increases. The relationship between MPP and MC is shown on Figure 10–1. They are mirror images of each other. MC reaches its minimum at the point where MPP is at a maximum.

AVERAGE COSTS

To determine if a firm is making a profit, one must know about average costs. We will consider three types of average costs: (1) average fixed costs (AFC), (2) average variable costs (AVC), and (3) average total costs (ATC). Each of the average costs is calculated by dividing the corresponding total cost figure by output. Averaged fixed cost is found by dividing total fixed cost by the level of output, and average variable cost is obtained by dividing total variable cost by output. Average total cost can be calculated in two ways: (1) dividing total cost by output or (2) summing AFC and AVC.

TABLE 10–2 Total and Marginal Cost

(1) Output (TPP)	(2) Labor (days)	(3) TVC	(4) TC	(5) MC
0	0	0	1,000	—
100	10	$1,000	2,000	$10.00
800	20	2,000	3,000	1.43
2,000	30	3,000	4,000	.83
2,900	40	4,000	5,000	1.11
3,600	50	5,000	6,000	1.43
4,200	60	6,000	7,000	1.67
4,600	70	7,000	8,000	2.50
4,800	80	8,000	9,000	5.00

FIGURE 10–1 Relationship between Marginal Physical Product and
Marginal Cost

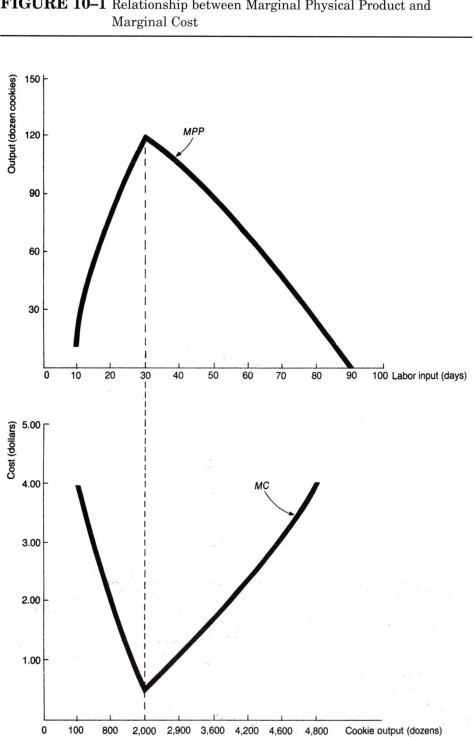

These measures become more meaningful by calculating their values from the cookie production example. The values of ATC, AVC, and AFC for this example are shown in Table 10–3. Labor is priced at $100 per day, and fixed cost is assumed to be $1,000.

Looking briefly at these average costs, AFC becomes smaller at larger levels of output. We might expect this, since fixed cost is spread across more units at larger output levels so each unit bears a smaller share of the cost. Perhaps most interesting is the behavior of AVC and ATC. Note that AVC declines over a range of output or inputs, reaches a minimum point, and then increases. The same pattern is observed for ATC, only these figures continue to decline until a slightly larger output is reached before they begin to increase.

RELATIONSHIP BETWEEN AVERAGE VARIABLE COST AND AVERAGE PHYSICAL PRODUCT

Notice that AVC starts at a relatively high figure, declines over a range, and then begins to increase. This U-shaped configuration of AVC stems from the inverted U-shaped APP curve. Recall that the inverted U-shaped marginal and average physical product curves have their origin in the law of diminishing returns. At some point the MPP of every input begins to decline, causing its corresponding MPP curve to turn down after reaching a maximum. When MPP starts to decline, the point where APP reaches its maximum and starts to decline is not far behind (see Figure 8–1, panel B).

TABLE 10–3 Average Costs

Output (TPP)	Labor (days)	ATC	AVC	AFC
0	0	—	—	—
100	10	$20.00	$10.00	$10.00
800	20	3.75	2.50	1.25
2,000	30	2.00	1.50	.50
2,900	40	1.72	1.38	.34
3,600	50	1.67	1.39	.28
4,200	60	1.67	1.43	.24
4,600	70	1.74	1.52	.22
4,800	80	1.88	1.67	.21

The same relationship holds for APP and AVC as exists for MPP and MC. When APP of an input is increasing, increasing quantities of output are forthcoming from each unit of the input. Therefore the average cost of each unit of output is decreasing, that is, the AVC curve is declining. Conversely, when APP is decreasing, progressively smaller amounts of output are forthcoming from each unit of the input. In turn this means that the AVC of each unit of output is increasing. Thus, when APP is increasing, AVC is declining, and when APP is decreasing, AVC is going up. Also, when APP reaches it maximum, AVC is at its minimum. In other words, the APP and AVC curves are mirror images of each other. This is illustrated in Figure 10–2.

FIGURE 10–2 Relationship between Average Physical Product (APP) and Average Variable Cost (AVC)

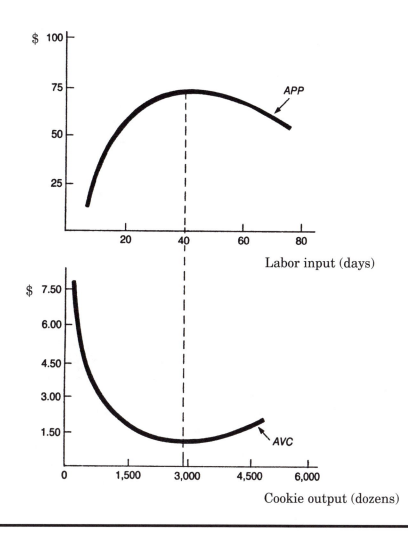

RELATIONSHIP BETWEEN MARGINAL AND AVERAGE COSTS

To understand the concept of supply, one must understand the relationship between marginal and average costs. They are easiest to see represented by a diagram. In Figure 10–3, the ATC and AVC curves and the marginal cost curve are superimposed on the same diagram.

Perhaps the most important characteristic is that MC intersects both AVC and ATC at their minimum points. The explanation of this characteristic is the same as that for MPP intersecting APP at its maximum point: If the marginal unit is below the average, it pulls the average down; if it is above the average, the average will rise. The effect of this quarter's or semester's grade point average on your overall grade average is an example. If this term's grade average (the marginal term) is above the overall average, the overall average will improve, and vice versa.

The same reasoning applies to marginal and average costs. Marginal costs will pull AVC and ATC lower as long as MC is below the averages. Notice that MC can be increasing during this time, as it is just left of the intersections with AVC and ATC. To the right of the intersections, MC is above the averages and pulls them up. It also follows that MC must intersect AVC and ATC at their minimum points.

The most important thing about the AFC (average fixed cost) curve is that it is not important. Thus, it is not shown in Figure 10–3. If AFC were plotted on a graph, it would slope down and to the right—-coming close to the horizontal axis but never reaching it.

You might have noticed that the three cost curves are drawn in a U-shaped configuration. This common shape of the marginal and average cost curves stems from the law of diminishing returns. At the point where MPP begins to decline, MC rises. When MC rises, the points where AVC and ATC begin to increase are not far behind.

PROFIT-MAXIMIZING RULE

In establishing the profit-maximizing rule, visualize a firm that produces varying quantities of a product at a given or constant price. This may not be precisely true for the cookie firm, but such a firm comes close to this situation. In Chapter 15, we will look at a firm that meets this criterion exactly.

To maximize profits, a firm should produce a unit of output only if the additional revenue obtained from its sale is at least as large as the additional cost incurred by producing it. The additional revenue obtained by selling one more unit of a product is called marginal revenue (MR). For the firm that can vary the quantity it sells without having to change the price of its product, marginal revenue is the same as product price. If the firm sells an extra dozen cookies for $2, MR is $2.

FIGURE 10-3 Relationships between Marginal and Average Costs

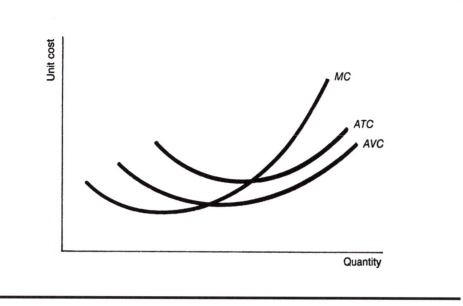

A firm will maximize its profits by increasing its output up to the point where:

$$MR = MC.$$

An easy way to see why profits are maximized only where MR = MC is to select an output level that does not correspond to this point and then see what happens. In Figure 10–4, suppose the firm produces Q_0 output. At this output level, MC is $1.50. However, MR, or price of the product, is $2. Thus, if the firm produced $Q_0 + 1$ units of output, it increases its profits (or decreases its losses) by 50 cents. (Figure 10–4 does not provide enough information to tell if the firm is making a profit or a loss at Q_0. This information is added in the next chapter.) If the firm is interested in maximizing profits, it will produce $Q_0 + 1$. At this output level, should $Q_0 + 2$ be produced? The answer is yes—because MR again exceeds MC—the extra unit brings in more than it costs to produce it. The question will continue to be answered in the affirmative as long as the actual quantity produced corresponds to a point where MR exceeds MC.

If the output level corresponds to a point where MC exceeds MR, to the right of Q_1 on Figure 10–4, profits will be increased by reducing output. For example, at Q_2, MC is $2.50 and MR equals $2. Thus, a one-unit reduction of output at Q_2 will reduce costs by $2.50 and reduce sales by $2. In this case, profits are increased (or losses decreased) by fifty cents by reducing output by one dozen. The same rationale is true between Q_2 and Q_1.

Total profits are maximized at the output corresponding to the point where MC = MR. If the firm is one unit to the left of this point, profits can be increased by increasing output. At one unit to the right, profits will be increased by decreasing output.

FIGURE 10–4 Maximization of Profits Where Marginal Revenue Equals Marginal Cost

---

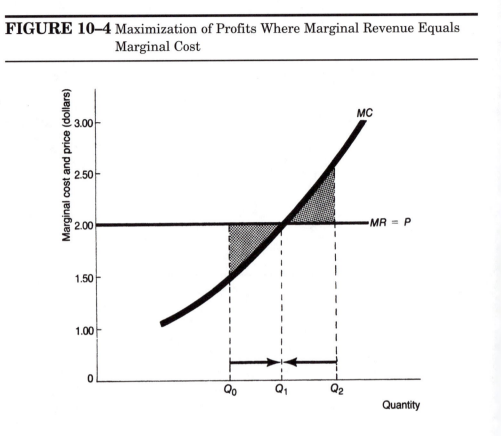

QUESTIONS

1. Distinguish between:
   a. Explicit and implicit costs.
   b. Fixed and variable costs.
2. a. What are normal profits?
   b. How will the total amount of normal profits of a firm be related to who owns the assets utilized by the firm?
3. Some people who own and operate small firms have willingly earned less in their firms than what they could earn working for someone else.
   a. Is this rational behavior?
   b. For these firms, are implicit costs greater or smaller than normal profits? Explain.
4. a. What are pure profits and why do they exist?
   b. What role do pure profits play in a market economy?
5. Over the past 40 years business firms have become larger. Has this increase in firm size led to higher profit rates? Explain.

6. a. What is marginal cost?
    b. From the figures below, calculate the marginal cost of producing an extra unit of output at each of the output levels.

Output	Total Cost
0	$100
1	150
2	230
3	350
4	500

7. a. What is the relationship between the MPP and MC curves? Why are they so related?
    b. What is the relationship between the APP and AVC curves? Why are they so related?
    c. What is the relationship between the MC, AVC, and ATC curves? Why are they so related?
8. a. What is the profit-maximizing rule?
    b. Why are profits not maximized if this rule is not met?

SELF TEST

1. Explicit costs are:
    a. fixed.
    b. variable.
    c. out-of-pocket expenses.
    d. paid by cash rather than check.
2. Which of the following would not be an explicit cost?
    a. wages paid to hired labor
    b. rent on building
    c. value of owner-operator's time
    d. interest paid on borrowed funds
3. Implicit costs are:
    a. fixed.
    b. variable.
    c. cost of the firm's own resources.
    d. paid by check rather than cash.

4. Which of the following would be an implicit cost?
    a. value of the owner-operator's time
    b. value of the owner-operator's capital
    c. interest in borrowed money
    d. a and b
5. Fixed costs are:
    a. those that do not change during inflation.
    b. those that do not change with changes in the level of output.
    c. the same as explicit costs.
    d. the same as implicit costs.
6. Variable costs:
    a. are the same as explicit costs.
    b. are the same as implicit costs.
    c. are more sensitive to inflationary conditions than fixed costs.
    d. change with the level of output.
7. In the long run all costs are
    a. fixed
    b. variable
    c. implicit
    d. explicit
8. Normal profits are about the same thing as _____ costs.
    a. fixed
    b. variable
    c. implicit
    d. explicit
9. Pure profits are:
    a. the return over all costs, implicit and explicit.
    b. about the same as explicit costs.
    c. about the same as implicit costs.
    d. about the same as normal profits.
10. Normal profits exist because:
    a. large firms have monopoly power.
    b. some resources are owned by the firm.
    c. knowledge is imperfect and the future unknown.
    d. knowledge is perfect and the future known.

11. Pure profits exist because:
    a. large firms have monopoly power.
    b. some resources are owned by the firm.
    c. knowledge is imperfect and the future unknown.
    d. knowledge is perfect and the future known.

12. Accounting profits include:
    a. only pure profits.
    b. only normal profits.
    c. both normal and pure profits.
    d. both fixed and variable profits.

13. During the post-World War II period, accounting profits of U.S. manufacturing corporations averaged about _____ cents per dollar of sales.
    a. 5   c. 15
    b. 10   d. 20

14. Marginal cost is the cost of:
    a. the lowest quality output.
    b. adding another unit of output.
    c. adding another unit of an input.
    d. the lowest quality unit of an input.

15. Marginal cost is computed by dividing the change in _____ by the change in _____ .
    a. output; total cost
    b. total cost; output
    c. total variable cost; output
    d. b and c

16. The marginal cost (MC) curve is a mirror image of the _____ curve.
    a. AVC   c. ATC
    b. APP   d. MPP

17. The MC curve eventually begins to increase because of:
    a. the law of diminishing returns.
    b. the decrease in output price.
    c. the increase in input prices.
    d. b and c.

18. The average variable cost (AVC) curve is a mirror image of the _____ curve.
    a. MC   c. AFC
    b. ATC   d. APP

19. AVC will increase if MC is:
    a. decreasing.
    b. increasing.
    c. above AVC.
    d. below AVC.

20. If MC is below ATC, ATC will be:
    a. increasing.
    b. decreasing.
    c. at a maximum.
    d. at a minimum.

21. Marginal revenue is the additional revenue obtained by:
    a. using one more unit of a variable input.
    b. selling one more unit of the product.
    c. adding an extra dollar to its sales.
    d. using one more dollar of a variable input.

22. To maximize profits, a firm should produce the quantity that corresponds to the point where _____ equals _____ .
    a. MR; MC
    b. input price; MC
    c. total costs; total revenue
    d. average cost; average revenue

23. If the quantity of output is less than that which maximizes profits, _____ is greater than _____ . Therefore when output is _____ more is taken in than is paid out.
    a. MR; MC; increased
    b. MC; MR; increased
    c. MR; MC; decreased
    d. MC; MR; decreased

24. If the quantity of output is more than that which maximizes profits, _____ is greater than _____. Therefore when output is _____ more is saved than is lost through the reduction in sales.
    a. MR; MC; increased
    b. MC; MR; increased
    c. MR; MC; decreased
    d. MC; MR; decreased

Chapter 11

Supply and Elasticities

Key Concepts

Supply defined

Marginal cost and supply

Average cost and supply

Stages of production and supply

Market supply

Elasticity of supply

Factors affecting elasticity of supply

Supply shifts

Supply shifters

Chapter 11 combines material from the last three chapters to construct the theory of supply. The main idea is that producers place more of a product on the market when its price is high than when it is low. The second half of the chapter focuses on the responsiveness of producers to price changes.

SUPPLY DEFINED

Supply is defined as a positive relationship between price and quantity, as in Figure 11–1. Other things equal, the higher the price of a good, the greater the quantity supplied. Just as with demand, it is important to distinguish between supply and quantity supplied. Supply is the entire price-quantity relationship. Quantity supplied refers to a particular quantity on a specific supply curve—such as Q_0 or Q_1 in Figure 11–1.

The positive relationship between price and quantity along a supply curve stems from the profit-maximizing goal of producers. When the price of a product increases, holding constant all other output and input prices, the profitability of producing the good also increases. This prompts producers to shift resources from the production of less profitable products into the more profitable good.

MARGINAL COST AND SUPPLY

The marginal cost curve becomes a supply curve by imposing the assumption

FIGURE 11–1 Supply

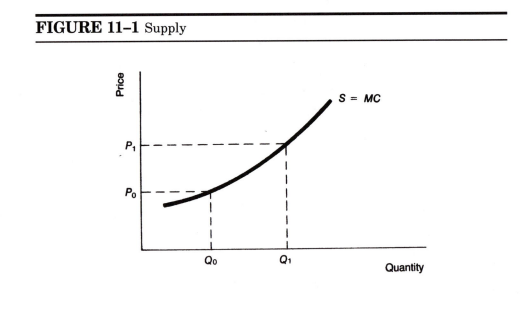

FIGURE 11–2 Marginal Cost, Average Costs, and Supply

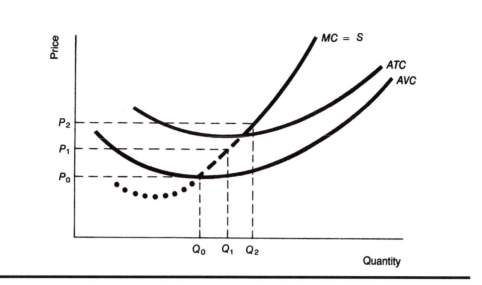

of profit maximization. This is shown in Figure 11–1. Recall that profits are maximized when quantity produced corresponds to the point where MR = MC, or P = MC. If price equals P_0, the profit-maximizing quantity will be Q_0. At P_1, quantity supplied is Q_1, and so on. Thus, the MC curve coupled with the profit-maximization assumption is a supply curve.

AVERAGE COSTS AND SUPPLY

The idea that the MC curve also is a supply curve has a qualification; only the portion of MC contained in Stage II of the three stages of production is supply. To see why, it is necessary to reintroduce the average variable cost (AVC) and average total cost (ATC) curves discussed in Chapter 10. Recall that each is calculated by dividing the corresponding total cost figure by output. The U-shaped ATC and AVC curves, along with MC, are shown again in Figure 11–2.

STAGES OF PRODUCTION AND SUPPLY

Now we can see why production only occurs in Stage II. First, MC cannot be drawn in Stage III. Recall that in Stage III, the output declines when an input and cost increase. Thus, Figure 11–2 only includes Stages I and II. If price is P_2, output will be Q_2 if the firm maximizes profits. At P_2, the firm is earning pure profits because product price exceeds ATC. The ATC curve tells us how much it costs to produce each unit on the average. Thus, if price exceeds ATC, the firm earns a pure profit. If price is below ATC, the firm incurs a loss.

FIGURE 11–3 Relationship of Stages of Production and Cost Curves

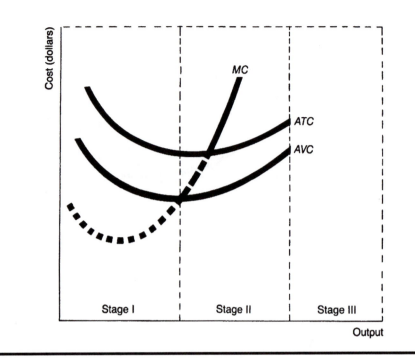

If price is P_1, output will be Q_1. However, in this case, the firm will not cover all costs because price is below ATC. The firm makes all its variable costs but not all its fixed costs. In this case, the firm incurs a loss. Will the firm produce at price P_1? It will in the short run if the fixed costs already have been paid at the beginning of the period, or cannot be avoided because of a contractual agreement.

In the long run, the firm would not produce if price is below the minimum ATC unless it was willing to accept a lower return on its resources than they could earn in an alternative occupation or use.

If price is below P_0, the firm will not produce. In this region, which is Stage I, the price is so low that the firm does not even make back its variable costs. It is like paying a person \$2 to produce a good that sells for \$1; it is better not to produce the good.

Now we can identify the supply portions of the MC curve. The dotted-line portion below the AVC curve is not supply. This is in Stage I. The dashed-line portion between AVC and ATC can be supply in the short run if fixed costs cannot be avoided or if the firm is willing to settle for less than maximum return on its resources. The portion of MC above ATC is always supply. The relationship between the stages of production, the MC, and average cost curves is summarized in Figure 11–3.

MARKET SUPPLY

Although it is necessary to focus on the individual producer or firm to derive supply, the concept is most useful when applied to the entire market. Market supply is obtained by summing the quantity supplied by all producers in the market at the various possible prices.[1] To simplify, suppose there are three producers in the market. Each has a specific supply curve as shown by the first three frames

FIGURE 11–4 Deriving Market Supply

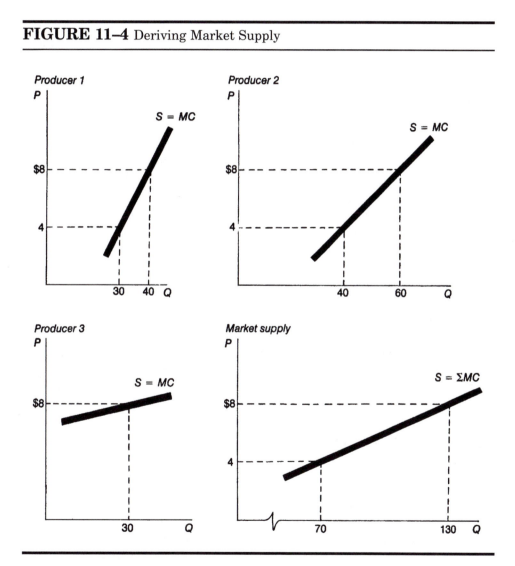

---

1 This procedure requires the assumption that input prices remain constant as quantity supplied in the market increases.

of Figure 11–4. To obtain the market supply curve shown in the fourth frame, we sum the three quantities at each price as indicated in this table:

	Quantity Supplied by Producer:							
Price	*1*		*2*		*3*		*Market Supply*	
$4	30	+	40	+	0	=	70	
8	40	+	60	+	30	=	130	

The increase in quantity placed on the market when price increases comes from two sources. First, there is an increase in the quantity supplied from existing producers in the market as illustrated by producers 1 and 2. Second, the price increase is likely to bring new producers into the market as illustrated by producer 3.

SUPPLY OF PREVIOUSLY PRODUCED GOODS

Not all goods supplied to markets have been produced in the period immediately preceding their sale. Examples include land, vintage automobiles, and old paintings. What does the market supply of these products look like? In these cases, the sum of the MC curves cannot be used as a market supply because production costs are nonexistent for natural resources or irrelevant for items produced years ago.

One might conjecture that the supply of such goods will be perfectly vertical because there is a fixed quantity of each. But that is incorrect. A vertical supply curve implies that people who own such goods will place the same quantity on the market at a low price as at a high price, which is unreasonable. If you owned a vintage '55 Chevy and someone offered you $100 for it, most likely you wouldn't sell. If someone offered you $10,000, you would be more likely to sell. Thus, the quantity you placed on the market at a high price will be greater than at a low price. When all owners of such goods are taken into consideration, some will sell at lower prices than others. Thus the market supply will be a continuous upward-sloping line.

ELASTICITY OF SUPPLY

Thus far, we have indicated only that product supply is an upward-sloping line, meaning that producers are willing to produce larger amounts when they expect higher prices. We have not considered how responsive producers are to a price change. Economists use a concept known as elasticity of supply to measure the responsiveness of producers to a price change. We will see that this concept is similar to price elasticity of demand—presented in Chapter 7.

Elasticity of supply (E_s) is defined as the percentage change in quantity sup-

plied resulting from each one percent change in price. The formula for computing E_s is the same as the price elasticity of demand formula:

$$E_s = \cfrac{\cfrac{Q_0 - Q_1}{Q_0}}{\cfrac{P_0 - P_1}{P_0}}$$

In computing E_s, however, the quantities Q_0 and Q_1 refer to the beginning and
ending quantities supplied rather than quantities demanded.

A simple example is worked out by inserting the numbers in Figure 11–5 into
the E_s formula. Let $4 be the initial price, P_0; $5 the new price, P_1; 100 the initial quantity, Q_0; and 150 the new quantity, Q_1:

$$E_s = \cfrac{\cfrac{100 - 150}{100}}{\cfrac{4 - 5}{4}} = \cfrac{\cfrac{-50}{100}}{\cfrac{-1}{4}} = \cfrac{-0.5}{-0.25} = 2$$

The elasticity coefficient of 2 in this example means that quantity changes by
2 percent for each 1 percent change in price. Supply elasticity is useful because
it tells us the change in quantity supplied resulting from a given percent change
in price. For example, if E_s is 2, a 10 percent increase in price will result in a 20
percent increase in quantity supplied.

Since the formula for computing E_s is the same as the formula for finding the
price elasticity of demand, it suffers from some of the same problems. First, it is

FIGURE 11–5 Elasticity of Supply Computation

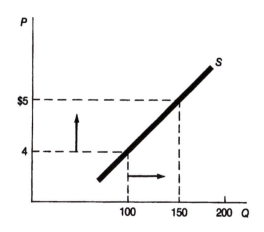

a point elasticity formula, so it should be applied to only small changes in price and quantity. In measuring E_s for actual products, economists use a statistical technique that measures small changes. This technique is studied in intermediate level statistics courses and also in a specialized area of economics known as econometrics.[2]

Economists classify E_s similarly to E_d. If E_s is less than 1, it is inelastic, whereas a supply elasticity coefficient greater than 1 is elastic. As E_s approaches zero (a vertical supply curve) E_s is described as highly inelastic. Similarly, when it approaches infinity (a horizontal supply curve) E_s is described as highly elastic.

FACTORS AFFECTING ELASTICITY OF SUPPLY

All products or producers do not exhibit the same elasticity of supply. Some products exhibit a highly elastic supply; a slight price change brings a large change in quantity. For others, supply is highly inelastic; a price change has little effect on the quantity supplied. Why are there differences in the size of E_s?

There are two major factors that influence the size of the elasticity of supply of a product: (1) the availability of substitute inputs that can be taken from other uses and (2) the time allowed for adjustment to occur. Regarding the first factor, if the production of a product utilizes inputs that are commonly used to produce other products, it will tend to have a more elastic supply than if it uses specialized inputs suited only for its production. In cookie production, for example, the resources used are widely available. Thus, one expects the supply of this product to be elastic.

The second factor, time for adjustment, is important because most production activities cannot be changed in scale overnight. If price increases, for example, some additional output will likely be forthcoming from increasing the amount of variable inputs; for instance, more labor can be hired and machines and facilities can be used more intensely by operating two or three shifts. However, relatively large changes in output usually cannot be attained until the level of fixed inputs can be changed, and it takes time to construct facilities and manufacture machines.

The ability to adjust outputs differs among industries. For example, changes in retail trade, where temporary facilities can be set up, are likely to take less time than changes in the output of heavy industry where specialized plants and equipment are required. In any given industry, the longer the time that elapses after a price change, the greater the change in output that is physically possible and the more elastic the supply will be.

In addition to the purely physical constraints on changing output, particular-

---

2 The "arc elasticity" or "midpoints" formula used to calculate the price elasticity of demand also can be applied to the elasticity of supply computation.

ly increasing it, the economic aspects are important. Even if it is physically possible to adjust output, it may not be profitable to do so immediately after a price change. The major consideration is the length of time the price change is expected to remain in effect. If the price change is expected to be temporary, there is little incentive for a producer to change the level of output substantially, because changes in output usually involve additional expense. To increase output, it maybe necessary to purchase new equipment, buildings, and so forth; or to decrease production one might have to let fixed inputs remain idle but still bear the fixed cost. Unless producers expect the price change to remain in effect for a time, it may not pay to incur the expense necessary to adjust output. As an analogy, you generally do not bother to put on a coat to pick up the morning paper on your doorstep on a cold day, but when you expect to be out for an hour, putting on a coat is worth the effort.

No producer has a crystal ball to accurately predict whether a price change will be temporary or long run in nature. Most producers have an opinion on the duration of a price change based on information about the market, but none can be absolutely sure. The longer a price change remains in effect, the more information producers will have and the more certain they will be as to the duration of the change. As a result, we should not expect to observe much change in output resulting from short-run, month-to-month fluctuations in output price. Rather, we expect producers to respond mainly to changes in the overall average level of prices that exists over a period of time.

SUPPLY SHIFTS

The supply curve can shift from one position to another—the same as demand. Representing the supply curve by a two-dimensional diagram makes it necessary to hold constant the other factors that can affect supply. If these factors do not remain constant, which is usually the case, there will be a shift in the supply curve from one position to another. Both an increase and decrease in supply are illustrated by Figure 11–6.

An increase in supply, illustrated by a shift from S_1 to S_2 in Figure 11–6, can be interpreted in two ways. First, at a given price, say P_1, producers will offer a larger quantity on the market: Q_2 instead of Q_1. A second way of interpreting a supply increase is that producers will supply the same quantity, say Q_1, at a lower price. Both ways of looking at a supply increase have the same meaning.

The meaning of a decrease in supply, as illustrated by S_0 in Figure 11–6, is strictly parallel to an increase. At a given price, say P_1, the quantity supplied declines from Q_1 to Q_0 Or, looking at it the second way, the price suppliers will require for quantity Q_1 increases from P_1 to P_2.

As in the case of demand, it is important to distinguish between a change in supply (increase or decrease) and a change in quantity supplied. The former refers to a shift of the entire supply curve, whereas the latter means a move-

---

FIGURE 11–6 Supply Shifts

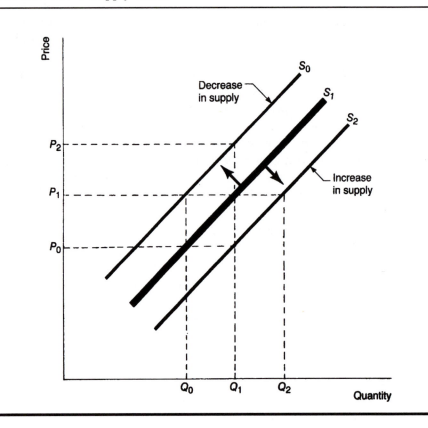

ment up or down a given supply curve. For example, an increase in product price, other things equal, results in an increase in quantity supplied, not an increase in supply.

SUPPLY SHIFTERS

There are five major factors that can shift the supply of most products. They are summarized below. A more thorough discussion of the supply shifters and how they affect market prices is presented in Chapter 12.

1. *Changes in the Prices of Resources.* A decrease in the price of resources (hence a decrease in production costs) has the effect of increasing the supply of the item produced, that is, shifting its supply to the right. As costs decline, producers can sell an item for a lower price and still retain their previous profit margins. (Bear in mind that an increase in supply—also means that producers are willing to supply a given quantity for a lower price.) Of course, an increase in resource prices has the opposite effect, namely to decrease supply or shift it to the left.

2. *Changes in Prices of Alternative Items that May Be Produced.* If prices of other goods or services that require about the same kinds of resources to produce decline, then we can expect the supply of the item in question to increase. For example, a firm that is producing both footballs and basketballs will be likely to increase its supply of footballs if the market price of basketballs declines. On the other hand, an increase in the price of an item can be expected to decrease the supply of alternative goods or services.

3. *Changes in Expectations of Producers Regarding Future Prices.* If producers expect the price of their own product to decrease in the future, they may sell off part of their inventory, thereby increasing present supply, in order to take advantage of favorable prices at the present. Accordingly, if producers expect higher prices in the future, they may decrease present supply in order to have more to sell when price is expected to be higher.

4. *Changes in Technology.* A change in technology always has the effect of increasing the supply of the item being produced because it has the effect of lowering production costs. Unless the new technology lowered production costs, producers would have no incentive to adopt it.

5. *Changes in Number of Producers.* The total market supply of an item will increase if the number of producers increases, assuming the average size of the producers remains constant. Finally, the supply of a good or service will decline or shift to the left with a decrease in the number of producers, again assuming no change in the average size of producers.

The five supply shifters listed above include those that apply to most goods and services. There may be other supply shifters which occur because of special circumstances. For example, in the production of agricultural products changes in weather or growing conditions represent an important supply shifter. Unusually good weather should bring forth an increase in supply of these products while unfavorable conditions such as drought likely will decrease supply, that is, shift the supply curve to the left.

CROSS ELASTICITY OF SUPPLY

Recall that one of the five supply shifters is a change in the price of a related good that can be produced. The responsiveness of producers to a change in the price of a related good is measured by the cross elasticity of supply. Specifically *cross elasticity of supply (E$_{cs}$)* is defined as the percent change in the supply of one good in response to a one percent change in the price of an alternative product. It is computed with the following formula:

$$E_{cs} = \frac{\% \, \Delta \, Q_i}{\% \, \Delta \, P_j}$$

The change in quantity is taken at any price—such as the difference between Q_0 and Q_1 at price P_1 in Figure 11–6.

The value of the cross elasticity coefficient can be negative or positive. It is negative for most pairs of products. This means they are substitutes in production. For example, a leather goods firm might produce belts and basketballs. If the price of belts decreases, other things equal, basketballs become more profitable, so the firm allocates some of its resources away from belts toward basketballs. Thus, the relationship between the price of belts and the quantity of basketballs is negative.

A positive cross elasticity of supply implies that the two goods are complements in production. By *complements,* we mean two goods that are produced together, such as gasoline and diesel fuel. If the price of gasoline increases, more petroleum is refined, which causes an increase in the supply of diesel fuel.

QUESTIONS

1. Differentiate between supply and quantity supplied.
2. a. What is the economic meaning of an upward-sloping supply curve?
   b. Why do producers or suppliers behave in this fashion?
3. a. Why is the MC curve also a supply curve?
   b. What portion of the MC curve is supply?
4. a. Why will producers never wish to be in Stage III?
   b. Why will producers never wish to be in Stage I?
   c. Will it ever pay to produce at a loss? Explain.
5. a. Using the figures below, plot the market supply curve on a diagram.

	Quantity Supplied by Producer:		
Price	1	2	3
40	10	12	20
30	5	8	12
20	0	5	10

   b. Would you expect the market supply curve to be more or less elastic than the supply curve of the average firm in the market? Explain.
6. a. Compute the elasticity of supply from the following data:

	Price	Quantity Supplied
Initial situation	$10	1,000
New situation	15	2,000

   b. What does the elasticity coefficient mean?
7. What factors influence the elasticity of supply of a product?

8. State how each of the following changes would affect the market supply of cookies. Illustrate with diagrams.
   a. An increase in the wage rate.
   b. An increase in the price of pies, an alternative product that can be produced.
   c. Robots are adopted that are less costly to employ than humans.
9. a. What is cross elasticity of supply?
   b. When will the cross elasticity be negative? Positive?

SELF-TEST

1. Supply is a _____ relationship between price and _____.
   a. negative; quantity
   b. positive; quantity
   c. negative; profits
   d. positive; profits
2. Because of the profit-maximizing rule, the _____ curve also is the firm's supply curve.
   a. ATC   c. MC
   b. AVC   d. AFC
3. If product price is higher than the minimum point on a firm's ATC curve, the firm will:
   a. make a pure profit.
   b. incure a loss.
   c. make a normal profit.
   d. close down.
4. If product price is equal to the intersection of the MC and ATC curves, the firm will:
   a make a pure profit.
   b. incur a loss.
   c. make a normal profit.
   d. close down.

5. If product price is between the intersections of the MC curve with the ATC and AVC curves, the firm will:
    a. make a pure profit.
    b. make a normal profit.
    c. incur a loss and close down.
    d. incur a loss but stay open if fixed costs cannot be avoided.

6. A firm definitely will not produce if product price is below the intersection of the firm's MC and _____ curves. At these prices the firm cannot cover its _____ costs.
    a. ATC; fixed   c. AVC; fixed
    b. ATC; variable   d. AVC; variable

7. Production will not take place in Stage I because in this region product price is too _____ to cover the firm's ____ costs.
    a. high; variable   c. high; fixed
    b. low; variable   d. low; fixed

8. Stage II of the three stages of production begins where the MC curve intersects the _____ curve.
    a. ATC   c. AVC
    b. AFC   d. MPP

9. The firm's supply curve extends up from the _____ of stage ____ .
    a. end; II   c. start; I
    b. end; III   d. start; II

10. Any point on a firm's supply curve implicitly assumes that:
    a. input prices are equal.
    b. input MPPs are equal.
    c. input price/MPP ratios are equal.
    d. all of the above.

11. Market supply is obtained by adding at each _____ all the firms' ____ .
    a. quantity; prices
    b. price; quantities
    c. quantity; costs
    d. price; costs

12. If the quantity of Rembrandt paintings which are offered for sale on the market increases as their price increases, we can infer that the supply curve for these paintings is _____
    a. downward sloping
    b. upward sloping
    c. vertical
    d. horizontal

13. Elasticity of supply is defined as the ____ change in _____ for each _____ change in ____ .
    a. unit; quantity; dollar; price
    b. dollar; price; unit; quantity
    c. percent; price; one percent; price
    d. percent; quantity; one percent; price

14. Compute the elasticity of supply from the following information.

	Price	*Quantity*
Initial situation	$20	1,000
New situation	25	1,500

    a. .50   c. 2
    b. .25   d. 1.25

15. If the elasticity of supply of a product is .75, a 10 percent change in the price of the item will bring forth a ____ percent change in quantity supplied.
    a. .75   c. 75
    b. 7.5   d. 750

16. Elasticity of supply of a product will be higher the _____ the availability of substitute inputs that can be drawn from other uses, and _____ the time has elapsed after the price change for adjustment to take place.
    a. greater; shorter
    b. smaller; shorter
    c. greater; longer
    d. smaller; longer

17. Which of the following would cause a change in supply?
    a. increase in product price
    b. decrease in product price
    c. increase in the price of an alternative good
    d. a and b

18. Which of the following would cause an increase in the supply of cookies?
    a. increase in the price of cookies
    b. increase in the price of energy
    c. decrease in the price of doughnuts, an alternative good that can be produced
    d. increase in the wage rate

19. Cross elasticity of supply is the _____ change in the supply of one good in response to a _____ change in the _____ of another good.
    a. unit; dollar; price
    b. percent; one percent; price
    c. dollar; unit; quantity
    d. percent; one percent; quantity

20. Two goods that exhibit a negative cross elasticity of supply are known as _____ in production. Those that have a positive cross elasticity are _____ common and are called _____ .
    a. substitutes; more; complements
    b. complements; more; substitutes
    c. substitutes; less; complements
    d. complements; less; substitutes

Part IV

Product Markets

_____

Chapters 12-13

Chapter 12

Demand and Supply

Key Concepts

Price determination
Surplus
Shortage
Demand shifts
Demand shifters
Supply shifts
Supply shifters
Simultaneous shifts
Time for adjustment

This chapter combines material from the previous eight chapters to construct the framework for price determination—demand and supply. After deriving equilibrium price, the second half of the chapter deals with the factors that cause the demand and supply curves to shift, which in turn cause changes in equilibrium price and quantity.

PRICE DETERMINATION

The first step is to superimpose the demand and supply curves on the same diagram, as shown by Figure 12–l. This is possible because both curves have price on the vertical axis and quantity on the horizontal axis. When the two curves are superimposed, they intersect. The price that corresponds to the point of intersection is the *equilibrium price,* while the corresponding quantity is the *equilibrium quantity. Equilibrium* is defined as a state of stability or balance where there are no forces causing movement, or there are equal opposing forces. If price is not at equilibrium, forces in the market will push price toward the equilibrium.This can be seen most easily if we choose a price that is not at equilibrium and see what happens.

Consider price P_1 in Figure 12–1. At this high price, a small amount is demanded, Q_0^d in the diagram. On the other hand, a large amount is supplied, Q_1^s in the diagram. Thus, at price P_1, the quantity supplied is greater than the quantity demanded. Hence, there is a surplus in the market; more goods or services are offered for sale than are bought, and inventories pile up, or people who offer the services remain under utilized. The inevitable result of this situation is a downward pressure on price. Sellers attempting to dispose of the surplus are forced to take a lower price. To make money, suppliers must sell what they produce. Some sellers, therefore, will begin to cut price to entice buyers to buy from them rather than from other sellers. When some sellers cut price, others must follow to remain competitive. Of course, buyers also are likely to exert pressure, reminding sellers who are reluctant to cut their price of the existing surplus and price reductions taking place. Thus, if price is above the equilibrium, the resulting surplus causes downward pressure on price and pushes it toward the equilibrium.

What happens if price is below the equilibrium, such as P_0 in Figure 12–1? At price P_0, quantity demanded, Q_1^d is greater than the quantity supplied, Q_0^s At such a low price, there is an incentive for people to buy more of the good, but at the same time, there is little incentive for producers to supply it. Consequently, there is a shortage; the product disappears from shelves, inventories fall, or people who provide the services are swamped with customers. The inevitable result is an upward pressure on price. Some buyers will not be able to obtain as much of the product as they would like, and they are likely to offer sellers a higher price if they will sell to them rather than to someone else. Other buyers must also offer higher prices. Sellers, seeing the shortage and realizing they can sell

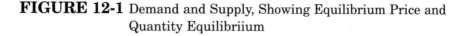

FIGURE 12-1 Demand and Supply, Showing Equilibrium Price and Quantity Equilibriium

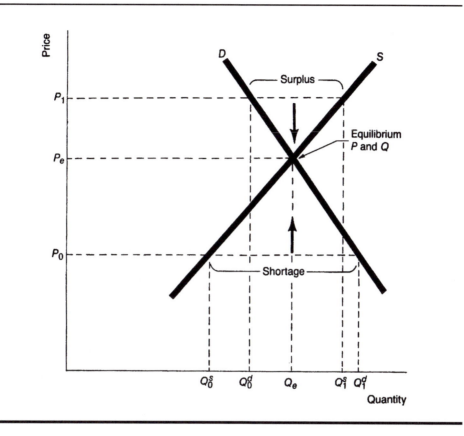

all they produce at a higher price, are likely to cooperate happily in the process by asking for higher prices. Thus, if price is below the equilibrium, there is an upward pressure on price caused by the resulting shortage. Only at price P_e will buyers take off the market exactly what sellers place on the market, that is, there will be neither a surplus nor a shortage.

DEMAND SHIFTS

As explained in Chapter 6, an increase in demand means that people wish to buy a larger quantity for any given price or will pay a higher price for a given quantity. An increase in demand is illustrated by an increase or shift to the right by the demand curve, as shown by the shift from D_1 to D_2 in Figure 12–2. Notice here that both the equilibrium price and quantity increase. A decrease in demand, illustrated by the shift in demand from D_1 to D_0 in Figure 12–2, results in a decrease in the equilibrium price and quantity. Also, recall from Chapter 6

FIGURE 12-2 The Effects of Shifts in Demand on Equilibrium Price and
Quantity

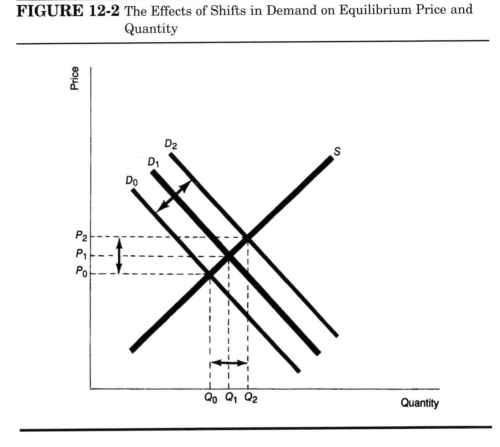

that there are five main demand shifters. Let us consider each demand shifter
to see how they affect price and quantity in the product market.

DEMAND SHIFTERS

1. Changes in Money Incomes

An increase in consumers' money incomes results in an increase in the
demand for many products. Some of the increase comes from using the product
more frequently, such as having eggs more times per week or from additional
consumers in the market. For example, people tend to enter the luxury car market as their incomes approach the $80,000 to $100,000-per-year bracket. The
more people in this income bracket, the greater the demand for luxury cars.
Economists refer to goods that increase in demand with higher incomes as superior goods. This name does not necessarily imply that such goods are made bet-

ter or last longer than other goods. It is a name for the category of goods or services that exhibits an increase in demand as incomes increase. Recall that the income elasticity of demand for such goods is a positive number.

There are examples of other goods or services that decrease in demand as incomes increase. For example, people tend to buy fewer starchy, high-calorie foods as their incomes grow. With higher incomes, they buy more meat, fruit, fresh vegetables, and convenience foods. Thus, the demand for starchy foods declines, or shifts to the left, as incomes increase. Economists refer to these goods or services as inferior goods, again without any intention to describe the durability or quality of the good. Also recall that the income elasticity of demand for such goods is a negative number.

It is possible that a change in income will have no effect on the demand for a good. For example, the per capita demand for all food as a composite good in high-income countries remains relatively stable when incomes increase. In this case the income elasticity is zero or close to it. In poor countries, food is a superior good; demand increases as incomes increase.

2. Changes in Prices of Related Goods

Substitutes. An increase in the price of a substitute has the effect of shifting the demand curve for a good to the right, as illustrated by the shift in demand from D_1 to D_2 in Figure 12–2. For example, if the price of Volkswagens increases, car buyers begin to substitute lower-priced Japanese and American-built cars in their place. As a result, there is an increase in the demand for Japanese and American autos. Consequently, the equilibrium price and quantity of the goods in question both increase. As people switch from the higher-priced substitute toward the good depicted in Figure 12–2, the demand for the good increases and, as a result, consumers pay more for it while they increase the amount purchased. The increased demand for the good causes its price to increase.

The opposite occurs if a substitute decreases in price. As people turn to the lower-priced substitute, the demand for the good in question decreases. This is illustrated by the shift from D_1 to D_0 in Figure 12–2. Consequently, the price of the good in question decreases along with the decrease in the quantity exchanged. In this case, it is the decreased demand for the good that causes the price to decline.

Shifts in demand resulting from changes in the price of a substitute cause the price of the good to move in the same direction as the substitute. Thus, the prices of two or more goods that consumers regard as close substitutes tend to rise and fall together.

Complements. An increase in the price of a complementary good causes the demand for the good in question to decrease, as illustrated by the shift in demand from D_1 to D_0 in Figure 12–2. The increase in the price of the complementary good causes people to buy less of it, and as a result, they also buy less of the good depicted in Figure 12–2. For example, an increase in the price of gasoline, which can be considered a complement to automobiles, will decrease the demand for automobiles, especially those that offer the lowest gas mileage. In this case, the price of the good in question (gas-guzzlers in this example) decreases along with a decrease in quantity exchanged.

The appearance of completely new products on the market may change the demand for existing products. If a new product is a substitute for an existing product and offers consumers more for their money (more MU per dollar), the demand for the existing product will decline. In this case, the entry of the new substitute product on the market has the same effect as a decline in the price of an existing substitute. Similarly, the appearance of a new complement increases the demand for a given product. It is as if an existing complement decreased in price. Thus, we can treat new products as if there was a decrease in the price of substitutes or complements, providing the new products offer more for the money than products already on the market.

3. Changes in Consumer Expectations Regarding Future Prices and Incomes

Since no one knows the future with certainty, our present actions are influenced by what we expect the future to bring. This is important in product demand. If, for example, you expect a product to be scarce and high-priced in the future, you will likely increase your purchases (demand) now to avoid the higher future price. An expected higher price will result in a shift to the right in demand, as illustrated by the shift from D_1 to D_2 in Figure 12–2. Expecting a lower price in the future has the opposite effect; present demand will decrease, such as the shift from D_1 to D_0 in Figure 12–2, as buyers wait for more favorable prices.

Anticipated changes in income also affect present demand. If you expected a rich uncle to leave you $1 million dollars in one or two years, you would likely be more liberal in your spending habits even now—well in advance of the date you actually receive the money. Thus your demand for many products or services would shift to the right, as shown by D_2 in Figure 12–2. Or, if you expected your present income source to dry up, you would become more frugal, so your demand for some items would shift to the left.

It is important to realize that current demand depends heavily on your long-run expected income. College students illustrate this idea well. They tend to enjoy a higher standard of living while in college than people with similar incomes who do not have much hope of substantial income growth in the future.

4. Changes in Tastes and Preferences

There are a few products and services whose demand is influenced by the changing whims of consumers. These items are fads that often change in style. For example, there is not much demand nowadays for high-button shoes. On the other hand, there has been a resurgence in demand for blue jeans. In economic terms, the demand for goods that are "out" shifts to the left, as in D_0, whereas the demand for items that are "in" shifts to the right, D_2 in Figure 12–2.

When attempting to explain changes in consumer purchasing behavior, it is tempting to ascribe too much importance to a change in tastes and preferences. Except for fads or fashions, tastes of large groups of people (markets) are quite stable. Before relying on changes in tastes and preferences to explain consumer behavior, it is good to exhaust all other possibilities. Be careful to include changes in price as a possible reason for changes in consumer behavior. For example, it has been argued that Europeans had different tastes than North Americans regarding small cars. But during the 1950s and 1960s, gasoline prices in the United States were between one-fourth and one-third the prices that existed in Europe because of high taxes on gasoline there. When gasoline prices increased to high levels in the United States, U.S. consumers also switched to smaller, more fuel-efficient cars. The reason is the relative increase in the price of gasoline—not a change in tastes.

5. Changes in Population

Since the market demand for a good or service is the sum of all individual demands, the greater the number of individuals in the market, the greater the market demand. Population growth, therefore, is an important factor in shifting demand to the right, such as D_2 in Figure 12–2. It is about the only factor shifting the demand for all food to the right, for example. In fact, the demand for most goods and services is shifting steadily to the right because of the growth in population.

Although these five demand shifters are the major economic factors that influence the position of the demand curve, there are other special circumstances that also can shift the demand curve. For example, as will be discussed in Chapter 13, passing a law that restricts or forbids the purchase of an item will decrease demand for that good or service.

To fully understand demand and the behavior of consumers, it is as important to be aware of the possible demand shifts as it is to know about the downward-sloping nature of the demand curve. Without a knowledge of these shifts and the factors that can cause them, it is not possible to understand consumer behavior. For example, if the demand curve for an item shifts to the right, consumers will increase their purchases at the same price or at a higher price. To the uninformed, it appears that price has no relationship to quantity demanded. But if one knows why the demand curve has shifted, the observed changes in price and quantity are reasonable and expected.

SUPPLY SHIFTS

As explained in Chapter 11, an increase in supply means that producers are willing to place more on the market at any given price or are willing to sell the same quantity for a lower price. An increase in supply is illustrated by the shift from S_1 to S_2 in Figure 12–3. Note that the equilibrium price decreases but quantity increases. A decrease in supply, illustrated by the shift in supply from S_1 to S_0 in Figure 12–3, results in an increase in the equilibrium price and a decrease in quantity. Also, recall from Chapter 11 that there are five main supply shifters. Let us consider each supply shifter to see how it affects price and quantity in the product market.

FIGURE 12–3 The Effects of Shifts in Supply on Equilibrium Price and Quantity

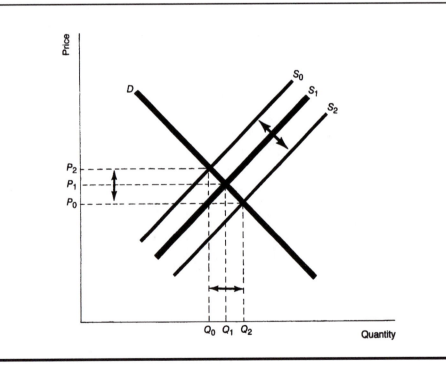

SUPPLY SHIFTERS

1. Changes in the Prices of Alternative Products

Most firms produce or have the capability to produce more than one product. The decision of how much of each product to produce depends on the price (profitability) of the other(s). There are two categories of related goods: substitutes and complements.

Two products are substitutes in production when an increase in the price of one product causes a reduction in the supply of the other product. Belts and basketballs were examples in Chapter 11. Two products are complements in production when an increase in the price of one product causes an increase in the supply of the other product, such as gasoline and diesel fuel. Complements usually are products that are produced together, or one is a by-product of the other product.

2. Changes in Prices of Inputs

As noted in Chapter 11, product supply is the same as marginal cost. Thus, anything that changes production costs eventually changes supply. If, for example, there is an increase in the price of labor, the total variable cost of a given output increases, which will increase the marginal cost—the added cost of an extra unit of output. Thus, an increase in input prices or cost decreases supply, shifting it upward and to the left, as shown by So in Figure 12–3. Conversely, a decrease in input prices increases supply, shifting it to the right (S_2 in Figure12–3).

A change in input prices causes the opposite change in supply. In graphic terms, this is easy to show. If the price of labor for the cookie firm increases to $100 from $50 per day, the marginal cost at any level of output is higher. Graphing the MC curve, where labor is priced at $100, results in a line above and to the left of the original curve. In terms of supply, this is a decrease. Thus, an increase in costs causes a decrease in supply, and vice versa.

From an economic standpoint, this relationship is reasonable. When input prices increase, producers must obtain a higher price for output to cover the higher cost of production. This means that supply decreases.

3. Changes in Producer Expectations of Future Prices

Since producers are human beings and therefore cannot know the future with certainty, many present production decisions are based on what they believe will happen in the future. If producers have a reason to expect changes in future prices, either in the prices of the product they presently produce or in prices of products they could produce, they will likely begin to adjust their production capacity accordingly. However, it is not possible to generalize across all situations the effect of, say, an expected increase in price. Each situation must be analyzed separately. For example, if the product can be stored, an expectation of higher future prices may lead to a reduction in the present supply as producers build up their inventories to have more to sell when they expect prices to be higher. The expected price increase must at least compensate for storage costs. For products that cannot be stored, the expectation of higher future prices may lead to an increase in the present supply as producers begin to expand capacity for the future.

Another important item is the expected duration of a price change. If producers expect only a temporary rise in future prices, they will be less willing to make extensive changes in productive capacity than if they expect higher prices to prevail for many years. Thus, the magnitude of the supply shift depends on the length of time the price change is expected to stay in effect. If the expected duration is short, the supply shift will be small, and vice versa.

4. Changes in Technology

In general, new technology makes presently used inputs more productive by improving their quality or by creating new inputs that are more productive than the old ones; both result in higher productivity. We can define higher productivity as decreasing the cost of a given level of output, say Q_1 in Figure 12–3, or increasing the level of output for a given cost, such as P_1 in Figure 12–3. Both of these changes describe an increase in product supply. Thus, new technology always increases supply. If new technology did not reduce costs, producers would have no incentive to adopt it.

5. Changes in Number of Producers

Other things being equal, an increase in the number of producers of a given size causes the supply curve of a product to increase. The same phenomenon can occur if the average size of the firms in the market increases. As more firms come into the market, supply shifts to the right, price declines, and quantity increases. The opposite occurs when the number or size of firms decreases. In later chapters, we will see that changes in the number of firms in response to pure profits or losses play a key role in either reducing pure profits or restoring normal profits.

Although these five supply shifters are the major economic factors that influence the position of the supply curve, other shifters may be important for certain products. For example, a change in the weather or growing conditions is an important supply shifter for agricultural products. A period of adverse weather may decrease the supply of certain products, while unusually good weather may increase their supply. Also, as will be discussed in Chapter 13, a law that prohibits the production or sale of an item will decrease its supply, particular1y if the penalty is severe.

SIMULTANEOUS SHIFTS IN DEMAND AND SUPPLY

To simplify the preceding discussion, we considered only one shifter at a time. We have no guarantee that actual market situations will be so simple. One or more of the demand shifters may operate in the market at the same time as one or more of the supply shifters. For example, an increase in money incomes may cause an increase in demand at the same time as an increase in wage rates results in a decrease in supply. This condition is what occurs during inflation. Other combinations of demand and supply shifts also are possible. Therefore, it is useful to list and illustrate the possible combinations of demand and supply shifts to observe what happens to price and quantity under each circumstance. There are four possible combinations of demand and supply shifts: (1) demand increases, supply increases; (2) demand increases, supply decreases; (3) demand decreases, supply increases; and (4) demand decreases, supply decreases. Each of these shifts can be caused by any one (or more) of the five demand shifters and by any one (or more) of the five supply shifters. The four combinations are illustrated in Figure12–4.

In panel A of Figure 12–4, an increase in both demand and supply causes quantity to increase. However, in this example, the upward pressure on price caused by the increase in demand is offset by the downward pressure exerted by the increase in supply. Consequently, price remains constant. One could construct the example so that price either increases or decreases. If demand increased more than supply increased, the price would rise, whereas price would decline if supply increased more than demand. Thus, the direction of price movement in this case is uncertain; it may stay the same, increase, or decrease. This example depicts the long-run behavior of most goods. Demand for most items, at least large categories of goods, tends to increase over time because of the growth in income and population. Supply tends to increase because of the growth in the number or size of firms.

The same idea applies to the other three combinations. In panel B the demand increase and the supply decrease both exert an upward pressure on price so that it increases. But, they exert offsetting pressure on quantity, so it is not possible to say how quantity will change. As mentioned, this example depicts the behavior of markets during inflationary times because of the increase of money incomes and input prices.

In panel C, the decrease in demand and increase in supply both exert a downward pressure on price causing a decrease in price. But, these shifts exert offsetting pressure on quantity, so it is not possible to say what happens to quan-

FIGURE 12–4 The Effects of Simultaneous Shifts in Demand and Supply on Equilibrium Price and Quantity

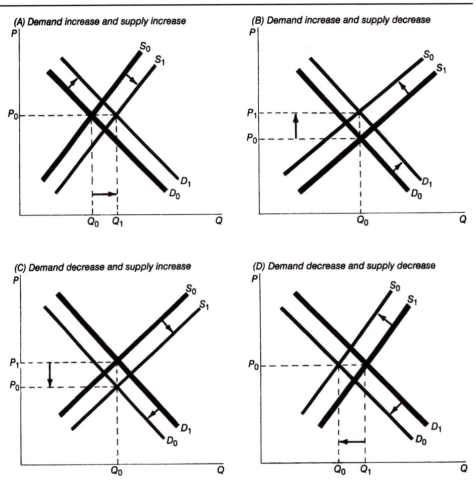

tity; perhaps there will be no change as shown. Finally, the decrease in demand and decrease in supply shown by panel D cause a certain decrease in quantity, but the change in price cannot be predicted with certainty. The last two examples, panels C and D, represent less common occurrences, although they can happen in specific instances.

SUMMARY OF PRICE AND QUANTITY CHANGES

It is evident that there is much more to demand and supply than the downward and upward slopes of the two curves and their interaction to determine the equilibrium price and quantity. Unless one knows the possible shifts that occur in demand and supply, there may appear to be no order to markets. Sometimes price increases while quantity decreases; at other times, both price and quantity increase. Or, price may increase without any change in quantity. With knowledge of the demand and supply shifters and how they affect demand and supply and price and quantity, a person can explain why markets behave as they do and can predict future changes in the demand and supply shifters. Although it is better to utilize a diagram each time you wish to determine a price and/or quantity change rather than memorizing the changes, the following summary helps synthesize material from the preceding sections:

Change in:		*Resulting Change in:*	
Demand	*Supply*	*Price*	*Quantity*
Demand Shifts			
Increase	None	Increase	Increase
Decrease	None	Decrease	Decrease
Supply Shifts			
None	Increase	Decrease	Increase
None	Decrease	Increase	Decrease
Simultaneous Shifts			
Increase	Increase	Uncertain	Increase
Increase	Decrease	Increase	Uncertain
Decrease	Increase	Decrease	Uncertain
Decrease	Decrease	Uncertain	Decrease

TIME FOR ADJUSTMENT

In the preceding chapter it was mentioned that the longer the time allowed for adjustment to occur, the greater the supply elasticity. At this point, it will be useful to explain in more detail the difference between short-run and long-run adjustments on both the demand and supply sides of the product market.

On the demand side of the market, we know from experience that a change in price may not precipitate an immediate response. For example, if the price of our favorite toothpaste increases, it may take us a certain amount of time to even find out about it. The first time we buy another tube the price may seem a bit high, but not having considered another brand, we go ahead and buy it. By the time we are ready for the next tube, however, we might well compare the prices of various brands; if our favorite brand is out of line with the others, we might try a lower-priced alternative.

The same process can go on in the event of a price decrease of a good or service. If we are not already buying it, the lower price may not come to our immediate attention. After we have had time to find out about the lower price and something about the good itself, we may give it a try. It is reasonable to believe, therefore, that the longer time consumers have to adjust to a price change, the more responsive they will be.

This idea can be represented by demand curves with differing slopes or elasticities. If only a short time is taken for adjustment to a price change, the demand curve will be relatively steep, or less elastic, than if a long period of time is considered. This is illustrated in Figure 12–5. D_s represents a demand with only a short time to adjust, while D_l represents a demand where adjustment by consumers takes place over a longer period. If supply shifts from S_1 to S_0 (decrease) and price increases, some consumers begin to decrease their purchases. The quantity sold then begins to decline, approaching Q_{s0} rather quickly. However, as more and more consumers adjust to this price increase, the quantity decreases further, eventually reaching Q_{l0}.

Figure 12–5 also can be used to represent a price decrease that might take

Figure 12–5 Effect of Time for Adjustment on Demand

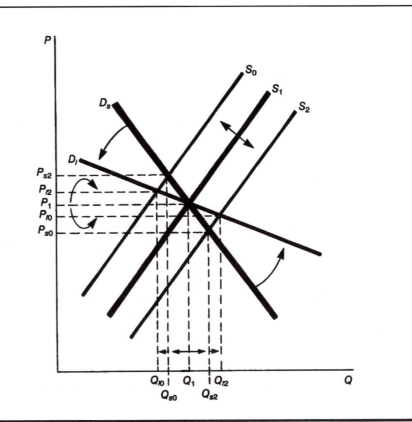

place following an increase in supply, as illustrated by supply shifting from S_1 to S_2. Here a few consumers increase their purchases soon after the price fall, so that the quantity increases to Q_{S2}. Then, as more consumers adjust, the quantity continues to increase, eventually approaching Q_{l2}.

It is important to note as well the pattern of price changes that take place. With a decrease in supply, the price moves upward rather rapidly. Then, as consumers are able to adjust their purchases toward other products, the price levels off and even decreases somewhat. With an increase in supply, the price falls rather abruptly, but as consumers take note of this and adjust their purchases toward this product, the price reaches a minimum and begins to ease upward slightly.

Time for adjustment is perhaps even more important for supply than for demand. There are two reasons producers do not adjust immediately to a price change. First, from a technical standpoint, it generally is not physically possible either to acquire fixed inputs rapidly or, because of market conditions, to dispose of them quickly. Second, from an economic standpoint, changing the level of production to a sizable extent generally requires additional expense. To increase output, new facilities and equipment will have to be bought and additional personnel hired. Thus producers want to be sure that a price increase will stay in effect for a fairly long period of time before they incur this expense. Similarly, producers who dispose of machines or structures before they have been substantially depreciated may have to bear a substantial loss. Thus producers may try to ride out a period of low prices, hoping for higher prices in the future.

Because of these factors, the elasticity of supply that allows a long period of time to adjust is higher (more elastic) than is elasticity that allows little time to adjust. This is illustrated in Figure 12–6, where price is assumed to change because of shifts in demand. If demand declines, say to D_0, the quantity produced will at first decline relatively little, to Q_{so}. But if the price remains low for a time, more adjustment will take place, reducing the quantity supplied even more, to Q_{lo}. The same rationale applies to an increase in demand where the quantity supplied increases first to Q_{S2} and later to Q_{l2}.

Notice also, as with demand, that the process of moving to a longer time for adjustment affects the price of the good or service. For example, there is a rather abrupt decline in price as demand decreases, but after producers adjust their production downward, the price eases back up slightly. The same phenomenon can be observed for an increase in demand, only here the price rises rather abruptly and then eases back down a little as producers adjust their production upward.

One important point that should be kept in mind when thinking about this process of adjustment by either producers or consumers is that not every producer or consumer needs to change the quantity produced or consumed when the price changes. All that is required to obtain a market response to a price change is that some people change the quantities they buy or sell. The fact that not everyone may change the quantity demanded or supplied with a price

FIGURE 12—6 Effect of Time for Adjustment on Supply

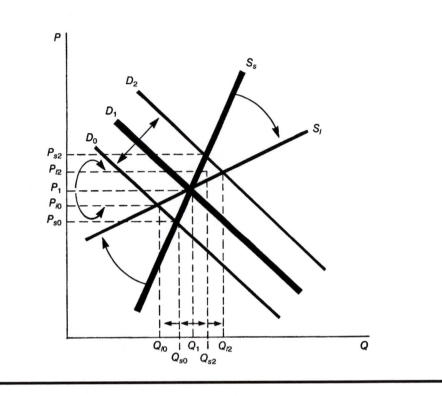

change has led some people to the erroneous conclusion that price has little effect in the market. Indeed, if everyone reacted to a price change, there would tend to be relatively large changes in the quantities exchanged in markets in response to just minor changes in price.

QUESTIONS

1. a. Define equilibrium price.
   b. If actual price is above the equilibrium, what will force it down?
   c. If actual price is below the equilibrium, what will force it up?
2. a. Plot the corresponding demand and supply curves from the figures below, showing equilibrium price and quantity.

Price	Quantity Demanded	Quantity Supplied
$100	10	50
80	20	40
60	30	30
40	40	20
20	50	10

   b. If price was $100, would there be a surplus or a shortage? How much?
   c. If price was $20, would there be a surplus or a shortage? How much?
3. Water, one of the basic necessities of life, is in most places cheap, if not free. Diamonds, on the other hand, nonessential items in our lives, are expensive. Can you explain this perverse behavior of price?
4. State how the stipulated changes in each of the following demand shifters would change the equilibrium price and quantity of new U.S. cars? Assume all other shifters remain constant except the one under consideration:
   a. An increase in money incomes of the car-buying public. Assume new cars are a superior good.
   b. A decrease in the price of foreign cars, a substitute for U.S. cars.
   c. Consumers expect less unemployment in the near future.
   d. Consumers tastes shift in the direction of European styling.
   e. Population increases.

5. State how the stipulated changes in the following supply shifters change the equilibrium price and quantities of personal computers. Assume all other shifters remain constant except the one under consideration:
   a. A decrease in the price of word processors an alternative product that can be produced.
   b. A decrease in the price of silicon chips.
   c. Producers expect prices to be lower next year.
   d. Advances are made in electronics technology.
   e. There is a decrease in the number of manufacturers of this product.
6. For some goods, such as rooms at summer resorts, both price and quantity increase during certain times of the year. For other products, such as fresh strawberries, price is negatively correlated with quantity. Why does price increase when quantity increases for one good while price decreases when quantity increases for the other?
7. a. Is it possible for the equilibrium price of a good or service to change without a change in the equilibrium quantity exchanged in the market? (Assume that neither the demand nor supply curve is perfectly inelastic.) Explain.
   b. Is it possible for the equilibrium quantity of a good or service to change without a change in the equilibrium market price? Assume that neither the demand nor the supply curve is perfectly elastic. Explain.
8. a. Trace the short-run and long-run effects on price and quantity in the new automobile market of a sudden decrease in demand for new cars.
   b. Trace the short-run and long-run effects in the coffee market of a freeze in Brazil that kills many coffee trees.

SELF-TEST

1. If actual price is above the equilibrium price, there will be a _____ and price will_____ .
   a. shortage; increase
   b. surplus; increase
   c. shortage; decrease
   d. surplus; decrease

2. If actual price is below the market equilibrium, there will be a _____ and price will_____ .
   a. shortage; increase
   b. surplus; increase
   c. shortage; decrease
   d. surplus; decrease

3. An increase in money incomes will _____ the demand for a superior good, causing its price to _____ and quantity to ____ .
   a. increase; increase; increase
   b. increase; decrease; decrease
   c. decrease; increase; increase
   d. decrease; decrease; decrease

4. If airplane and bus transportation are substitutes in consumption, a decrease in airline fares will cause the demand for bus transport to _____ which, in turn, will cause bus fares to _____ and bus quantities to _____ .
   a. increase; increase; increase
   b. decrease; decrease; decrease
   c. increase; decrease; increase
   d. decrease, increase; decrease

5. If gasoline and automobiles are complements in consumption, a decrease in the price of gasoline will _____ the demand for automobiles, causing auto prices to _____ and quantities to _____ .
   a. increase; increase; increase
   b. decrease; decrease; decrease
   c. increase; decrease; increase
   d. decrease; increase; decrease

6. If people expect the price of gold to increase in the near future, the current demand for gold can be expected to ____ , causing its current price to _____ .
   a. increase; remain unchanged
   b. decrease; decrease
   c. increase; increase
   d. decrease; remain unchanged

7. Prewashed jeans have become popular among young people. This change in tastes caused the demand for this product to _____ and its price to _____ .
   a. increase; decrease
   b. increase; increase
   c. decrease; decrease
   d. decrease; increase

8. Consider a company that can produce both word processors and typewriters. A decrease in the demand for typewriters can be expected to _____ the price of typewriters and _____ the supply of word processors.
   a. decrease; increase
   b. increase; increase
   c. decrease; decrease
   d. increase; decrease

9. Energy is an important input in the production of automobiles. An increase in the price of energy would _____ the supply of autos and _____ their prices.
   a. increase; increase
   b. increase; decrease
   c. decrease; increase
   d. decrease; decrease

10. A mining company that has large stocks of copper on hand is observed to increase its sales. From this we might infer that the company expects the future price of copper to _____ .
    a. decrease
    b. increase
    c. remain unchanged

11. An improvement in the technology of producing personal computers will lead to _____ in the supply of computers and _____ in their prices.
    a. a decrease; an increase

b. a decrease; a decrease

c. an increase; an increase

d. an increase; a decrease

12. During times of inflation, demand_____ and supply _____ , causing prices to increase and quantity to _____ .

    a. increases; decreases; either increase or decrease

    b. increases; decreases; increase

    c. decreases; increases; either increase or decrease

    d. decreases; increases; decrease

13. Water is cheap because _____ is large relative to _____ . Diamonds are expensive because _____ is large relative to _____ .

    a. demand; supply; supply; demand

    b. supply; demand; demand; supply

    c. supply; demand; supply; demand

    d. demand; supply; demand; supply

14. During the summer, strawberry prices tend to be lower than in the winter months. This can be explained by _____ during the summer. However, rooms at summer resorts tend to go up in price during the summer. This can be explained by _____ during the summer.

    a. a decrease in demand; a decrease in supply

    b. an increase in supply; an increase in demand

    c. a decrease in supply; a decrease in demand

    d. an increase in demand; an increase in supply

15. It is possible for the price of a good to increase without observing a change in its quantity. This can be explained by _____ in demand coupled with _____ in supply.

    a. a decrease; an increase

    b. a decrease; a decrease

    c. an increase; an increase

    d. an increase; a decrease

16. It is possible for the quantity of a good to increase without observing a change in price. This can be explained by _____ in demand coupled with _____in supply.

    a. a decrease; an increase

    b. a decrease; a decrease

    c. an increase; an increase

    d. an increase; a decrease

17. In the long run, demand is _____ elastic than in the short run, and supply is _____ elastic than in the short run.

    a. more; less   c. more; more

    b. less; more   d. less; less

18. If there is an increase in demand, the price increase will be _____ in the short run than in the long run. The quantity increase will be _____ in the short run than in the long run.

    a. greater; smaller

    b. greater; greater

    c. smaller; smaller

    d. smaller; greater

19. If there is an increase in supply, the price decrease will be _____ in the short run than in the long run. The quantity increase will be _____ in the short run than in the long run.

    a. greater; smaller

    b. greater; greater

    c. smaller; smaller

    d. smaller; greater

Chapter 13

Government in the Market

Key Concepts

Rules of the game

Environmental quality

Ceiling prices and shortages

Support prices and surpluses

Sales and excise taxes

Illegal goods and services

Rationing

Resource allocation

This chapter deals with the impact of government action on markets, particularly how it affects prices and quantities. Among other things, we see how government action can result in market shortages or surpluses.

INTRODUCTION

The discussion in Chapter 12 on the determination of price and quantity and their changes focused on market-oriented factors. It is well known that government at all levels intervenes in markets either through direct action, such as setting price, or through legal regulations that affect buyers and/or sellers. Much disagreement exists regarding the optimum amount of government intervention. People with a conservative political viewpoint tend to believe that markets can run themselves within the legal framework of society. People with a liberal view tend to prefer a greater amount of government intervention in markets. We will not argue one point of view over the other; instead, we will attempt to identify the major types of government intervention and evaluate their effects.

ESTABLISHING THE RULES OF THE GAME

Although we will not dwell at length on the legal aspects of markets, for any market to function properly, both buyers and sellers must obey certain rules. Although markets such as those for illegal drugs exist without government sanction, or even in spite of the best efforts of government to stamp them out, government can improve the efficiency of markets by establishing basic rules of behavior and enforcing them.

Perhaps the most basic rule is the law requiring buyers to pay sellers for goods purchased or services rendered and for sellers to deliver the goods and services for which they receive payment. For most people, payment of one's debts or the willingness to deliver upon receipt of payment is a matter of personal integrity. But for others who may attempt to defraud the other party in the exchange, such laws and the threat of punishment are necessary to keep such behavior to a minimum. Failure to pay for goods or to deliver what has been paid for is in principle a theft. Granted there may at times be disagreement between buyer and seller on the terms of the exchange. An inability to reach an agreement may require a court settlement. Fortunately the vast majority of all transactions do not require this.

A second important role of government in market operation is to provide information about products to buyers or to require that this information be available. As noted in Chapter 4, a consumer maximizes utility by equating the marginal utilities per dollar for all goods purchased. If information about the product or its price is lacking or wrong, it is not possible to compare the marginal utility per dollar of the product with the alternatives. Most of us have purchased goods or services that we would not have bought had we known their true characteristics or price. The truth-in-packaging and truth-in-lending legislation attempts to improve buyer information in the market. As a rule, it is easier and more successful to provide buyers with correct information and let competition take its course than to regulate sellers closely.

Government also is active in setting standards and testing products before they are put on the market. This is particularly important for potentially harmful products such as drugs and food. Harmful products eventually come to the attention of buyers and are forced off the market, but unnecessary injury or death can be avoided if these products are identified beforehand.

MAINTAINING ENVIRONMENTAL QUALITY

The increase in pollution awareness and society's attempts to overcome it have necessitated government at all levels to establish and enforce environmental standards. In an open competitive market, each firm attempts to produce at the lowest possible cost to maximize profits and compete with other firms that also attempt to minimize costs. Consequently, in industries emitting pollution, each firm has an incentive to dispose of waste as cheaply as possible. Usually, this means disposing such materials into the water, soil, or air. Even if some firms would rather not pollute because of social conscience, firms that do pollute can drive the nonpolluters out of business by underpricing them in the market.

The tendency for individual firms to get rid of waste materials as cheaply as possible and pollute the environment has been called *market failure*. As will be pointed out shortly, this phrase is not entirely accurate because pollution also existed in centrally planned or nonmarket economies, perhaps to a greater degree than in market economies. At any rate, if society wishes to improve the quality of the environment it is necessary for government to establish environmental standards that must be adhered to by all firms. It costs money to install pollution-control devices or in some way capture the pollutants, and this increases production costs. If all firms in an industry have to meet the same environmental standards, the production costs of firms that try to minimize pollution do not have to exceed the costs of those with less of a social conscience. An exception are foreign firms located in countries that have less stringent pollution-control laws,which can undersell domestic firms because of lower costs. In a later chapter, we will see the effects of environmental quality regulations on the costs and product prices of firms.

In regard to maintaining environmental quality, the government also monitors and regulates products that, when used by consumers, may be harmful to the environment or to people. Currently, extensive testing is required before potentially harmful products are placed on the market. Moreover, products that were developed before such testing was required are monitored for health or environmental damage. Examples of products that have been removed from the market include DES (a growth stimulant for cattle) and DDT (an insecticide used only by special permit). DES was suspected of causing cancer in humans, while DDT is not biodegradable. Consequently, DDT built up in the environment and living tissue-causing soft-shelled eggs in birds, which limited their reproductive ability; it was also suspected of harming humans. It is not that firms deliberately placed such products on the market knowing the damage they can cause. Rather, these firms did not always know the full impact of products that first appeared to be beneficial. The objective of extensive testing is to discover any harmful side effects before they can take a toll.

The need for government action to ensure environmental quality is not a problem specific to market or capitalist economies. Centrally planned economies also had pollution. The problem is one of property rights. Who is responsible for the pollutants, which are a special kind of *goods?* Perhaps it is more appropriate to call pollutants *bads.* If a *bad* is the opposite of a *good,* it should carry a negative price. To dispose of a pollutant, the seller should pay the buyer. The buyer, in the case of pollutants, is society. When pollutants are freely disposed into the environment, society unintentionally pays a high price for them. Restriction on disposal of pollutants through government action is a way for society to "purchase" fewer *bads.* Because of its importance, the pollution problem is discussed in greater detail in Chapter 19.

CEILING PRICES

There are times, generally during war, when society believes that the prices of certain goods or services are too high. This belief stems from the idea that excessive pure profits are earned in the production or supply of these items. Consequently, the government may enact legislation that establishes maximum prices of certain goods or services, which makes it illegal for suppliers to sell any regulated items for a higher price.

The established prices are known as ceiling prices because the selling price is not supposed to rise above the maximum. The ceiling price is below the market equilibrium price; otherwise it would not be a ceiling or have any effect on the market.

The consequences of a ceiling price are easily illustrated by the use of the traditional demand-supply diagram, as in Figure 13–1, where P_c represents the ceiling price, which is below the market equilibrium price, P_e. At P_c, the quantity demanded, Q_d, is greater than the quantity supplied, Q_s. At the price P_c, people want to buy more than what is offered for sale. Thus, some buyers have to settle for less than they would like. How should the available supply be allocated?

One option open to the government is to allocate the available quantity on a first-come, first-served basis. The problem with this approach is that it is waste-

FIGURE 13-1 Ceiling Price in a Market

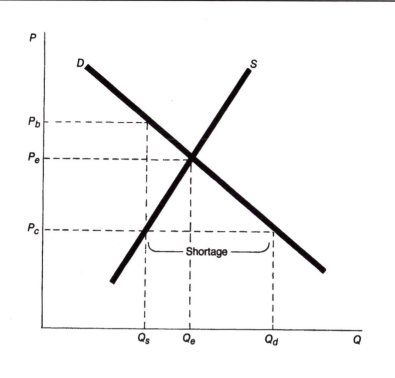

ful. Countless hours are spent by people standing in line to obtain a portion of the scarce item. The total output of goods and services to society could be increased if people devoted their energies to production rather than to standing in line or attempting to bribe the product's distributors.

An alternative and more efficient method of allocating the available output is to issue ration stamps equally among the population. Although many people cannot buy as much as they would like under this scheme, at least there is a little for everyone, and it eliminates much of the wasted effort mentioned above. It is important to recognize that a ceiling price inevitably creates a shortage in the market and consequently makes it necessary to impose a rationing scheme.

A second side effect of a ceiling price is that it reduces the quantity produced of the already scarce commodity. In Figure 13-1, before the ceiling price, output is at Q_e, and after the ceiling is imposed, output declines to Q_s. This happens because the lower price forces suppliers to reduce their production of the good or service in question—perhaps increasing their output of nonregulated items.

Because of food shortages and subsequent high food prices, the governments of numerous developing nations have set ceiling prices on food to hold down inflation. However, from our analysis of the effect of ceiling prices, it is evident that such a policy only makes the problem worse—because it further reduces the meager output of food. Low food prices also reduce the incentive for public and private research agencies to provide new technology for agriculture, and there is little increase (shift) in the supply curve of food.

A third effect of a government-imposed ceiling price is the creation of a black market where people who desire a larger amount than their quota are willing to pay a high price to obtain it. The black-market price can be determined from Figure 13-l. At quantity Q_s, the demand curve tells us that people are willing to pay the black-market price (P_b). This price is illegal because it is above the ceiling. Also, this price is substantially above the market equilibrium price, P_e. Thus, the black-market price is not a valid indicator of the price that would prevail without the ceiling.

SUPPORT PRICES

Occasionally, society decides that the market price of a good is too low, and as a result government action is undertaken to keep price above the equilibrium level. The motivation for this action generally stems from a belief that producers of the supported products suffer from low incomes and that raising the price of their products will raise their incomes. Agriculture is an example.

The effect of a support price is shown by Figure 13–2. At the support price, P_s, the quantity supplied, Q_s, exceeds the quantity demanded, Q_d. As a result, there is a surplus in the market amounting to the difference between Q_s and Q_d. The only way the government can maintain the support price, therefore, is to buy the surplus and keep it off the market. Otherwise, the excess output will exert a downward pressure on price and drive it toward equilibrium.

The stocks of agricultural commodities accumulated by the U.S. government over the years, mainly grains and dairy products, are examples of surpluses resulting from support prices. Western European countries also have accumulated surpluses of agricultural commodities due to similar policies. At times, countries have attempted to dump surplus commodities on the world market at subsidized prices. But, this practice generally brings howls of protest from nations that normally export these products at nonsubsidized prices.

The existence of a support price provides an incentive for producers to produce even more of an overabundant product. At the equilibrium price, P_e, Q_e is supplied, whereas at the higher support price, P_s, Q_s is offered for sale. To reduce this surplus, the government has restricted the use of land by producers who wish to sell at the higher support price. Unfortunately, restricting land has not been a successful means of restricting output because producers have increased output by increasing the use of inputs that substitute for land—particularly fertilizer, herbicides, and improved varieties of crops.

The ability of support price programs to substantially raise the income of producers who really need help is questioned increasingly. Support price programs have been ineffective as an income-supporting scheme because the low-income

FIGURE 13-2 Support Price in the Market

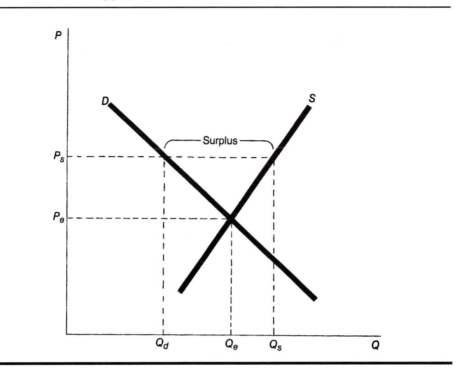

producers tend to be small producers. Doubling the price of wheat from $3 to $6 per bushel adds only $1,500 per year to the income of a 500-bushel-per-year producer, but it adds $60,000 per year to a 20,000-bushel producer. Thus, price support programs tend to help high-income producers more than low-income producers.

A further drawback of farm price support programs is that some of the resulting surpluses that are purchased by the government are shipped to low-income countries at zero or subsidized prices. This depresses farm prices in the recipient countries and retards the development of their agriculture. An alternative program for alleviating hunger in low-income countries, which would stimulate the demand for food and the development of their agriculture as well as the industries serving agriculture, is presented in Chapter 27 of the companion macro text.

SALES AND EXCISE TAXES

Common methods of obtaining government revenue, both state and federal, are sales and excise taxes. These taxes are levied as a percentage of the selling price of the goods or services they cover. Some items, particularly items that society regards as luxuries or nonessentials, such as liquor or jewelry, may be covered by more than one tax. Other items, such as food and clothing, may be taxed at a lower rate or not at all.

A supply-demand diagram also can be used to analyze the effects of a sales or excise tax. A convenient way of thinking about such a tax is that it increases the price of a given quantity of the item taxed. A sales or excise tax decreases the supply to consumers or shifts the market supply curve upward and to the left. Because of the tax, a given quantity will cost more to buy. The imposition of such a tax is illustrated in Figure 13-3, in which the supply curve after the tax is represented by S_0.[1]

Notice that the market equilibrium price increases from P_e to P_d after the tax is imposed. Also, recognize that with a downward-sloping demand and an upward-sloping supply, the price rise to consumers is less than the amount of the tax. Figure 13-3 shows that the total tax at quantity Q_t is the same as the distance from P_s to P_d on the vertical axis. This is the amount that the supply curve has been shifted up because of the tax.

However, the price that producers obtain after the tax is reduced by the distance between P_e and P_s. Although producers (sellers) collect price P_d from buyers, they must relinquish an amount equal to the tax—leaving them with a lower net price than before the tax—as long as the demand curve is downward sloping. Producers are left with a lower net price after the tax than before because they do not decrease quantity enough to push the selling price up by the full amount of the tax. Even though producers suffer a reduction in profits due to the lower net price received, they would suffer an even greater reduction in profits by forcing the price up by the full amount of the tax. This results from the large decrease in quantity sold that would occur if the price were increased by the full amount of the tax. Profits depend on both price and quantity. We will see this more clearly in the following chapters.

Because of the price increase to consumers and the decrease in the net price received by producers, it is sometimes said that consumers bear part of the burden of the tax according to the price increase they must pay, while producers bear a part of the burden according to the decrease in the net price they receive. In Figure 13–3, consumers bear a greater share of the burden than producers. In the long run as supply becomes more elastic, an even greater share of the tax is borne by consumers. In this case, the more elastic long-run supply curve shifts up by the amount of the tax and raises the price paid by consumers by almost as much as the tax. If the supply curve is horizontal, that is, perfectly elastic, consumers bear 100 percent of the tax. In this case, producers have

---

1 The supply shift is drawn to illustrate a tax of a given percent of the selling price. At higher prices the absolute difference between S_0 and S_1 is greater than at lower prices.

FIGURE 13-3 Effect of a Sales or Excise Tax

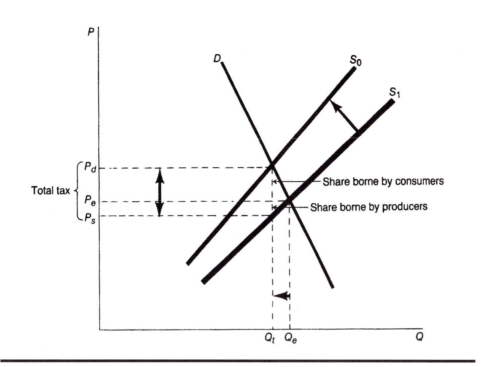

reduced output of the taxed items enough for the price to rise by the full extent of the tax.

Because of the reduction in the quantity of a taxed item demanded and supplied, the use of selective sales or excise taxes distorts the output mix of goods and services produced in an economy. The quantities of nontaxed or less heavily taxed items increase at the expense of items taxed at higher rates. This outcome has been of some concern to economists because it causes a reduction in the value of output to society from a given amount of resources used. An intuitive explanation for this outcome is that resources are pushed into the production of products that are less valued by society than the taxed items. We will say more about the effect of resource allocation on total value of output in the following section.

Sales and excise taxes also have been criticized for being regressive, that is, for falling most heavily on low-income people. This occurs if low-income people spend a larger share of their income on the taxed items than their higher-income counterparts in the long run. An attempt is made to mitigate this problem by taxing nonessentials, such as alcoholic beverages, tobacco, and luxury items, at relatively high rates and not taxing necessities such as food and clothing—or taxing them at lower rates. However, taxes on alcoholic beverages and tobacco also are regressive because they make up a larger share of the budgets of people with low incomes than of those with high incomes.

DEAD WEIGHT LOSS OR SOCIAL COST

When governments enact policies or laws such as ceiling or support prices, or sales taxes, the market prices of the affected goods are changed from what they would be in an undistorted market. The change in price in turn causes a change in quantity demanded and supplied. For example, a support price increases the market price and decreases the quantity demanded.

This change in price and quantity results in a decrease in the value of output produced in the economy. This decrease in value of output has come to be known as a dead weight loss or social cost to society. To understand why society suffers this loss it is first necessary to interpret the meaning of price as it is read off the demand and supply curves.

Along a demand curve, price reflects the value that society places on the marginal or last unit produced. If an item sells for $100, it is an indication that the last unit purchased is worth at least $100 to the buyer, or else the person would not have parted with the $100.

Along a supply curve, price reflects the value that society places on the goods given up to produce the marginal or last unit produced and sold—its opportunity cost. Recall from chapter 11, a supply curve also is a marginal cost curve. Marginal cost is the value of resources required to produce one more unit of the product. These resources could have been used to produce something else. Consequently marginal cost also is opportunity cost. When more of one good is produced, the added resources used in its production must be taken from some other use, resulting in a decrease in value of output of another good. The decrease in value of the next best alternative good that can be produced is called opportunity cost.

A dead weight loss occurs when a policy or law is enacted which drives a "wedge" between the demand price and the supply price. This is illustrated by Figure 13–4A. Suppose a ceiling price is imposed that lowers the market price to $75 from the $90 equilibrium price that existed in an undistorted market. The lower price prompts producers to reduce quantity supplied from Q_1 to Q_0. At quantity Q_0, the demand curve indicates that the value of the marginal unit to consumers is $100. However, the supply curve tells us that the value of alternative goods given up to produce the marginal unit is $75. You might ask, what is the problem since more is gained than is given up? The problem is that, if an additional unit of the good was in fact produced and sold, society would gain $100 of value and give up $75 resulting in a net gain of $25. In other words, a ceiling price causes an under allocation of resources to the good in question. The total dead weight loss of the ceiling price is shown by the shaded triangle in Figure 13–4A[2]. Moving from Q_0 to Q_1 the dead weight loss per unit becomes

FIGURE 13–4 Dead Weight Losses

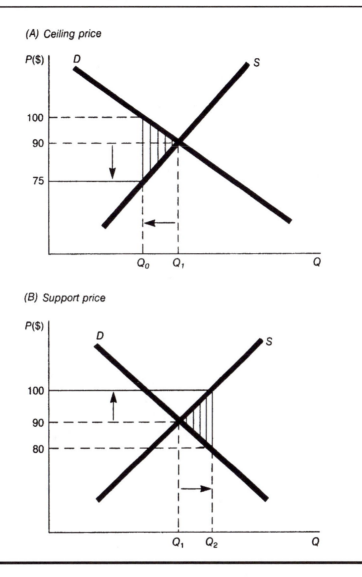

smaller and smaller, and disappears when the undistorted market equilibrium price is established.

A dead weight loss also occurs if price is maintained above the market equilibrium by a support price policy. As illustrated by panel B of Figure 13-4, the support price increases the price of the product to $100 from the $90 equilibri-

---

[2] A similar dead weight loss occurs when a sales tax is imposed on a specific good.

um. This prompts producers to increase quantity supplied from Q_1 to Q_2. At the larger quantity Q_2, the demand curve indicates that consumers value the marginal unit at $80. The supply curve tells us that at Q_2 the value of alternative goods given up to produce one more unit of this good is $100. In this case, society could gain $20 net if one less unit of this good was produced leaving more resources to produce other goods. In other words, a support price causes an over-allocation of resources to the good in question. The total dead weight loss of the support price is illustrated by the shaded triangle in Figure 13-1B. Moving from Q_2 to Q_1, the per unit loss becomes progressively smaller, reaching zero at Q_1.

In Chapter 16 the dead weight loss or social cost of monopoly is discussed. This loss occurs because of the ability of a monopoly to charge a price higher than would exist in a competitive market. It should also be mentioned that the preceding discussion assumes the absence of pollution. When producers emit pollutants into the air or water, the undistorted market price leads to a social cost. In this case too much of the good is produced. This problem will be discussed in Chapters 18 and 19.

ILLEGAL GOODS OR SERVICES

Most societies enact laws that forbid the use of certain goods or services. These laws stem from the belief that consumption of illegal items harms either the individual who consumes them or the people with whom the person comes in contact. Examples of currently illegal goods and services in the United States include mind-distorting drugs, pornographic literature, prostitution, and certain kinds of gambling. Unfortunately, passing a law against the use of a good or service does not eliminate the demand for it. Indeed, there would be no need for such a law if the demand for the good or service did not exist.

Just as for any other good or service, we can visualize both a supply and demand for the illegal item. We have no reason to believe that its demand curve will not slope downward and to the right, like any other market demand curve. There probably will not be as many demanders in such a market because most people do not buy illegal items. Moreover, as the equilibrium price increases, the number of people who buy in these markets will decline, as well as the quantity demanded per person.

Regarding the market supply of illegal goods, there is no reason to believe that higher prices would not bring forth additional quantities. As long as there is a demand for the item, there will always be entrepreneurs ready to supply it for a profit. As prices increase, so do profits; this provides more incentive for illicit suppliers.

Although the market demand and supply of illegal goods and services can be represented by the traditional downward-sloping and upward-sloping lines, there is one important consideration with such goods and services that is not present for their legal counterparts—the penalty for getting caught. The penalty is a demand shifter if it applies only to the person consuming the good or service. If the penalty applies only to the supplier, it is primarily a supply shifter. If it applies to both parties, we would expect the penalty to shift both demand and supply.

In general, the imposition of a penalty or an increase in the harshness of the penalty decreases (shifts to the left) the demand, the supply, or both. For example, imposing a suspended sentence will not decrease the demand for marijuana as much as a definite five-year prison term. Thus, we can expect that increasing the harshness of the penalty on buyers will shift demand to the left, reducing the market price and the quantity exchanged, as illustrated in Figure 13-5A.

On the other hand, if there is an increase in the penalty on suppliers, we can expect a decrease in supply. For example, many prostitutes would find alternative ways of making a living if the penalty for practicing their trade consisted of a $10,000 fine compared with a $100 fine. The effect of a penalty on suppliers is illustrated in Figure 13-5B.

Although a penalty on either the demander or supplier decreases the quantity of an illegal good or service, the price change depends on who is penalized. Goods or services for which only the supplier is penalized tend to have a higher price than in a free market. Most illegal goods or services fit this description. It is not clear why most societies have penalized suppliers more harshly than demanders for dealing with illegal goods and services. Imposing a more severe penalty on consumers will lower the market price from what it would be in a free market, or from what it would be if only suppliers were penalized.

DRUG LEGALIZATION?

Although the majority of U.S. citizens probably favor tough drug laws, especially against sellers, there is a growing sentiment for changing the approach for controlling drug use. It has become apparent that current drug laws have been no more successful than the attempt to stop the consumption of alcoholic beverages during Prohibition. Hundreds of millions of dollars have been spent on the war on drugs, thousands of people have been sent to prison for selling and/or using drugs; and many lives have been lost in the law enforcement process. Yet there is little to show for it.

As pointed out in the preceding section, efforts to control the use of an illegal substance which focus on the supply side result in a couple of undesirable side effects. First the decrease in supply causes an increase in their price. The high prices of mind-distorting drugs yields the potential for enormous profits. The lure of quick riches is especially appealing to young people from poor neighborhoods, drawing them into the business. Many end up dead or in prison, their lives ruined.

A second drawback of focusing on the supply side to control the drug traffic is the high cost of drug addiction. This means that drug addicts have to engage in

FIGURE 13–5 Effects of Penalties in the Market for Illegal Goods and Services

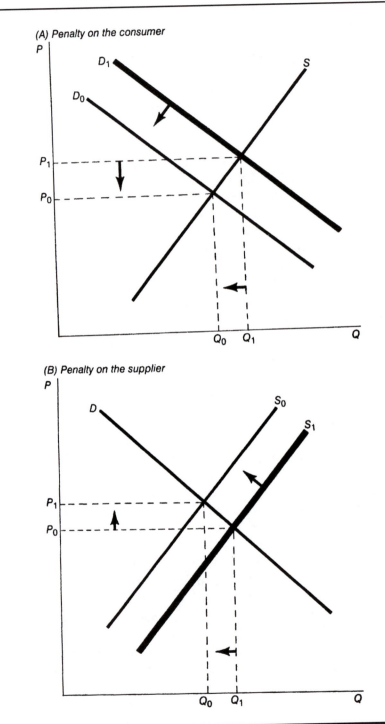

more crime against people and property to raise the money to support their habits. Law-abiding citizens who are victims of this crime also suffer from the war on drugs. And taxpayers are called upon for increasing amounts of money to increase police forces, build more prisons, and house an ever-increasing prison population.

Recognizing that supply-side drug control doesn't work, there have been proposals to focus on the demand side—catching and punishing drug consumers. This policy would decrease the demand for drugs and decrease drug prices. In turn this should decrease other types of crime such as muggings and robbery. However when the police begin to haul in wealthy and influential citizens on drug charges, society probably will begin to lose its zeal for strict drug law enforcement. It is easier for society to send a young minority person to prison than an otherwise respected member of the community. One can envision in this case a relaxation of drug enforcement efforts, toward what might be called *de facto* legalization. Drug laws would still remain on the books but the police would not actively pursue the enforcement of these laws. This policy has been in effect for some time in the Netherlands and appears to be working. The ill effects of using drugs do not appear to be greater in the Netherlands than in the United States.

Of course, this would not mean that people would be free to injure others while under the influence of drugs. Spaced-out drivers are as dangerous as drunken drivers. Laws against such behavior would have to be rigorously enforced. Moreover, efforts toward educating young people on the hazards and sheer stupidity of drug use would have to continue.

There will never be a drug-free society, just as there will never be an alcohol- or tobacco-free society. But society can minimize the damage caused by these substances by using a more reasonable approach of education and compassion rather than of ignorance and coercion.

RATIONING

Rationing generally conjures up a scheme where the government issues ration coupons that allow consumers to purchase a specified amount of the good in question. This circumstance arises when the government places a control or ceiling on the maximum price sellers can obtain. Coupon rationing is most often used in times of national emergency such as wars, at least in the United States and other market economies. In more normal times, coupon rationing is rarely used in these countries.

One might ask, since every nation's ability to produce goods and services falls short of its citizens' desires, why isn't it necessary to always employ rationing to dole out the available output? The answer is that every nation employs a rationing scheme. The one most commonly used in market economies is market price. Recall that if there is a shortage in a market, the price will rise to the equilibrium level. At this level, buyers will purchase exactly what sellers place on the market. Hence, price is the rationing device.

That people rarely think of price as a rationing device attests to its success in this role. It works well because people impose rationing on themselves. If a good becomes scarce and its price rises, the MU per dollar received by consumers declines. This gives them an incentive to consume less of the item and substitute for it more of something that offers a higher MU per dollar. With coupon rationing, the limit of how much we can consume is set by an outside authority, the government. If the price is set low, causing MU per dollar to be high, people have an incentive to circumvent the regulation—attempting to buy more of the scarce item. Resources must then be employed to police people's behavior, and if they are caught breaking the law, more resources must be used to punish them.

Another undesirable consequence of coupon rationing is that the price ceiling reduces the incentive of producers to supply the already scarce goods-making them even more scarce. As time elapses and supply and demand become more elastic, the gap between quantity demanded and quantity supplied becomes wider. People then resort more to black markets until the official price becomes meaningless.

Even with coupon rationing, market price still performs part of the rationing task. The only time coupon rationing would perform 100 percent of the rationing function is when price is zero. As long as market price is some positive value, it contributes to rationing.

RESOURCE ALLOCATION

In any economy, millions of decisions must be made each day regarding how the nation's resources are used to produce the available output. How many resources will be used to produce food, how many for clothing, shelter, medical care, entertainment, or investment in capital goods?

There are two general methods of answering these questions: by a central planning authority or by the millions of participants in markets. The first method was utilized by Communist societies, which is why they are often referred to as centrally planned economies. The second method is used by market economies.

In a Communist society or centrally planned economy, all the nation's non labor resources were owned by the government and just about everyone worked for the government. Thus, the people in charge of allocating resources, the central planning committee, had the authority to issue orders or quotas telling producers how much they should produce and by what means. The quotas were not always met, but the resources generally went where the planning committee wanted them. Labor had to also receive permission from the authorities to change jobs and/or place of residence.

In a market economy, the resource allocation decisions are more diverse. The underlying source of information upon which these decisions are made is market price. Consider a situation where more of a good is produced than consumers want to buy at the prevailing market price. A surplus occurs and as a result, the price of the item declines. The lower price reduces the profitability of the item, which causes producers to look for other, more profitable products to produce. In turn, they reduce the output of the surplus item. Thus, resources are allocated away from the production of less popular goods and services toward more popular items. In this process, market price is both a source of information and an incentive mechanism. As the price of something declines, producers know it is amply supplied to consumers, and the decline in price and profitability gives them the incentive to act on this information. The opposite occurs when too little of a good or service is produced. The shortage causes an increase in the price and profitability of the good or service, giving producers the stimulus and the incentive to increase production. Hence, resources are allocated toward increasing the output of goods that consumers want.

Since market price allocates resources between alternative goods and services, government policies that change market prices, such as ceiling or support prices on selected items, also change the pattern of resource allocation in the economy. Consider a ceiling price. If the price of a good or service is maintained at an artificially low level, producers have an incentive to look for more profitable items to produce, and there is a tendency for resources to leave these areas in search of more profitable opportunities elsewhere.

Unfortunately, this outcome is the opposite of what we want. If the price of an item is relatively high, it indicates that the item is scarce relative to the demand of consumers. But the imposition of a ceiling price drives some resources away from its production, which makes the item more scarce than it was before the ceiling. An example of the effect of ceiling prices is rent control in New York City. Not only has a shortage been created for apartments, particularly in the central part of the city, but landlords also have little incentive to maintain their buildings, which hastens the deterioration of living units in the city. In the long run, resources that otherwise would have gone to repair the rent-controlled buildings have gone elsewhere in search of higher returns. Also people living in rent-controlled apartments are reluctant to leave even though they could afford better ones as their incomes increase. This makes it more difficult for low-income people to find housing they can afford. The nationwide shortage of gasoline, and long lines at the pumps, that occurred during the 1970s is another example of how price controls cause shortages. In this case the shortage of gasoline was alleviated by the increasing imports of foreign oil.

An opposite problem occurs when the price is set artificially high, that is, when there is a support price. In this case, the equilibrium price is low because the supply is large relative to the demand of consumers. The existence of a support price that is higher than the equilibrium price draws even more resources into the production of an already abundant good. Again, the result is the opposite of what is desired.

Sales and excise taxes also have an impact on the allocation of resources. By driving a wedge between the prices that consumers pay and producers receive, a sales or excise tax reduces the profitability of producing the taxed item, and it tends to drive some resources away from its production. The higher price that consumers pay also discourages its use.

Market prices, in general, do not allocate resources to the production of public goods and services. Many products, such as roads, police protection, and the military, do not have a market price. The objective of people in charge of this allocation should be to produce the amount and mix of public goods and services that maximize the welfare of society—given the wishes of people for private goods and services. This is a difficult job, not only because no one knows what an optimal allocation is, but also because it differs for different people. For example, politically conservative members of society prefer a smaller proportion of all output to be public goods, or at least goods and services provided by government than their liberal counterparts. The anticipated benefits from public goods in relation to the amount of taxes one has to pay will also influence a person's desire for such goods. Few people like to pay for public goods and services that do not appear to be a good buy in relation to the private goods and services available. People who receive public goods without paying substantial taxes for them are not as likely to call them a bad buy.

As we saw earlier, market prices provide signals that enable producers to decide upon the amount and mix of private goods and services produced in the economy. The signals that guide public decision makers who allocate resources to public goods and services are more complex. Sometimes a shortage of such goods occurs as in the case of crowding in our national parks or congestion on our streets and highways. In other cases, the representatives of citizen groups, such as the Sierra Club or Common Cause, may petition public decision makers to reorder their priorities. Professional lobbyists representing special-interest groups also influence the amount and mix of public goods produced. It is also common for people with a special interest to demonstrate or picket a government agency in an attempt to change the allocation of resources. Sometimes the demonstrations become violent and turn into riots, which is a destructive way to reallocate resources.

In Communist economies, most of the resources used in the production of public and private goods were allocated by government orders. One drawback of allocating resources by political decree as opposed to price signals is that it forced people to act against their self-interest, which hurts incentives. As an extreme example, you would not be happy if a government official ordered you to quit college or your job and take a job in the coal mines if there was a shortage of fuel. Nor would you be happy if you were ordered to use coal rather than fuel oil or gas to heat your dwelling. On the other hand, if the wages of coal miners rose substantially relative to other occupations, many people would voluntarily enter this occupation to increase their incomes. Similarly, if the price of oil and gas increased relative to coal, people would tend to voluntarily increase their use of coal while conserving oil and gas. Another problem of resource allocation by a central planning committee is that it is impossible for the committee to gather sufficient and accurate information to know where the resources would yield the greatest benefit to society. Hence, this type of economy is subject to making colossal mistakes of either producing too much or too little of various goods. Finally, political pressure may preclude making adjustments even when the committee knows that they should be made.

QUESTIONS

1. Cite the laws or regulations that improve the workings of markets.
2. a. A ceiling price, if it is below the market equilibrium price, will cause a shortage of the good or service in question. True or false? Explain.
   b. A support price, if it is above the market equilibrium price, will cause a surplus of the good or service in question. True or false? Explain.
3. a. Assuming upward-sloping supply and downward-sloping demand curves, a sales or excise tax raises price to consumers by the amount of the tax. True or false? Explain.
   b. In the long run, when supply becomes more elastic, will consumers or producers bear the major burden of such a tax? Explain.
4. The demand for mind distorting drugs is inelastic. If so, should organized crime be in favor of tighter or looser controls over drug traffic? Explain.
5. Most illegal goods and services are high priced. Why?
6. a. Why is it necessary to ration every good and service?
   b. What are some alternative methods of rationing the available output?
   c. Why is price a desirable rationing device?
   d. How can government policies take away the rationing function of price?
7. a. How do market prices allocate the nation's resources to their most valuable uses?
   b. How can ceiling and support price policies distort the allocation of resources?

SELF TEST

1. Shoplifting _____ the cost of doing business and causes prices paid by honest people to be _____ than they would otherwise be.
   a. increases; lower
   b. increases; higher
   c. decreases; lower
   d. decreases; higher
2. False or misleading information makes it more difficult for consumers to maximize utility because:
   a. prices are higher.
   b. prices are lower.
   c. MU/P ratios cannot be accurately assessed .
   d. demand cannot be measured.
3. If environmental regulations were absent, _____ firms would pollute in order to produce at a _____ cost .
   a. less; higher
   c. more; higher
   b. less; lower
   d. more; lower

4. The inability of a competitive market to prevent pollution is known as:
   a. ceiling prices.
   b. price supports.
   c. market failure.
   d. market power.

5. Ceiling prices or price controls are commonly imposed during times of _____ . Such a policy causes _____ to occur.
   a. unemployment; surpluses
   b. unemployment; shortages
   c. inflation; surpluses
   d. inflation; shortages

6. A black market is the result of _____ . The black market price is _____ than the price that would have prevailed in an uncontrolled market .
   a. support prices; higher
   b. support prices; lower
   c. ceiling prices; higher
   d. ceiling prices; lower

7. Support prices cause_____because at these prices, quantity supplied is _____ than quantity demanded.
   a. surpluses; greater
   b. surpluses; less
   c. shortages; greater
   d. shortages; less

8. Support prices have been most prevalent in:
   a. agriculture.
   b. petroleum.
   c. coal mining.
   d. the auto industry.

9. If the supply curve is upward sloping, a sales or excise tax _____ the price paid by consumers and _____ the net after-tax price received by producers.
   a. increases; increases
   b. decreases; increases
   c. increases; leaves unchanged
   d. increases; decreases

10. In the long run, as supply becomes more elastic, a major portion of sales or excise taxes is borne by
    a. producers
    b. consumers
    c. the government
    d. retailers

11. When a ceiling price is placed on a good the value of the last unit to consumers is _____ than the value of goods given up to produce it. Therefore too _____ of this good is produced relative to other goods.
    a. less; much
    b. less; little
    c. greater; little
    d. greater; much

12. When a support price is imposed on a product the value of the last unit of this good to consumers is _____ than the value of goods given up to produce it. Therefore too _____ of this good is produced relative to other goods.
    a. less; much
    b. less; little
    c. greater; little
    d. greater; much

13. If the major penalty for dealing in illegal goods and services falls mainly on buyers or demanders, their prices will be _____ and quantities _____ than in an unrestricted market.
    a. higher; smaller
    b. higher; larger
    c. lower; smaller
    d. lower; larger

14. If the major penalty for dealing in illegal goods and services falls mainly on sellers or suppliers, their prices will be_____ and quantities_____ than in an unrestricted market.
    a. higher; smaller
    b. higher; larger
    c. lower; smaller
    d. lower: larger

15. In the United States, penalties for dealing in illegal goods and services fall most heavily on_____ causing their prices to be relatively_____ .
    a. buyers; low
    b. buyers; high
    c. sellers; low
    d. sellers; high

16. Laws prohibiting the production and sale of mind-distorting drugs have:
    a. increased crimes against people and property.
    b. increased the prison population.
    c. decreased the prices of drugs.
    d. a and b.

17. With coupon rationing, the amount of each good or service consumed is determined by:
    a. consumers themselves.
    b. producers.
    c. the government.
    d. the cost of ration coupons.

18. With price rationing, the amount of each good or service consumed is determined by:
    a. consumers themselves.
    b. producers.
    c. the government.
    d. the cost of ration coupons.

19. In centrally planned economies, resources were allocated to alternative uses by:
    a. market prices.
    b. producers.
    c. the government.
    d. no one.

20. In market economies, resources are allocated to alternative uses by:
    a. market prices.
    b. multinational corporations.
    c. the government.
    d. no one.

21. If prices of goods and services are set artificially high, too _____ of these items will be produced; whereas, if they are set artificially low, too _____ will be produced.
    a. few; many   c. few; few
    b. many; few   d. many; many

22. Private incentives tend to work to the benefit of society when _____ allocate(s) goods and services to their most productive uses.
    a. the government
    b. market prices
    c. multinational corporations
    d. a central planning committee

Part IV

Market Structures

_____

Chapters 14-18

Chapter 14

Returns to Scale and Firm Size

Key Concepts

Long run average total cost curve

Economies of scale

Constant returns to scale

Diseconomies of scale

Management factor

Increasing cost industry

Constant cost industry

Decreasing cost industry

Long run supply

This chapter and the next four chapters classify the firms in a market economy. This chapter explains why firms vary in size. The explanation is called returns to scale. *Returns to scale* are determined by the firm's long-run average total cost curve.

LONG-RUN AVERAGE TOTAL COST CURVE

The long-run average total cost (LRATC) curve of a firm is defined as an envelope of all possible short-run ATC curves. At any point in time, a short-run ATC curve can be drawn for a firm at a given level of fixed inputs such as land, buildings, and machinery. Because of the law of diminishing returns, each short-run ATC curve is U-shaped. When the firm is small, the minimum point on its short-run ATC curve corresponds to a small quantity. When the fixed inputs are small, output is small.

The short-run ATC curve for a small firm, say one with 1,000 square feet of floor space, is denoted by ATC_1 in Figure 14–1. One can visualize similar ATC curves drawn for larger firms as denoted by ATC_2, ATC_3, and so on. As a firm's fixed inputs increase in size, the minimum point on its corresponding ATC curves occurs at successively large quantities. The curve that envelopes all the short-run ATC curves is the long-run ATC (LRATC) curve. Any point on the LRATC curve represents the lowest possible cost of producing a given level of output at the existing technology and input prices.

A. Economies of Scale

As the firm increases the size of its fixed inputs, the building in this example, the minimum points on its corresponding ATC curves occur at lower levels, which is an expected outcome. The larger building can accommodate more people with each person better able to spend time on tasks that he or she does best. Also, the large space can accommodate larger and more efficient machines.

When the minimum points on successively larger ATC curves occur at lower levels, as shown by ATC_1 to ATC_3 in Figure 14–1, the LRATC envelope will slope down and to the right. The reduction in LRATC at larger-sized firms is called *economies of scale.*

B. Constant Returns to Scale

After a firm reaches moderate size, it may not be possible to capture additional unit cost savings. Additional specialization of tasks may not be feasible, and machines are increased in number rather than becoming larger as the size of the firm increases. In this case, the minimum points on successively larger short-run ATC curves can level out at a constant level, as shown by ATC_3 to

FIGURE 14–1 Long-Run Average Total Cost Curve

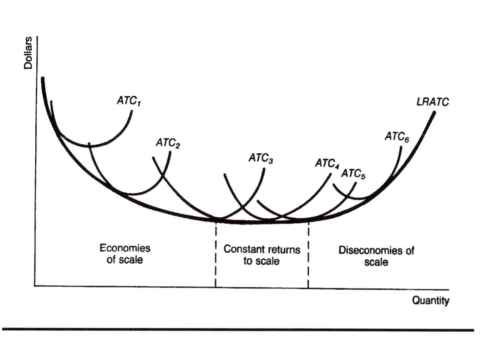

ATC$_5$ in Figure14–1. The LRATC envelope of such ATC curves is horizontal. This denotes constant returns to scale. No additional unit cost savings are attained as the firm becomes larger.

C. Diseconomies of Scale

As the firm increases in size, the minimum points on the corresponding ATC curves can become higher, indicating that unit costs increase as the firm grows. This phenomenon generally is attributed to management difficulties for large firms. Managers are further removed from the production process and have to obtain information second- or third-hand. This leads to inaccuracies and mistakes. As the firm grows, the increase in unit costs is called *diseconomies of scale*. The region of diseconomies of scale corresponds to the upward-sloping portion of the LRATC curve.

FIRM SIZE

Returns to scale is a long-run concept, enough time for firms to change the level of inputs that are fixed in the short run—land, buildings, and machines. It behooves a firm to grow to a size that enables it to capture any economies of scale but not so large as to encounter diseconomies. This size corresponds to the lowest possible point on the LRATC curve. Or, if the curve has a flat portion (constant returns),the firm should strive to be here. When average total cost is minimized, the firm has the best opportunity to earn pure profits—or at least escape losses.

The shape of the LRATC curve for the typical firm in an industry has an important bearing on the size of firms in an industry. If the LRATC curve turns upward at a small size, the average size of firms in that industry will be small. In such an industry, large firms exhibit higher unit costs and therefore cannot compete with small firms. In the long run, the price of the product will correspond to the lowest point on the typical firms' LRATC curve. If product price is higher than this, the existence of pure profits will attract new firms or resources. In turn, industry output increases and price declines. The opposite occurs if product price is lower than the minimum point on LRATC.

If the shape of the typical firm's LRATC curve is such that its low point occurs at a large level of output, the average size firm in the industry also will be large. In this case, small firms cannot compete with large ones. Product price will be competed down to the point where the most efficient, large firms can just cover their costs.

Another possibility is a LRATC curve that exhibits a relatively long, flat portion—constant returns to scale. In this situation, there can be a large difference in the size of firms. Small firms can coexist with large ones; neither has a cost advantage.

The Management Factor

From the preceding discussion, one can conclude that if the typical firm in an industry is able to capture significant scale economies, the industry will be made up of a few large firms. Conversely, if scale economies are exhausted at relatively small output levels, the industry will consist of many small firms. This is not to say, however, that all firms in an industry will be of equal size. The ability of a firm to survive in a competitive market and its ultimate size depend very much on the quality of its management.

A well-managed firm will exhibit a LRATC curve that lies below one from a poorly managed firm and will continue to slope down to greater levels of output. Of two firms that start up at the same time, the one with better management will more likely grow to a larger size and survive at that size than the one with poorer management.

What are the characteristics of a good manager or a well-managed firm? This is a question for an entire MBA program, but a few general points can be made. The better-managed firm will come closer to equalizing the input price/MPP ratios in order to minimize cost at each level of output. Also the good manager maximizes the potential of the firm's employees as well as maximizing the

MPPs of other inputs, given their level of use. A good manager is adept at dealing with people, both employees and customers. This includes an ability to identify and hire capable and hard-working employees. Retaining good people also requires a willingness to give employees responsibility and to compensate them accordingly. The better manager also is alert to the market, utilizing the firm's resources to produce the goods or services most demanded by consumers, and paying attention to quality control. In short, the quality of management is determined by the accuracy and quality of thousands of management decisions made each year.

Management ability may in part be learned through training and experience but it also is likely to be a part of one's inherent skills, such as the ability to play the piano, do mathematics, or run 100 meters in 10 seconds. It also requires a willingness to work hard and think.

PRODUCTION COSTS: THE FIRM VERSUS THE INDUSTRY

A. Increasing Cost Industry

Although the preceding discussion of economies and diseconomies of scale focused on the individual firm, remember that a firm's production costs can be affected by other firms in the industry. This can happen through the price of resources. If just one or a few firms expand or contract, there will not likely be any change in the price of resources because they use a small part of the industry total. A change in output by all firms in the industry or a substantial change in the number of firms, however, might change the price of the resources used in this industry. A substantial contraction by the industry, for example, releases resources that must find alternative employment. To do this, they might be required to accept lower prices. On the other hand, if there is interest in attracting a substantial quantity of additional resources, their price might rise to draw them away from other industries.

In addition to resource price increases, expansion by the entire industry can affect the individual firm's cost curves through what economists call technical diseconomies. The most common example of these is waste disposal. If the industry is small and its firms are scattered, disposing of waste tends to be less costly than if the industry is large and highly concentrated. For example, one or a few small firms may release wastes into the environment without causing public alarm. But with growth of the industry, each firm may have to construct costly waste disposal facilities, which increases the cost curves of all individual firms.

Economists refer to industries that experience a rise in costs, either through resource price increases or through technical diseconomies, as increasing cost industries. As this kind of industry expands, the minimum point on each firm's LRATC curve increases so that the zero pure-profit price rises. Thus, as the industry grows larger, the long-run equilibrium price for the industry increases. The situation is illustrated in Figure 14–2A, in which it is assumed that the industry expands by adding additional firms.

B. Constant Cost Industry

Although increasing costs are expected in many industries, it is possible to visualize one that can expand its output without increasing costs. This could happen if the resources used by the industry make up a small proportion of the total employment of these resources. Cookie production, for example, employs a small proportion of the total land, labor, and other resources that are available in the economy. Also, no technical diseconomies are likely to be present. Economists refer to such an industry as a constant-cost industry because each firm's cost curves and the long-run equilibrium price do not change as the industry expands to larger levels of output, as in Figure 14-2B.

C. Decreasing Cost Industry

There is a third possibility, a decreasing cost industry, in which costs decline as the industry grows. This is less common than the first two cases. Decreasing costs can occur if the price of the industry's resources declines as the industry grows. This phenomenon usually occurs in new or developing areas. If only a few firms are present, many of the resources will have to be shipped in from distant places or produced locally on a small scale at high costs. If the industry is small and insignificant, there likely will be no public effort to establish institutions to serve it or to train people to work in it if special skills are required. On the other hand, an industry that becomes a significant part of an area's economy can expect to enjoy special advantages. Supporting industries that can supply resources at a minimum cost will emerge; financial institutions will consider it a better risk and will loan money at a lower rate of interest; and public schools might offer special training to young people who want to find employment in the industry. Economists refer to these circumstances as *external economies*. In this case, the entrance of additional firms lowers costs for all firms. It is not totally unexpected, therefore, that industries tend to concentrate in specific areas rather than spread out. Decreasing costs are illustrated in Figure 14–2C.

An industry might exhibit all three situations at different stages of development.When an industry is young and becoming established, it might enjoy decreasing costs. Then, when it is moderate in size, it might expand with constant costs. Finally, as it becomes a major industry using a significant proportion of the resources it employs, it may have increasing costs.

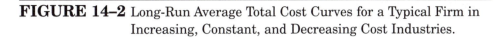

FIGURE 14–2 Long-Run Average Total Cost Curves for a Typical Firm in Increasing, Constant, and Decreasing Cost Industries.

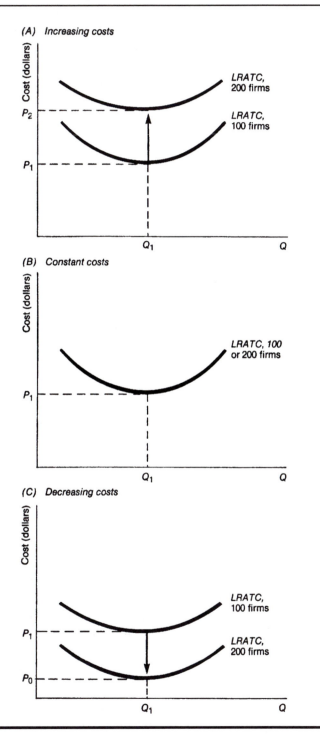

LONG-RUN SUPPLY

In the long run, competitive forces make each firm in an industry produce the quantity of output that corresponds to the minimum point of its LRATC curve, Q_1 in Figure 14–2. If a firm does not produce at this point, other firms that succeed in producing at the minimum-cost point will produce at a lower cost and drive the high-cost firms out of business. This occurs because the price of the product will be competed down to the minimum point of the LRATC curve, and any firm that does not operate at this point incurs losses.

Consider what happens in an increasing-cost industry. At the low price, P_1, there are 100 firms of a given size in the industry, each producing Q_1, as shown in Figure 14–3. Thus, in the long run, the total output of the industry at price P_1 is 100 Q_1. This is illustrated by Figure 14–3. Now suppose the demand for the industry's product increases and the resulting short-run increase in the price of the product draws 100 more firms of equal size into the industry so that the industry doubles in size. If the growth of the industry causes the price of one or more of the industry's resources to increase, the LRATC curve for the typical firm will shift upward as shown in Figure 14–2A. In the long run, the price of the industry's product will settle at P_2. Thus, in the long run, the total output of the industry at price P_2 is 200 Q_1. This is also illustrated in Figure 14–3. Connecting the two points we have just derived yields an upward-sloping, long-run supply curve as shown in Figure 14–3. Thus, in an increasing cost industry, the long-run supply is upward sloping.

In a constant cost industry, the expansion of the industry leaves the LRATC curve of the typical firm unchanged. Consequently, product price remains at P_1 at both 100 Q_1 and 200 Q_1. Plotting these points on a diagram similar to Figure 14–3 yields a horizontal line. Therefore, the long-run supply curve in a constant cost industry is horizontal, or perfectly elastic. Finally, in a decreasing cost industry, the growth in size from 100 to 200 firms lowers the LRATC curve to each firm, as shown in Figure 14–2C. Now, when output increases from 100 Q_1 to 200 Q_1, the price of the product declines to P_0 from P_1. Plotting these points yields a downward-sloping line. Consequently, the long-run supply for a decreasing cost industry is downward sloping. Try to plot the long-run supply curves for the constant and decreasing cost industry cases on your own.

The downward-sloping long-run supply for a decreasing cost industry may at first appear rather strange. All of the discussion on supply in preceding chapters depicted it as an upward-sloping line. Bear in mind that long-run industry supply is derived in a different way than summing the individual firm MC curves to obtain supply. In summing the individual firm supply curves, input prices and the prices of competing products are held constant. When they change, supply shifts. In deriving the long-run supply by plotting the minimum points on firms' LRATC curves, input prices are allowed to vary as the industry expands. If input prices decrease as the industry becomes larger, a downward-

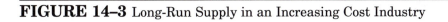

FIGURE 14–3 Long-Run Supply in an Increasing Cost Industry

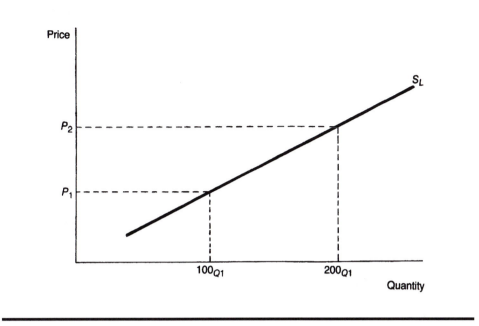

sloping long-run supply is possible. Thus the normal upward-sloping market supply presented in earlier chapters and the downward-sloping long-run industry supply of this chapter are derived under a different set of assumptions. Both are correct.

QUESTIONS

1. a. Why might the minimum points of a firm's short-run average total cost curves decrease as the firm expands?
    b. Why might the minimum points increase?
2. Define:
    a. Economies of scale.
    b. Constant returns to scale.
    c. Diseconomies of scale.
3. Under conditions of economies of scale, is it possible for a large firm that produces a small quantity to experience a higher average total cost than a smaller firm that produces a quantity at the lowest point of its ATC curve? Explain.
4. Illustrate the shape of the LRATC curve for the typical firm in an industry:
    a. Made up of small firms.
    b. Made up of large firms.
    c. Made up of large and small firms.
5. Define the following:
    a. Increasing cost industry.
    b. Constant cost industry.
    c. Decreasing cost industry.
6. a. What conditions give rise to increasing, decreasing, and constant cost industries?
    b. What kinds of firms would you find in each of the above industries?
7. What conditions cause:
    a. An upward-sloping, long-run supply curve?
    b. A horizontal long-run supply curve?
    c. A downward-sloping, long-run supply curve?
8. Is it possible for the long-run supply curve of an industry to slope down if the industry's short-run supply is obtained by summing all the individual firms' MC curves which slope upward? Explain, and derive a downward-sloping long-run supply curve.

SELF TEST

1. The LRATC curve is _____ of all possible short-run _____ curves .
    a. a summation; MC
    b. a summation; ATC
    c. an envelope; MC
    d. an envelope; ATC
2. Each short-run ATC curve is drawn for a given level of:
    a. sales.
    b. variable inputs.
    c. fixed inputs.
    d. total inputs.
3. Economies of scale exist when the firm's short-run ATC curve _____ as the firm expands output.
    a. does not shift
    b. shifts outward at the same level
    c. shifts up and to the right
    d. shifts down and to the right
4. Constant returns to scale exist when the firm's short-run ATC curve _____ as the firm expands output.
    a. does not shift
    b. shifts outward at the same level
    c. shifts up and to the right
    d. shifts down and to the right
5. Diseconomies of scale exist when the firm's short-run ATC curve _____ as the firm expands.
    a. does not shift
    b. shifts outward at the same level
    c. shifts up and to the right
    d. shifts down and to the right
6. In the region of economies of scale, the firm's LRATC curve:
    a. slopes down.
    b. slopes up .
    c. is horizontal.
    d. is vertical.

7. In the region of constant returns to scale, the firm's LRATC curve :
   a. slopes down.
   b. slopes up.
   c. is horizontal.
   d. is vertical.

8. In the region of diseconomies of scale, the firm's LRATC curve:
   a. slopes down.
   b. slopes up .
   c. is horizontal.
   d. is vertical.

9. Economies of scale stem mainly from:
   a. management difficulties.
   b. more efficient utilization of fixed inputs.
   c. lower prices paid for inputs.
   d. higher prices received for the output.

10. Diseconomies of scale stem mainly from:
    a. management difficulties.
    b. more efficient utilization of fixed inputs.
    c. higher prices paid for inputs.
    d. lower prices received for the output.

11. If there are few very large firms in an industry, it is an indication that _____ exist in the industry.
    a. diseconomies of scale
    b. economies of scale
    c. constant returns of scale

12. If there are many small firms in an industry, it is an indication that large firms are subject to:
    a. diseconomies of scale.
    b. economies of scale.
    c. constant returns to scale.

13. If an industry is made up of small firms and large firms operating side by side, it is an indication that the LRATC curve for the typical firm:
    a. slopes down.
    b. slopes up.
    c. has a long horizontal section.
    d. has a long vertical section.

14. A good manager:
    a. equalizes input price/MPP ratios.
    b. maximizes MPPs of employees and other inputs
    c. hires quality people, gives them responsibility, and compensates them accordingly.
    d. does all of the above.

15. The LRATC curve of a well-managed firm lies _____ the LRATC for a poorly managed firm and begins to slope up at a _____ quantity of output.
    a. above; larger
    b. below; larger
    c. above; smaller
    d. below; smaller

16. In an increasing cost industry, expansion of the industry causes a(n) _____ in prices paid for inputs and shifts each firm's LRATC _____ , causing long-run output price to _____ .
    a. increase; upward; increase
    b. increase; upward; decrease
    c. decrease; downward; decrease
    d. decrease; downward; increase

17. In a decreasing cost industry, expansion of the industry causes a(n) in price paid for inputs and shifts each firm's LRATC , causing long-run output price to
    a. increase; upward; increase
    b. increase; upward; decrease
    c. decrease; downward; decrease
    d. decrease; downward; increase

18. In a constant cost industry, expansion of the industry _____ each firm's LRATC curve, causing long-run output price to _____ .
    a. increases; increase
    b. decreases; decrease
    c. does not affect; remain constant

19. An industry's long-run supply curve is made up of the minimum points of its firms' _____ curve.
    a. MC   c. AVC
    b. ATC   d. LRATC

20. The long-run supply curve of an increasing cost industry is:

    a. upward sloping.

    b. downward sloping.

    c. horizontal.

    d. vertical.

21. The long-run supply curve of a decreasing cost industry is:

    a. upward sloping.

    b. downward sloping.

    c. horizontal.

    d. vertical.

22. The long-run supply curve of a constant cost industry is:

    a. upward sloping.

    b. downward sloping.

    c. horizontal.

    d. vertical.

23. To obtain the normal upward-sloping market supply, input prices are _____ . In deriving the long-run industry supply by plotting the minimum points on firms' LRATC curves, input prices are _____ .

    a. allowed to change; held constant

    b. held constant; allowed to change

    c. held constant; held constant

    d. allowed to change; allowed to change

Chapter 15

Perfect Competition

Key Concepts

Perfect competition defined

Characteristics of a perfectly competitive firm

Demand facing a perfectly competitive firm

Three kinds of demand curves

Long run adjustment

The search for lower costs

Economic efficiency

This chapter focuses on the small end of the size distribution of business firms—perfect competition. After establishing the two characteristics common to all perfectly competitive firms, the discussion turns to the profit-maximizing behavior of such firms. Here we will see that each firm in an attempt to maximize its own profits also maximizes the value of output to society.

PERFECT COMPETITION DEFINED

A perfectly competitive firm is one that has no power to alter the price it receives for its product. For this reason, the perfectly competitive firm is sometimes called a price taker. The firm takes the price of its product as determined in the market. The agricultural firm or farm is the only firm that meets this criterion. Therefore, agriculture is a perfectly competitive industry of perfectly competitive firms. The small size of each firm relative to the industry's size suggests a lack of significant scale economies.

CHARACTERISTICS OF A PERFECTLY COMPETITIVE FIRM

There are two basic reasons that a perfectly competitive firm must accept the price that is determined by the market: (1) it sells a product that is undifferentiated from the product of all other firms in the market and (2) it sells a small proportion of the total market.

That a perfectly competitive firm sells a product indistinguishable from what is produced by other firms in its market means that buyers have no preference for the product of one firm over another. Thus, every firm must sell its product at the price all the other firms obtain. Why should buyers pay $3.25 per bushel of wheat from farmer Jones if 10,000 other farmers are selling the same product for $3 per bushel? In other words, each producer must conform to the market price.

We also know that because of the downward-sloping nature of market demand curves, market price can be changed only if the quantity sold is changed; quantity must decrease to obtain a higher price, or any increase in the quantity demanded must be accompanied by a price reduction. But, because the perfectly competitive firm sells a minute fraction of the market, each firm cannot alter market price by producing more or less. For example, suppose farmer Jones decides that the market price of wheat is too low. What can he do about it? If he reduces his production by half (a drastic measure for any firm), the total market supply would remain unchanged, because taking a few hundred or thousand bushels from a market in which millions of bushels are traded has an imperceptible effect; it's like taking a handful of sand away from a beach. Thus, no matter what quantity the firms decide to produce, within reason, the market price remains the same.

Thus, the characteristic of an undifferentiated product requires each perfectly competitive firm to sell at the same price as all other firms, that is, the market price; and the characteristic of producing a small fraction of the market means that each perfectly competitive firm has no power to alter the market price.

DEMAND FACING A PERFECTLY COMPETITIVE FIRM

We can obtain a better understanding of the relationship between a perfectly competitive firm and the market in which it sells by diagrams. The traditional market demand and supply curves are depicted in Figure 15–1A. The equilibrium price and quantity that prevail in this market are denoted by P_e and Q_e. The price that each firm will face, therefore, is P_e, if the market is allowed to reach an equilibrium.

The individual perfectly competitive firm operating in this market is represented by Figure 15–1B. Its supply curve, as we know, is the marginal cost (MC) curve above the point where it intersects the average variable cost curve if it is already committed to its fixed costs. The price that the firm will receive for its product is P_e, as determined by market supply and demand. This price, P_e, is the demand facing this firm. The price line, P, is a demand curve in that it tells the firm what price it will receive for its product. The fact that the demand curve is a perfectly horizontal line (perfectly elastic) means that the firm can produce and sell any output within reason at this price. In other words, the market stands ready to buy any reasonable quantity from this firm at price P_e. Thus, the line showing the price is the demand curve facing this firm.

In an actual market situation, the prevailing market price need not be the equilibrium price. For example, if market demand had recently shifted to the right and the market price had not adjusted to the new, higher equilibrium level, the actual market price probably would be less than the equilibrium. However, as explained previously, forces then would occur and push the actual price up toward the new equilibrium. During the adjustment, the price line facing the individual firm would rise in accordance with the existing market price. In other words, we would not expect the price line to shift instantaneously from one equilibrium position to another.

From our discussion relating to product supply, we know that a producer of this nature maximizes profits by producing a quantity that corresponds to the point where price equals marginal cost. This quantity is represented by Q_f in Figure 15–1B. Notice that the units of measure on the quantity axis differ greatly between the market and the firm. The market quantity might be measured in terms of millions of units, whereas the firm's quantity might be measured in number of units. The units of measure on the price axes are the same for the market and the firm.

Let us summarize the three kinds of demand curves we have studied. The first is the demand of an individual consumer, represented by a downward-sloping

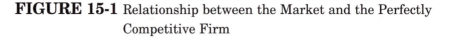

FIGURE 15-1 Relationship between the Market and the Perfectly
Competitive Firm

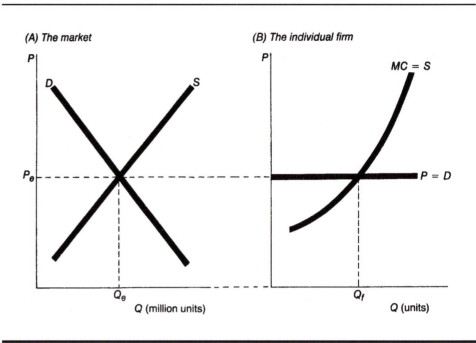

line indicating that quantity increases as price decreases, and vice versa. The
second demand curve is market demand—the sum of all individual demanders
in the market. This is also represented by a downward-sloping line, as in Figure
15–1A. The third is the demand curve facing an individual firm. For the perfectly competitive firm, this demand curve is a perfectly horizontal line, indicating that the market will take any reasonable quantity the firm wishes to sell
at the going market price.

PRICE, COSTS, AND PROFITS

The perfectly competitive firm takes the price as determined in the market
and decides whether or not it should produce; and if so, how much. Recall from
the supply discussion in Chapter 11 that pure profits are earned only if price is
greater than the average total cost at the quantity the firm chooses to produce.
Also recall from Chapter 10 that a firm will maximize profits, or minimize losses, by producing the level of output corresponding to the point where marginal
revenue equals marginal cost. For a perfectly competitive firm marginal revenue equals product price. This occurs because the firm can sell any quantity it
wishes, within reason, without lowering its price. Therefore a perfectly compet-

FIGURE 15–2 Possible Profit or Loss Positions of Perfectly Competitive Firms

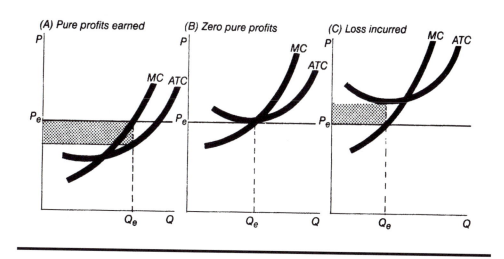

itive firm maximizes profits by producing an output which corresponds to the point where product price equals marginal cost.

The three diagrams in Figure 15–2 illustrate the three possible profit positions for perfectly competitive firms. The price, P_e, that is shown is determined by market demand and supply, as illustrated in Figure 15–1A. The firm that earns pure profits in its business is illustrated in Figure 15–2A. The resources (inputs) used in this production activity earn more than they could in other kinds of work. The total pure profits for the firm are represented by the shaded area. Notice that total profits are maximized at a level of output beyond the point where profit per unit is the largest, that is, the point where the distance between price and average total cost (ATC) is the greatest. Such an outcome is reasonable because the firm is interested in maximizing its total profits rather than profit per unit.

The situation depicted in Figure 15–2B, zero pure profits, is one in which the resources employed by this firm are earning just what they could earn in some other alternative occupation. This situation is the only one of the three shown in which the firm produces a quantity corresponding to the minimum point on its ATC curve. The case of a firm that is not covering its costs (implicit plus explicit) is shown in Figure 15–2C. In this example, the resources employed by the firm earn less than what they could in other occupations. This does not necessarily mean, however, that this firm's cash expenses are greater than its total sales because, as noted in Chapter 11, the ATC curve includes a charge for the resources owned by the firm as well as its cash expenses.

If we could measure perfectly the costs of individual firms at any point in time, we would probably observe all three of these situations in a given market or industry. There would be a few well-managed, low-cost firms making pure profits, as illustrated in Figure 15–2A. There would be other firms breaking even but doing as well as they could in any other occupation. There would also be a few firms making less than they could in other occupations, perhaps looking for a chance to sell their assets and begin another line of production.

Figure 15–2C need not depict a badly managed, slipshod enterprise. The costs for this firm might be high because it has better alternatives than the other firms in the market. For example, the owner of the firm might be a highly educated wheat farmer who has the opportunity of working in a nearby bank at a salary much higher than his neighbors could obtain in their best alternative occupations. Thus, a firm's cost might be high either because the owner is a bad manager or because the person has superior talents that are in demand elsewhere. It is not valid to conclude, therefore, that an industry in which the number of firms is decreasing is losing its least productive people. it may lose some of them, but at the same time, it can lose its most productive people because they have superior opportunities elsewhere.

LONG-RUN ADJUSTMENT

Economists have precise definitions for the terms short run and long run as they apply to production and supply. The short run is the length of time that is too short to change the level of fixed inputs used or the number of firms in the industry but long enough to change the level of output by changing variable inputs. Essentially, the marginal physical product curve and its mirror image, marginal cost, reflect short-run changes in production.

The long run is a period of time long enough to change either the level of fixed inputs used by firms or the number of firms. Unfortunately, it is impossible to designate a period of time that constitutes the long run for all types of firms or even for different situations. The length of this period differs among firms, depending on how difficult or costly it is to change fixed inputs. If production requires extensive fixed inputs, say extensive irrigation or drainage facilities, the length of time to reach a long-run adjustment will be longer than for firms that pursue production in small rented facilities, such as barber shops.

The length of time to reach a long-run adjustment also depends on how profitable it is to adjust. If it is profitable for a firm to expand its fixed inputs or for new firms to enter the industry, the adjustment time will be shorter than if it barely pays to change the level of output or to enter or leave the industry. For example, if it is profitable to expand facilities, most contractors will step up the completion date if they are paid to do so. A higher fee enables them to pay their employees for overtime work to finish the job more quickly.

In looking at long-run adjustment for a perfectly competitive industry in more

FIGURE 15-3   Short-Run Market Equilibrium with Pure Profits Made by the Average Firms

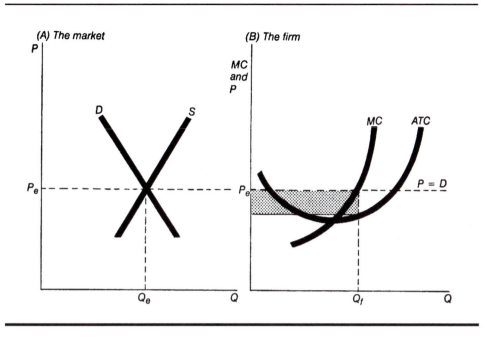

detail, we will start where the market is in equilibrium, that is, where price corresponds to the intersection of supply and demand, as shown in Figure 15–3A. Suppose that the typical firm in the industry is making substantial pure profits, as shown in Figure l5-3B. Assume as well that each firm maximizes its profits by producing an output that corresponds to the point where price is equal to marginal cost, Q_f in Figure 15–3B. These two conditions—market price is at the point where the quantity demanded equals the quantity supplied and price equals marginal cost for each firm—constitute a short-run equilibrium for an industry. This situation is illustrated in the two diagrams in Figure 15–3.

If each firm makes pure profits, however, we can expect that existing firms will expand their facilities (increase their fixed inputs) and/or additional firms will enter the industry to get a piece of the action. We need not assume that all firms are making substantial pure profits for this to happen. In fact, some businesses might be characterized by Figures 15-2B and C. All that is necessary is that a sizable portion of existing firms make pure profits.

Recall from the discussion on product supply that an increase in the number of firms or an increase in the size of firms shifts the market supply curve to the right, as shown in Figure 15–4A. An increase in supply reduces market price. As the market price falls, so does the price that faces each firm. Thus, as the supply shifts right and market price falls, the pure profits that each firm is making are competed away. This process is illustrated in Figure 15–4A and B.

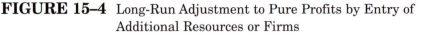

FIGURE 15–4   Long-Run Adjustment to Pure Profits by Entry of
Additional Resources or Firms

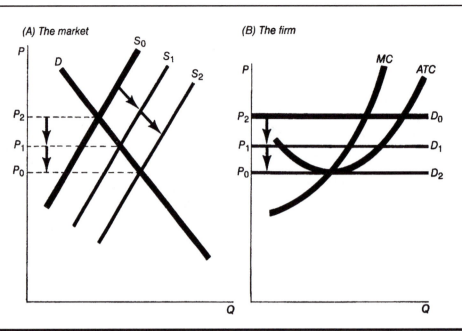

This process of new resources coming into an industry to compete away pure profits is most noticeable at high levels of pure profits. Then, as price falls closer to the zero pure-profit point (P_0 in Figure 15–4), the entry of additional resources will slow down as the prospects for pure profits diminish, although it is not uncommon to observe situations where firms have built up optimism over time and continue to expand until price falls below the zero pure-profit point. As soon as this happens, some firms find more profitable opportunities elsewhere, move out of the industry, and contribute to a decrease in supply, which eventually pulls price up toward the zero pure-profit equilibrium.

An opposite process of adjustment occurs if a large share of the firms in a market or industry are suffering losses or negative pure profits. Here, firms move to more profitable opportunities, decreasing the market supply, and raising market price.

The existence of pure profits or losses results in a long-run adjustment characterized by the corresponding entry or exit of resources or firms. It is also possible to observe adjustments on the cost side. In the production of wheat, for example, there may be a few firms that enjoy some special advantage, such as productive soil. The entry of new firms might push price down to the zero-profit position for every firm in the industry except the privileged few. They might continue to reap pure profits. Eventually, these unusually profitable firms will

FIGURE 15-5   Long-Run Adjustment to Pure Profits by Increases in Cost
of Resources to the Individual Firm

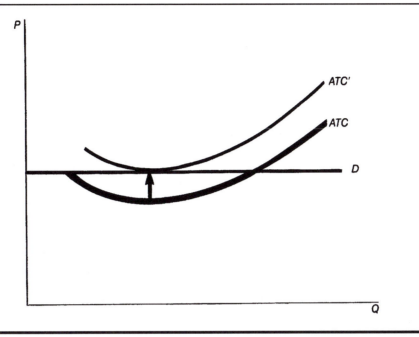

be sold to new owners, and the price paid for these firms reflects the pure profits that can be expected in the future. The new owners are willing to pay more
for productive land than for poor land. With an increase in the land price, there
will be an increase in the cost of production, mainly because of the increase in
the interest charge (explicit or implicit) and taxes. If the sellers of these productive firms are shrewd bargainers, they will obtain a price that pushes average total cost (ATC) just about up to the expected future price as illustrated by
Figure 15–5. Economists refer to this situation as a capitalization of pure profits into the value of land.

This phenomenon of cost adjusting to price has been particularly important in
U.S. agriculture. As pointed out in Chapter 13, the government has attempted
to increase incomes by establishing support prices of various products. Prices
are fixed, but over the years, pure profits have been eroded away because of the
bidding up of land prices. Eventually, producers are forced back to the same zero
pure-profit position that existed before support prices. The people who owned
the land during its price rise, however, enjoyed a capital gain. Also remember
that for this phenomenon to occur, a necessary condition is that the product
price be maintained at the artificially high level, such as by price supports.
Without the price support, competitive forces would drive the product price
down to the zero pure-profit level, as illustrated by Figure 15–4.

Again, adjustment will not be instantaneous. Pure profits or losses exist for different firms at any point in time. But, if pure profits or losses exist, we can observe an adjustment toward a long-run zero pure-profit position in a perfectly competitive industry.

THE CONTINUAL SEARCH FOR LOWER COSTS

Even though all firms in a perfectly competitive industry face a common market price, there are substantial differences in costs among firms. High costs may be due to low productivity resulting from inept management, or they may stem from high-paying opportunities in other lines of work. A perfectly competitive firm has no control over the price of its product, and such a firm cannot alter the opportunities existing elsewhere. In fact, high implicit costs stemming from superior opportunities elsewhere are welcomed because they represent opportunities to increase income.

However, most perfectly competitive firms can do something about the efficiency of their production processes. The more efficient a firm is in transforming inputs into output, the lower its production costs and the higher its profits. Thus, most firms continually search for new cost-reducing inputs or techniques to increase profits. The effect of achieving a cost reduction in production is illustrated by Figure 15–6. Average total cost (ATC) is shifted downward, and marginal cost (MC) is shifted downward and to the right. If price is at P_0, then the firm can move from a zero pure-profit position to a position of positive pure profits after the cost reduction.

In addition to creating pure profits for the firm in this example, a second effect of a cost reduction is the shift downward and to the right of the MC curve. This tells us that the firms now can produce an additional or marginal unit more cheaply than before. But remember that the MC curve is also the firm's supply curve. At the original MC, Q_0 is produced by the firm, whereas at the new lower MC^1, Q_1 is produced. If a few firms find a way to reduce costs and shift their supply curves, there is no perceptible effect in the market. Increasing the production of wheat by 1,000 bushels, for example, will not be noticed in a market where millions of bushels are traded.

Although the increased production from a single firm has no appreciable effect on the market, similar action by many firms will shift the market supply curve to the right, which reduces the market price. Furthermore, the lower market price squeezes the newly created pure profits out of firms that have achieved lower costs.

Once a significant proportion of firms adopts a new cost-reducing input or technique and the market price begins to fall, the firms that have not reduced costs find their profit positions eroding, and consequently they must also adopt these inputs or techniques so they will not suffer losses and have to leave the industry. This process of the early adopters reaping pure profits and the subse-

FIGURE 15–6 Effects of a Cost Reduction

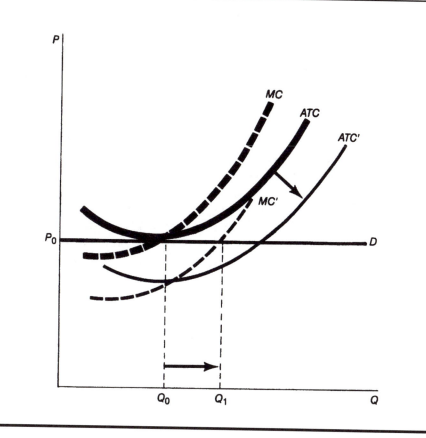

quent erosion of profits to these firms (and losses to the remaining firms) is like a treadmill; each firm must run faster (decrease costs more and more) to stay even. Although each firm may not appreciate this continuous struggle, consumers and society generally gain from it, because more output is obtained from the nation's scarce resources.

ECONOMIC EFFICIENCY

A perfectly competitive industry frequently is used by economists as a standard by which to judge other industries. The reason is that a perfectly competitive equilibrium (short-run or long-run) results in maximum economic efficiency. At this point, resources are allocated such that the value of society's output is maximized. Three criteria are required to obtain economic efficiency. First, there must be maximum technical efficiency. This means that a physical output obtained from a given level of inputs is at its maximum. In other words, resources are not being wasted. For example, a given amount of labor and capital might produce only 20 bushels of wheat if time were wasted or the machines used inappropriately. But, if the inputs were fully and correctly utilized, 30 bushels might be produced. Technical efficiency also means that the firm is on the highest isoquant for a given input mix.

A second criterion necessary to obtain economic efficiency is that a given level of output is produced at the least possible cost. Recall from Chapter 9 that a given output can be produced by various combinations of inputs, but only one combination will result in the lowest possible cost. This is the combination that results in the equality of the P/MPP ratios or that corresponds to the tangency point between the isoquant and the lowest possible isocost line. This is the cost-minimizing condition. Actually, any firm, whether it is perfectly competitive or not, can meet these first two conditions: the attainment of maximum technical efficiency and the cost-minimization condition.

The third criterion necessary for maximum economic efficiency is that the level of output for each good corresponds to the point where the marginal cost of producing an extra unit is equal to the price of the good. This is the profit-maximizing level of output for each perfectly competitive firm. In the next three chapters, we will see that an imperfectly competitive firm will not produce this level of output. Hence, only perfect competition meets the three criteria required to reach maximum economic efficiency (i.e., the maximum value of output). The next question is: Why does the P = MC equality result in the maximum value of output, given the amount of resources available to a country? To understand why, recall what price and marginal cost represent.

As explained in Chapter 13, the price of a product is the value that society assigns to a marginal unit. For example, if the price of wheat is $4 per bushel, we can infer that society values an extra bushel of wheat at $4 or it would not choose to buy it for this price.

Marginal cost (MC), on the other hand, represents the cost to society in terms of other products given up to obtain an extra unit of this product. For example, if the MC of wheat is $4, to produce an extra bushel, $4 worth of another good or service must be given up, assuming that this other good is produced in an industry where price and MC also are equal.

It is easiest to understand why the equality of price and MC results in a maximum value of output if we first look at a situation where price does not equal marginal cost. Suppose that, for some reason, the price of a bushel of wheat is $4 and its MC is $3. This means that society values an extra bushel at $4 and values the goods or services given up to produce this extra bushel at $3. Now, if one extra bushel of wheat is produced, society gains $4 and gives up $3, leaving a net gain of $1. Thus, it behooves society to increase the production of wheat under these circumstances, because the value of total output is increased using the same amount of resources. There is an underallocation of resources to the production of a good or service if its price is greater than its MC.

In the opposite situation, say price is still $4 but MC is $5. By decreasing the production of wheat by one bushel, society gives up $4 worth of wheat but gains $5 worth of other goods and services, resulting in a net gain of $1. Thus, if MC is greater than price, there is an overallocation of resources to the production of this product because by reducing its production, the total value of output is increased with a given amount of resources. The value of output is maximized only if price equals marginal cost because when this occurs, it is impossible to reallocate resources to increase the total value of output. Perfectly competitive firms attempt to produce at the point where price equals MC. Thus, an advantageous characteristic of perfect competition for society is that producers attempting to maximize their profits by equating price and marginal cost also maximize the value of output to society.

However, perfect competition is not the ultimate goal in all industries. We will see in the following chapters that the nature of most products precludes perfect competition in their production. However, the further removed an industry is from the perfectly competitive model, the greater the chance that society will suffer a significant reduction in the value of output for a given amount of resources.

The idea of competitive forces working for the good of society was introduced by the eighteenth-century Scottish economist and philosopher Adam Smith in *The Wealth of Nations,* published in 1776. He called this phenomenon the "invisible hand." Each firm that attempts to maximize its own profits also maximizes the value of output to society, as though guided by an invisible hand.

QUESTIONS

1. a. What is a perfectly competitive firm?
    b. What are the two characteristics that give rise to such a firm?
    c. What industry comes closest to perfect competition?
2. a. Distinguish between the demand by consumers for a product produced by a perfectly competitive firm and the demand facing such a firm.
    b. What is the shape of the demand curve facing a perfectly competitive firm?
    c. What is implied by such a demand curve?
3. A simple method for determining the most profitable level of output for a perfectly competitive firm is to find where the difference between product price and ATC is the greatest and then produce the corresponding quantity of output. True or false? Explain.
4. Wheat production in the United States is carried on by many firms, each selling a product undifferentiated from that of other firms in the market. Explain how the price of wheat is determined and how this price is related to the individual producer.
5. An increase in market supply, say because of favorable growing conditions, will cause a decrease in the demand facing the firm. True or false? Explain.
6. a. Differentiate between short-run and long-run adjustment to price changes.
    b. What are the two ways in which pure profits are competed away in a perfectly competitive industry?
    c. It is common practice for governments to set the support price of wheat at the average cost of production for the industry. What happens to the price of land that is more productive than the industry average? What happens to the industry average cost of production?

7. Plant breeders continually develop new varieties of wheat that yield more than old varieties.
    a. Explain the effect of a new variety on the costs and profits of the alert, early-adopting farmer.
    b. Explain the long-run adjustment of the wheat-producing industry to this new development.
    c. Explain what would happen to producers who do not adopt a new variety.
8. a. What is economic efficiency?
    b. What are the three criteria necessary to achieve economic efficiency?
    c. Why does perfect competition result in maximum economic efficiency?

SELF-TEST

1. A perfectly competitive firm is defined as one which has no control over:
    a. its costs.
    b. its output.
    c. its profits.
    d. the price of its product.
2. A perfectly competitive firm has no control over the price it receives for its product because:
    a. it sells a small share of the market.
    b. it sells a homogeneous product
    c. it cannot earn a pure profit.
    d. a and b.
3. The industry comprised of perfectly competitive firms is:
    a. education.
    c. medical care.
    b. agriculture.
    d. retail trade.
4. The demand facing a perfectly competitive firm is:
    a. perfectly elastic.
    b. perfectly inelastic.
    c. upward sloping.
    d. downward sloping.

5. The demand curve facing a perfectly competitive firm tells the firm that the market will take any quantity the firm is willing to produce at the _____ price.
   a. profit-maximizing
   b. cost-minimizing
   c. market
   d. profit-minimizing

6. The demand facing a perfectly competitive firm corresponds on the vertical axis to :
   a. the market price.
   b. the profit-maximizing price.
   c. the cost-minimizing price.
   d. the profit-minimizing price.

7. The demand for the product sold by a perfectly competitive industry is:
   a. perfectly elastic.
   b. perfectly inelastic.
   c. upward sloping.
   d. downward sloping.

8. Which of the following demand curves is not downward sloping?
   a. demand facing the perfectly competitive firm
   b. demand for the product of a perfectly competitive industry
   c. demand by an individual consumer for the product produced by a perfectly competitive firm

9. The profit-maximizing quantity of output by a perfectly competitive firm corresponds to the point where _____ equals
   _____ .
   a. MC; ATC
   b. market price; ATC
   c. market price; MC
   d. MC; AVC

10. If market price exceeds ATC at the profit-maximizing level of output, _____ will be experienced.
    a. normal profits
    b. losses
    c. pure profits

11. If market price is less than ATC at the profit-maximizing level of output ,_____ will be experienced.
    a. normal profits
    b. losses
    c. pure profits

12. A perfectly competitive firm will earn normal profits if price equals:
    a. MC.
    b. AVC.
    c. MC = ATC.
    d. MC = ATC = AVC.

13. A perfectly competitive firm may incur losses because:
    a. it is badly managed.
    b. its owner-operator may have a high opportunity cost.
    c. market price is low.
    d. all of the above.

14. In the short run, output:
    a. cannot be changed.
    b. can be changed by changing variable inputs.
    c. can be changed by changing fixed inputs.
    d. can be changed by changing all inputs.

15. In the long run,_____ inputs are variable.
    a. no
    b. the firm's own
    c. purchased
    d. all

16. In the long run, the existence of pure profits leads to_____ , _____ and _____.
    a. entry of firms; decreased supply; higher prices
    b. entry of firms; increased supply; lower prices
    c. exit of firms; decreased supply; higher prices
    d. exit of firms; increased supply; lower prices

17. In reference to question 16, the adjustment squeezed out:
    a. losses.
    b. pure profits.
    c. normal profits.

18. In a perfectly competitive industry, market price will settle in at the point where _____ and _____ are earned.
    a. MC = ATC; pure profits
    b. MC = ATC; normal profits
    c. MC = AVC; pure profits
    d. MC = AVC; normal profits

19. Firms which have a special cost advantage over other firms in the production of a product such that their short-run ATC is less than product price, will:
    a. continue to earn pure profits for all time to come.
    b. continue to incur losses for all time to come.
    c. have the pure profits capitalized into the value of their assets, causing ATC to increase.
    d. have their pure profits capitalized into the value of their assets, causing ATC to decrease.

20. Which of the following conditions is not required to reach maximum economic efficiency?
    a. absence of pure profits
    b. maximum technical efficiency
    c. cost minimization
    d. price equals MC

21. Perfect competition maximizes the value of output to society because each firm attempts to maximize profits by producing that level of output corresponding to the point where product price equals:
    a. MC.
    b. ATC.
    c. AVC.
    d. AFC.

Chapter 16

Pure Monopoly

Key Concepts

The three types of firms discussed in this and the following two chapters, pure monopoly, monopolistic competition, and oligopoly, are commonly grouped in the broad category called imperfect competition. This chapter defines an imperfectly competitive firm, and then focuses on pure monopoly. A major consideration is the profit-maximizing price that a monopoly would charge if it were free to do so.

IMPERFECT COMPETITION DEFINED

An imperfectly competitive firm is one that can exercise some control over the price it receives for its product. There are two main reasons a firm might have some control over the price it charges: (1) each firm produces a sizable share of the market and (2) each firm sells a product that is distinguishable from competitors' products. These two reasons are the opposite for a perfectly competitive firm. It is sufficient for a firm to fulfill either of these requirements to be imperfectly competitive. Some firms exhibit both characteristics.

In examining why these two characteristics allow a firm to have some control over the price of its product, consider a firm that sells a large share of the total market, such as U.S. Steel. If U.S. Steel reduced its annual output by 10-20 percent, we would observe a noticeable decline in total steel output in the United States and an increase in the price of steel, providing the market demand for steel is downward sloping. As a result of its production cutback, U.S. Steel could raise the price of its product by a small amount. Similarly, a comparable increase in output by U.S. Steel would add a noticeable amount to total steel output and result in at least a small decline in the market price of steel. In this case, U.S. Steel would have to accept a lower price for its product. The main point is that such a firm can manipulate the price it receives for its product by changing its level of output.

A firm that sells a product that differs somewhat from its competitors' products can also exercise some control over the price of its product. In the above example, we considered a firm that sells a large share of the market with a product that is the same as its competitors' to keep the effect of product differentiation separate from share of the market. Now we will consider a firm that sells a small share of the market but whose product is slightly different from its competitors'—say, the local Amoco station in your neighborhood. It might appear that such a firm's main product, gasoline, is the same as that sold by other Amoco stations. However, a retail firm's specific location and the kind of service it renders can result in some difference in its product. If some of the firm's customers prefer its product to the product of competing stations, the station in question probably could raise its price a few cents a gallon over its competitors without having its gasoline sales go to zero. The people who found the station a convenient place to stop or for some reason liked the service probably would continue to patronize it, at least for a time. On the other hand, if the station low-

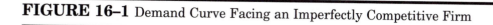

FIGURE 16-1 Demand Curve Facing an Imperfectly Competitive Firm

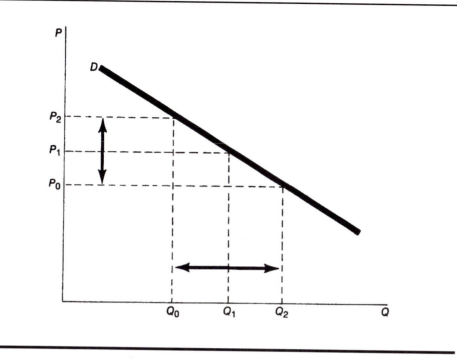

ered its price a few cents below its competitors, it would attract additional customers. A firm that sells a product that is somewhat different from its competitors' products has some leeway in the price it charges.

DEMAND FACING AN IMPERFECTLY COMPETITIVE FIRM

The imperfectly competitive firm's ability to alter the price of its product is translatable to the demand curve facing such a firm. Chapter 15 showed that the perfectly competitive firm faces a perfectly horizontal (perfectly elastic) demand curve, reflecting the fact that it has no control over the price it receives. For an imperfectly competitive firm, its ability to raise the price and sell a smaller quantity, or lower the price and sell a larger quantity, means that the firm faces a downward-sloping demand curve. This is illustrated in Figure 16-1.

If the firm raises its price, say from P_1 to P_2, it is forced to reduce its sales from Q_1 to Q_0. Or, if the firm wishes to increase sales, say from Q_1 to Q_2, it must lower the price from P_1 to P_0. Thus, the demand curve of all imperfectly competitive firms is downward sloping. Remember, however, that even though this downward-sloping demand curve facing the individual firm resembles the market-demand curve for the product, it is not the same as market demand. (Pure monopoly, to be discussed shortly, is an exception.) As long as there is more than one firm selling in a market, the demand curve facing each firm is considerably more elastic than the market demand curve. For a pure monopoly, the demand curve facing the firm is the same as the market demand curve because there is just one firm.

MONOPOLY DEFINED

Pure monopoly exists when a single firm supplies a product. Private, unregulated monopoly is not allowed in the United States. The firms that come closest to a pure monopoly are the public utilities such as natural gas and electric companies. These firms have exclusive rights to operate in an area to capture scale economies and to avoid a duplication of facilities. The motivation for having such firms is to lower the product's cost for consumers from what it would be in an open, competitive market. In electric power, the main source of increased costs is the duplication of transmission lines. The same is true for natural gas supply.

The definition of monopoly depends on how one defines the industry. For example, an electric power company has a monopoly in selling electricity but not in selling all power. Fuel oil and gas are alternatives, although imperfect for lighting. Similarly, the post office has a monopoly in delivering first-class mail but not all mail or communication. Thus, to have a monopoly, one must narrowly define the industry.

A monopoly is not a natural economic phenomenon. To preserve a monopoly, the government must keep out competition by issuing licenses to existing firms. If there are profits to be made, other firms would be attracted and the monopoly would disappear.

What about small towns or rural areas where a single grocery store, service station, or barber shop serves the entire community? Aren't these firms monopolies in their communities? No. If a single firm in a small community started to charge unusually high prices, customers, especially persons living in the fringe area next to another supplier, could easily switch. Also, the threat of a competitor moving in if a firm becomes too greedy can temper a desire to monopolize. Thus, there is little concern over the apparent lack of competition for such firms.

Firms that hold licenses to operate free of competition in an area are closer to the pure definition of monopoly. For this reason, such firms are regulated by government agencies. Standards of performance and prices are established, and the firm's behavior is monitored. However, in recent years, an increasing amount of criticism has been directed at government-sanctioned monopolies, which has led to the deregulation of several industries such as airlines, trucking, telephones, and certain financial services. The evidence suggests that regulation actually increased the price paid by consumers. For example, during regulation, the airfare from Los Angeles to San Francisco, which was an intrastate route and not regulated, was about half the regulated fare from

Chicago to Minneapolis-St.Paul, approximately the same distance. There is nothing like a little competition, even one or two competitors, to keep a firm efficient and innovative.

MARGINAL REVENUE AND PRICE

To determine the profit-maximizing price for a monopoly, it is necessary to reintroduce the concept of marginal revenue (MR). Recall that marginal revenue is the additional revenue obtained by selling one more unit of output. It is computed as:

$$MR = \frac{\Delta TR}{\Delta Q}$$

where ΔTR is change in total revenue and ΔQ is change in quantity of output sold.

For a firm that faces a perfectly elastic demand, such as perfect competition, marginal revenue is equal to product price. Selling one more unit of a product, say for $5, adds $5 to the firm's sales or revenue. For a firm that faces a downward-sloping demand curve, such as monopoly, marginal revenue will be less than the price received for the product. The reason is that the firm must sell all of its output at the same price. If the firm wishes to sell more, it must lower the price. This lower price must apply to all units sold. The firm cannot sell the additional output to its newest customers at a lower price than it charges old customers. Therefore, the slight reduction in price of all previous units sold causes the added revenue obtained from the additional units sold to be less than the price received for them.

For example, suppose an electric company wishes to increase sales. To do so, it must lower its price:

Initial situation:	price:	$10
	quantity:	100
New situation:	price:	$9
	quantity:	150

$$\text{Marginal revenue} = \frac{\Delta TR}{\Delta Q} = \frac{1,350 - 1,000}{150 - 100} = \frac{350}{50} = \$7$$

Although the price of the marginal unit is $9, MR is $7. The $1 reduction in price on the previous 100 units sold causes the MR to be $2 less than the new lower selling price of the product. Because MR is less than price at any given quantity, when the demand curve facing the firm slopes down, the line graphing MR lies below the demand curve, as in Figure 16–2.

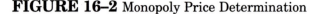

FIGURE 16–2 Monopoly Price Determination

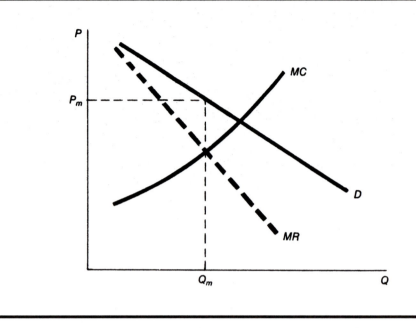

MONOPOLY PRICE DETERMINATION

The profit-maximizing rule stated in Chapter 10, MR = MC, is true for all firms—including monopolies. To maximize profits, the monopoly firm should produce the quantity corresponding to the point where MR = MC. This is denoted as Q_m in Figure 16–2. The price that the firm charges is determined by the demand curve. At Q_m, the firm's customers are willing to pay P_m. Thus, the firm will set price at P_m. Any other price and quantity will reduce profits. At a smaller quantity and higher price, MR is greater than MC. This means that the firm can take in more than it lays out if it lowers price slightly and increases output. Conversely, if output is greater than Q_m, MC is greater than MR. Now the firm can do better by reducing its quantity. Quantity Q_m is the best place to be because at any other quantity profits will increase (or losses decrease) by moving toward Q_m.

MONOPOLY PROFIT OR LOSS

To determine if a monopoly is earning a profit or incurring a loss, the ATC curve must be superimposed on the diagram. The three possible cases where the firm is earning a pure profit, normal profit, and a loss are illustrated in Figure 16–3 diagrams A, B, and C, respectively.

FIGURE 16–3 Monopoly Profit and Loss

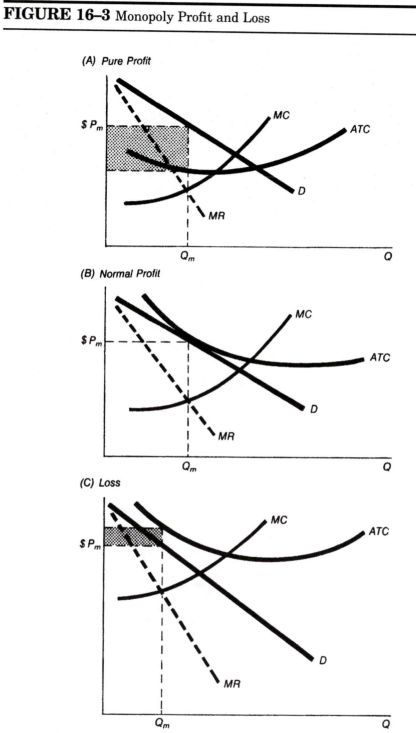

(A) Pure Profit

(B) Normal Profit

(C) Loss

A pure profit will be earned if the profit-maximizing price exceeds ATC at the profit-maximizing quantity. The shaded rectangle in Figure 16–3A represents the pure profits earned by the firm during a specified time period.

Figure 16–3B illustrates the case where the monopoly is making a normal profit. In this case output price equals ATC. Here the firm's resources are earning as much as they could earn in their next best alternative uses.

A pure monopoly could also incur a loss. This would occur if the ATC curve lay above the firm's demand curve as illustrated by Figure 16–3C. The loss is shown by the shaded rectangle. This situation could happen if demand for the firm's product is insufficient to cover its costs, or if its costs become too high. Should this prevail for long the firm would eventually go out of business.

SOCIAL COST OF MONOPOLY

Most people dislike monopoly, except persons who enjoy the privilege. The dislike stems from the knowledge that the price charged by a monopoly will be higher than what occurs in a more competitive market.

In addition, it can be shown that monopoly is undesirable because it causes a misallocation of resources in the economy. This results in a reduction in the value of output for society. The economic rationale for this reduction is easier to understand with a diagram such as Figure 16–4. Notice that the profit-maximizing price exceeds marginal cost. Again, product price is an indication of how much consumers value an extra unit. Marginal cost reflects the value of alter-

FIGURE 16–4 Social Cost of Monopoly

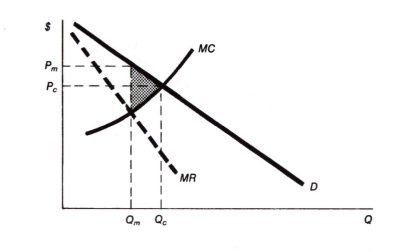

native products given up to produce an extra unit (opportunity cost). Therefore, at the profit-maximizing price, the value of the marginal unit produced by a monopoly exceeds the opportunity cost of this unit. At first glance, this may appear desirable. But society could do better if the monopoly produced more and other industries produced less. Each additional unit of output past Q_m yields a net gain to society of the difference between the demand curve (price) and the MC curve. By moving to Q_c from Q_m society gains the value of the shaded triangle in Figure 16–4. At Q_c price is P_c. If the monopoly was, instead, a perfectly competitive industry and had the same costs as the industry, it would produce Q_c and have price P_c. Thus, the shaded triangle represents the social cost of monopoly as opposed to perfect competition.

A regulatory agency that wished to duplicate the perfectly competitive outcome would set price at P_c. At this price, the firm's customers would purchase Q_c output. If the firm makes normal profits, it should be willing to produce Q_c.

Any situation where price is greater than marginal cost causes a misallocation of resources, resulting in a smaller total value of output for society, given the resources available. Therefore, the same criticism can be levied against any firm that faces a downward-sloping demand curve (i.e., imperfectly competitive). But economists have found that the loss of output in the U.S. economy because of a misallocation of resources from monopoly power of firms is small.[1] Also, politicians and the public are not very concerned about a misallocation of resources, probably because they cannot envision the total value of output without the misallocation.

MONOPOLY POWER

It is common to refer to the degree of monopoly power held by firms, particularly large corporations, even though private monopoly is illegal in the United States. Monopoly power, however, is a vague term. The most precise measure of monopoly power is the ratio of the product price to the marginal cost of producing the last unit of the product. Recall from Chapter 15 that in a perfectly competitive industry, each firm produces the quantity corresponding to the point where P = MC. In other words, the P/MC ratio for firms with no monopoly power (perfectly competitive) is equal to one.

With imperfect competition, each firm maximizes profits by producing the quantity that corresponds to the point where MR = MC. Because an imperfectly competitive firm faces a downward-sloping demand curve, its profit-maximizing price is greater than MC as shown in Figures 16–3 and 16–4. Thus, the P/MC ratio for all imperfectly competitive firms is greater than one. This ratio becomes larger,the steeper (less elastic) the demand curve facing the individual firm. Given the elasticity of the market demand for the product, the greater the

---

1 See Arnold C. Harberger, "Monopoly and Resource Allocation," *American Economic Review,* May 1954, pp. 7787.

share of the market enjoyed by each firm (the closer it comes to a pure monopoly), the steeper the demand curve facing the firm and the higher the P/MC ratio. Thus, the size of the P/MC ratio is a precise measure of monopoly power.

The main difficulty in using the P/MC ratio to measure monopoly power is the lack of information on the marginal cost of firms. The next best monopoly power measure for the largest firms in a market or industry is market share. Given the market elasticity of demand for the product, the larger the share of the market, the greater the monopoly power of large firms.

The increase in foreign competition and imports have decreased the market share and monopoly power of large U.S. firms. Over the years the demand faced by these firms has become more elastic. Foreign competition also has had the effect of improving the quality of U.S. manufactured products. This is particularly noticeable in the automobile and electronics industries.

MONOPOLY POWER AND INFLATION

During times of increased inflation, people tend to blame large firms for rising prices. Since businesses are raising prices, it is understandable why people come to that conclusion. Although a full explanation for inflation is best left to a macro economics course, each imperfectly competitive firm, regardless of its monopoly power, has only one profit-maximizing price for a given set of demanded and cost curves. This price is read off the demand curve at the quantity corresponding to the intersection of MC and MR. If firms decided to raise prices without a change in their demand and cost curves, they would experience reduced profits, which would be irrational. Thus, we can be certain that the underlying cause of inflation is not due to a sudden increase in greed by businesses, for such behavior leads to lower profits. Indeed, there is no reason to believe that the desire for profits is any greater during inflation than during periods of stable prices.

However, businesses do raise prices during periods of inflation. This behavior is the result of the desire to maximize profits or minimize losses (the latter also occurs during inflation). Price increases result from an increase in the demand facing the firm and/or an increase in the cost of production. The demand facing the firm increases because of consumers' higher money incomes, although not necessarily higher real incomes. Recall that a change in money incomes is a demand shifter. In addition, higher prices paid for labor, capital, and raw materials increase the firm's marginal and average cost curves—shifting them up and to the left. Both shifts result in a higher profit-maximizing price.

The shifts in the demand and cost curves that occur during inflation are out of the individual firm's control. If the firm had control over them, it would want to decrease costs to put more distance between price and ATC. The firm wants to experience an increase in demand for its product, but this desire is not limited to inflationary times. At any rate, the desired shifts in costs and demand, if the firm could control them, would not necessarily lead to an increase in product price. Thus, we should look for a reason other than the monopoly power of businesses for the underlying cause of inflation.

QUESTIONS

1. a. How does an imperfectly competitive firm differ from one that is perfectly competitive?

   b. If an imperfectly competitive firm wishes to increase quantity sold, what must it do to price? What if it wishes to increase price?

2. What is monopoly and how does its definition depend on how the industry is defined?

3. At expressway service stops, a single gasoline company is generally given exclusive right to do business at one location. Is this service station a monopoly? Explain.

4. Small towns in rural areas may have just one service station, one cafe, and one grocery store. Would each of these businesses be a monopoly? Explain.

5. a. What is marginal revenue (MR) and why is MR less than price for a firm facing a downward-sloping demand curve?

   b Draw a demand curve facing an imperfectly competitive firm and its corresponding marginal revenue curve. Do the same for a perfectly competitive firm.

6. a. Compare the profit-maximizing price and quantity for a monopoly with the values in a perfectly competitive industry. Assume the same marginal cost and demand for both.

   b. In attempting to maximize profits, do owners of a monopoly act differently than owners of perfectly competitive firms? Explain.

   c. The higher the price charged by a monopoly the higher its total profits. True or false? Explain.

7. Why is monopoly considered socially undesirable?

8. The United States and other market economies will always suffer from inflation because of the desire of large corporations having monopoly power to maximize profits. True or false? Explain.

SELF-TEST

1. An imperfectly competitive firm is one that exercises _____ control over the price of its product.
   a. no
   b. some
   c. complete

2. An imperfectly competitive firm has some control over the price it receives for its product because it sells a _____ share of the market, and/or it sells a(n) _____ product.
   a. large; undifferentiated
   b. small; differentiated
   c. large; differentiated
   d. small; undifferentiated

3. A firm sells a product that is slightly different from the products of competing firms can raise its price without:
   a. having its market share go to zero.
   b. having the quantity it sells decline.
   c. precipitating a price war.
   d. reducing its profits.

4. A firm sells a large share of the market can raise its price because:
   a. customers have to buy its product or go without.
   b. the market does not notice the action of a single firm.
   c. the total market supply declines.
   d. each buyer purchases a small share of the firm's sales.

5. The distinguishing characteristic of all imperfectly competitive firms is that they face a _____ demand curve.
   a. perfectly elastic
   b. perfectly inelastic
   c. upward-sloping
   d. downward-sloping

6. If an imperfectly competitive firm wishes to raise the price of its product, it must:
   a. increase its quantity sold.
   b. decrease its quantity sold.
   c. suffer a reduction in profits .
   d. obtain permission from the Price Control Commission.

7. If an imperfectly competitive firm wishes to increase its sales, it must:
   a. decrease its price.
   b. increase its price .
   c. suffer a reduction in profits.
   d. obtain permission from the Production Control Administration, an agency of the U.S. government.

8. Pure monopoly exists where there is (are) _____ firms(s) in the market.
   a. zero
   b. one
   c. two
   d. many

9. In the United States, pure monopoly is:
   a. the most common type of firm.
   b. is illegal but flourishes.
   c. is illegal and therefore does not exist in its pure form.
   d. is legal but does not exist because of low profits.

10. In order for a monopoly to exist, entry into the market must be _____ . The most effective method of accomplishing this is:
    a. open; licensing.
    b. blocked; licensing.
    c. open; collusion.
    d. blocked; collusion.

11. In the United States, firms that come closest to a pure monopoly are:
    a. the multinational corporations.
    b. small-town grocery stores.
    c. the oil companies.
    d. public utilities.

12. A single firm selling groceries and gasoline in a small town _____ be considered a monopoly because:
    a. can; there's only one firm in the market.
    b. can; entry of new firms is blocked.
    c. cannot; the firm's customers have alternatives and entry of new firms is not blocked.
    d. cannot; the government regulates prices it charges and the quality of its services.

13. Government regulation of firms can result in _____ prices than would exist in an unregulated market because of the absence of _____ .
    a. higher; collusion
    b. higher; competition
    c. lower; collusion
    d. lower; competition

14. Marginal revenue is calculated by dividing _____ by _____ .
    a. total revenue; quantity sold
    b. quantity sold; total revenue
    c. change in total revenue; change in quantity sold
    d. change in quantity sold; change in total revenue

15. Compute marginal revenue from the following figures.

	Price	Quantity
Initial situation	$1.00	1,000
New situation	.75	1,600

    a. $1.00
    b. $ .75
    c. $ .50
    d. $ .33

16. Marginal revenue for an imperfectly competitive firm is _____ than price. For a perfectly competitive firm, it is _____ price.
    a. less than; equal to
    b. equal to; less than

c. less than; greater than

d. greater than; less than

17. If an imperfectly competitive firm lowers its price to sell a larger quantity, MR will be _____ than the new lower price because:

    a. greater than; the firm must sell all previous units at the new lower price as well as the extra units.

    b. less than; the firm can sell all previous units at the original higher price and the extra units at the new lower price.

    c. greater than; the firm can sell all previous units at the original price and the extra units at the lower price.

    d. less than; the firm must sell all previous units at the new lower price as well as the extra units.

18. A pure unregulated monopoly will maximize profits by producing a quantity corresponding to the point where:

    a. ATC = demand.

    b. MC = demand.

    c. MC = ATC.

    d. MR = MC.

19. The profit-maximizing price charged by a pure unregulated monopoly corresponds to the point where:

    a. MC = demand.

    b. ATC = demand.

    c. the profit-maximizing quantity equals demand.

    d. the profit-maximizing quantity equals supply.

20. A monopoly will earn a pure profit if price is_____, and will incur a loss if price is _____

    a. less than MC; greater than MC

    b. greater than MC; less than MC

    c. less than ATC; greater than ATC

    d. greater than ATC; less than ATC

21. The existence of monopoly causes a(n) _____ allocation of resources to these industries because at the profit-maximizing quantity _____ is greater than _____.

    a. over; MC; price

    b. under; MC; price

    c. over; price; MC

    d. under; price; MC

22. The socially optimum price for a monopoly corresponds to the point where:

    a. MC = demand.

    b. ATC = demand.

    c. the profit-maximizing quantity equals demand.

    d. the profit-maximizing quantity equals supply.

23. The most precise measure of monopoly power is the P/MC ratio. The value of this ratio is _____ for perfect competition and _____ as the market moves toward pure monopoly.

    a. one; increases

    b. one; decreases

    c. zero; increases

    d. zero; decreases

24. During times of inflation, the profit-maximizing price of large, imperfectly competitive firms increases because costs _____ and demand _____ .

    a. increase; decreases

    b. decrease; increases

    c. increase; increases

    d. decrease; decreases

Chapter 17

Monopolistic Competition

Key Concepts

Monopolistic competition defined

Price determination

Pure profits or losses

Long run adjustment

Advertising

Marginal cost and supply

Chapters 17 and 18 consider the majority of nonagricultural firms in a market economy. In numbers of firms, most are in the monopolistic competition group, the topic of this chapter. After establishing the two conditions common to all monopolistically competitive firms, their adjustment to pure profits or losses is considered. The discussion then turns to advertising, and the chapter ends with an explanation of why the marginal cost curve of an imperfectly competitive firm is not strictly a supply curve, which it is for perfect competition.

MONOPOLISTIC COMPETITION DEFINED

Monopolistic competition bears some similarity to both monopoly and perfect competition, but it is more closely related to the latter. The two distinguishing characteristics of monopolistic competition are: (1) there are many firms, each selling a small proportion of the market, and (2) each firm sells a product that is slightly different from competitors' products.

The characteristic of monopolistic competition that is similar to perfect competition is that there are many firms, each selling a small proportion of the market. However, the fact that each firm sells a product slightly different from that of its competitors results in a downward-sloping demand curve facing each firm. Because its product or service is slightly different from competitors', the firm has some control over the price it charges.

The multitude of firms engaged in retail trade are the best examples of monopolistic competition; service stations, barber shops, department stores, grocery stores, florists, and repair shops are examples. In addition, all of the small and medium-sized manufacturing firms fall into this category. In numbers of nonagricultural firms, the majority are monopolistically competitive.

It may appear strange to say that two retail outlets that sell the same brand of product, such as two Amoco service stations, sell a slightly different product. In retail trade the physical appearance and service provided by the store are important. Stores that offer a clean, pleasing environment in which to shop and are staffed by courteous and knowledgeable personnel in a sense sell more desirable merchandise than do less pleasing establishments. Location also is important. Other things equal, goods and services more accessible also are more desirable. This location factor can be translated into a price difference. The added transport cost of shopping at out-of-the-way or far-off locations makes this merchandise more expensive relative to that sold in easily accessible or close-by locations. Finally, the time required to shop is an important consideration for busy people. This helps explain the popularity of clusters of stores in shopping centers and of fast-food restaurants which save time for shoppers and diners.

Another factor that distinguishes two seemingly identical products is service. Some people prefer to purchase their clothing in intimate little shops where the clerk is friendly, knowledgeable, and readily available for assistance. Others buy their clothes in large department stores with little assistance and impersonal checkout counters. Even though the physical characteristics of the items sold in the two stores can be identical, the customer who wants to consume more service along with the item will buy from the small, intimate shop, although the latter generally sells higher quality merchandise to attract higher income shoppers.

However, providing services involves a cost, so we should expect to pay a higher price where more service is provided. For example, gasoline is cheaper at self-service pumps because you buy less service than at full-service pumps. As individual consumers, we must decide whether the marginal utility per dollar for these services is at least equal to the marginal utility per dollar of other things we buy.

PRICE DETERMINATION

The fact that the goods or services sold by monopolistically competitive firms differ in some respect, either physically or because of location or services, allows a particular firm some flexibility in the price it charges. This does not mean that a service station could charge $1.50 per gallon for gasoline when other stations in the neighborhood are charging $1.25 to $1.30 per gallon without losing most of its sales. If the station manager feels that the station can clear more net profit by a narrow-margin, high-volume operation, the manager will probably charge a bit less than the competition. If the manager thinks the station can make more with a wider-margin, lower-volume business, the price will be higher than average.

In monopolistic competition, the price range within which the firm can operate is determined largely by the average price of its closest competitors. The individual firm may diverge slightly from the average market price, depending on the kind of business it wishes to operate. It is a mistake, however, to believe that just because a firm selling under conditions of monopolistic competition places a price tag on its product that it can charge any price it pleases. Most firms in this kind of market are restricted to a narrow range of price. They have a bit more freedom, however, than the perfectly competitive firm, which has no leeway in the price it charges.

With perfect competition, we were more precise in determining the price and output for an individual firm. Recall that a perfectly competitive firm maximizes profits if it produces a quantity that corresponds to the point at which marginal cost is equal to market price. We illustrated this with a diagram. We can utilize a similar technique for monopolistic competition, only in this case, we must remember that the firm faces a slightly downward-sloping demand curve. Therefore, the marginal revenue of an additional unit sold is somewhat less than the price of this unit because the new lower price must apply to all units sold. There is no difference in the way costs are derived between perfect competition and monopolistic competition, so we can continue to apply the average and marginal cost concepts utilized in Chapters 15 and 16.

Like a monopoly, a monopolistically competitive firm maximizes profits if it sells a quantity that corresponds to the point at which marginal cost is equal to marginal revenue. Recall that marginal cost (MC) is the cost of producing or selling an additional unit of output, and marginal revenue (MR) is the additional revenue obtained from this extra or marginal unit sold. For example, if it costs a service station 90 cents to sell an extra gallon of gasoline, and the marginal revenue from this extra gallon is 95 cents, the station can increase its profits (or decrease losses) by 5 cents if it sells this extra gallon.

Moreover, it benefits the firm to increase output as long as MR is greater than MC. Why this is so is illustrated in Figure 17–1. Suppose we cut in at a quantity of output just short of the point where MC equals MR, Q_0 If we increase output by one additional unit past Q_0 our total costs increase by the distance from the horizontal axis up to the MC curve. However, our total revenue increase is shown by the distance between the horizontal axis and MR. The difference between these two distances represents the additional profit that the firm captures by producing this extra unit.

If we continue to increase output, the distance between MC and MR continues to grow smaller, but as long as there is any distance between them, total profits can be increased by increasing output. Total profits are maximized (or losses minimized) at the quantity where MR equals MC, Q_1 in Figure 17–1. To stop producing short of this point, say at Q_0 means that the firm needlessly forgoes profits (or incurs unnecessary losses) equal in value to the area of the shaded triangle.

Also, we can use Figure 17–1 to illustrate the profit-maximizing price that a monopolistically competitive firm charges. If the firm chooses to maximize profits and produce or sell Q_1, the demand curve facing this firm indicates that the price its customers are willing to pay is equal to P_1. The firm would not want to charge a lower price because in so doing it would throw away profits. On the other hand, it could not charge a higher price because its customers will pay only price P_1 for quantity Q_1.

PURE PROFITS OR LOSSES

In Figure 17–1, there is no indication however, that the firm is making a pure profit or incurring a loss. All we can tell is that P_1 and Q_1 are the optimum price and quantity, respectively, meaning that either the firm's losses are minimized or its profits are maximized. To determine the profit or loss, we must know the average total cost (ATC). If ATC is below the price at the optimum quantity, the firm reaps a pure profit; if ATC is above the price, the firm incurs a loss.

Figure 17–2A illustrates a situation where the firm makes a pure profit, meaning that the resources used by the firm are earning more than they could make in some alternative activity or occupation. The total dollar value of the

FIGURE 17-1 Profit-Maximizing Price and Quantity for a Monopolistically Competitive Firm

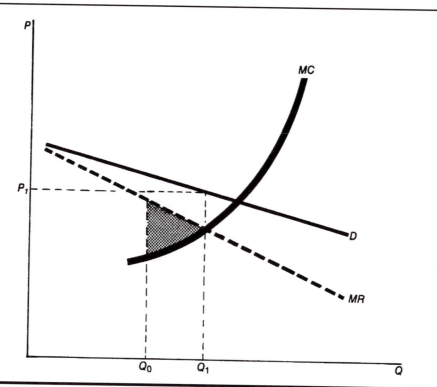

pure profit is illustrated by the shaded area. A firm can find itself in this envi-
able position for two reasons: (1) The firm is managed so well that its costs are
low, or (2) the firm sells a desirable product so that the demand curve it faces is
high relative to competitors' demand curves.

Figure 17–2B depicts a firm incurring a loss. In this situation, the resources
used by the firm earn less than they could in alternative employment. The total
dollar value of the loss is illustrated by the shaded area. A firm can be in this
circumstance if its costs are high because of either high-paying alternative
employment for its resources or poor management. Or, the firm can incur losses if the product it sells is not as desirable to consumers as the products sold by
its competitors, so that the demand it faces for its goods is relatively low.

To summarize this procedure, we determine the profit-maximizing quantity
for a monopolistically competitive firm by the intersection of the MR and MC
curves. The profit-maximizing price is then determined by extending the vertical line drawn through the intersection of MR and MC up to the demand curve.
The point where this vertical line touches the demand curve corresponds to the
profit-maximizing price on the vertical axis. The price line is not drawn over

FIGURE 17–2 Profit and Loss Situations for a Monopolistically
Competitive Firm

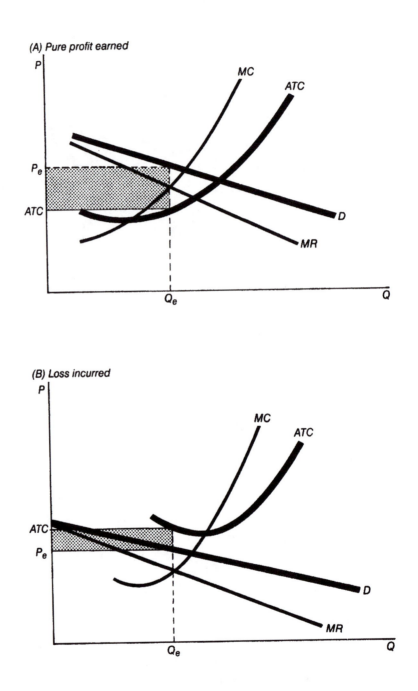

from the intersection of MR and MC because the price is determined by the demand curve.

If price as determined by the demand curve is greater than the ATC at the profit-maximizing quantity, then the firm is making a pure profit. The average profit per unit is given by the distance between price and ATC at the profit-maximizing quantity. If we multiply this average profit per unit by the total units sold (the profit-maximizing quantity), we obtain the total pure profits. This is illustrated by the shaded rectangle in Figure 17–2A. Similarly, if price is less than ATC at the profit-maximizing quantity, losses will occur. The average loss per unit is equal to the distance between price and ATC, and the total loss is equal to the rectangle, as illustrated in Figure 17–2B.

To summarize, we use MR and MC to determine the quantity to produce and the demand to give us the profit-maximizing price at that quantity. The profit (or loss) is determined by the difference between price and ATC. This procedure applies to any firm that faces a downward-sloping demand curve, that is, any imperfectly competitive firm, including one that is monopolistically competitive.

LONG-RUN ADJUSTMENT

The existence of either pure profits or losses for a substantial number of firms in a monopolistically competitive market will cause adjustments in the industry. For example, if a substantial share of firms reap pure profits, this is a signal for existing firms to enlarge their enterprises or for new firms to enter. In either case, the demand curve facing each firm begins to decrease, shifting downward to the left. A decrease in demand has two meanings: (1) the firm's consumers will now buy a smaller amount at a given price, or (2) its consumers will buy a given amount only if the price is lower.

This phenomenon is easier to understand if you visualize yourself as the owner of a restaurant that is making substantial pure profits. Seeing a good opportunity, another firm builds a restaurant across the street and begins to take some of your customers, perhaps by selling at a slightly lower price. As some customers leave, the demand curve facing your firm begins to decrease. You lower your price to compete with the new firm and adjust to the new lower demand and marginal revenue curves. As the demand curve facing your firm decreases (shifts left), the profit-maximizing price and quantity declines. As a result, your pure profits decline and you approach a zero pure-profit position, as illustrated in Figure17–3A.

There is no reason why every monopolistically competitive firm has to end up at a zero pure-profit or tangency position. Some firms may continue to reap pure profits because they own or control certain specialized inputs that other firms cannot duplicate. In retail trade, each firm's location is unique, and some are more accessible to customers than others. The choice of a superior location may be due to the skill of the original owner or manager, to luck, or to circumstances

FIGURE 17–3 Long-Run Adjustment by Individual Firms to Pure Profits in Monopolistic Competition

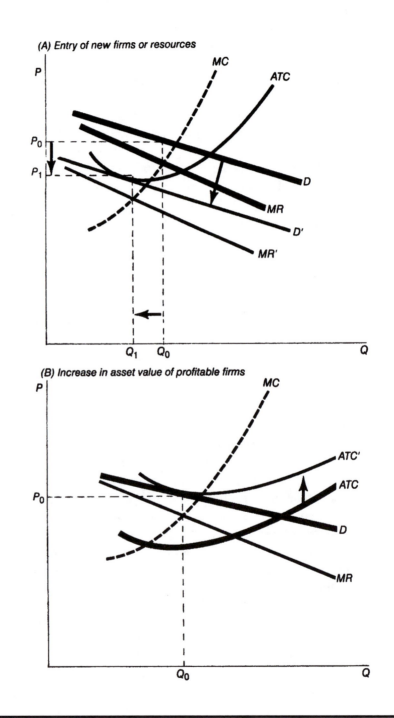

beyond the firm's control, such as the construction of a housing development nearby. In other cases, a firm may have built up goodwill among its customers over the years,which cannot be duplicated by new entrants into the market. Also the owners of some firms may possess superior entrepreneurial ability that cannot be duplicated by competing firms.

Will the owners of such firms continue to reap pure profits? Yes and no. The fact that other firms cannot duplicate the firm's superior inputs means that the product price probably will not be bid down any further and that the firm can retain the profits. On the other hand, the market value of the profitable firm's assets will increase to reflect its superior profit position. We would expect potential buyers to pay more for the assets of a highly profitable firm than for the assets of a firm that earns normal profits or incurs losses. Economists would say that the pure profits are capitalized into the firm's value. If the owner correctly calculates implicit costs, mainly forgone interest on the increased equity value in the firm, the average total cost curve will increase as illustrated by ATC^1 in Figure17–3B. The pure profits disappear into the increased capitalized value of the firm. However, the current owner does not lose these profits because they have contributed to an increase in the value of the person's assets.

Since owners have finite life spans, profitable firms eventually change hands. If the original owner or seller is a shrewd bargainer, it is possible to obtain a price that will give the new owner a normal profit or a normal return on the investment. The phenomenon is the same for corporations, whose owners (stockholders) may number in the thousands, while the firm's equity value is reflected in the value of its stock certificates.

In any industry, circumstances continually change. Thus, it is unlikely that every firm is at a zero-profit, long-run equilibrium. It is more realistic to visualize a situation where there is continual movement toward equilibrium but few instances where it is ever reached. We would expect to observe at any time a wide variety of profit positions by firms; some might enjoy substantial pure profits; others earn what is earned in other industries, and others incur losses.

We could go through the same analysis for a case in which a substantial proportion of the firms in a monopolistically competitive market suffer losses. The opposite would occur, compared with the pure-profit situation. Firms would leave the industry-shifting the demand curve that faces the remaining firms to the right.

Persistent losses also can change the asset value of a firm. As an example, consider a service station or restaurant built on a busy two-lane highway that is replaced by a new expressway. The firm will suffer a major decline in sales because of losing most of the highway traffic, and may go out of business. If the owner sells the structure, it will bring considerably less than it would have in its original use. The new owners may turn the service station into a bicycle repair shop, or the restaurant may be converted to a day-care center. If the new owners are shrewd bargainers, they will not pay any more for the structure than what assures them a normal profit in the new business.

Firms such as a service station, clothing store, or restaurant that realize losses often go out of business. After a few months of remaining vacant, they may open under new management in the same kind of business. If the previous owner could not make a normal profit, how can the new owners expect to do any better? They may have ideas on how to improve things, but it is likely that they have purchased the structure at a price that enables them to expect a normal profit. Or, if the new owner is a shrewd bargainer, the person may buy the property at a price low enough to yield pure profits, at least for a time.

A change in costs because of a revaluation of assets, either up or down, does not affect the price of the product sold or produced. Here, costs are price-determined. In a case where costs are changed because of changes in production technology or input prices, the market price will change because of a change in supply. In the latter case, costs are price-determining.

ADVERTISING

Advertising is common to all imperfectly competitive firms, particularly with monopolistic competition and oligopoly, although perfectly competitive firms and public utilities also engage in this practice. It includes a wide range of activities. The homemade for-sale sign on an automobile, the want ads in the newspaper, roadside signs, radio and TV commercials, and magazine layouts are examples of advertising. Some advertising is done by buyers, such as help-wanted ads, although the majority is done by sellers.

Advertising is divided into two major types: informational and persuasive. Informational advertising informs prospective customers about what is for sale, its characteristics, and its price. An example of informational advertising is the grocery store newspaper advertisement telling the prices of items that can be bought at a particular store. Persuasive advertising, on the other hand, attempts to persuade people to buy one product rather than another. Most of the advertising on television and radio is persuasive, although such advertising also contains some information by making us aware of certain product characteristics.

All advertising attempts to accomplish one objective: increase the firm's profits. The main way to increase profits is to increase the demand for the firm's product. Advertising attempts to increase demand by telling consumers what the firm is selling, together with some characteristics of the firm's product (informational advertising). Also advertising tries to convince consumers that the firm's product is better than other products on the market, and that it is just what the buyer needs (persuasive advertising). In the process of increasing the demand for the firm's product, advertising also attempts to differentiate the product from other products in the market. This has the effect of decreasing the elasticity of demand facing the firm. The less elastic the demand facing the firm, the more monopoly power is enjoyed by the firm, and the greater the discretion it has to set the price of its product.

Advertising costs money; thus when a firm or group of firms decides to advertise, we conclude that the marginal revenue obtained from the extra products sold due to advertising is at least as great as the marginal cost (including advertising expense) of the extra units sold; otherwise, firms would not advertise.

Much disagreement exists about the merits of advertising. Most people, including economists, agree that informational advertising is beneficial. For consumers to maximize utility, they must know what is for sale, something about the good or service being sold, and the selling price. In addition, advertising increases competition between buyers and sellers and between different sellers of the same product. If buyers are informed through advertising that a given product is available at a lower price than what is asked by a particular seller, they can bargain with the seller to lower the price or they will buy elsewhere. Similarly, if sellers see other sellers offering lower prices, they will follow to remain competitive. For example, the average price of eyeglasses in states where eyeglasses advertising is banned was found to be more than twice the average price paid in states where advertising is not restricted.[1]

Much less agreement exists, however, about persuasive advertising. The advertising industry argues that advertising stimulates the economy by enticing people to spend. Others, particularly persons who have recently endured a nauseating commercial, argue that persuasive advertising is pure waste because the effect of one firm's advertising cancels out the advertising of other firms.

An objective appraisal of advertising, if possible, would rate it somewhere between these extreme views. Advertising stimulates spending on the item being advertised or it would not pay to advertise. But, it is less clear whether advertising makes people spend a larger share of their income. Expenditures on advertising have increased greatly during the past five decades, but on the average, people spend about the same proportion of their income today as they did 50 or 60 years ago. Nor is it clear that it is desirable for people to spend a larger share of their disposable income on consumer goods.

It has been suggested that the government ban persuasive advertising and allow only informational advertising. The problem, however, is to separate the two. One could argue, for example, that telling people product A is superior to all competitive products is really informational advertising. Banning persuasive advertising also would result in much waste from lawyers' fees and court costs. The litigation cost would be borne by consumers through higher product prices and higher taxes.

---

1. Lee Benham, "The Effect of Advertising on the Price of Eyeglasses," *Journal of Law and Economics.* 1972.

MARGINAL COST AND SUPPLY

Throughout the discussion on imperfect competition thus far, use of the word *supply* has been avoided. This is because an imperfectly competitive firm does not have a supply curve as such. Recall that in perfect competition, the firm's marginal cost (MC) curve is its supply curve. The firm, faced with a given price, maximizes profits by producing up to the point where price equals MC. The MC curve, therefore, is the supply curve because it denotes the quantity that will be produced at a given price.

The MC curve of an imperfectly competitive firm, however, is not its supply curve, because for a given quantity, the price charged will depend on the demand curve facing the firm. Thus, we cannot determine both price and quantity from the MC curve alone. We have to know both MC and demand to determine the price and quantity for a firm operating in imperfect competition.

However, the factors that shift the MC or supply curve of a perfectly competitive firm also shift the MC curve of a firm in imperfect competition. Moreover, the result of a shift in MC is the same as a shift in supply. For example, a shift to the left, or an increase in MC, reduces the quantity and increases the price in imperfect competition, which is the same as a decrease in supply in perfect competition. Remember from our discussion of product supply that an increase in costs results in a decrease in supply, and vice versa. Because of these similarities, we do not commit a gross error by referring to the supply of automobiles or gasoline, for example, even though these products are sold by imperfectly competitive firms.

QUESTIONS

1. a. What are the two characteristics that give rise to monopolistic competition?
   b. Give some examples of monopolistically competitive firms.
   c. How can two retail stores that sell the same brand of product be considered as selling differentiated products?

2. Suppose by lowering its price from $1.20 to $1.15 per gallon, a service station can sell 15,000 gallons of gasoline per week as opposed to 10,000. Can we infer from these figures that the marginal revenue of an extra gallon sold in this range of output is $1.15? Why or why not? What is MR in this case?

3. a. Using the appropriate diagram, illustrate the profit-maximizing price and quantity for a monopolistically competitive firm.
   b. Explain why any other price or quantity will not maximize profits.

4. Using the appropriate diagrams, illustrate the case where a monopolistically competitive firm is making:
   a. pure profits.
   b. just normal profits.
   c. a loss.

5. Describe the process of adjustment that would occur if a grocery store in an expanding resort area is making pure profits.

6. What are the two ways in which pure profits are competed away in a monopolistically competitive industry?

7. a. Why do firms advertise?
   b. Would society be better off if advertising was banned? Explain.

SELF-TEST

1. Monopolistic competition includes those firms that sell a _____ share of the market, and sell a _____ product .
   a. large; differentiated
   b. small; differentiated
   c. large; undifferentiated
   d. small; undifferentiated

2. Retail stores that sell the same brands of merchandise can be viewed as selling _____ products because of:
   a. undifferentiated; service and location.
   b. differentiated; product quality differences.
   c. undifferentiated; product quality differences.
   d. differentiated; service and location.

3. The profit-maximizing quantity for a monopolistically competitive firm corresponds to the point where _____ equals _____ .
   a. MC; demand
   b. MC; MR
   c. MR; demand
   d. MR; price

4. The profit-maximizing price for a monopolistically competitive firm corresponds to the point where the _____ equals _____ .
   a. MC; MR
   b. MC; demand
   c. profit-maximizing quantity; demand
   d. profit-maximizing quantity; MR

5. If the actual quantity sold by a monopolistically competitive firm is less than the profit-maximizing quantity, profits can be increased by increasing the quantity sold because the _____ of an extra unit is greater than its _____ .
   a. MR; MC
   b. price; MR
   c. MR; price
   d. MC; MR

6. A monopolistically competitive firm will earn a pure profit if _____ is greater than _____ at the profit-maximizing quantity.
   a. MC; product price
   b. product price; MC
   c. ATC; product price
   d. product price; ATC

7. A monopolistically competitive firm will incur a loss if _____ is greater than _____ at the loss-minimizing quantity.
   a. MC; product price
   b. product price; MC
   c. ATC; product price
   d. product price; ATC

8. A monopolistically competitive firm will earn normal profits if _____ equals_____ at the profit-maximizing quantity.
   a. ATC; AVC
   b. ATC; product price
   c. ATC; MR
   d. MR: product price

9. If existing monopolistically competitive firms are making pure profits, _____ causing the demand curve facing each firm to _____.
   a. firms will leave; increase
   b. firms will leave; decrease
   c. new firms will enter the market; increase
   d. new firms will enter the market; decrease

10. As new monopolistically competitive firms enter a market, the demand facing each firm in the market _____ , causing the price received by each firm to ____ . In a long-run equilibrium _____ profits are earned.
    a. decreases; increase; pure
    b. increases; decrease; pure
    c. decreases; decrease; normal
    d. increases; increase; normal

11. As monopolistically competitive firms leave a market, the demand facing each firm in the market _____ causing the price received by each firm to _____ . In a long-run equilibrium _____ profits are earned.
    a. decreases; increase; pure
    b. increases; decrease; pure
    c. decreases; decrease; normal
    d. increases; increase; normal

12. A firm that has special characteristics or a special product that cannot be duplicated by competitors and is making pure profits will experience _____ in the value of its assets and earn _____ profits in the long-run.
    a. an increase; normal
    b. a decrease; normal
    c. an increase; pure
    d. a decrease; pure

13 A firm that is incurring a loss and is sold to a new owner can earn a _____ for the new owner if the firm's assets are revalued _____.
    a. loss; downward
    b. normal profit; downward
    c. loss; upward
    d. normal profit; upward

14. When assets of a firm are revalued up or down because the firm is making either a pure profit or a loss, costs are said to be:
    a. price determining.
    b. price determined.
    c. fixed.
    d. variable.

15. It has been argued that _____ advertising is wasteful.
    a. all
    b. persuasive
    c. informational
    d. price

16. It has been observed that where advertising is banned, prices are _____ because:
    a. higher; of a reduction in competition.
    b. higher; of higher costs.
    c. lower; of increased competition.
    d. lower; of lower costs.

17. For a perfectly competitive firm, the _____ curve is also a supply cure. For an imperfectly competitive firm, price and quantity depend on both _____ and _____.
    a. MR; MC; MR
    b. MC; MC; demand
    c. MR; MC; demand
    d. MC; MR; demand

Chapter 18

Oligopoly

Key Concepts

Oligopoly defined

Price determination

Kinked demand curve

Interdependence of firms

Price searching

Mergers and conglomerates

Collusion and anti-trust legislation

Summary of demand facing the firm

This chapter deals with the market organization called oligopoly where three or four large firms supply the major share of the market. Although the model for portraying an oligopoly is similar to the monopoly and monopolistic competition cases, a special problem is addressed—the possibility of collusion among firms to divide the market and set a higher than competitive price.

OLIGOPOLY DEFINED

Oligopoly is derived from the Greek word *oligos*, meaning few. This definition provides a hint about the kind of industry characterized by an oligopoly. An oligopoly is an industry in which a few firms, say three or four, produce the major share of the market. Oligopoly is commonly found in heavy industry or in products marketed nationally. Autos, steel, airplanes, drugs, construction equipment, minerals, petroleum, and computers are products produced by oligopolies.

Industries in which a few large firms produce the major share of the output occur mainly because large firms can produce the product more efficiently than small firms, that is, because of economies of scale. For example, it is hard to visualize the auto industry consisting of several thousand or even several hundred firms. Each firm would be too small to utilize the most efficient mass-production techniques.

Unlike monopolistic competition, the firms in an oligopolistic market do not necessarily produce a differentiated product. In fact, petroleum, steel, and minerals could all be classified as homogeneous products. A ton of steel produced by U.S. Steel is essentially the same product as a ton produced by Bethlehem Steel or Jones and Laughlin. There are oligopolies that produce differentiated products such as automobiles or appliances. Thus, the distinguishing characteristic of an oligopoly is the small number of firms in the market.

PRICE DETERMINATION

The fact that each firm sells a substantial share of the market or sells a differentiated product allows each firm to somewhat influence the price of its product. For example, if one of the large steel companies reduced its output, there would be a decline in the amount of steel on the market, providing that steel imports do not make up the difference. This would result in an increase in steel prices. Thus, each firm has some control over the price of the product it sells. In other words, each firm in an oligopoly faces a downward-sloping demand curve.

However, each firm's ability to influence the price of its product is limited by the substitute products available. Each firm, therefore, must sell its product at a price in line with the prices of competitors. Ford would not sell many cars if its price were several hundred dollars higher than comparable Chevrolet models. For homogeneous products produced in an oligopolistic market, there is less opportunity for price differentials to exist. Disregarding transportation charges, no one would buy steel from U.S. Steel if it charged more than its competitors.

We should not be surprised, therefore, when all firms in an oligopoly market change their prices at about the same time. This indicates that consumers regard the products of firms in an oligopoly market as close substitutes. If a firm's price rises out of line with the prices of other firms, its customers soon discover substitute products that give them more for their money. If the products of firms in an oligopolistic market are close substitutes for one another, as in steel or petroleum, for example, there will be no price difference between the products. For products such as luxury automobiles, which consumers regard as less perfect substitutes, wider price differences between firms occur.

Also, all firms in a particular industry use about the same technology and resources. Therefore, if resource prices change, the MC and ATC curves for each firm will shift by about the same amount. Consequently, the profit-maximizing price will change by about the same amount for each firm.

In dealing with the prices of oligopolistic products, one must distinguish between the list price, the price on the window sticker for automobiles, for example, and the actual price that consumers pay. The difference between the two prices can be substantial for differentiated products. For example, during most years, the actual selling price of new U.S.-made cars is about 15 percent lower than the list or sticker price. In times of unusually low demand, or for certain models that are not selling well, the discount may be even greater, particularly at the end of the model year. On the other hand, in times of strong demand for certain makes or models, actual prices can exceed sticker prices. One should regard the actual price—rather than the list price—as the profit-maximizing (or loss-minimizing) price. When cars sell below list price, auto makers would like to obtain the higher price. But, in many cases, the demand is such that firms would end up with large, unsold inventories at the end of the model year and, as a result, earn lower total profits, or incur greater losses than if they cut the price and sell the extra units.

Oligopolistic price determination is illustrated with Figure 18–1. The same diagram used for illustrating the optimum price and quantity for a monopoly and a monopolistic competition firm can be used for oligopoly. We might expect, however, that an oligopoly would face a less elastic demand curve than a monopolistically competitive firm because by definition it sells a larger share of the market. It is risky to generalize about this because of differences in the degree of product differentiation between the two types of firms and because of possible differences in the elasticity of the market demand for the general category of product, such as steel versus cars. Other things equal, the demand facing an oligopolist selling a homogeneous product is more elastic than for one selling a product different from its competitors.

The three types of firms, monopoly, monopolistic competition, and oligopoly, are similar in that the oligopoly also attempts to equate MC with MR to determine the most profitable output. The price charged by the firm is determined by the demand facing the firm at this output. This profit-maximizing price, shown

FIGURE 18–1 Profit-Maximizing Price and Quantity for an Oligopoly

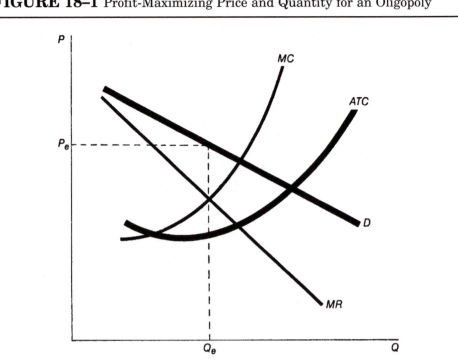

in Figure 18–1, is actual price, not list price.

In this example, price is greater than average total cost, so the firm earns a pure profit. Of course, this is only an example. If the ATC curve was everywhere above the firm's demand curve, the firm would have to take a loss or shut down.

THE KINKED DEMAND CURVE

Another apparent characteristic of an oligopolistic market is the relative "stickiness" of product price. Compared with perfectly competitive and monopolistically competitive firms, oligopolies tend to change the price of their products infrequently. For example, once an auto manufacturer announces the list prices of its new cars, it tends to stick with them, often for the entire model year except in periods of relatively high inflation. We should bear in mind, however, that these are list prices, not actual prices.

In an effort to formulate a theory that takes this characteristic specifically into account, the "kinked' `demand curve facing the firm was developed. The basic assumption of this theory is that each firm attempts to retain its present customers or attract new ones. Let us see how the kinked demand curve is derived. Suppose General Motors raises its price. It is assumed in this case that

FIGURE 18–2 Kinked Demand Curve

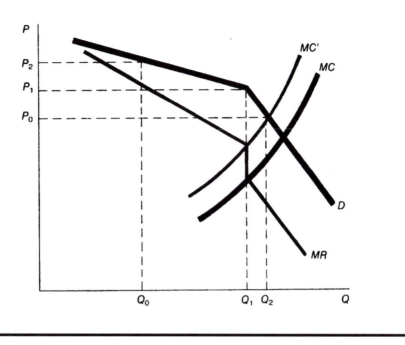

the other auto manufacturers will hold to their original price in order to take GM's customers.[1] Thus GM experiences a substantial reduction in sales, as shown in Figure 18–2, where price increases from P_1 to P_2 and quantity declines from Q_1 to Q_0 On the other hand, if GM reduces prices from P_1 to P_0, it is assumed that other firms will also reduce their prices. Thus GM is able to obtain only a modest increase in sales, say from Q_1 to Q_2. Therefore we have a kink in the demand curve facing the firm.

Notice also that the kinked demand curve results in a discontinuous MR curve. The more elastic portion of the MR curve is derived from the more elastic segment of the demand curve, and the less elastic portion of MR is derived from the lower, less elastic portion of the total demand curve. The resulting two segments of the MR curve are joined by a vertical line. Now if MC should intersect MR at some point within this vertical section, a shift in MC, as shown in Figure 18–2, would not change the optimum price and quantity for the firm. That is, the profit-maximizing price and quantity would remain at P_1 and Q_1 respectively, for either MC or MC[1]. As a result, the kinked demand curve is

---

1. Notice that this assumption implies that the other firms do not attempt to maximize profits by producing where MC equals MR.

sometimes used to explain why oligopoly prices do not exhibit a large amount of fluctuation.

The theory of the kinked demand curve has fallen out of favor among economists and is not used much any more for several reasons. For one thing, it is not possible to derive from the kinked demand curve how the going price and quantity come to be what they are. These magnitudes have to be assumed as given. Second, it is doubtful that oligopolistic prices are as inflexible as generally assumed. Even though list prices might remain unchanged over a long period, actual prices may vary considerably. For example, the actual price of a new car tends to fall from the beginning to the end of the model year, even though the list price stays the same. The same is true for appliances. Or if an oligopolistic firm mistakenly produces more of an item than it thought would sell at the list price, price cuts are in evidence in order to get rid of the excess inventory. Finally, as pointed out in footnote 1, the assumptions imply that competing firms do not attempt to maximize profits by equating MR with MC.

INTERDEPENDENCE OF FIRMS

An inevitable result of the few firms in an oligopolistic market is that the action of any major firm significantly affects the sales and/or price of the other firms in the market. For example, suppose General Motors grants a wage increase to its employees, which leads to an increase in production cost, as shown in Figure 18-3A. We can see from Figure 18–3A that it is in GM's interest to raise the price of its cars from P_0 to P_1 and reduce the quantity sold from Q_1 to Q_0 to again equate MC and MR. If they continued to charge P_0 and sell Q_1, MC would be greater than MR; they would lose money on the marginal units produced.

Recall from our discussion of consumer demand that when the price of a good increases, there is an increase in demand for substitute goods. We can predict, therefore, that an increase in the price of GM cars will lead to an increase in demand for other makes, as shown in Figure 18–3B. Consumers will try to avoid the higher price of GM cars by purchasing more of other makes. But, an increase in the demand for other makes will lead to an increase in both price and quantity of these cars, as the other firms attempt to equate MC with MR, as shown in Figure 18–3B. We see, therefore, that an increase in the costs and price of products of just one of the major firms in an oligopolistic market leads to an increase in the price of other firms' products as well. The other auto firms eventually will experience the same increase in labor costs as GM, so everyone's cost curves will end up at about the same level.

Also, the increase in demand and price shown in Figure 18–3B will lead to a slight increase in demand for GM cars, resulting in a slightly greater increase in price for these cars than originally specified in Figure 18–3A. In fact, we can trace this process of cause and effect back and forth indefinitely. As a rule, how-

FIGURE 18–3 Effects of an Increase in Manufacturing Costs of General
Motors Automobiles

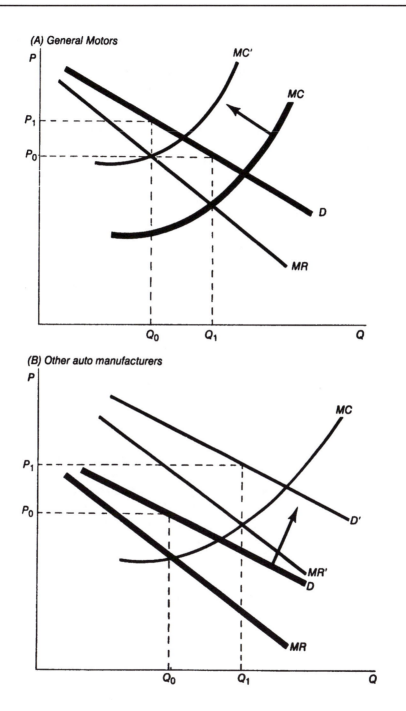

ever, the largest changes come on the first round, so the second- or third-order effects are of less importance.

It is common to observe oligopolies in a specific industry raising or lowering their prices at about the same time. This behavior has caused some people to suspect that the firms are colluding to set prices. But it is not necessary to have collusion for firms to exhibit this behavior. Firms change prices because of changes in the demand facing the firm, and/or because of a change in costs. When one or both of these changes occur they tend to affect all firms in the industry. For example, if the demand for U.S.-made cars increases, the demand facing most U.S. car makers will increase. This in turn increases the profit-maximizing price, so firms raise their prices.

The same thing happens when costs increase. Since all firms producing the same kind of product, such as cars, utilize the same resources and the same basic technology, an increase in the price of one or more of these inputs increases marginal and average costs. This in turn increases the profit-maximizing price, so all firms raise their prices.

Notice that when demand suddenly increases the price increase is accompanied by an increase in quantity. However, when costs increase, the price increase results in a decrease in quantity if demand has not shifted.

PRICE SEARCHING

Although diagrams are helpful in providing a framework for thinking about the operation of an oligopolistic firm and market, we should not lose sight of the complexities involved, particularly regarding price determination by the individual firm. It is one thing to equate marginal cost with marginal revenue, follow the line up to the demand curve, and determine price and quantity. It is quite another thing to learn what these magnitudes are.

Each large oligopolistic firm has a staff of economists, cost accountants, market researchers, and the like to assess costs and market demand. But, there is still plenty of trial and error in price determination. This is particularly true for a new product or an entirely new firm. If there are similar products already on the market, the firm wants to set a price somewhere in line with established items. The firm also wants to compare such a price with its unit production costs. It will have a good idea of average costs and may have some idea of marginal costs.

Once a price is set and a production decision has been made, the firm will receive information from the market and from its own cost and profit figures. If the product is not selling and inventories are piling up, it may indicate that the product is overpriced. When introducing a new product, it is usually necessary to offer consumers a bit more for their money than they receive from established items, or else they have little incentive to change. As sales increase (i.e., demand facing the firms increases or shifts to the right), the firm may want to adjust the price slightly upward, especially if production cannot keep up with sales. Of course, in times of inflation, with increased wages and prices of raw materials, product price must be increased or the firm will find its average total costs exceeding product price.

Each firm must watch its major competitors. If the firm is small or new in the business, it might decide to play follow-the-leader. If the large, dominant firm increases price, the small firm follows suit; or, if the large firm lowers price, so does the small one. This behavior, common in oligopolistic markets, is referred to as price leadership. In addition to relieving the small firm of periodically deciding on its product price, this practice reduces the likelihood that the small firm will provoke the large one into a price war, possibly wiping out the small firm.

Even with price leadership, at least one firm in an oligopolistic market must bear the responsibility of setting a price. One such procedure is sometimes called average cost pricing. Here, the firm determines the average total cost of an item, adds a certain percent of that figure for profit, and uses this figure for its price. Of course, this does not guarantee the firm a profit regardless of its costs. If the firm becomes inefficient, other firms may decide that they can sell at a lower price and still cover their costs, including a normal profit. Thus, even a so-called dominant firm has no guarantee of remaining dominant. In addition to contending with the up-and-coming firms on the home scene, it may have to contend with foreign competition. Competitive forces from foreign firms are especially evident in such industries as autos, steel, shipbuilding, shoes, electronics, petroleum, and textiles.

Also, the potential competition of each firm is not limited to existing firms in its industry. If excessive pure profits are evident in an industry, there is usually nothing to stop established firms in other industries from moving in to get a piece of the action. For example, if bicycle manufacturing becomes very profitable, there is nothing to stop General Motors or Ford from getting into the bicycle business. Many of today's conglomerates are involved in several industries simultaneously.

MERGERS AND CONGLOMERATES

Many firms are in a situation where they must become larger to become more efficient (that is, attain economies of scale) and remain competitive in their field. Since internal growth is often a relatively slow and difficult process, the merging of two or more firms is a popular vehicle for growth. A better appreciation for its popularity can be gained by looking at the advantages of a merger. Two or more firms that become one can gain some advantages of specialization by devoting entire plants to the production of one or two components of their overall product. For an auto firm, one plant might manufacture engines, another bodies, and so on. One may also gain some scale economies by sharing a common management and administrative structure. Instead of having two or three main offices and staffs, the merged firm can get by with one. A larger firm can take advantage of a more efficient advertising medium, such as nationwide television, or borrow at a lower rate of interest, or it can sell stock more easily.

In addition to pure scale economies, some firms have obtained tax savings through merger. For example, if a firm incurring losses merges with one reaping pure profits, their overall tax bill may be reduced by writing off the one's losses against the other's profits. Another advantage is the possibility of easing the competitive pressure faced by each firm. The merger of two intense rivals would make life easier for both firms. However, where the merger of two competing firms results in a monopoly, the Justice Department is likely to step in and forbid the merger.

Merger is not limited to firms in the same industry. When two or more firms in separate industries merge, they form a conglomerate. A well-known conglomerate is International Telephone and Telegraph (ITT), which has holdings innumerous industries. Large firms such as ITT often have sufficient assets to acquire control of other firms and their management, as opposed to working out a mutual agreement, as in a merger.

HOSTILE TAKEOVERS

The practice of acquiring control of a firm without the consent of the acquired firm's management is a hostile takeover. In this case, a firm or person buys the majority of the voting stock in another firm. The acquiring party can then replace the acquired firm's management and sell off parts of that firm. Actually, the word hostile describes the view of the acquired firms management who fear losing their jobs. The owners or stockholders of the acquired firms are not forced to sell their stock; they willingly sell when the price of the stock is bid up in the market.

Some states have passed legislation making it more difficult for hostile takeovers to occur. It has been questioned whether such legislation is in the best interest of society. If weak firms are taken over by strong ones, efficiency is improved and society gets more out of its resources. Sometimes it is argued that the acquiring firms reorganize or assimilate the acquired firms so that their products are no longer recognizable. This may be true, but the acquiring firms have no incentive to make the resources of their takeover objects less profitable than before; to do so would reduce profits.

COLLUSION AND ANTITRUST LEGISLATION

The few firms in an oligopolistic market allow the possibility for two or more rival firms agreeing not to compete. Agreements of this nature can be informal, with rivals agreeing to maintain a certain price or to divide up the market.

There is also the possibility that participating firms will enter into formal agreements where each firm agrees to a specified price and quantity of the product each will produce. This arrangement is referred to as a cartel. A cartel or even an informal agreement results in a market resembling a monopoly. It is as though there were only one firm in the market. As a consequence, we expect a higher price than if there were many firms competing in the market.

The two main legal tools that the government uses to fight nonsanctioned monopolies or cartels are the Sherman Antitrust Act of 1890 and the Clayton Antitrust Act of 1914. The Sherman Act makes restraint of trade or any attempt to monopolize trade a misdemeanor, that is, a criminal offense against the federal government. The Clayton Act essentially duplicates the Sherman Act and details the various illegal activities that might lead to a monopoly or cartel. The intention of this act was curbing a monopoly before it occurred, rather than punishing it after the fact. The Federal Trade Commission (FTC), also set up in 1914, has the power to investigate unfair business practices and take legal action if required.

In addition to government action against monopolies or cartels, there is a market force that acts as a continual deterrent. This is the temptation by colluding firms to cheat on one another. As shown in Figure 18–4, an industry that becomes a monopoly or cartel must reduce its output to raise price. Thus, each firm that agrees to collude must agree to reduce its output for the scheme to work. But, if each firm is maximizing profits by equating MR with MC before the collusion occurs, then after they agree to reduce quantity and raise price, MR for each firm will be greater than MC, as shown in Figure 18–4. Before collusion, each firm maximizes profits by producing Q_1—the quantity that corresponds to the intersection of the MC and MR curves. During collusion, each firm reduces its output to Q_0 We cannot, however, illustrate the new higher price that results from collusion on the diagrams in Figure 18–4 because these are the demand curves that face each firm, not the market demand. We can only assume that the new higher price results in higher net profits for each firm, or else it would not pay to collude.

During collusion, each firm is in a situation where MR is greater than MC. Thus, it is in the interest of each firm to sell a few extra units of output under the table. By doing so, the firm can increase its profits even more. But when all or most firms participating in the collusion cheat in this manner, the market price falls; otherwise, the additional output cannot be sold. Unless the colluders can impose a penalty on the cheaters, collusive agreements tend to break down. But it is difficult to enforce any kind of penalty against a firm for refraining from an illegal activity.

The Organization of Petroleum Exporting Countries (OPEC), a well-known cartel, provides a good example of this phenomenon. For a while during the mid-to-late 1970s this group of countries was able to increase petroleum prices faster than the rate of inflation. However the power of the cartel to set world petroleum prices began to erode when some of its members, principally Saudi Arabia,

FIGURE 18–4 Effect on Individual Firms of Colluding to Reduce Quantity and Raise Price

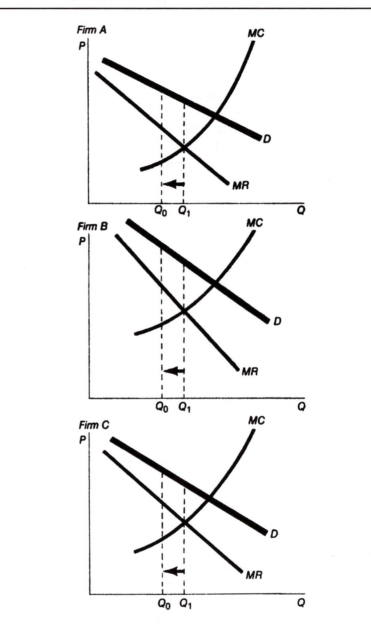

began to sell at prices below the agreed upon level in order to increase their export revenues. Soon other countries followed suit, and by the mid-1980s petroleum prices declined to levels below the l930s after adjusting for inflation.

A SUMMARY OF DEMAND FACING THE FIRM

It is useful at this point to summarize and compare the demand curve facing each of the four types of firms we have studied. We began in Chapter 15 with the perfectly competitive firm that faces a perfectly elastic demand. In Chapters 16-18 we have looked at three types of imperfectly competitive firms: pure

FIGURE 18–6 Summary of Demand Curves Facing the Firms in the Four Major Types of Market Situations

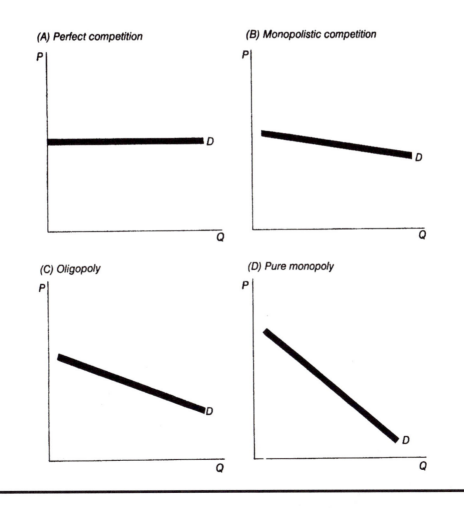

monopoly, monopolistic competition, and oligopoly. Each of these firms faces a downward-sloping demand. In general, the fewer the firms producing a particular good or service and the more differentiated the product of each firm, the steeper or less elastic the demand facing each firm. The demand curve facing the individual firm in each of four market situations is illustrated in Figure 18–6.

It is best to think of these four types of firms as a continuous distribution, from perfect competition to pure monopoly, rather than four hard-and-fast categories. These categories are useful in that they identify where in the distribution a given firm is located. Most firms fall somewhere between the two extremes of perfect competition and pure monopoly.

QUESTIONS

1. a. What is an oligopoly?
    b. What characteristics are necessary to have an oligopoly?
2. Using the appropriate diagram, illustrate the profit-maximizing price and quantity for an oligopoly.
3. a. Draw a kinked demand curve for a firm and identify the region on the corresponding MR curve where a shift in the MC curve will not change the profit-maximizing price or quantity.
    b. Why is the upper portion of the kinked demand curve drawn to be more elastic than the lower portion?
    c. In constructing the kinked demand curve, what is assumed about the profit-maximizing behavior of competing firms?
4. During the 1970s, an inflationary period accompanied by above-average unemployment, U.S. automakers raised the prices of their products, while the number of vehicles they sold decreased. At the time some people argued that this was irrational. How might one explain this phenomenon as rational, profit-maximizing behavior?

5. Comparable models of GM, Ford, and Chrysler cars sell for about the same price, and when one company changes its price, they all change prices by about the same amount. From these observations can we conclude that the Big Three automakers are colluding to set prices? Explain.
6. a. What is a cartel, and why does society consider cartels undesirable?
    b. Why do cartels tend to break down?
7. In recent years, hostile takeovers have been well-publicized. How can a hostile takeover occur? If one firm doesn't want to sell to another, can it be forced to do so? Explain.
8. a. What factors determine the elasticity of the demand curve facing a firm?
    b. Rank the four types of firms according to those facing the most to the least elastic demand.

SELF-TEST

1. An oligopoly consists of a market where there are _____ firms, each selling a _____ share of the market.
    a. many; large
    b. many; small
    c. few; large
    d. few; small

2. The distinguishing characteristic of an oligopoly is that each firm sells a:
    a. differentiated product.
    b. large share of the market.
    c. undifferentiated product.
    d. small share of the market.

3. Some oligopolies sell a large share of the market and a differentiated product, while others sell a _____ share of the market and _____ product.
    a. small; a differentiated
    b. small; an undifferentiated
    c. large; an undifferentiated product
    d. a and b

4. The demand curve facing an oligopoly should be _____ the demand facing a monopolistically competitive firm.
    a. the same elasticity as
    b. more elastic than
    c. less elastic than

5. An oligopoly will maximize profits by producing the quantity that corresponds to the point where _____ equals:
    a. ATC; demand.
    b. MC; demand.
    c. MC; ATC.
    d. MC; MR.

6. An oligopoly will maximize profits by setting a price that corresponds to the point where:
    a. MC = MR.
    b. the profit-maximizing quantity corresponds to demand.
    c. the profit-maximizing quantity corresponds to MR.

    d. MC = demand.

7. According to the kinked demand curve theory, when a firm increases the price of its product, competing firms _____When a firm lowers its price, other firms _____ .
    a. raise their prices; hold their prices constant
    b. hold their prices constant; lower their prices
    c. hold their prices constant; raise their prices
    d. raise their prices; lower their prices

8. If General Motors increases the price of its cars, the _____ facing Ford Motor Co. will _____ .
    a. demand; increase
    b. demand; decrease
    c. supply; increase
    d. supply; decrease

9. Prices of comparable makes and models of automobiles are quite similar because:
    a. consumers view them as close substitutes.
    b. each firm employs similar technology and pays about the same for inputs.
    c. firms collude to set price and divide up the market.
    d. a and b.

10 . New products which appear on the market generally are priced:
    a. as high as possible.
    b. where MC = MR.
    c. at what the market will bear.
    d. in line with the competition.

11. A hostile takeover of one firm by another is frequently opposed by:
    a. the stockholders of the acquired firm.
    b. the stockholders of the acquiring firm.
    c. the management of the acquired firm.
    d. the management of the acquiring firm.

12. "Corporate raiders" that engage in hostile takeovers defend their action by arguing that they:

a. promote competition.

b. reduce speculation in the stock market.

c. improve the management of weak firms.

d. increase employment of middle management personnel.

13. Two or more firms which collude to raise the prices of their products are known as a:

a. holding company.

b. cartel.

c. conglomerate.

d. public utility.

14. Two or more firms that collude to raise their prices must:

a. announce their intentions to the Justice Department.

b. increase their quantities.

c. decrease their quantities.

d. lower their profits.

15. If collusion occurs, each colluding firm is producing a quantity where _____ is greater than _____ .

a. MR: MC

b. MR; demand

c. MC; MR

d. MC; demand

16. As a consequence of the situation described in question 15, each firm has an incentive to _____ the other firms by selling at a slightly _____ price than the agreed-upon colluding price.

a. cooperate with; higher

b. cooperate with; lower

c. cheat on; higher

d. cheat on; lower

d. consumer cost.

17. Which of the following firms face the most elastic demand?

a. perfect competition

b. monopolistic competition

c. oligopoly

d. pure monopoly

18. Which of the following firms face the least elastic demand?

a. perfect competition

b. monopolistic competition

c. oligopoly

d. pure monopoly

Part VI

Market Topics

_____

Chapters 19-20

Chapter 19

Externalities And The Environment

Key Concepts

Externalities

Over-allocation of resources

Market failure

Pollution permits

Subsidizing waste disposal

Optimal level of pollution

Environmental regulations and economic growth

In recent years society has become more concerned about the pollution that firms emit into the soil, water, or air during the course of producing their products. This pollution can result in health problems for people, birds, and animals, and/or cause an unsightly environment.

EXTERNALITIES DEFINED

Externalities is a word that has long been in the economist's vocabulary. It refers to costs borne by society over and above those incurred by the firm or individual. These costs are commonly called social costs. Pollution is a social cost. If a firm pipes waste material into a river, for example, people downstream suffer the consequences. They may suffer health problems, or find that they no longer can enjoy the recreational value of the river. Thus they suffer a cost that is not taken into account by the firm doing the polluting. In other words, the cost of disposing the waste exceeds the cost of the pipe in which it is transported.

RESOURCE ALLOCATION

In Chapter 10 we saw that the firm maximizes profits by producing the level of output corresponding to the point where marginal cost equals marginal revenue. When externalities or social costs exist, the marginal cost as viewed by the firm is lower than the full or true marginal cost borne by society. Society's cost includes the cost incurred by the firm—the firm is part of society—but also includes the social cost over and above the firm's cost.

Social cost for an imperfectly competitive firm is illustrated by Figure 19–1. MC is the private marginal cost as viewed by the firm whereas MC^1 is the true or full marginal cost borne by society. If the firm disregards social costs, it produces quantity Q_1 and charges price P_0. If the firm is required to "clean up its act" so as to eliminate its pollution, the marginal cost is now higher at MC^1. The elimination of pollution could be accomplished by installing pollution control devices, or treating the waste before discharging it into the environment. Alternatively the firm could contract with another firm that specializes in waste treatment to neutralize the pollutants. Either way, the firm incurs a cost that is reflected in MC^1.

Notice that when the firm internalizes the externalities or social cost, the profit maximizing level of output decreases to Q_0 from Q_1. At the same time, the profit maximizing price increases from P_0 to P_1. When a firm does not take into account the added social cost of pollution, it produces too much. Economists would say that there is an overallocation of resources to firms and industries that pollute. Too much of these goods are produced and not enough of other goods, including pollution control services. Thus pollution results in a misallocation of the nation's resources.

Because it costs more to carry on production without polluting the environ-

Figure 19–1 Effect of Pollution Control

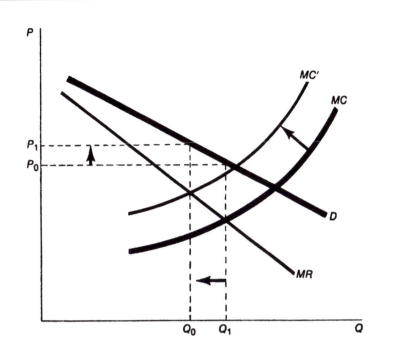

ment, the prices of goods produced also must increase. Consumers then are purchasing a cleaner environment along with conventional goods and services.

CAN POLLUTION BE CONTROLLED?

In order for a firm to stay in business, it must sell its product at a competitive price and at the same time cover its costs, i.e., make at least a normal profit. Firms that are owned or operated by socially responsible people who wish to avoid pollution have a problem. If they install pollution control devices, or treat their wastes, their costs will increase. If their production costs exceed the prices of competitor's products, these socially responsible firms may be driven out of business. All it takes is for a few unscrupulous firms that pollute and thereby produce at a lower cost to take over the market. Thus, firms are in a sense driven to the lowest common denominator. This phenomena is sometimes called "market failure." However, the term is not entirely accurate because some of the world's worst pollution occurred in Eastern Europe and the former Soviet Union where markets did not exist.

At any rate, if private firms are left to their own devices, competitive pressure forces each to produce at the least possible cost to stay in business. Thus in order to control pollution it is necessary for some outside authority, namely some level of government, to establish the "rules of the game." If all firms have to abide by certain standards, then those who desire to behave responsibly and avoid polluting are not placed at a competitive disadvantage.

Setting environmental standards that all firms must adhere to is one way to control pollution. To carry on production, each firm is required to install pollution control equipment, such as "scrubbers" in smokestacks, or modify its technique to meet the standards. A problem with imposing uniform standards across all firms is that conditions differ and the cost of meeting these standards differ among firms and industries. Hence some people will feel they are discriminated against if the standards are the same for everyone. On the other hand, if the standards are not the same, then those having to meet stiffer standards will voice the same complaint.

Another technique that has been suggested is to levy a tax on pollutants. Setting the tax rate would be a problem with this approach. How high should it be? Should the tax be uniform across firms or industries or should it differ? If it is uniform, firms that find it expensive to control pollution will be penalized more. If the tax varies, fairness and favoritism will be issues.

A third technique that can be applied in certain cases is to tax inputs that cause pollution. For example, in agriculture nitrogen fertilizers and chemicals can contaminate surface and ground water. By placing a tax on these inputs, they become more expensive and less are used. Countries in Western Europe have adopted this approach with some success.

POLLUTION PERMITS

The newest technique for reducing pollution is for the government to auction off pollution permits to the highest bidders. In the first auction, conducted by the Chicago Board of Trade in 1993, each permit gave the purchaser the right to emit one ton of sulphur dioxide during the year. The permits, which are issued by the Environmental Protection Agency (EPA), first sold in 1993 at prices ranging from $200 to $250 each. Most were purchased by electric utilities—firms that emit sulphur dioxide from their coal-burning electric generation facilities.

This is a novel approach to controlling pollution that has advantages over strict regulations. First, the firms that find it most costly to control pollution should be willing to pay the highest prices for the permits. Thus, the firms that can decrease this pollution the cheapest will do so instead of buying the permits. With this procedure, the greatest reduction in pollution is obtained for a given cost.

This procedure also allows the EPA to gradually reduce the amount of pollution by reducing the number of permits. As the quantity of permits declines, their prices will increase. As this occurs, firms will find it more economical to install pollution control devices. Another advantage of this approach is that environmental groups can buy the permits and choose not to exercise their right to pollute. By so doing they help clean up the environment. Contributors to environmental groups decide in effect how much clean air is worth to them. Previously, these groups have had to lobby for more strict environmental standards. This can be frustrating if their lobbying efforts do not bear fruit.

PUBLIC POLLUTION

While it is common to blame business firms for pollution, governmental units also should be included among the list of polluters. Cites and municipalities that do not adequately treat sewage and water runoff also pollute rivers and other bodies of water. And landfills that contain dangerous chemicals can leak and contaminate the soil and ground water. Military bases and munitions plants owned by the federal government are additional sources of pollution.

Probably the greatest pollution caused by the military was that left by the Soviet army when it vacated its bases in Eastern Europe. As information becomes more available, it is becoming apparent that some of the world's greatest environmental damage was caused by the governments of the nonmarket, centrally planned, communist countries. For many decades public dissent was repressed, and their governments' actions were not held up to public scrutiny. Unfortunately the citizens of these countries are now paying the price for the irresponsible behavior of their former repressive regimes.

Ordinary citizens are not blameless either. A major pollution source is the emissions of private automobiles. The more we drive, the more we pollute. Granted, the new models of cars are less pollution prone than the old "gas-guzzlers" of years ago. Much environmental pollution also is caused by irresponsible people who throw trash from car windows onto public roadways. While this pollution may not be health threatening, everyone suffers a reduction in their standard of living because of the unsightly environment caused by this behavior. The same is true of debris thrown into lakes and rivers by those who should know better.

Private citizens cause pollution for much the same reason that business firms and governments do; it is cheaper or more convenient to discard waste than to dispose of it, or to recycle the products that can be recycled. Many states levy stiff fines on people throwing debris from car windows, or dumping it on the side of the road. But the offenders are hard to catch. The provision of convenient garbage disposal containers in public places helps to minimize the amount of trash thrown on sidewalks, streets, and highways. Most people care enough about the environment to dispose of their trash at collection points if it is reasonably convenient to do so.

WHO SHOULD PAY?

The cost of garbage pick-up from residences and places of business is another issue that every community must deal with. Should this cost be paid by individuals, or should it be paid by the community at large through taxes? It can be argued that people who generate the most waste should pay more for its disposal than those who do not. Also when waste is costly to dispose of, people will have an incentive to recycle more, and be more careful to minimize the amount of waste they generate. At the same time, if garbage pick-up fees become excessive, people will have an incentive to dump the waste onto the public roadways, or on someone else's property, public or private. The high private cost of hazardous waste disposal has caused some irresponsible people to dispose of this waste in an illegal manner.

If garbage pick-up and waste disposal is subsidized by public tax funds, people will not have an incentive to dump waste illegally, but rather place it in containers for pick-up. The drawback of this policy is that people then will not have much incentive to minimize garbage and waste production, which might be called "bads" or opposed to "goods." In view of the fill-up of public land-fills, particularly surrounding large cities, the problem of garbage disposal is becoming more acute. Also, in the interest of fairness, those who generate a lot of waste such as business firms, ought to pay more for waste pick-up than households. Some combination of cost sharing by public tax monies and private payment appears to be most feasible.

Certain products such as batteries, tires, anti-freeze, oil, appliances, and packaging probably ought to carry a "disposal tax" when sold new. Then when the time comes to dispose of the products, the people who purchased them and benefitted from their use would pay for the cost of their disposal or recycling. Such a tax would be easy to levy, although it would likely be opposed by the manufactures of the products. Educational efforts are needed to convince manufacturers that it is in their long run interest to place society's welfare above their short run profits.

WHAT IS THE OPTIMAL LEVEL OF POLLUTION?

At first glance, the question posed above seems rather odd. If pollution is bad, should not society strive to eliminate it entirely? Probably not. Although a pristine environment would be the ideal, the cost of achieving such a state of the world would likely be prohibitive. Many products such as cars and appliances would either disappear or greatly increase in price, making them unaffordable to all but the very rich. Food also would greatly increase in cost if commercial fertilizers, herbicides, and insecticides were banned. Again, it would be the poor who would suffer the most.

It is necessary to recognize that a trade-off exists between a pollution free environment and conventional goods. The more society demands of the former, the less there will be of the latter. No doubt, most people would prefer to have a cleaner environment without giving up conventional goods. As technology improves and adapts to efforts to clean up the environment, some progress can be made in this direction. But there comes a point where society will have to say, in effect, this is as much as we are willing to pay towards a pollution-free environment. At this point society is in effect saying that the value of a cleaner environment no longer exceeds the cost of obtaining it in terms of higher priced products. Of course, as in all matters of public debate, there will be differences among people on the so-called "optimal" level of pollution. The debate will never be settled. As, or if, the per capita income level increases, people may well decide to spend part of their increase in income on "environmental goods" such as clean air and water, and the opportunity to enjoy nature in its natural state. In the world's poorest nations, the environment is not high on the agenda of society's problems. The problem of obtaining enough food to stay alive for another day crowds out concerns over the environment, especially for the poorest of the poor. Thus economic growth can be viewed as environmentally friendly. When people become richer, they can turn their attention towards environmental goods, in addition to the necessities of life.

THE ENVIRONMENT VERSUS ECONOMIC GROWTH?

We know, countries that have experienced economic growth and attained a high standard of living also have the best record on the environment. Yet there is a lingering concern that stricter environmental regulations will be detrimental to growth. Business and political leaders have expressed concern that firms and jobs will leave states which pass stringent environment legislation and locate in more environmentally lenient states. Is there any evidence to justify this concern?

According to a recent study by Stephen M. Meyer of MIT, during the 1980s, states with stronger environmental policies had a better record of economic growth than state with less stringent regulations. In other words, the data revealed a positive relationship between states' environmental record and economic growth—just the opposite of what many have feared.

The underlying reasons for the positive relationship between the strength of environmental regulation and economic growth are not clear. It is possible that the relationship is spurious. In other words, there may be a third factor causing both to occur. One possibility might be that states that favor strong environ-

---

[1]Meyer, Stephen M. "Environmentalism and Economic Prosperity: Testing the Environmental Impact Hypothesis." Massachusetts Institute of Technology, Project on Environmental Politics and Policy. Bldg/Room E38-628, Cambridge, MA 02139, October 5, 1992.

mental policies also may be those more willing to invest in such things as education, research, health, transportation, and communications—investments that stimulate economic growth. Nevertheless, even if this is the case, the strong environmental regulations of these states have not offset the growth enhancing effects of their public investments.

An alternative explanation for the positive relationship between the environment and economic growth is that skilled and well educated workers are attracted to states or regions that promote a cleaner and healthy environment. Firms and employment opportunities follow these people. Such firms are more likely to be high-tech in nature; growth of these firms and industries has been higher than in the older, mature industries. It is also possible that firms facing stronger environmental legislation react by investing more in cleaner and newer methods of production, rather than moving to another state where they may face the same regulations sometime in the future. Investment in new technology, in turn, results in higher economic growth.

DANGEROUS PRODUCTS

Following World War II, advances in chemical technology made possible the production of many new products, particularly pesticides. When products like DDT first appeared on the market, they were viewed as a safe and effective way of controlling harmful insects. At the time, there were few if any tests of possible side-effects. It wasn't until Rachael Carson's book, *Silent Spring,* that people became aware of the harmful side-effects on the environment, particularly birds. Even after the book appeared, respected scientists attempted to discredit it. The passage of time has revealed that Rachael Carson was right and the scientists were wrong. Now most scientists have a deep respect for Carson's early work, and products are thoroughly tested before releasing them to the market. The Environmental Protection Agency (EPA) requires thorough testing of both new and older established products. As a result of this testing, some products were taken off the market, DDT probably the best known. It was found that DDT caused soft-shelled eggs of birds thereby harming their reproductive capacity.

Further discoveries of possible cancer producing chemicals in foods heightened the public's concern over food safety. The Delaney Clause passed by Congress during the Eisenhower Administration, prohibited even a tiny amount of carcinogens in foods. This standard has been lowered slightly because in earlier years the testing apparatus was not as accurate as that now in use. Modern testing equipment is so sensitive as to be able to detect a teaspoon of foreign substance in the Great Lakes. Many have questioned whether such minute amounts represent any danger to health.

Even if there is a health risk stemming from a substance, is there an acceptable level of this risk, or does it have to be zero? For example, if one person out of a million dies from the use of a pesticide, should the pesticide be banned? If so, how can society justify the use of other goods such as automobiles, tobacco, alcohol, and electricity where the risk of premature death is much greater? Smoking alone is estimated to cause over 500,000 deaths per year in the United States. If one in a million is deemed an acceptable risk, what is the threshold where it becomes unacceptable?

There is also the problem of measuring the effects on health of potentially harmful substances. Some have argued that the large doses fed to laboratory animals, mainly rats, over a short period far exceed the level consumed by humans over a life-time. This is not to say that the effects of all potentially harmful substances have been exaggerated. But society is scared to death of the unknown and the unseen. Small but unknown risks seem to carry more weight than the familiar and known such as automobile travel or smoking. As a result there is danger that society may over-react to even unsubstantiated claims of some minute risk, and call for laws to prohibit such products.

QUESTIONS

1. What is an externality, and why do externalities cause a misallocation of resources in the economy?
2. Is the full cost of driving one's car to school or work borne by the individual? Explain.
3. Why is it necessary for government to become involved in efforts to reduce pollution?
4. What are the advantages of auctioning off pollution permits over strict regulations as a means of decreasing pollution?
5. Give some examples where governmental units cause pollution. Do the same for private citizens.
6. Should the cost of garbage pick-up and disposal be subsidized by tax monies? Defend your answer.
7. The environment generally is less pleasing to the eye in poor neighborhoods than in rich ones. Why?
8. It is a concern of some people that stricter environmental regulations will decrease economic growth. Is this concern supported by the evidence? Explain.
9. Suppose you are a member of the Environmental Protection Agency (EPA) charged with making a decision on the acceptability of a new pesticide. What factors would need to be considered in making this decision?

SELF-TEST

1. Externalities result in____costs. Such costs result in a situation where the cost to society of a product____the cost to the firm.
    a. lower; is less than
    b. social; is greater than
    c. lower; is greater than
    d. social; is less than

2. The existence of social costs results in a(n)____of resources to the production of the product in question because the marginal cost facing society____the marginal cost facing the firm.
    a. overallocation; exceeds
    b. overallocation; is less than
    c. underallocation; exceeds
    d. underallocation; is less than
3. If social costs are internalized, product price will____and quantity produced will____.
    a. decrease; decrease
    b. decrease; increase
    c. increase; increase
    d. increase; decrease
4. Socially responsible firms that try to minimize pollution and incur____costs than competitors, as a result:
    a. higher; can enjoy a competitive advantage
    b. lower; can enjoy a competitive advantage
    c. higher; may be driven out of business
    d. lower; may be driven out of business
5. The phenomenon described in question 4 is sometimes called:
    a. externalities
    b. social cost
    c. excess profits
    d. market failure
6. Correcting the phenomenon labelled in question 5 requires____.
    a. an excess profits tax
    b. a government subsidy
    c. government intervention
    d. consumer education
7. Strictly speaking, market failure____an accurate term because pollution was (is) a problem in____.
    a. is; market economies
    b. is not; nonmarket economies
    c. is not; the public sector
    d. b and c

8. The main problem of controlling pollution by setting government standards that must be met by all firms:
    a. nonpollutors are penalized
    b. circumstances differ among firms and industries
    c. the measurement of pollution emissions
    d. costs increase more for polluters than nonpolluters

9. The main problem of controlling pollution by taxing pollutants:
    a. nonpollutors are penalized
    b. production costs are increased more for polluters than nonpolluters
    c. setting the proper tax rates
    d. polluters are penalized

10. The practice of auctioning off pollution permits:
    a. provides an incentive to first reduce pollution that is cheapest to control
    b. does not allow environmental groups to influence the amount of pollution
    c. encourages firms to pollute
    d. requires firms to first reduce the pollution that is most expensive to control

11. The problem(s) of subsidizing garbage pickup by using tax money:
    a. the incentive to reduce garbage is diminished
    b. recycling is discouraged
    c. dumping of garbage in public places is cheaper
    d. a and b

12. The problem of assessing the full cost of garbage pickup to businesses and home-owners:
    a. the incentive to reduce garbage is diminished
    b. recycling is discouraged
    c. dumping of garbage in public places is cheaper
    d. a and b

13. The optimal level of pollution:
    a. zero
    b. when the value of a cleaner environment no longer exceeds the cost of reducing pollution
    c. when the cost of a cleaner environment exceeds the value of the environment
    d. when the cost of improving the environment is at a minimum

14. High income communities and countries tend to have a____environment than their poorer counterparts. In the world's poorest nations the main concern is____.
    a. cleaner; pollution
    b. more polluted; hunger
    c. more polluted; pollution
    d. cleaner; hunger

15. A____relationship has been observed between economic growth and environmental standards. This can be attributed to:
    a. negative; the movement of firms to states with lower standards
    b. positive; the desire by well educated people to live in a clean environment
    c. positive; investment by firms in new technology that decreases pollution
    d. b and c

Chapter 20

Agriculture And Food

Key Concepts

Homestead Act
Farm Size
Agricultural Mechanization
Labor push vs. labor pull
Productivity Growth
Farm Programs
Farm Price Instability
Food Stamps
Engel Curve

United States agriculture consists largely of family farms. With the growth in farm size, there has been a concern that large corporate or factory farms will someday take over agriculture. Although such farms do exist, only about two percent of farm and ranch land in the U.S. is owned by nonfamily corporations. The large corporate farms are most commonly found in poultry production and livestock feeding which do not require large land holdings.

HOMESTEADERS

The family farm structure in the United States owes a lot to the settlement pattern of the country. Unlike some countries where royalty or the government bestowed large tracts of land to wealthy and prominent families, U.S. agriculture has been characterized by small freeholders. The framers of the U.S. constitution saw this as a desirable social structure. Among these, Thomas Jefferson stands out as an advocate of the family farm, although he himself owned 10,000 acres and nearly 200 slaves.

Probably the most significant piece of legislation affecting the structure of U.S. agriculture was the Homestead Act of 1862. Under the provisions of this act, families received clear title to 160 acres provided they lived on the land for at least 5 years. During the 30 years after the passage of the Homestead Act, most of the land west of the Mississippi river was settled. The 1890s is commonly referred to as the closing of the frontier. However, the number of farms in the country did not peak until 1935 at 6.8 million, and land in farms reached its maximum in 1950 at 1,159 million acres. In 1992, there were 2.1 million farms and 980 million acres of land in farms.

THE TREND TOWARDS FEWER AND LARGER FARMS

As economic growth occurred and per capita incomes increased, economic forces came into being that reshaped the structure of U.S. agriculture in favor of fewer but larger farms. During the nation's settlement period and extending into the 1930s, farm people could earn an income comparable to nonfarm people with the amount of land provided by the Homestead Act. Granted, farm incomes were depressed in the Great Depression of the 1930s, but few people left farms for the cities because of the high unemployment rate. During, and particularly after World War II, off-farm earnings prospects improved. As veterans of World War II returned to the farm, many soon realized that their incomes would be improved by leaving agriculture and taking nonfarm occupations. The GI Bill which financed further schooling facilitated the move. The same desire to increase incomes was true of people who had farmed during the war.

Migration out of agriculture peaked in the 1950s when over one million people left the farms each year in search of higher incomes elsewhere. Most succeeded. But it was not without costs. When a city person changes jobs, or even occupation, place of residence and lifestyle can remain virtually unchanged. But farming is a way of life as well as an occupation. Changing occupations, for most farm people means a change in place of residence, leaving behind familiar surroundings, friends, and relatives. No doubt, many had second thoughts about the wisdom of their move. But a few years after settling into their new homes, and having made new friends, the adjustment became less painful. Their higher incomes allowed a standard of living that could not have been achieved had they remained on farms.

The migration of people out of agriculture left the remaining land to be divided up among fewer but larger farms. Larger farms made it possible for the people remaining in agriculture to increase their incomes along with the incomes of nonfarm people.

FARM MECHANIZATION

The family farm is aptly named because it is typically owned and operated by a family. Some of the larger farms have hired hands, and others are partnerships such as siblings or parent-son or-daughter operations. But in the United States over 97 percent of the farm land is in the hands of families.

We know that in order to increase output, which occurs when farm size increases, there must be an increase in inputs. We know also that the amount of labor per farm in the United States has remained relatively constant over the past 60 years. The increase in land per farm and output per farm has been made possible by increasing the machinery input. The increase in the opportunity cost of farm labor relative to the cost of machinery services made the increase in machinery and land per farm economically feasible.[1]

The use of more and larger machines allowed farm families to operate larger farms and in so doing increase their incomes along with the income growth of nonfarm people.

DID MACHINES DISPLACE PEOPLE?

The decline in number of farm people along with the growth of farm mechanization has prompted some to argue that machines have pushed people off of farms. This could happen if the cost of machinery services decreases relative to the cost of labor. As a result there could be a decrease in the demand for labor which in turn would decrease labor earnings and in a sense force people out of

---

[1]Kislev, Yoav and Willis Peterson, "Prices, Technology, and Farm Size." *Journal of Political Economy,* 90 (Nov. 1982) pp. 578-95.

farming. This phenomenon might be called the labor-push hypothesis.

An alternative argument is that higher wages in nonfarm occupations have enticed people to leave agriculture. This can be described as a decrease in supply of labor to agriculture. In this case quantity of labor is decreased, similar to the case described above, but wages and labor earnings in agriculture are increased. This phenomenon could be termed the labor-pull hypothesis.

Which of the two alternative hypotheses explains the decrease in farm labor? Of course, both could occur simultaneously. Then the question becomes, which is dominant? A study of the mechanical cotton harvester in the United States revealed that 79 percent of the decline in hand picking of cotton was due to the increase in nonfarm wages—the pull effect; the remaining 21 percent was attributed to the reduced cost of machine harvesting—the push effect.[2]

Since the mechanical cotton harvester is viewed by many as the classic case of labor push, it appears that most of the reduction in number of farm people overall resulted from the increase in nonfarm wages. The relatively high economic growth that took place during the 1950s and 1960s, increased nonfarm incomes at a rapid rate and prompted millions of farm people to leave the land in search of higher incomes in the cities. Although the farm population in the United States has stabilized, rural to urban migration is an ongoing phenomenon in the developing countries.

PRODUCTIVITY GROWTH

Productivity is defined as units of output per unit of input. It can be measured as output per unit of a single input, called partial productivity, or output per unit of all inputs as a package. The latter is called total factor productivity. Both partial and the total measures are used to describe productivity growth in agriculture. The two most common partial productivity measures used in agriculture are land and labor productivity—crop yields per acre and output per unit of labor. In countries where population density is high and land is expensive relative to labor as in Asia, land productivity is of most interest. In countries such as the United States and Canada where population density is lower but labor is more expensive, labor productivity takes on greater importance, although crop yields are considered important indicators in these countries too.

The main problem with partial productivity measures, such as crop yields or labor productivity, is that they are influenced by the use of other inputs. Crop yields or land productivity is increased when more fertilizer and chemicals are applied per acre. Thus, higher output per acre which might give the impression that farmers are becoming more efficient, simply reflects the application of more

---

[2]Peterson, Willis and Yoav Kislev, "The Cotton Harvester in Retrospect: Labor Displacement or Replacement?" *Journal of Economic History,* Vol. XLVI, No. 1 (March 1986) pp. 199-216.

nonland inputs per acre. The same is true of labor productivity. Higher output per unit of labor occurs mainly because of greater mechanization.

The total factor productivity measure where output is divided by a measure of all inputs, removes the problems mentioned above. But an increase in total productivity also gives the impression that more output is forthcoming per unit of input. Strictly speaking, this is impossible. Unless there is a change in the basic laws of physics, biology, and chemistry, more output cannot be obtained without more inputs. How, then, can there be an increase in total factor productivity?

At the present, inputs used in agriculture, as well as in all other industries, are much different than they were decades ago. Over time, new inputs have appeared on the scene and virtually all inputs, including labor, have increased in quality. If these new and improved inputs are not completely and accurately measured, the denominator in the output/input ratio will be understated. As a result it will appear that more output is forthcoming per unit of input. In reality, more output is forthcoming because of the use of more inputs. Higher quality inputs are in a sense more inputs than those of lower quality. Thus the observation that productivity has increased should not be taken to mean that the added output is a free gift of nature. It takes money and resources to improve the quality of inputs.

PRODUCTIVITY GROWTH AND FARM INCOME

At first glance, one would be inclined to believe that growth in agricultural productivity is a phenomenon to be desired by both farmers and consumers. As noted previously, new technology has the effect of decreasing costs and increasing supply, that is, shifting the supply curve to the right. This results in a larger quantity exchanged in the market, and lower prices paid by consumers. Consumers like this. However, lower product prices received by farmers are not welcomed by them.

If the demand for products sold by farmers is inelastic, an increase in supply causes price to decline more in percentage terms than the increase in quantity. As a result, the total revenue received from the sale of farm products can decline when supply increases. Thus farm income decreases. For farmers as a group, technological change decreases farm income from what it would otherwise be.

The phenomenon described above is most likely to exist for products consumed domestically. In this case, demand is likely to be inelastic. For products exported on the world market, demand facing agriculture will be more elastic. This is because the Unites States is only one of many sellers in the world market. Each seller does not have a big impact on world market price when it changes the quantity it exports. In this case, total revenue will increase when technology improves and supply increases.

Although farmers can suffer a short run loss of income during times of rapid technological change, in the long run they will benefit by the increase in overall economic growth. Farmers which are part of a high income society have higher incomes than those in a poor society. High income societies also have more generous farm programs.

FARM PROGRAMS

Typically, average incomes of farm families have lagged behind those of nonfarm families, although by 1991 the difference was not great. Median income of farm and nonfarm families in that year was $32,889 and $36,002 respectively. However, the difference was relatively large during the Great Depression of the 1930s. In addition to low farm product prices, the widespread drought of that period decreased the saleable output. Income also lagged by a relatively large amount during the 1950s and 1960s. High economic growth during these decades resulted in a rapid growth of nonfarm incomes. Moreover, rapid technological change on farms caused supply to increase more rapidly than demand, thereby causing prices received by farmers to be depressed.

In an attempt to improve farm incomes, the U.S. government initiated farm price support programs during the 1930s. Essentially the programs consisted of the government purchasing surplus products in order to remove them from the market and bolster prices. Farmers fared well during World War II, although subsides on certain products were continued in an effort to stimulate production. During the post World War II era, the programs continued. Price supports were established on certain products, mainly corn, wheat, milk, tobacco, and sugar crops. In an effort to hold down the resulting surpluses, the government either paid farmers to take land out of production, or required them to do so to be eligible for the higher support prices. However surpluses still accumulated because farmers took the poorest land out of production and utilized more chemicals and fertilizer as land substitutes. (Surpluses always occur when market price is supported above the market equilibrium.) Except for a brief time during the world food scare of the mid to late 1970s, farm programs have contributed substantially to farm income. In 1992, government payments amounted to 18 percent of net farm income in the United States.

Farm programs have come under increasing criticism in recent years. For one thing, the programs provides the greatest income support to the largest farms. This occurs because the payments are based on production and/or ownership of land. For example, if the price of wheat is increased 50 cents per bushel because of the program, a small farmer that sells 500 bushels receives $250 in income support. A large farm that sells, say, 50,000 bushels receives $25,000 in payments. It has been reported that the large, land owning families have received payments of a million dollars or more per year for not growing crops on their land. Programs that increase the incomes of the well-to-do with tax money taken from low and middle income people are hard to justify.

A third unwanted outcome of farm programs is the accumulation of surpluses. Essentially this amounts to producing products no one wants to buy at the higher support prices. The practice wastes resources. Of greater importance, the government sells the surplus commodities to the less developed countries at free or subsidized prices. The subsidized surplus commodities compete with domestically produced food in the recipient countries, and lowers farm prices in these countries. This makes agriculture less profitable in these countries and retards their development.

One might defend the practice of distributing cheap or free food to starving people in the less developed countries as a humanitarian gesture. But the question then becomes, is there a better way to help these people other than penalizing their domestic agriculture and setting back their economic development?

FARM PRICE INSTABILITY

Compared to the prices of most other goods and services, prices received by farmers tend to be unstable. Prices change because of shifts in demand, supply, or both. For products consumed domestically, demand is quite stable. Food consumption does not fluctuate very much; people have to eat. Most of the price instability in the domestic market comes from supply shifts. These shifts are caused by year-to-year changes in growing conditions, which are primarily weather, insects, and disease related. In a year of good growing conditions, yields are high and supply shifts to the right. This causes lower prices. Conversely in poor crop years, yields are smaller, supply decreases, and market price increases.

It is also important to note that demand for agricultural products in the domestic market is rather inelastic, at least for broad categories of products.

Figure 20–1 Price Changes with Elastic and Inelastic Demand

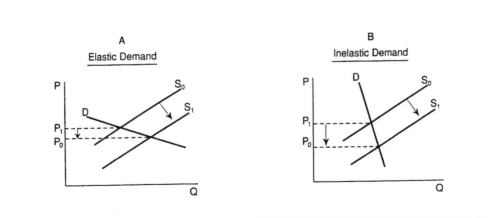

This occurs because stomachs are rather inelastic; people do not eat a lot more if price declines, nor a lot less if price increases. The inelastic nature of food demand causes a wider fluctuation in price than if demand were more elastic. This is illustrated in Figure 20–1, A and B. Both have the same shift (increase) in supply. In panel A, demand is drawn to be elastic; in panel B, inelastic. Note that the price decline resulting from the given increase in supply is greater in panel B than in panel A.

Years of favorable growing conditions and bumper crops are considered good by most people, farmers and consumers alike. But the low prices that accompany high yields can decrease farm income. Recall that when demand is inelastic total revenue declines when supply increase because price declines proportionately more than quantity increases.

The situation for products exported on the world market is somewhat different. Mainly these are wheat, corn, and soybeans. In 1990, 58 percent of the total U.S. wheat crop was exported. For corn and soybeans, exports were 38 and 35 percent of total production respectively.

Demand for exported crops also can be unstable. This occurs because of changes in growing conditions around the world. If a region or country experiences a crop failure, it will increase its demand for commodities imported from other countries. Thus one can expect greater year-to-year fluctuations in demand for exported commodities than for those produced mainly for the domestic market.

This is not to say that prices will be more unstable for exported crops. It depends on the correlation between demand and supply shifts. If export demand increases when domestic supply increases, there may not be much of a decrease in price. On the other hand, a demand decrease coupled with a supply increase will cause an even greater price decline than if the product were sold mainly in the domestic market.

FOOD STAMPS

The distribution of surplus food began in the 1930s during the Great Depression. After the end of World War II when surpluses became a problem again, renewed efforts were made to increase demand for agricultural products. As a result, in 1961 a pilot food stamp program was begun under the Kennedy Administration. The official Food Stamp Act was passed in 1964 during the Johnson Administration.

The initial motivation for the use of food stamps probably came from the dual desire to dispose of surpluses and to improve the diets of the needy. Now the program is viewed mainly as an income supplement to low income people, although it no doubt has the effect of increasing the demand for food. Studies have found that food stamp recipients increase their spending on food in the range of 20 to 35 cents for each dollar of food stamps received.

Until 1979, food stamp recipients, except for the very poorest people, were required to purchase the stamps. This requirement was dropped at the time because of the difficulty of recipients to raise the cash to buy the stamps. The utilization of food stamps increased rapidly during the 1970s and the early 1980s, periods of inflationary conditions and/or high unemployment. By 1992 about 25 million persons participated in the program; 10 percent of the U.S. population.

The value of stamps received by a family depends on income and family size. To be eligible, a family's income cannot exceed 130 percent of the official poverty level for that household size. Also there are limits on a family's assets. Recipients cannot own a car worth more than $4,500 (in 1992) unless it is required for work, and cannot have over $2,000 in cash or liquid assets; $3,000 for the elderly. If a family increases its income, the value of stamps received decreases by 30 cents for each extra dollar of income earned. In 1992, actual food stamp benefits per recipient averaged $821. This amounts to about 75 cents per meal. Food stamps do not allow for a lavish diet but they do help to stave off hunger.

Although the food stamp program has come under some public criticism, it is viewed by experts as a desirable method of income transfer. It is an efficient program, not subject to a high bureaucratic overhead, and unlike the farm program, it helps those most in need of help. It also meets with the humanitarian objectives of society by increasing the access of the poor to a basic necessity, namely food. Of course, it should be recognized that recipients increase their purchases of other things as well as food. The stamps release income from food purchases that can be used for nonfood items.

Most of the criticism of the food stamp program has come from the sale of stamps for cash by recipients, or their use to pay for nonfood items. This is an indication that the marginal utility per dollar of nonfood items is greater than it is for food. Thus the requirement that recipients buy food with the extra food stamp money forces them to a lower level of utility than if they received cash that they could spend as they see fit.

THE ENGEL CURVE

A discussion of food would not be complete without touching on the Engel curve. Ernst Engel, a German statistician who lived during the 19th Century, observed in his study of the spending habits of Belgian families that "The poorer the family, the greater the proportion of its total expenditure that must be devoted to the provision of food." In other words, as income increases, expenditures on food increase less rapidly. The relationship between income and food expenditures, referred to as the Engel Curve, is shown in Figure 20–2. At some point, one might expect the curve to become horizontal. There is a limit to how much one can eat.

Figure 20–2 The Engel Curve

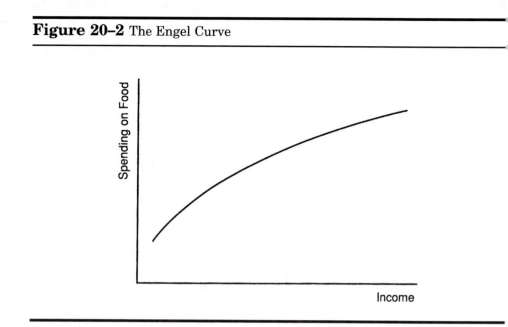

Although Engel's observation in the 19th century still holds true today, a substantial proportion of what people think of as food purchases is in reality services and packaging. Most items found in grocery stores have been processed or altered in some way from their original state. Bread and cookies are baked, meat is dressed and cut into individual servings, canned goods and breakfast cereals are processed, and so on.

Even more services are embodied in food when it is purchased in restaurants. And the amount of services purchased varies a lot among restaurants. At one end of the spectrum is the fast food place serving a limited menu, prepared by a part-time fry cook. At the other end of the scale, more services are purchased when food is consumed in an elegant restaurant, rich in ambiance, and prepared by a skilled chef. There is considerable leeway in how much one spends on food when services are added.

QUESTIONS

1. In the early 1900s the typical family farm consisted of about 160 acres. In the late 1900s average farm size is about 460 acres. Why the growth in farm size?

2. What change in relative prices made possible the increase in size of family farms?

3. John Steinbeck in his book *Grapes of Wrath* argued that farmers have been "tractored off the land." Translate this statement into a supply and demand framework. What is an alternative explanation for the migration off farms?

4. Productivity growth reflects the fact that more output is obtained from a given quantity of inputs. Comment.

5. a. Why have farm programs created surpluses?
   b. In addition to surpluses, what are the other undesirable side-effects of farm programs?

6. Why are farm prices more unstable than prices of most other commodities?

7. Some food stamp recipients sell their stamps for cash but at a discount from what the stamps could buy at the grocery store. The practice is against the law. Why do recipients do this?

8. What is implied by the Engel Curve about the income elasticity of demand as incomes increase?

SELF-TEST

1. Economic growth which results in higher incomes of nonfarm people:
   a. results in a rural to urban migration
   b. results in a shortage of food
   c. causes a decrease in farm size
   d. has little effect on agriculture

2. Families have been able to enlarge the size of their farms by:
   a. working harder and longer hours
   b. hiring nonfamily workers
   c. relying on more mechanization
   d. changing the crop mix towards less labor intensive crops.

3. Incomes of farm families have increased along with incomes of nonfarm families by:
   a. increasing the number of family workers per farm
   b. increasing the prices that farmers receive for their products
   c. the greater use of unpaid family labor and less of hired employees
   d. increasing farm size

4. The utilization of more machinery per farm worker was made possible by:
   a. higher prices of labor relative to machinery
   b. higher prices of machinery relative to labor
   c. higher farm product prices
   d. government price supports on farm products

5. According to research findings, the majority of people who left agriculture did so because of:
   a. higher wages in nonfarm occupations, the labor push effect.
   b. higher wages in nonfarm occupations, the labor pull effect.
   c. lower prices of machinery services, the labor push effect.
   d. lower prices of machinery services, the labor pull effect.

6. Growth in total factor productivity in U.S. agriculture can be attributed to:
   a. the increase in farmers' ability to obtain more output from a given amount of input
   b. the reduction in use of high quality inputs
   c. the decline in number of farmers
   d. unmeasured quality improvements in inputs

7. Technological change_____supply and

_____ farm income if demand is inelastic.

a. increases; increases

b. decreases; increases

c. decreases; decreases

d. increases; decreases

8. The phenomenon described in question 7 above is most likely to occur with:

   a. products produced for the domestic market

   b. products produced for the export market

   c. products produced for home consumption by farmers themselves

   d. wheat and corn

9. The main beneficiaries of farm programs:

   a. consumers

   b. small farmers

   c. large farmers

   d. small town businesses

10. Undesirable side-effects of farm programs:

    a. higher applications of chemicals and fertilizers

    b. unwanted surpluses

    c. retardation of agricultural development in LDCs

    d. all of the above

11. Farm product prices tend to be_____stable than other prices because demand is_____and supply is_____

    a. less; inelastic; unstable

    b. less; elastic; unstable

    c. more; inelastic, stable

    d. more; elastic; stable

12. Food stamps are now utilized by about_____percent of the population. To be eligible a family's income cannot exceed_____percent of the official poverty level.

a. 10; 30

b. 10; 130

c. 30; 30

d. 30; 130

13. An attempt by food stamp recipients to sell their food stamps for cash is an indication that their marginal utility per dollar for other goods and services_____the marginal utility per dollar of food. Making the sale of food stamps illegal forces recipients to act:

    a. is less than; in their own best interest

    b. is less then; against their self interest

    c. is greater than; in their own best interest

    d. is greater than; against their self interest

14. According to the Engel Curve, as family income increases they spend:

    a. more in total on food

    b. less in total on food

    c. a larger proportion of their income on food

    d. a smaller proportion of their income on food

15. As family income increases beyond the middle income range that now exists in the United States, the increase in expenditures on food that does occur is due mainly to:

    a. larger families

    b. people eating more

    c. purchase of more services

    d. higher prices in affluent neighborhoods

Part VII

Factor Markets

_____

Chapters 21-24

Chapter 21

Labor Markets

Key Concepts

Demand for Labor

Profit maximizing rule for input use

Supply of labor

Wage determination

Shifts in demand for labor

Labor demand shifters

Shifts in the supply of labor

Wage and employment changes

Wage differences

The next four chapters deal with the markets for the two primary factors of production—labor and capital. The main objective of this chapter is to show how wages are determined and why they differ among occupations.

THE DEMAND FOR LABOR

The labor market, like the product market, consists of demanders and suppliers. The price of labor (wage or salary) is determined by the interaction of demand and supply. Certain groups in society may not like the market-determined wage and may attempt to change the wage. But, let us first see how the market functions before we study attempts to modify it.

The basic concept of demand for labor was presented in Chapter 8—marginal physical product (MPP) of an input. Recall that MPP is units of additional output obtained from one additional unit of an input. To derive the demand for labor we only need to assign values to MPP.

The value of marginal physical product (VMP) is defined as the value of additional output that is obtained from one more unit of the input. The VMP of an input for a perfectly competitive firm is obtained by multiplying the price of the output (P) by MPP:

$$\text{VMP} = \text{P x MPP}$$

The VMP label is commonly used in conjunction with perfectly competitive firms—ones that face a perfectly elastic demand.

A parallel concept for imperfectly competitive firms that face a downward-sloping demand is referred to as marginal revenue product (MRP). Its definition is the same as VMP. The difference is that MRP is calculated by multiplying MR times MPP.

$$\text{MRP} = \text{MR x MPP}$$

Since product price equals MR for a perfectly competitive firm, MRP can be used for either type of firm.

A graph of VMP or MRP of an input is a demand for that input. The explanation is given in terms of VMP, but the same is true for MRP.

Because of the law of diminishing returns, the MPP of an input declines as more of it is used. Therefore, the graph of MPP is a downward-sloping line as in Figure 21–1A. The VMP curve shown in panel B is the same shape; the only difference is that the VMP graph has value or dollars on the vertical axis.

If a firm wishes to maximize profits, it increases the use of an input up to the point where the input price is equal to VMP. If a firm stops short of this point, it gives up profits unnecessarily. This is illustrated in Figure 21–1B. Suppose the price of labor is $75 (per day) and the firm hires 40 labor days. The fortieth day of labor adds $100 to the firm's output. Therefore, if the firm hired one more day of labor beyond 40 it would add roughly $25 to its net profits. Naturally, the

FIGURE 21–1 Relationship between Marginal Physical Product and Value
of Marginal Product

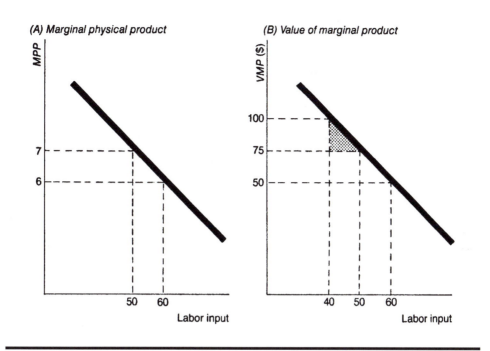

firm would do so. By continuing to add labor up to 50 days it adds to its profits
a value equal to the shaded triangle in Figure 21–1B. Consequently, if labor
received a wage of $75 per day, the firm would hire 50 days, say, per week. At
$100 per day, 40 days are hired. And at a $50 wage, 60 days are hired.
Therefore, the firm's VMP curve of an input also is its demand curve for the
input. Remember, though, that it assumes profit maximization by the firm.

PROFIT-MAXIMIZING RULE FOR INPUT USE

In deriving the demand for an input such as labor, we have implicitly derived
the profit-maximizing rule for input use: hire an input until the price of the
input (P_x) equals the VMP of the input:

$$P_x = VMP_x$$

It is proven in the appendix to this chapter that the profit-maximizing rule for
input use is equivalent to the profit-maximizing rule for output use, $P = MC$,
presented in Chapter 10.

The market demand for labor is the summation at each wage of the amount demanded by all employers in the market. The procedure is similar to what is used to obtain the market demand for a product.[1]

THE SUPPLY OF LABOR

Labor supply is the other half of the labor market. Similar to the definition of product supply, the supply of labor is a positive relationship between price (wage) and quantity. This implies that people supply more labor when wage is high (other things equal) than when it is low.

It is useful to investigate in a bit more detail the main factors that determine a person's willingness to supply labor. Assume there are two uses of a person's time: work and leisure. The latter includes sleep and any activity that takes up a person's time when he or she is not working for a wage or salary. The money earned by working can be converted into goods and services or saved. If the wage rate increases, the amount of goods that can be purchased also increases. Therefore, if a person takes a day off with a high wage, more goods and services are given up than if the wage was lower. The opportunity cost of leisure is the goods and services given up by not working. When the wage increases, the opportunity cost increases. Another way of saying this is that when the wage increases, the cost of leisure increases. Therefore, we can expect people to "buy" less leisure (work more) when its price is high. This is called the substitution effect. People substitute goods (work) for leisure when the price of leisure (wage) increases.

There is, however, a second offsetting factor: the income effect. When wage and income increase, people have more money to "purchase" leisure; they may, therefore, work less. It is not possible to predict which of the two effects is stronger. If the substitution effect dominates, the person's labor supply curve will be upward sloping. If the income effect is stronger, the labor supply curve will bend backwards. If the two effects offset each other, the supply of labor will be vertical or perfectly inelastic. The relative magnitude of the two effects can vary from a low wage to a high wage as shown in Figure 21–2.

Over the last half-century, the length of the workweek in the United States has not changed much. This indicates that the two effects offset each other as the wage rate has risen over time. Of course, supply has continually increased due to population growth.

There may be some question whether people have much choice over the length

---

[1] This procedure requires the assumption of a constant output price. In reality, the market demand will be less elastic than the summation of individual employer demand curves because as more labor is hired and output increases, product price decreases, which in turn decreases the VMP of labor.

FIGURE 21–2 Wage Response and Market Supply of Labor

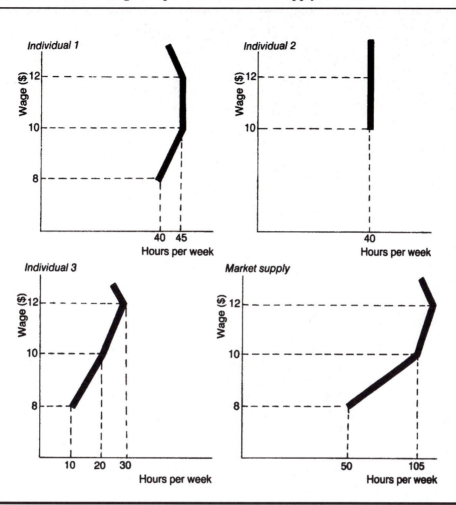

of the workweek; most jobs entail 40 hours. However, if people really wanted to work a shorter week, employers who responded to this wish would be preferred and could have a greater choice in whom they hire. Other employers would follow suit, which would cause the nation's workweek to decrease in length.

The differing response to wage increases is illustrated in Figure 21–2. The first three diagrams represent the supply of labor by three individuals. At $8 per hour, individual 1 is willing to supply 40 hours a week of labor. As the wage increases to $10 per hour, she increases her workweek to 45 hours. At $12 per hour, she works the same amount, 45 hours, and at wages exceeding $12, she reduces the length of her workweek. In other words, at the $12 and over wage, the substitution effect does not override the income effect. Individual 2, on the other hand, does not enter the labor force until wages rise to $10 per hour. In the range of wages considered, the workweek remains at 40 hours. Individual 3 increases hours worked from 10 to 30 as wages rise from $8 to $12 per hour. These are examples of what we might expect from different individuals. The first person might be the breadwinner of a family, the second might be semiretired and decide to enter the labor market at a $10 wage, and the third might be a college student holding a part-time job.

If we assume, to keep the example simple, that the three individuals compromise the available supply of labor, the market supply can be derived by adding together the quantity supplied at each price. At $8 per hour, individuals 1 and 3 supply 40 and 10 hours, respectively, making a total of 50 hours. At the $10-per-hour wage level, individual 2 is included in the labor force. Thus, along with the slight increase in labor offered by individuals 1 and 3, raising the wage to $10 obtains a total of 105 hours supplied.

Note that the market supply of labor will be more elastic than the supply of individuals currently working in the market. This is because of the entrance of people into the labor market as wages rise. The result is greater response to wage increases for the market than is true for the average individual in the market.

WAGE DETERMINATION

Wages are determined in the labor market in the same way that prices of ordinary goods and services are determined in their respective markets—by demand and supply. The intersection of the two curves sets the equilibrium wage. If actual wage is above the equilibrium, quantity supplied exceeds quantity demanded and a surplus results. In the labor market, a surplus is called unemployment. At a wage below the equilibrium, there is a shortage. If the labor market acted like other markets, a surplus should drive the wage down and a shortage should drive it up. The latter seems to occur, but institutional and psychological factors can keep the wage from declining. The apparent inflexibility of wages on the downside is discussed later.

A. Perfectly Competitive Employer

A perfectly competitive employer of labor hires a small share of the labor market and therefore has no control over the market wage. Such an employer faces a perfectly elastic supply of labor as illustrated in Figure 21–3B. The supply facing the firm corresponds to the wage determined in the market as shown in panel A. To maximize profits, the firm hires Q_1 of labor. Stopping at Q_0 reduces the firm's profits by the area of the shaded triangle in panel B.

Virtually all employers are perfectly competitive buyers of labor because they hire a small share of the market. Even a large firm in a small town can add to its labor force by advertising in out-of-town newspapers. Thus, it can attract

FIGURE 21–3 Wage Determination: Perfect Competition in the Labor Market

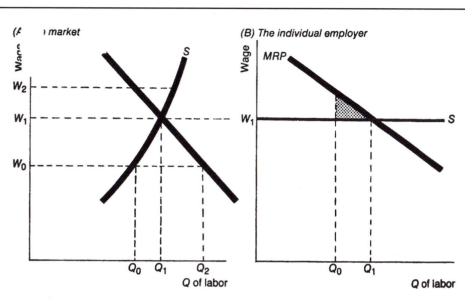

workers from the entire country. No single employer hires a large share of the nation's working population.

B. Imperfectly Competitive Employer

Although it is not common to find employers that are imperfectly competitive, to round out the discussion the imperfectly competitive case is presented. An imperfectly competitive employer faces an upward-sloping supply of labor. This means that the firm must increase wages if it wishes to expand its labor force. Or, it can lower wages if it hires fewer people.

A consequence of an upward-sloping labor supply for a firm is that the additional or marginal cost of adding more labor exceeds the wage of the extra workers. The reason is that the firm must pay a higher wage to attract additional employees, and this higher wage must be paid to all employees.

The cost of adding additional labor is called the marginal resource cost (MRC) of labor. At any level of labor hired, the MRC of labor is greater than the wage paid. Thus, if we wish to represent this relationship on a diagram, the MRC curve lies above the supply curve and rises at a faster rate, as shown in Figure 21–4.

Note that marginal resource cost on the buying side of the labor market is analogous to marginal revenue (MR) on the selling side of the product market.

FIGURE 21–4 Wage Determination: Imperfect Competition in the Labor Market

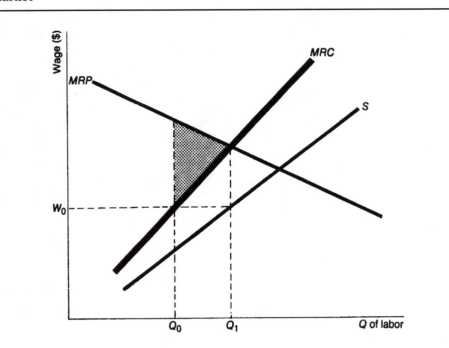

Marginal revenue is less than price because to sell more, the price reduction must apply to all units sold; MRC is greater than the wage because to hire more, the higher wage must apply to all labor employed—not just the marginal workers. In other words, the MRC of an additional worker is the wage paid to the worker plus the small increase in total wages that must be paid to each of the firm's other employees.

If the firm wishes to maximize profits, it attempts to equate the MRC of its labor with labor's MRP, and it hires Q_1 of labor. If it stopped short of this point, say at Q_0, the contribution of a marginal unit of labor would exceed its cost. As we saw in the preceding section, increasing the labor hired from Q_0 to Q_1 results in an addition to total profits that is equal in value to the shaded triangle in Figure 21–4.

Also note in Figure 21–4 that the wage paid by the imperfectly competitive employer of labor is equal to W_0, the point on the supply curve corresponding to Q_1 the quantity of labor hired. At this quantity of labor, people are willing to work for W_0. Unlike the situation for a perfectly competitive employer, MRP is greater than the wage. This is not to say that the imperfectly competitive firm exploits labor. By attempting to maximize profits, this type of firm behaves exactly the same as a perfectly competitive employer. It is hiring labor up to the point where the additional cost of adding another unit of labor (MRC) is equal to the contribution of that worker to the value of output (MRP).

Wages paid by a perfectly competitive buyer of labor should not be any different from wages paid by an imperfectly competitive buyer of comparable labor in the same market. If wages were not equal, employees would quit the low-paying employer and switch to the higher-paying one.

It is not necessary for all employees to be mobile to prevent long-run wage differences between individual employers or markets. When wages paid by an employer differ from wages paid elsewhere, the movement of a small percentage of all employees from low- to high-wage employers usually is enough to force wages up in low-wage markets and bring them down in high-wage jobs. Also, an inequality of wages between areas or regions usually results in some employers moving to the low-wage areas, as illustrated by the movement of northern industry to the South after World War II. This increases labor demand in the low-wage areas and decreases demand in the high-wage areas. As a result, wage differences narrowed.

To differentiate imperfect competition on the buying side of the market from the selling side, a market where there are few buyers is called an *oligopsony*. This is comparable to an oligopoly, which characterizes a situation of few sellers in a market. If there were only one buyer of labor, the firm would be called a *monopsony*, comparable to a monopoly on the selling side.

This does not mean, however, that an oligopoly on the selling side results in oligopsony on the buying side, or vice versa. The same is true of a monopsony. For example, a local light and power company might have a monopoly on the sale of electricity, but it is a perfectly competitive buyer of labor since the firm can draw its employees from a regional or even national labor market where there are many thousands of people possessing the required skills.

SHIFTS IN DEMAND FOR LABOR

We have studied how wages are determined in two kinds of labor markets. Now, we will explain changes in wages and levels of employment. As noted in Chapter 12, if a product market is in equilibrium, the only way a change in price can occur is by a change or shift in either demand or supply of the product, or both. The same is true for labor. Wages change in response to a change in market demand, supply, or both.

Let us look at changes or shifts in the demand for labor. Most of what we say about shifts in demand for labor can be applied to the demand for any input. Recall from the product market discussion that an increase in demand occurs when it shifts upward and to the right, as shown by D_2 in Figure 21–5A or MRP_2 in Figure 21–5B. Notice that the equilibrium or profit-maximizing wage also increases. Conversely a decrease in labor demand results in a decrease in wages, as illustrated by D_0 or MRP_0 in Figure 21–5.

FIGURE 21–5 Shifts in the Demand for Labor

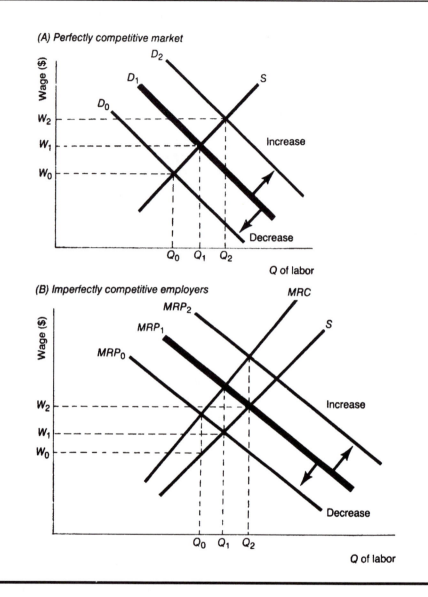

Because the value of marginal product (VMP) for a perfectly competitive buyer of labor is derived by multiplying marginal physical product (MPP) times product price, we expect either a change in product price or a change in MPP of labor to shift the demand for labor. The same is true for an imperfectly competitive buyer of labor because a change in price also results in a change in marginal revenue. We can conclude, therefore, that the demand for labor will shift in response to a change in product price or a change in the productivity of labor. The same is true for any input.

DEMAND SHIFTERS

The following are the main labor demand shifters.

A. Changes in Product Price. A rise in product price results in a higher VMP or marginal revenue product for a given level of input use. The opposite is true for a decline in product price.

B. Changes in Marginal Physical Product. There are three major factors that can change or shift an input's MPP. These are:

1. Changes in Quantity or Quality of Complementary Inputs. A complementary input is defined as one which increases the MPP of a given input when the use of the complement is increased. Consider, for example, a worker digging a hole with a spade. When given a back-hoe, the worker's productivity or MPP increases. Thus, the back-hoe is a complement to labor, as are all kinds of raw materials. Without bricks, mortar, or lumber, for example, a construction worker would not be productive.

An increase in the quality of a complementary input has the same effect as an increase in its quantity; that is, it increases or shifts to the right the MPP curve of the input. For example, a secretary with a new personal computer will be more productive than she would be with a slow manual typewriter.

2. Changes in Quantity or Quality of Substitute Inputs. A substitute input is defined as one that decreases the MPP of a given input when the substitute use is increased. For example, the use of a second worker on one spade reduces the MPP of the first worker who could use it only part of the time.

It is not obvious in a given production activity whether two inputs are complements or substitutes. Furthermore, this relationship can change at different levels or mixes of input use. For example, adding the back-hoe to the two workers with the spade increases the MPP of the worker who operates the machine, but it decreases the MPP of the second worker if that person just stands and watches.

For some labor, therefore, capital or machines are complements; they increase labor's productivity. For other labor, however, usually persons with the lowest skills or seniority on the job, capital may be a substitute that forces them to find other employment. It is this situation that we hear about most regarding automation and unemployment.

An increase in the quality of a substitute input also is similar to an increase in the quantity of such an input. In this case, quality improvement decreases or shifts to the left the MPP curve of the input. For example, an increase in the speed and capacity of a computer decreases the MPP of a bookkeeper if it leaves the person with nothing to do.

3. Changes in Quality of the Input. This factor is especially important for labor. Through education and training, people have become more productive; they have increased their MPP, which has resulted in an increased demand for their labor.

SHIFTS IN THE SUPPLY OF LABOR

Labor supply tends to be more stable than labor demand. The overall supply of labor for the entire economy depends on the population. The more people, the more labor supplied at a given wage. Thus, the aggregate supply of labor in the United States has increased with its population. The proportion of the population participating in the labor force also affects the labor supply. Recently in the United States, increasing numbers of women have joined the labor force-increasing the overall supply of labor. Also a greater proportion of high school and college students is working part-time, which adds to the nation's labor supply.

The increase in education and skills of the labor force also contributes to the supply of labor. If we measure labor in homogeneous efficiency units, a given number of highly skilled people is equivalent to more labor than an equal number of less-skilled people. In the previous section, we mentioned that an increase in people's skills tends to increase their productivity and, hence, their MPP and demand. An increase in the wages from increased skills requires, therefore, that the demand for skills increase more than the supply of skills.

The supply of labor facing a given industry or area also depends on the area's population, although in this case, the supply of labor can also shift in response to a change in wages in another industry or area. Suppose, for example, there is a sudden increase in the demand for labor, as with the oil discoveries in northern Alaska. The increase in wages for people to operate oil rigs attracted more labor to this occupation. But, this reduced (shifted to the left) the supply of labor to other nearby industries such as mining, fishing, and the service trades, causing wages in these occupations to increase as well.

WAGE AND EMPLOYMENT CHANGES

There has been a long-run, upward trend in wages and employment in the United States. Because of our population growth and the increased participation of women in the labor force, the supply of labor has been increasing or shifting to the right. In order for wages to increase, the demand for labor must shift to the right more rapidly than the labor supply. Otherwise, there cannot have been an increase in wages and employment, as occurs in the 1950s and 1960s. Since then supply has increased more rapidly than demand, causing some decrease in real wages.

The two main factors that shift labor demand to the right and raise wages are: (1) an increase in the use of complementary inputs, mainly capital, and (2) an increase in the quality of the labor force through education. Recall from the preceding section that these two factors increase the productivity or MPP of labor and thereby increase labor demand.

For individual geographic areas, industries, or firms, however, there are instances of a decrease in the demand for labor. This can occur if there is a decreased demand for the good or service produced. As a result, the firms involved reduce the quantity of inputs used that are complementary to labor, mainly capital and raw materials. There is a corresponding decline in labor's MPP and consequently a decline in labor demand, as shown in D_0 in Figure 21–5A.

The logical expectation in this situation is a decline in wages and employment. If we were dealing with a nonhuman input, this would occur. But with labor, it is unwise for a firm to immediately reduce the wages of its employees in response to a decrease in its marginal revenue product (MRP) of labor. An across-the-board wage cut affects all employees and, to say the least, leaves them unhappy. Disgruntled employees are not conducive to high labor productivity and profits. Moreover, if labor is represented by a union, the wage contract may forbid any wage decrease.

Rather than reduce wages when there is a decline in demand for labor, most firms choose to lay off some people, at least in the short run. A layoff affects the firm's marginal employees leaving the remainder virtually untouched. The people who are laid off may be disgruntled, but they are not around to affect the firm's productivity. In the event of a severe and prolonged decline in the demand for labor in an area or by an industry, we would see some downward adjustment in money wages, such as occurred during the Great Depression and again in the 1980s and early 1990s.

The stickiness of wages on the downside causes a surplus of labor known as unemployment. If wage rates were completely flexible, any decrease in demand for labor would cause a reduction in wage rates. As soon as wages settled to lower equilibrium levels, the surplus labor (i.e., involuntary unemployment) would disappear.

There are occupations in which wages have increased substantially over the years but the productivity of workers has not increased much. Some examples include teachers, barbers, and taxi drivers. One can explain the wage increase by the upward shift in the supply curve of labor facing these occupations. If most other occupations have experienced wage increases, people will not enter occupations in which labor productivity has not increased unless they receive wages comparable to what they could earn in occupations in which labor productivity has increased. The relative prices of goods and services will increase in areas where wages increase without productivity gains, however. Therefore, certain occupations that do not experience gains in labor productivity still can enjoy wage increases if most other occupations in the economy experience a gain in labor productivity.

WAGE DIFFERENCES

The large differences between the wages or salaries of different people or groups sometimes seem unjustified. The movie star or professional athlete may earn several million dollars per year, possibly working six months, while others have to toil from dawn to dusk for the minimum wage. Why?

Wage differences are explained by demand and supply. A person lucky enough to possess scarce talent in high demand, such as throwing a baseball or football exceedingly well, tends to enjoy a high wage. Other talents, such as pushing or pulling a lever on a machine all day, which are in abundant supply relative to their demand, are not as well paid.

Some occupations require lengthy training periods, which reduces the supply. The doctor, lawyer, or college professor who spends 8 to 10 years preparing for a profession must be compensated for the investment, or it would not pay to enter the profession. Substantial wage differences exist within and between professions even though the educational requirement is similar. For example, the internationally known heart surgeon or Nobel Prize winner often enjoys an income that is substantially larger than unknown colleagues. Salary or income differences reflect differences in ability and productivity. One does not enjoy an international reputation without some special accomplishment.

Some professions enjoy a higher average level of income than others with similar educational requirements because of a strong union. Medical doctors, for example, tend to earn more than college professors with a Ph.D. The former are represented by a strong "union," the American Medical Association (AMA),while college professors are not, for the most part, unionized. We will discuss how unions and organizations such as the AMA influence the incomes of members in the next chapter.

There are certain occupations where, in order to enter, one must pay a substantial entrance fee. Two well-known examples are seats on the stock exchange and taxicab medallions in New York City; each sells for thousands of dollars. The existence of an entrance fee indicates that employment in these occupations is not open to all who are qualified and, as a result, the hourly earnings of persons who buy their way in are larger than what could be earned in alternative occupations. For new entrants, the opportunity cost of the money invested in the entrance fee equalizes the net earnings of occupations with other alternatives.

Wages or salaries also reflect differences in working conditions. An occupation that requires exposure to the elements or special hazards tends to pay a higher salary than jobs that provide comfortable, safe working conditions. Construction workers, for example, earn substantially more per year than bank clerks or shoe salespersons. Similarly, steel workers who assemble the superstructure of today's skyscrapers are well paid for their physically demanding work and the risks they take. In general, jobs that present special risks or disadvantages, such as working in remote areas, must offer higher salaries to attract people. The supply of people for these jobs is small relative to the demand, so their wages are high. The relatively high wages of construction workers are also attributed in part to a strong union, and to the seasonality of their work. The wages lost during days when work is impossible because of bad weather are made up during the days when they can work.

On the other hand, occupations that allow one to work in air-conditioned comfort tend to offer somewhat lower salaries, given the educational requirements that accompany such jobs. People who work in these jobs take part of their salaries in attractive working conditions. For these jobs, the supply of people is large relative to the demand, so wages are lower than in less-attractive jobs.

The impact of working conditions and skills on wages is shown in Table 21–1. The highest hourly wage rates are in mining and construction—occupations requiring workers to bear considerable risk of injury or death, or to work in extreme heat or cold. The skill premium shows up in the wages of construction workers in the special trades—electricians, plumbers, bricklayers, and so forth. Not only do these occupations require considerable skill, they also involve harsh working conditions.

The pleasant working conditions of office or store work are reflected in the lower wages of workers in retail trade, finance, and services. In the latter category, skill differences appear by comparing hotel workers with persons offering repair services. Also the low hourly pay of hotel workers and restaurant employees is offset by tips. People will work for lower hourly wages if they receive tips from customers.

The figures in Table 21–1 do not include the highest-skilled professionals such as scientists, medical doctors, lawyers, and corporate executives whose salaries are likely to be in the $100 to $200 per hour range and beyond. Successful business entrepreneurs enjoy similar earnings. Their special skills enable them to do interesting work in pleasant surroundings and be highly paid at the same time.

JOB DISCRIMINATION

In recent years the women's movement has drawn our attention to existing inequalities in women's salaries and opportunities in comparison with those available to men. Over a long period of time certain occupations, such as nurse, secretarial worker, and airline stewardess, have traditionally become associated with women, while other occupations, such as construction worker, truck driver, and stevedore, have been generally considered to be in the domain of men. Many people are now questioning whether these traditional roles of men and women are justified.

No doubt a large part of the reason for the dominance of one sex or the other in certain occupations is the roles accepted by both men and women because of culture and tradition. Some occupations were regarded as women's work; others were men's work. Society is indebted to the women's movement for opening up new opportunities for women by changing the thinking of many people of both sexes concerning the capabilities of women. No nation can afford to lose the talent and energy of half its population. Nor should a woman have to forgo a career that appeals to her simply because it is not regarded as women's work. This is

TABLE 21–1 Hourly Earnings of Nonsupervisory Workers. Private Nonagricultural Payrolls, September 1995

| | Hourly Wage Rate | |
Occupation	Average	Specific
Mining	$15.34	
Metal		$16.88
Coal		18.51
Oil and gas.		14.46
Nonmetal minerals		13.69
Construction	$ 15.29	
General building		$14.44
Heavy construction		15.12
Special trades		15.62
Manufacturing	$12.45	
Durable goods		$13.02
Nondurable goods		11.67
Wholesale trade	$12.48	
Durable goods		12.96
Nondurable goods		11.81
Retail trade	$ 7.77	
Lumber and hardware stores		$9.27
General merchandise stores		7.56
Food stores		8.20
Auto dealers		10.61
Apparel stores		7.51
Furniture		10.27
Restaurants		5.64
Finance, insurance, and real estate	$ 12.38	
Banking		9.64
Credit agencies		12.71
Insurance agencies		14.91
Services	$ 11.47	
Hotels		$7.93
Personal services		7.59
Business services		10.70
Auto repair		9.97
Misc. repair		11.71
Health services		12.54
Legal		16.13
Total private	$ 11.56	

Source: "Employment and Earnings," U.S. Dept. of Labor, Bureau of Labor Statistics 42, no. 11 (Nov. 1995).pp. 96–115

not to deny the importance of activities in the home. The many services provided by homemakers such as rearing children, preparing meals, and in general keeping families together amount to thousands of dollars per year per family if they could be purchased in the market. Women who choose to devote full time to such activities are still contributing much to their family's and society's welfare.

It might be argued, of course, that some jobs require certain characteristics that are more likely to be inherent in women than in men, or vice versa. For example, women on the average probably have greater manual dexterity than men, but they do not possess as great physical strength. This may at least partly explain why typists tend to be women and construction and dock workers tend to be men. To the extent that physical differences between men and women do exist and these differences are important to certain jobs, the mix of men and women can be expected to be different. If the occupations that require staffing by men exhibit harsh working conditions such as exposure to the elements and hard physical labor, additional compensation may be required in order to attract qualified people, and we can expect the average salaries of men to be somewhat higher than those for women. As technology progresses and fewer jobs require brute strength, women should enjoy an increasing advantage in the job market, at least in comparison to times past. For example, the greater manual dexterity of women should give them an advantage in working with computers.

It is, of course, possible to find occupations in this country in which women are doing basically the same work as men but are earning lower salaries. Mainly it is these situations that give rise to charges of discrimination. It is, however, possible to explain at least part of these wage differences without resorting to the discrimination argument. It is common for married women to drop out of the labor force, at least for a time, during their childbearing years. More frequent changing of jobs and interruption of employment means that women on the average build up less seniority than men, which reduces their chances of moving up to higher-paying management positions.

It should be noted that discrimination against women or minorities by employers is irrational. If women are equally productive as men but receive lower salaries then their VMPs (or MRPs) will exceed their wage rates. In this case an employer can increase profits by hiring women rather than men. Employers who refuse to hire women will have higher costs and will not be able to compete with firms that do not discriminate. The same is true of minorities.

Appendix: Proof of the Equivalence of the Profit-Maximizing Rules for Output and Inputs

Recall from Chapter 10 that profits are maximized when a firm's output corresponds to the point where product price (P) equals MC.

$$P = MC$$

Also recall that MC is the cost of producing one more unit of output. As pointed out in Chapter 8, the cost of producing one more unit of output using more of an input (x) is P_x/MPP_x.

$$\text{Therefore MC} = P_x/MPP_x$$

$$\text{Consequently } P = P_x/MPP_x,$$

$$\text{or } P_x = P \bullet MPP_x.$$

$$\text{Since VMP}_x = P \bullet MPP_x,$$

$$\text{then } P_x = VMP_x$$

This proves that the last expression, $P_x = VMP_x$, the profit-maximizing rule for inputs, is equivalent to the first, P = MC, the profit-maximizing rule for output.

QUESTIONS

1. Why is the VMP or MRP of an input also a firm's demand for the input? What assumption is required?

2. a. Suppose you apply for a job that pays $20,000 per year. What must be true of your VMP or MRP to obtain this job and keep it?

    b. Several of the top entertainers in the United States earn over $50 million per year, while factory, office, service workers, and teachers toil for a fraction of this wage. Are entertainers overpaid? Are low-wage people underpaid for their labor? Explain.

Wage per Hour	Hours per Week Supplied by Employee:		
	1	2	3
$8	0	0	40
10	0	40	40
l2	40	40	40

3. a. Using the above figures, plot the market supply of labor from the figures for individual employees.

    b. Is the market supply more or less elastic than the supply of each individual? Why?

4. Suppose you own a small business and employ 10 people. One of your main problems is absenteeism. To ease this problem, you consider raising your employees' wages from $9 to $10 per hour. Do you think this raise would reduce the number of days missed? Explain.

5. a. Using diagrams, illustrate how wage is determined in a market made up of perfectly competitive buyers of labor, and how this wage relates to the individual employer.

    b. Using a diagram, illustrate how wage is determined by an imperfectly com-petitive buyer of labor.

6. a. What happens to the demand for labor when there is a decrease in demand for consumer or investment goods?

    b. Why does this phenomenon cause an increase in unemployment?

7. Barbers, taxicab drivers, and teachers probably are not much more productive nowadays than they were 40 to 50 years ago. Yet, their real wages have increased substantially. Why?

8. Explain how each of the following circum-stances will affect the demand for labor:

    a. A decrease in demand for the product produced by labor.

    b. An increase in the use of capital that is complementary to labor.

    c. An increase in the use of capital that is a substitute for labor.

    d. An increase in the skills of labor.

9. Why is discrimination against women or minorities irrational for a firm that wish-es to maximize profits?

SELF TEST

1. Marginal physical product (MPP) is:

    a. the units of input required to obtain one more unit of output.

    b. the units of output obtained from using one more unit of an input.

    c. dollars of input required to obtain one more unit of output.

    d. dollars of output obtained from one more unit of an input.

2. Value of marginal product (VMP) of an input is:

    a. the value that an extra unit of output adds to total sales or revenue.

    b. the cost of adding one more unit of output.

    c. the cost of adding one more unit of input.

    d. the value of extra output obtained by adding one more unit of the input.

3. VMP is obtained by multiplying MPP by:
   a. input price.
   b. output price.
   c. APP.
   d. MC.

4. Marginal revenue product (MRP) is obtained by multiplying MPP by:
   a. input price.
   b. marginal revenue.
   c. APP.
   d. MC.

5. The VMP curve relates to _____ competitive firms and the MRP curve relates to _____ competitive firms.
   a. imperfectly; perfectly
   b. perfectly; imperfectly
   c. profitable; unprofitable
   d. unprofitable; profitable

6. To maximize profits a firm should expand the use of an input until its VMP _____ the price of the _____ .
   a. exceeds; input
   b. equals; input
   c. exceeds; output
   d. equals; output

7. Because of the profit-maximizing rule set forth in question 6, the VMP curve of an input also is its _____ curve.
   a. demand
   b. supply
   c. MTC
   d. ATC

8. The profit-maximizing rule for output:_____. The profit-maximizing rule for input use: _____ . These rules are
   a. $P_x = VMP_x$; $P = MC$; unrelated
   b. $P = MC$; $P_x = VMP_x$; unrelated
   c. $P_x = VMP_x$; $P = MC$; equivalent
   d.. $P = MC$; $P_x = VMP_x$; equivalent

9. The price of leisure is equal to:
   a. the cost of entertainment.
   b. zero, because money cannot buy happiness.
   c. wages forgone by not working.
   d. zero, because leisure is not bought and sold.

10. If an employer increases wages of his or her employees to reduce absenteeism, employees will take fewer days off if the _____ effect exceeds the _____ effect.
    a. wage; income
    b. substitution; income
    c. wage; substitution
    d.. income; substitution

11. If wages are higher than the equilibrium wage in a labor market, the resulting _____ is called _____.
    a. shortage; inflation
    b. surplus; inflation
    c. shortage; unemployment
    d. surplus; unemployment

12. A perfectly competitive employer of labor faces a labor _____ that is perfectly _____ .
    a. supply; elastic
    b. supply; inelastic
    c. demand; elastic
    d. demand; inelastic

13. Most employers are _____ competitive buyers of labor because most hire a _____ share of the total labor market.
    a. perfectly; large
    b. perfectly; small
    c. imperfectly; large
    d. imperfectly; small

14. A perfectly competitive employer maximizes profits by hiring labor up to the point where the wage rate equals:
    a. the price of labor.
    b. the price of the product.
    c. the MR of the product.
    d. the VMP or MRP of labor.

15. An imperfectly competitive buyer of labor:
    a. hires a large share of the labor market.
    b. sells a large share of the product market.
    c. pays a lower than competitive wage.
    d. a and c.

16. An imperfectly competitive buyer of labor will maximize profits by hiring employees up to the point where the last employee's _____ is equal to his or her _____ .
    a. MRP; wage
    b. MRP; MRC
    c. wage; MRC
    d. MRP; MPP

17. An imperfectly competitive buyer of labor will maximize profits by paying:
    a. a zero wage.
    b. a wage corresponding to the profit-maximizing quantity point on the supply curve of labor facing the employer.
    c. a wage corresponding to the intersection of MRC and MRP.
    d. a wage corresponding to the intersection of MRP and the supply of labor facing the employer.

18. An increase in the price of the product _____ the _____ labor.
    a. increases; demand for
    b. increases; supply of
    c. decreases; supply of
    d. decreases; demand for

19. If consumers decrease their demand for products and wages do not decrease, there will be _____.
    a. wage increases
    b. unemployment
    c. inflation
    d. strikes

20. Two inputs are complements if an increase in the quantity of one _____ the _____ of the other.
    a. increases; MPP
    b. decreases; MPP
    c. increases; supply
    d. decreases; supply

21. Two inputs are substitutes if an increase in the quantity of one _____ the _____of the other.
    a. increases; MPP
    b. decreases; MPP
    c. increases; supply
    d. decreases; supply

22. The demand for skilled people is _____ than the demand for those with less skills because their _____ are higher.
    a. greater; wages
    b. greater; MPPs
    c. less; wages
    d. less; MPPs

23. The productivity of people in certain occupations such as teaching and driving a taxi has not increased appreciably over the past several decades. Yet their real wages have increased. This can be explained by the increase in real wages in alternative occupations which had the effect of_____ the _____ labor to teach and drive a taxi.
    a. increasing; demand for
    b. increasing; supply of
    c. decreasing; demand for
    d. decreasing; supply of

24. Which combination of characteristics results in the highest wages?
    a. high skill and pleasant working conditions
    b. high skill and disagreeable working conditions
    c. low skill and pleasant working conditions
    d. low skill and disagreeable working conditions

25. Discrimination by employers against women and minorities decreases the profits of their firms because the VMPs (MRPs) of those discriminated against are _____ than their wages. Profits for these firms could be increased by hiring _____ women and minorities.
    a. greater; more
    b. greater; less
    c. less; more
    d. less; less

Chapter 22

Labor Unions

Key Concepts

Working conditions
Job security
Higher wages
Industrial unions
Craft unions
Collective bargaining
Minimum wage laws

A discussion of labor is incomplete without considering labor unions. Unions have attempted to improve the welfare of their members in three areas: (1) better working conditions, (2) job security, and (3) higher wages. Most of this chapter centers on the third area, although the other two areas are important and are discussed briefly.[1]

BETTER WORKING CONDITIONS

Competition in the business world requires each firm to produce at the least possible cost to survive and to earn profits. Improving the working conditions of employees costs money; employers have not been in the forefront in this area. Employers especially sensitive to working conditions incur higher costs and can be driven out of business by competitors who are not as sensitive. Granted, their workers would be happier and more productive, but if the increased productivity does not compensate for the added cost, the firm would have to bear the net cost. There is also the uncertainty of whether and how much improved conditions increase worker productivity. In health and safety, the benefits may be a long time in coming. If all employers were required to play by the same rules, that is, if all are required to provide better working conditions, no single employer is penalized. This is like reducing pollution. Individual firms cannot do much to change conditions alone. But, when everyone must meet the same standards, no single firm is penalized and forced out of business.

Labor unions have been active in promoting better working conditions on two fronts: (1) in negotiating union contracts, and (2) in promoting legislation in Congress. If a union represents the majority of workers in an industry, it may persuade the unionized firms to improve conditions under threat of a strike. However the union has less power at this level than if legislation is passed—nonunion firms can still undercut unionized firms in the product market. By promoting legislation which specifies workplace standards, even nonunion firms must abide by the rules.

The recent increase in imports from low-income countries threatens working conditions of U.S. workers. It is the same as being undercut by nonunion firms that do not have to follow stringent rules.

JOB SECURITY

Anyone who has been an employee knows the uncertainty and anxiety that results from not knowing whether one's job will exist in the months and years

---

1 For added reading on labor unions, see Albert Rees, *The Economics of Trade Unions,* 3rd ed. (Chicago: University of Chicago Press) 1988.

ahead. Employees who have been laid off know this feeling well, and persons who have not found a job after being laid off know it even better. This is not to say that employers are free of such anxiety; their businesses also can disappear in this uncertain world.

Unions have attempted to promote members' job security by union contracts and legislation. For example, a railroad contract may specify that each train locomotive must have two people in the cab even though the company might argue that with the newest technology, one can do the job.

Attempts to promote job security by work rules have not been highly successful. If new technology makes a job obsolete, eventually it disappears. Unions have been more successful in promoting legislation that helped maintain full employment in the economy. The Full Employment Act of 1946 was a milestone in this area. In times of increased unemployment, unions have advocated increased government spending to reduce unemployment. Everyone's job security is increased when unemployment is low.

HIGHER WAGES

Labor unions have attempted to increase members' wages in three ways: (1) increase the demand for labor, (2) decrease the supply of labor, and (3) bargain for a union wage.

A. Increase the Demand for Labor

This method is probably the most desirable but the most difficult. It is desirable because it results in both a higher wage and greater employment, as illustrated in Figure 21–5 in Chapter 21. It is difficult because unions do not have much influence over the demand for labor.

One way to increase labor demand is to increase demand for the final product. In years past, unions utilized advertising urging consumers to buy union-made products; such advertising is less common nowadays.

Recently, unions have been active in discouraging imports of foreign-made products by lobbying for protective tariffs or quotas on imports. The success of this effort is questionable because limiting imports limits our exports. If we do not buy from other nations, they cannot obtain dollars to purchase goods from the United States. As a result, there is a decrease in the export demand of union-made products.

Increasing the productivity of labor (or the MPP) also increases the demand for labor. As a result, unions have attempted to improve working conditions and shorten the workweek to maximize each employee's potential. Unions also have encouraged education and have been active in apprenticeship programs, although apprenticeship programs have been a more effective device for limiting the supply of labor.

B. Decrease the Supply of Labor

Unions have been more successful in raising wages by limiting the supply of labor than by increasing demand. This is particularly true among the so-called craft unions representing skilled workers. The prime vehicle for limiting entry into the profession or trade is by controlling entry into the training or apprenticeship program.

Shifting the supply of labor, back and to the left from what it would be with free entry into the profession, increases wages and reduces the number of people employed. Trade unions and professional associations such as the AMA have utilized this technique successfully because the outcome (higher wages and less employment) does not, at least in the short run, harm established members of the trade or profession. Their wages are high, and they generally do not have to fear unemployment.

The people harmed by this technique are people who could have obtained higher incomes if they had been allowed to enter the profession; and consumers, who pay more for services rendered. If wages and the cost of services become excessively high, however, public opinion may result in government pressure to allow more freedom of entry. Also, substitute products will appear, as evidenced by mobile homes or factory-built housing which results in a decreased demand for the services of skilled tradespeople.

C. Bargain for a Union Wage

Collective bargaining is the most common means of increasing wages. Here, the union negotiates with the employer and under threat of strike attempts to set a wage higher than in a free-market equilibrium. This technique is used mainly by industrial unions—those that represent the workers of entire industries. Examples include the autoworkers, steelworkers, garment workers, and the teamsters (truck drivers).

Unlike the craft unions, which limit membership, the industrial union's goal is to bring all workers in the industry into union membership. The wisdom of this policy is clear when we remember that because the jobs represented by industrial unions do not require specialized training, there is always a large pool of substitute labor that can easily step in if union labor becomes costly than nonunion labor. In addition, the success of industrial unions hinges on the condition that all firms in the industry employ union members. When unionized firms pay a higher wage and hence incur higher costs, the lower-priced products of nonunionized firms can take over the market.

In bargaining for a union wage, unions attempt to obtain a higher wage for their members than what is determined in a free market. As explained in Chapter 21, this wage corresponds to the intersection of labor's demand and

FIGURE 22–1 Union Wages in the Labor Market

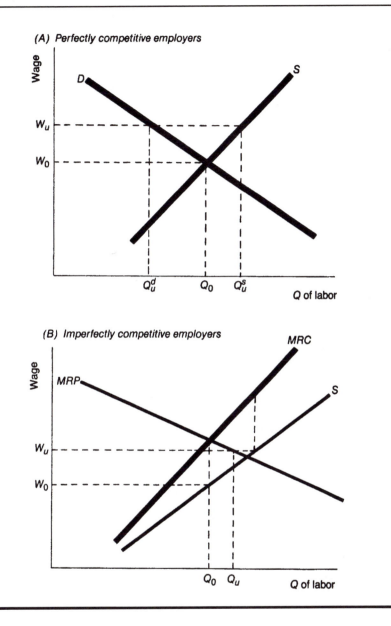

(A) Perfectly competitive employers

(B) Imperfectly competitive employers

supply in a perfectly competitive market, as illustrated in Figure 22–1A by W_0. The free-market wage in an imperfectly competitive labor market is also denoted in Figure 22–1B by W_0. The union wage is denoted by W_u in both diagrams.

In perfect competition, note that the imposition of the union wage reduces the quantity of labor employed in the market from Q_0 to Q_u^d For employers to pay the higher wage, they must reduce employment until labor's MRP rises to the wage level. If they did not reduce personnel, the wage of the marginal workers would exceed the value of what they produce. The resulting decline in employment is a check on the union's bargaining power, however. Unions like to minimize unemployment, along with achieving higher wages. Moreover, unions traditionally have not enjoyed a large, loyal membership during high unemployment periods.

Notice also in Figure 22–1A that the quantity of labor seeking employment in the union wage industry increases from Q_o to Q_u^s, resulting in an unemployed fringe equal to the distance between Q_u^d and Q_u^s. This represents the waiting list of hopeful employees.

The outcome of a union wage in an imperfectly competitive labor market, illustrated in Figure 22–1B, is surprising. Note that in a free market the imperfectly competitive buyer of labor pays W_0 and hires Q_o But when the union bargains for a wage, say W_u, the employer increases employment up to Q_u This occurs because the union wage nullifies the firm's original MRC curve. At wage W_u, the firm can hire any quantity of labor without paying more for additional workers. The firm's MRC curve under a union wage, therefore, consists of the dashed line that begins at W_u on the vertical axis, runs out to the supply curve, and then extends up to join the original MRC curve of the firm.

At first, the outcome depicted in Figure 22–1B appears highly beneficial to union members: Their wages are higher and their total employment has increased provided the union wage is set somewhere between the original free-market wage, W_0, and the point where the firm's original MRC curve intersects its MRP curve. We should point out, however, that this outcome is not likely to persist over the long run. As wages are increased, the firm's cost curves are shifted upward and to the left and profits are reduced. Firms making only normal profits will tend to leave the business, output will decline, and the total demand facing the union for its labor also will decline. So, labor still ends up with fewer jobs in the long run. Furthermore, the existence of imperfectly competitive employers should not be taken for granted. Virtually all employers hire a small proportion of the total labor force in their respective labor markets, which means that they face a highly elastic supply of labor, especially in the long run.

HAVE UNIONS INCREASED WAGES?

The answer to the above question may appear obvious: We continually observe negotiated wage increases in unionized trades or industries. Would the normal forces of supply and demand result in comparable wage increases? Based on empirical studies, unions have increased the wages of members by 10 to 15 percent.[2] These studies also show, however, that wages of nonunion workers are 3

---

2 Gregg Lewis, *Union Relative Wage Effects* (Chicago: University of Chicago Press, 1986).

to 4 percent lower than they would be in the absence of unionism. Since union membership accounts for only 12 percent of the U.S. labor force, it appears that although unions have altered the structure of wages, they have not increased the overall average level of wages in the country.

It is easy to see why unions have been able to raise wages by collective bargaining and by restricting entry. But why should unions cause other workers to receive lower wages? First, an increase in wages in unionized industries results in fewer jobs in these industries or occupations than would otherwise be the case; that is, there is a movement up along the labor demand curve. The people who would have worked in these jobs are forced to find employment in other, nonunion occupations. This increases (shifts to the right) the supply of workers for these occupations. When supply increases from what it otherwise would be, price, or in this case, the wage, is lower.

This phenomenon is illustrated in Figure 22–2. The increase in wages because of union pressure from W_e to W_u and the resulting reduction in the quantity of labor demanded from Q_1 to Q_0 are shown in Figure 22–2A. (In this case, we assume the wage increase results from collective bargaining by an industrial union, but the same overall result would occur because of restricting entry into a unionized trade.) The reduction in people working in the unionized industry increases the supply of people in nonunion occupations, as illustrated in figure 22–2B. And, as a result, the wage level in a nonunion occupation is decreased.

The ability of unions to influence the overall level of wages appears to be decreasing over time because of the decline in the proportion of workers holding union membership. In 1990 only 12 percent of all employees in the private sector belonged to unions, down from 25 percent in 1973. Several reasons may be given for this decline. First, the proportion of workers employed in highly unionized industries such as autos, steel, and mining declined during this period. The service sector which is not so heavily unionized became a larger area of employment. Second, the relatively high unemployment rates of the early to mid-1980s and in the early 1990s likely contributed to the decline in union membership. During times of higher unemployment, union membership tends to decline. Workers become more interested in keeping their jobs than in pushing for higher wages or better working conditions. Also, when unemployment is high, unions have a hard time recruiting new members. Related to the above, the increased competition of foreign products drove many unionized firms out of business, and their former employees had to take jobs in lower-paying nonunion occupations. Unionized firms with high wages are especially vulnerable to competition, foreign and domestic, because of their higher costs. When foreign products became more readily available to U.S. consumers at lower prices and often at higher quality than domestic products, many U.S. firms began to lose money and had to shut down.

It is not clear that unions acted in the best interest of their members during the 1970s by pushing for higher wages and more restrictive work rules. During the 1980s many of these employees were forced into early retirement, or had to

FIGURE 22–2 Effect of Union Wage Increase on Union and Nonunion
Occupations

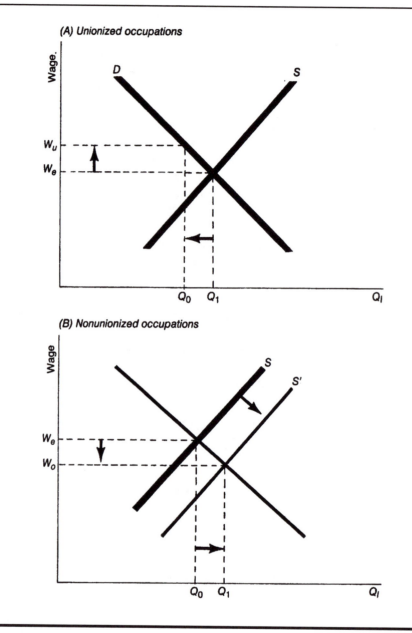

take jobs in nonunion occupations at substantially lower wages. Their wages in
the 1990s probably would have been higher if they could have remained in their
former occupations, at wages somewhat lower than they were getting when they
lost their jobs.

MINIMUM-WAGE LAWS

Although minimum-wage laws are not strictly union-inspired, they have similar effects to union wages set by collective bargaining. Also, unions have actively promoted enactment of minimum-wage legislation.

Society has attempted to protect itself against employers who pay excessively low wages through minimum-wage laws. A minimum-wage law requires employers to pay employees covered under the law an hourly wage at least as high as the stipulated minimum. There is a federal minimum-wage law that covers workers in manufacturing and industries engaged in interstate commerce. Many states, particularly northern industrial states, have their own minimum-wage laws, especially for employees not covered under federal law. The stipulated minimum wage has steadily increased in this country. The federal law, stemming from the Fair Labor Standards Act of 1938, began with a minimum wage of 25 cents an hour in 1940, increasing to $5.15 an hour in 1997. Over the years, the minimum wage has been adjusted upward to keep pace with inflation.

In an attempt to minimize the increase in unemployment among young people, recent minimum-wage legislation allows employers to pay a training wage equal to 85 percent of the federal minimum wage for three months. After three months on the job, the full minimum wage must be paid. The training wage applies only to workers 16 to 19 years of age. Of course, employers have the option of laying off a young person after three months, rather than paying the higher minimum wage, and then hiring someone else at the training wage. The result is a higher turnover of workers and probably poorer performance due to less experienced workers on the job.

The persons most affected by such legislation are at the low end of the wage scale, mainly teenagers working on their first jobs and people with relatively few skills. It may appear that a minimum wage is a boon to low-wage earners. After all, if the minimum wage is $5.15 an hour, take-home pay is larger than if you had to work for a market-determined wage of, say, $4.15 an hour. Although a minimum-wage law can guarantee that a worker receives a base wage, it cannot guarantee that a job will be available at that wage. In fact, if the minimum wage is above the equilibrium wage for occupations with low hourly pay, a decline in the jobs available to low-wage earners will occur.

If the market demand for labor affected by minimum-wage legislation is elastic, which is likely since there are ample substitutes for such labor, then raising the wage rate through minimum-wage laws reduces the total earnings of people at the low end of the wage scale. In this case, the percentage reduction in employment is greater than the percent increase in wage rates. Thus, such laws can make the income distribution more unequal.

This problem is best illustrated with a simple market demand and supply diagram for labor in Figure 22–3. Assume that the minimum wage, W_m, is above

FIGURE 22–3 Effect of a Minimum Wage Law on Low-Income People

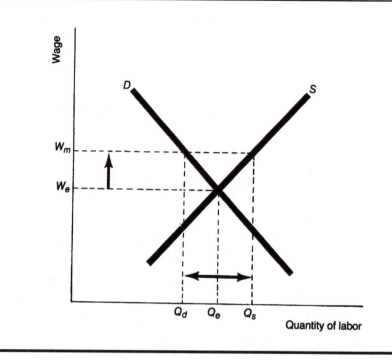

the market equilibrium wage, W_e. At the minimum wage, the quantity of labor demanded, Q_d, is less than the amount demanded at the equilibrium wage, Q_e. In other words, by imposing a minimum-wage law, people at the low end of the wage scale face a decrease in available jobs. Generally, employers substitute capital or machines for higher-priced labor. At the same time, the higher minimum wage draws more people into the market, as illustrated by the increase in the quantity of labor supplied from Q_e to Q_s. The gap between Q_d and Q_s, therefore, represents the number of people who would like to work at this wage but cannot find a job—the unemployed.

The results of minimum-wage laws predicted by our theoretical framework also are substantiated by empirical studies.[3] The impact of minimum-wage laws is felt most by teenagers, particularly teens from minority groups. It is doubtful, however, that many full-time semiskilled or unskilled workers in manufacturing are affected by such laws. Part-time jobs, particularly in service trades, are most affected.

---

3 See, for example, Douglas K. Adie, "Teen-Age Unemployment and Real Federal Minimum Wages," *Journal of Political Economy.* March-April 1973, pp. 435–41; and M. Kosters and F. Welch,"The Effects of Minimum Wages on the Distribution of Changes in Aggregate Unemployment," *American Economic Review,* June 1972, pp. 323-32.

QUESTIONS

1. a. At the present, relatively few business firms provide day-care facilities for children of employees. What must be true for a firm to willingly provide these facilities? Would it affect wages?

   b. If society decided that day care should be accessible to children of all employees in the country, is there any way this could be accomplished? Explain.

   c. Who would pay for these facilities?

   d. Would the cost of day care have any effect on the ability of domestic firms to compete in the world market?

2. By what means have labor unions attempted to improve working conditions?

3. By what means have labor unions attempted to increase job security?

4. a. How have craft unions attempted to increase wages?

   b. What are the limitations of this method?

5. a. How have industrial unions attempted to increase wages?

   b. What are the limitations of this method?

6. How is it possible for unions to have decreased the wages paid in nonunion occupations?

7. a. What effect do minimum-wage laws have on unemployment if wages are set above the market equilibrium? Explain.

   b. Who is most affected by these laws?

SELF-TEST

1. Business firms that undertake measures to improve working conditions of employees and in so doing incur higher production costs:

   a. will be assured of a market for their products.

   b. run the risk of being driven out of business.

   c. will be assured of pure profits for all time to come.

   d. can pass on higher costs to their customers.

2. If all domestic business firms in an industry are required to meet certain working conditions for their employees:

   a. no employees need to fear unemployment.

   b. all firms can be assured of a pure profit.

   c. an individual firm is not penalized for improving working conditions.

   d. the firms need not fear foreign competition- .

3. Unions have been active in promoting better working conditions by:

   a. promoting legislation in Congress.

   b. negotiating union contracts under threat of strike.

   c. urging people to buy union-made products.

   d. a and b.

4. Firms located in countries that do not require as favorable working conditions as does the United States:

   a. have a competitive advantage in the U.S. market.

   b. run the risk of losing the U.S. market because of high labor costs.

   c. produce inferior products that are not competitive in the U.S. market.

   d. will not be able to attract labor in their domestic labor market.

5. Labor unions have attempted to improve job security of their members by:

   a. increasing wages.

   b. union contracts.

   c. legislation.

   d. b and c.

6. Efforts by unions to increase job security by negotiating work rules _____ been very successful because:

a. have not; they tend to increase production costs.

b. have; they tend to decrease production costs.

c. have not; of legislation which forbids the practice.

d. have; they increase worker productivity.

7. Increasing wages by increasing the demand for labor is the _____ desirable method to accomplish this objective but (and) the _____ difficult to attain.

a. least; least

b. most; most

c. least; most

d. most; least

8. Which of the following efforts by unions is (are) aimed at increasing the demand for union labor?

a. raising wages

b. promoting legislation which restricts imports

c. advertising for consumers to buy union-made products

d. b and c.

9. Increasing wages by decreasing the supply of labor has been most effectively done by:

a. supplying birth-control information.

b. bargaining for a union wage.

c. urging people to buy union-made products.

d. restricting entry in training or apprenticeship programs.

10. Labor unions have been more successful _____ the _____ labor than _____ .

a. decreasing; supply of; increasing demand

b. decreasing; demand for; decreasing supply

c. increasing; supply of; increasing demand

d. increasing; demand for; increasing supply

11. Craft unions attempt to increase wages primarily by:

a. increasing demand.

b. decreasing supply.

c. increasing supply.

d. collective bargaining under threat of strike.

12. Craft unions tend to be _____ to get into, and represent mainly _____ workers.

a. hard; unskilled

b. easy; unskilled

c. hard; skilled

d. easy; skilled

13. Industrial unions attempt to increase wages primarily by:

a. increasing demand.

b. decreasing supply.

c. increasing supply.

d. collective bargaining under threat of strike.

14. Collective bargaining for a higher union wage can be successful if:

a. unemployment is high.

b. employers think profits will be reduced more by a strike than by higher wages.

c. employers think profits will be reduced more by higher wages than a strike.

d. nonunion firms have a substantial share of the market.

15. Industrial unions tend to be _____ to get into and represent mainly _____ workers.

a. hard; unskilled

b. easy; unskilled

c. hard; skilled

d. easy; skilled

16. Higher union wages in a perfectly competitive labor market _____ the quantity of labor demanded and _____ unemployment.

a. decreases; increases

b. increases; decreases

c. decreases; decreases

d. increases; increases

17. Higher union wages in an imperfectly competitive labor market can _____ employment in the _____ run.
    a. decrease; short
    b. increase; short
    c. increase; long
    d. b and c

18. The outcome of economic studies suggests that labor unions _____ altered the structure of wages in the country and (but) _____ raised the overall level of wages.
    a. have not; have
    b. have; have not
    c. have not; have not
    d. have; have

19. During the 1970s and 1980s union membership as a percent of the U.S. private sector work force _____ from _____ percent.
    a. decreased; 25 to 12
    b. decreased; 50 to 25
    c. increased; 12 to 25
    d. increased; 25 to 50

20. During the 1980s _____ unemployment and _____ imports led to the decrease in union membership.
    a. higher; increased
    b. lower; decreased
    c. lower; increased
    d. higher; decreased

21. If unions are successful in raising wages in unionized occupations, the _____ labor in nonunion occupations _____ , causing their wages to _____ .
    a. demand for; increases; increase
    b. demand for; decreases; decrease
    c. supply of; increases; decrease
    d. supply of; decreases; increase

22. Minimum-wage laws have the effect of_____ the quantity of labor demanded and _____ the quantity supplied causing unemployment to _____ .
    a. increasing; decreasing; increase
    b. decreasing; increasing; increase
    c. increasing; decreasing; decrease
    d. decreasing; increasing; decrease

23. Minimum-wage laws have the effect of _____ unemployment mainly among _____ .
    a. decreasing; young people
    b. increasing; young people
    c. decreasing; older established workers
    d. increasing; older established workers

Chapter 23

Capital and Interest

Key Concepts

Capital defined

Annual cost of capital

Depreciation

Marginal product of capital

Rate of return on capital

Capitalized value

Interest rate determination

Interest rate differences

Nominal versus real rate of interest

Rationing and allocating functions

Stock market

In all production, labor is combined with capital to yield an output. Since most capital lasts for more than one year, the question of how to measure its annual cost is considered in this chapter. Then, the discussion turns to measuring the profitability of capital—mainly its rate of return. The chapter ends with consideration of the market for loan funds, how loan interest rates are determined, and why they differ among borrowers.

CAPITAL DEFINED

In business or economics, the word capital has two different meanings. Businesspeople may think of capital as cash or money to operate a business, as in working capital. Economists, however, define capital as durable or long-lasting inputs such as land, buildings, machines, and tools that yield a flow of services over time. The quantity of capital is measured in monetary terms, however. Actually, this definition of capital also could apply to consumer durables such as housing, automobiles, and appliances. They are long-lasting and yield a flow of services over time. In view of the discussion of household production in Chapter 8, consumer durables are inputs in the production of utility. Consumer durables generally are not thought of as capital, however, so this chapter will focus on the narrower definition of the word.

The study of capital is separated from the study of labor because there are differences between these two inputs. The first and most obvious difference is that capital is an inanimate, nonliving input devoid of feelings or preferences. Although the owners of capital are concerned about the wage or return it receives, they do not care about its working conditions such as the length of its work week or whether it is employed in a prestigious occupation. Thus, many of the factors important for labor are not of concern in our discussion of capital.

A second difference is that capital is generally purchased for use over a long period. For example, you may purchase an asset this year that will produce for the remainder of your lifetime. Labor, or other inputs such as raw materials, are purchased only for immediate or current use. Granted, there may be an understanding between employer and employee about the length of time they will associate, but the employer of labor, unlike the employer of capital, does not usually pay the employee a lump sum for all future services; this difference is important.

A third difference between capital and labor is that the purchase of capital may involve an expenditure in advance of the date it begins to contribute to output. Economists refer to the time interval between the expenditure and the beginning of the output flow as the gestation period. This interval is especially important for investment in education, as explained in Chapter 25.

ANNUAL COST OF CAPITAL

What does capital cost? At first, the answer appears obvious. Surely the cost of capital is what buyers pay people who produce it. But the answer is not this simple. Consider the purchase of a $10,000 machine. It is unreasonable to charge the entire $10,000 against this year's sales. The machine likely will be available for service next year. But, it is also reasonable to charge a part of the $10,000 purchase price against the current year's production. Thus, this year's cost will be somewhere between $10,000 and zero; $10,000 is too high and zero is too low.

It is reasonable to charge the current year's production with at least the amount the machine depreciated during the year. Let's say that the market value of the machine decreased to $7,000, resulting in $3,000 depreciation.

The second component of the annual cost of owning a capital item is interest. If the $10,000 came from borrowed funds, the interest charge will be explicit and noticeable. However, even if the money came from the firm's own funds, an interest charge still should be made because of the money's opportunity cost. If the funds were not used to buy the machine, they either could be earning interest or invested in some other capital that yields a return.

Thus, there are two components of the annual cost of owning a capital item: depreciation and interest. If 10 percent could be earned on the money, the first year's interest charge would be $1,000, which makes a total cost of $4,000 for the first year.

In the second year the interest charge should be figured on $7,000 invested because $3,000 of the original $10,000 was written off at the end of the first year. At 10 percent, the interest charge would be $700 the second year. If the machine depreciated another 30 percent the second year, the depreciation charge would be .30 x $7,000 = $2,100. Thus, the total cost of ownership the second year would be $700 + $2,100 = $2,800.

DEPRECIATION

Because depreciation accounts for a large share of the annual cost of owning a capital item, it is useful to examine it in more detail. There are two reasons a capital item depreciates: (1) the wearing out or "using up" of the item, and (2) obsolescence. In regard to the first reason, remember that the current market value of a capital item reflects the present value of its expected future contribution to output. Thus, the older an item, the fewer the years of productive life that remain. For example, a new machine may have 10 years of service ahead of it, while a five-year-old machine may have only five years of life remaining. Even if the used machine could do about the same amount of work per day as the new machine, no one would pay as much for the used item because of the smaller number of work days left in it. Also, there is more uncertainty involved in buying a used machine. For example, the buyer may not know whether the previous owner had taken good care of it. The possibility of high future repair bills will lower the price that buyers are willing to pay.

In an age of change and technological improvement, capital also becomes obsolete. If something new comes on the market that reduces production costs or increases efficiency, the demand for the old capital will decline; hence its price will fall. Thus, the depreciation of capital depends on its own productivity and the productivity of the new capital produced. Because of this, it is difficult, if not impossible, to predict in advance how fast an item will become obsolete. Nor is it easy to separate how much of an item's depreciation is due to wearing out and how much is due to obsolescence; both reduce its market value.

Two widely used methods of estimating depreciation are (1) the straight-line method, and (2) the constant-percentage method. The resulting decline in value of the depreciated item for each of these methods is illustrated in Figure 23–1. The straight-line method amounts to decreasing the value of the capital by a constant number of dollars each year. For example, if you were depreciating the $10,000 machine by the straight-line method over a period of 10 years, you would assess $1,000 per year as depreciation.

If you use the constant-percentage method, you multiply each year's market value by a constant percentage. For example, if you depreciate the machine 30 percent per year, the first year's depreciation would be $3,000, the second year's $2,100, ($7,000 x 0.30), the third year's $1,470, and so on. With the second method, the annual depreciation is higher when the item is new, which results in a lower depreciated value during its early years of use. With this method, also, the item does not depreciate to zero, although it comes close.

The method of depreciation chosen and the length of time involved depend on the item to be depreciated. The constant-percentage method is more realistic for most items, since depreciation usually is higher during the first few years of ownership. An automobile, for example, tends to depreciate between 20 and 25 percent per year, depending on the make, model, amount of use, and the care it has received. If you purchase an $10,000 automobile, it depreciates $2,500 the first year if the 25 percent rate applies. In calculating the total cost of ownership the first year, include the interest charge, $1,200 if taken at 12 percent, together with gasoline, insurance, license fees, and so forth. With normal use, the total annual cost of an $10,000 automobile is about $5,000 for the first year of ownership. Is it worth it?

ThE MARGINAL PRODUCT OF CAPITAL

In deciding whether or not to purchase or keep a machine or other capital item, it is necessary to consider its cost and returns. In previous sections we looked at cost; let us now consider the returns of a capital item. Capital is similar to labor or any other input in that it contributes to the output of goods and

Figure 23–1 Straight-Line and Constant-Percentage Patterns of Depreciation for a $10,000 Asset

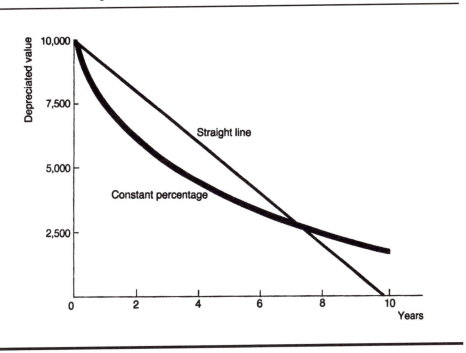

services. This contribution to output can be measured either in physical units of output by its marginal physical product (MPP), or in monetary units in terms of its value of the marginal product (VMP)—or marginal revenue product (MRP). Recall that MPP is the additional output obtained from an additional unit of the input—capital in this case—and VMP or MRP is the value of the additional output obtained from an additional unit of capital. To simplify the notation, we will refer only to the MRP of capital.

The MRP of capital is the value of the additional output made possible by utilizing a machine compared with what would be produced if it were not used.

Because we are interested in comparing capital's annual MRP with its annual interest plus depreciation charge, we ought to refer to the machine's annual "net" MRP. This is the value of additional annual output less the added expense incurred by owning and operating the machine, such as fuel, repairs, additional labor, and insurance.

THE RATE OF RETURN ON CAPITAL

Because a capital item generally is purchased for use over a number of years, it is common to express its contribution to output during a given year as a fraction of its value at the beginning of the year. The resulting figure is commonly referred to as a rate of return. The rate of return on capital is the amount each dollar earns each year after all expenses, including depreciation in this case, have been subtracted. It is commonly expressed as a percentage. For example, suppose after subtracting depreciation and other expenses from the gross MRP of the $10,000 machine that the first year's earnings are $1,200. During this year, its rate of return is equal to 0.12 or 12 percent (1,200/10,000). In other words, each dollar earns 12 cents during the year.

The rate of return on capital is the same idea as the rate of return on a savings account in the bank. However, unlike a savings deposit in a bank, which earns its stipulated rate of return year after year as long as the money is left in the account, the earnings of a machine or building can vary from year to year and eventually end as the item wears out.

CAPITALIZED VALUE

There is one kind of capital, however, that does not wear out or depreciate with normal care—land. Suppose you purchase a plot of land for $10,000 and expect it to remain at this price. Also, suppose you collect $1,000 per year return from the land for as long as you want to by renting it out. Assume that there are no other expenses, so the $1,000 is a net return.

For an asset that will yield a stream of returns for all time to come, its annual rate of return can be computed as follows:

$$r = \frac{\text{Annual net returns}}{\text{Capital value}}$$

In the land example above, the rate of return is:

$$r = \frac{\$1,000}{\$10.000} = 0.10 = 10 \text{ percent}$$

By manipulating this formula, we can derive another formula that is useful for deciding the maximum price you can afford for a piece of property. In the formula, r represents the interest rate of return, R represents the annual net return, and K represents the capital value. Now we have:

$$r = \frac{R}{K} \quad \text{or} \quad K \times r = R \quad \text{or} \quad K = \frac{R}{r}$$

The resulting formula, $K = R/r$, tells how much a piece of property is worth if we know its annual return and the interest charge. To purchase this plot of land, suppose you took out a $10,000 loan at 12 percent. Utilizing this formula, we find:

$$K = \frac{\$1,000}{0.12} = \$8,333$$

If you were assured an annual $ 1 ,000 net return on this land and the money to buy it cost 12 percent per year, you could have paid as much as $8,333 for the land. Economists refer to the K in this formula, or the $8,333, as the capitalized value of the property. In a competitive market, prospective buyers tend to bid the price of the property up to this amount. And sellers, knowing this, will set the selling price at the capitalized value. If you buy a piece of property for $10,000 that has a capitalized value of $8,333, it is not a good deal unless the price of land appreciates in the future due to inflation. In fact, land in the 1970s sold for three to four times its capitalized value; most likely this was due to the expectation of future inflation. When inflation subsided in the early 1980s land prices declined substantially. People revised their expectations to a lower rate of inflation.

For a given annual return R, the capitalized value K will vary inversely with the size of the interest rate r. If the interest rate paid on your loan was 20 percent, K would have been $5,000. A lower interest rate, such as 10 percent, would result in a higher capitalized value of $10,000.

Although the relationship between the interest rate and the capitalized value is an algebraic phenomenon—the larger the denominator, the smaller the quotient, and vice versa—it has an underlying economic rationale. At a high interest rate, say 20 percent, the income forthcoming in the future is more expensive to obtain than if the interest rate was lower. At high interest rates, borrowers must pay more for the distant income in terms of either an interest charge on borrowed funds or forgone interest from their own funds; hence, they cannot pay as high an initial price for the property.

In times of inflation, the value of land and other real assets increases faster than the general price level, particularly in the early stages of inflation. This occurs because of expected future inflation. As inflation persists, both buyers and sellers expect an increase in the future net returns and in the selling price when the land is sold. The increased future values are capitalized into the current price of land.

INTEREST RATE DETERMINATION

In the discussion thus far we have taken the interest rate as given. How is the interest rate on borrowed funds determined? The interest rate is the price of loan funds, and prices are determined in markets by demand and supply.

Looking at the demand for loan funds, we can identify two sources of this demand. First, there is the demand from businesses for financing new investment spending. Second, households demand loan funds to make large-scale purchases such as houses, cars, and appliances and for other purposes, including

FIGURE 23–2 Interest Rate Determination in the Loan Market

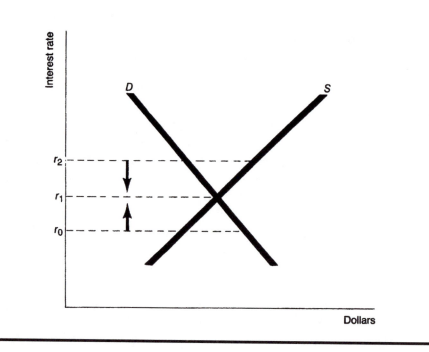

education, medical bills, and travel. The demand curve for loan funds is a downward-sloping line, as shown by Figure 23–2. The fact that some investments are less profitable than others (lower rate of return) means that a decrease in the interest rate will bring an increase in acceptable investments, which means that more loan money will be demanded to finance this added investment spending.

Turning to the supply side of the loan market, one might ask: Where do loan funds come from? In general, the supply of loan funds is the amount of money people are willing to divert from current consumption to saving. Businesses also save by retaining part of their earnings and returning it into the firm for investment. All firms are owned by people, so the definition holds. The supply curve of loan funds is an upward-sloping line, as illustrated by Figure 23–2. This implies that people will supply a greater number of dollars at relatively high interest rates than at relatively low rates, other things equal. The degree of savers responsiveness to interest rate changes is an unsettled question in economics. However, if people buy less of an item when its price increases and more when it becomes less expensive, we can expect some increase in the rate of saving (out of a given income) when the interest rate increases. As pointed out in Chapter 4, an interest rate increase raises the price of current consumption relative to future consumption.

As in any other market, there is one equilibrium price (interest rate) and quantity that prevails at any one time, given the demand and supply curves. This interest rate is illustrated by r_1 in Figure 23–2. At a higher rate, say r_2, a greater number of dollars are supplied than are demanded; that is, there will be a surplus of money in the loan market. Borrowers seeing this surplus of funds will press for a rate that is more favorable, while lenders will have to agree to the lower rate if they wish to loan out these funds. Similarly, if the interest rate was below the equilibrium, say r_0, there would be a shortage of funds, since a greater number of dollars would be demanded than supplied at this interest rate. As a result, lenders will press for a more favorable rate (to them), and borrowers will have to pay the higher rate or go without funds.

As in the product market and the labor market, the demand and supply curves of loan funds also will shift from one position to another. The demand for loan funds will be closely tied to investment opportunities. If prospects for future profits increase, we can expect some increase in the demand for funds to finance new investment. Or, if totally new and profitable investment opportunities arise, perhaps as the result of new technology, the demand for funds also will increase, or shift to the right.

Changes in the supply of loan funds also will affect the equilibrium rate of interest on these funds. Inflation is an important shifter of the supply of loan funds. An increase in the actual or expected inflation rate causes a decrease in the market supply of loan funds. People who lend money, or place it in a bank or savings institution, are aware that when the money is repaid it has less purchasing power than when it was lent. To compensate them for this loss, lenders (savers) require a higher rate of interest to make funds available. Unless they can obtain higher rates, they might just as well purchase consumer durables or other assets that rise with the price level such as precious metals or real estate.

INTEREST RATE DIFFERENCES

For simplicity, we have discussed the interest rate as if there was a single rate of interest prevailing in the economy at a point in time. There are, in fact, a number of rates of interest depending on the loan market under consideration. Banks charge a prime rate for their most favored customers and other, higher rates for small business, home, or auto loans. Banks and finance companies charge still higher rates for so-called personal loans, and loan sharks extract rates from their customers that are even higher.

What accounts for these differences? Basically, interest rate differences reflect different demand and supply conditions in the particular loan market under consideration. If the supply of funds is large relative to the demand, then the interest rate will be low, and vice versa.

The differences in interest rates between various borrowers and types of loans are largely the result of differences on the supply side of the market. The major consideration is the expected cost of making the loan. Two cost components are important. Perhaps most important is the risk of making the loan. Although lenders can never be 100 percent certain of being repaid, past experience tells them that certain loans are much less risky than others. For example, large, reputable companies that have been in business for many years and have built up good credit ratings will likely face a supply curve of funds that lies to the right of small, relatively unknown borrowers. As the risk of default increases, lenders are forced to charge a higher rate to pay for the money lost through non-payment of that type of loan. Lenders attempt to segregate potential borrowers by degree of risk to give lower rates to low-risk borrowers (mainly to get their business), while making high-risk borrowers pay a larger share of the cost of defaults.

In addition to risk, a second cost component that accounts for differences in the rate of interest charged is the administrative cost of making and collecting the loan. On a per dollar basis, this is higher for small loans. For example, the total cost of the paperwork necessary to process a $100,000 loan is not much different from the total administrative cost of making a loan of $1,000. Thus, the cost per dollar is higher for the smaller loan. To recoup these costs, the lender has to charge a higher rate on small loans. The cost of collecting also varies. At the extreme are lenders who employ a staff of "300-pound field men" to search out and persuade borrowers to pay up, or else! Since these lenders (the crime syndicate) must pay for these "services," they have to charge a high interest rate. If their rates are above the legal maximum, as usual, they also have to be compensated for the risk of getting caught and serving a prison term.

If loan sharks charge such high rates and use such violent methods of collection, why do people borrow from them? The answer is that not everyone can obtain loans from reputable lenders at the legal interest rates. Ceilings on interest rates, or usury laws, force people desperate for loans without adequate collateral or credit ratings into the clutches of unscrupulous lenders.

THE NOMINAL VERSUS THE REAL RATE OF INTEREST

The interest rate we have been discussing is the money or nominal rate. The real rate is the nominal rate adjusted by the rate of change of the general price level, that is, the rate of inflation. A simple example illustrates the effect of inflation on the interest cost and returns of a loan. Suppose you lend someone $100 at 12 percent interest, to be paid back with interest one year from now, and the inflation rate during this year is 5 percent. At the end of the year, you receive $112. But, the 5 percent inflation rate means that it now takes $105 to buy the same amount of goods and services that the $100 purchased at the beginning of the year. Thus, you have gained only $7 in real purchasing power by making the loan. In other words, you received a 7 percent real rate of interest on the loan. The formula for finding the real rate is:

Real rate = Nominal rate – Annual percent change in price level

In the preceding example, the real rate is:

$$7 = 12 - 5$$

If there were no restriction on the level of the nominal rate of interest, the loan market would establish an equilibrium nominal rate of interest high enough to compensate for the expected inflation plus something extra to provide a positive real rate of interest. In reality, upper limits on nominal interest rates as set by usury laws may restrict the nominal rate of interest from rising to its free market equilibrium. In years of high inflation, the real rate is often negative; that is, the nominal rate is smaller than the rate of inflation. Why do savers offer any funds under such circumstances? Lending, even at a negative real rate, is better than not lending at all and having inflation diminish one's cash even more rapidly. Also, if negative real rates prevail, loans will be selectively rationed to good friends of the lending agency or institution—usually large, low-risk borrowers.

RATIONING AND ALLOCATING FUNCTIONS OF THE INTEREST RATE

Market price is a rationing device whereby people voluntarily limit the use of goods and services that are not free, as noted in Chapter 12. Price also allocates scarce resources to production of goods and services most valued by society. The interest rate, being the price of investment funds, serves to ration and allocate these funds.

The potential amount of investment that could be undertaken during a given year exceeds the resources available to undertake it. As a result, the available funds have to be rationed and allocated to their most valuable uses. Since, in the private sector, investment will not be undertaken unless the expected rate of return is at least as large as the interest rate, the available investment funds are rationed or made unavailable to low-payoff, unprofitable investments.

Moreover, the interest rate allocates the available investment funds to areas where the expected rate of return is highest. The greater the expected rate of return in relation to the interest rate, the more incentive investors have to allocate funds to these areas because of expected profits. Thus, the interest rate keeps funds from being invested in low-return areas and pulls the funds toward more productive investments.

Much investment also takes place with public funds where profit is not a major consideration. Yet, public agencies also need to consider the interest rate. For a public investment to be socially profitable, its contribution to the output of society should be large enough to yield a rate of return at least equal to the before-tax marginal rate of return on alternative private investment.[1]

---

1 A figure of 15 percent is frequently used as the before-tax return to investment in the economy. See Willis Peterson, "Rates of Return on Capital: An International Comparison" KYKLOS, Vol. 2, 1989,pp. 203-17.

THE STOCK MARKET

The sale of stock represents an important source of funds to finance private investment. Although the loan market and the stock market are similar in economic terms and closely related, there is a legal difference in that the people who provide funds in the stock market become part-owners of the business they invest in. Although few stockholders actively participate in managing the companies in which they invest, they are the owners. Thus, money raised by sale of stock is sometimes called equity capital, while money raised by borrowing is known as debt capital.

The price of existing stock is determined by the forces of demand and supply. If the demand for stocks increases relative to the supply, their prices will increase, and vice versa. Many short-run fluctuations in the stock market stem from changing expectations of future business conditions and/or changing expectations of the future value of the stock. For example, if many people who own stock believe stock prices will fall in the near future, they may attempt to sell, thereby increasing supply and lowering stock prices. Thus, the psychology of the market is important in the short run. Over the long run, however, the value of each firm's stock tends to reflect the dividends paid and the growth in value of the firm's assets.

In assessing the value of a firm's stock, a helpful guide is the firm's price-earnings (P/E) ratio. This ratio is obtained by dividing the firm's current stock price by the past year's earnings on equity capital. These earnings are obtained by subtracting all expenses, including interest on borrowed funds and depreciation of capital from the firm's sales. If a firm has a P/E ratio of 5, it means that the firm's stock is selling for five times its earnings. This means that each $100 of stock earned $20. Another way of stating this is that the firm earned a 20 percent rate of return on equity capital. Of course, this does not mean that the firm's stockholders received a $20 dividend for each $100 of stock they own in the company. Most corporations pay out less than total earnings on equity capital choosing instead to return some earnings into the company. Retained earnings should increase the future value of the firm's stock because of the increase in value of assets and net worth of the firm.

QUESTIONS

1. a. What is capital?
   b. What do capital and consumer durables have in common?

2. a. What is the annual cost of owning a $10,000 automobile the first year of ownership if the rate of interest is 12 percent and the auto depreciates 25 percent per year? Assume insurance, license, and maintenance cost $1,000 per year and that the car is driven 15,000 miles per year at 20 miles per gallon of gasoline. Assume gasoline is $1.25 per gallon.
   b. What is the cost the second year of ownership?

3. a. Why does capital depreciate?
   b. What are the common methods of calculating depreciation?

4. a. What is capitalized value?
   b. What is the capitalized value of a parcel of land that yields $100 annual net returns if the interest rate is 15 percent?
   c. What is the capitalized value of the above parcel if the interest rate is 10 percent?
   d. During the 1970s, farm land in the United States sold for three to four times its capitalized value. Why?

5. a. Why do nominal interest rates rise during inflation?
   b. Can real rates of interest be negative? Explain.

6. a. What type of borrower pays the highest rate of interest?
   b. How do usury laws affect such borrowers?

7. How does the interest rate ration and allocate investment funds?

8. a. What determines stock prices?
   b. How is the price/earnings ratio related to the rate of return on money invested in the stock market?
   c. Why do stock prices change?

SELF-TEST

1. Capital is:
   a. money.
   b. Washington, D.C.
   c. inputs used up in the production process.
   d. long-lasting, durable inputs.

2. Which of the following characteristics differentiate capital from labor?
   a. it contributes to output
   b. it costs money
   c. working conditions are not so important
   d. it doesn't wear out

3. The two items that determine the annual cost of capital are:
   a. wear and tear.
   b. wages and prices.
   c. interest and depreciation.
   d. time and money.

4. Capital depreciates because:
   a. it wears out.
   b. it becomes obsolete.
   c. the future is unknown.
   d. a and b.

5. An interest charge should be included in the annual cost of ownership:
   a. only if the money to purchase the capital is borrowed.
   b. only if the money to purchase the capital is the owner's.
   c. only if capital depreciates.
   d. regardless of whether the money is borrowed or obtained from the owner's funds.

6. What is the annual cost of owning a $12,000 automobile the first year of ownership if the interest rate is 10 percent; it depreciates 25 percent; and gasoline, license, insurance, and repairs amount to $1,500 per year?
   a. $12,000   c. $4,200
   b. $5,700   d. $1,500

7. In reference to question 6, what is the cost of ownership the second year, assuming the same conditions?
   a. $4,650   c. $9,000
   b. $5,700   d. $3,150

8. Under a constant percent depreciation pattern the largest depreciation occurs the year of ownership.
   a. first   c. second
   b. last   d. next to last

9. With a straight-line depreciation pattern a capital item depreciates:
   a. a constant dollar amount each year.
   b. a constant percent each year.
   c. a decreasing dollar amount each year.
   d. an increasing dollar amount each year.

10. The MRP of capital is:
    a. interest plus depreciation.
    b. the additional income generated by utilizing the capital.
    c. the additional units of output obtained by utilizing the capital.
    d. interest plus depreciation plus operating expenses such as insurance and repairs.

11. The rate of return on capital is:
    a. annual interest plus depreciation expressed as a percent of the value of capital at the beginning of the year.
    b. the annual monetary contribution of capital expressed as percent of the value of the capital at the beginning of the year.
    c. the annual physical contribution of capital expressed as a percent of the value of capital at the beginning of the year.
    d. the annual monetary contribution of capital expressed in dollars.

12. The rate of return on capital is calculated by _____ the _____ by _____ .
    a. dividing; annual net returns; capital value
    b. dividing; capital value; annual net returns
    c. multiplying; annual net returns; capital valued.
    d. multiplying; capital value; annual net returns

13. Capitalized value tells us:
    a. interest plus depreciation expense.
    b. the value of capital after subtracting interest plus depreciation expense.
    c. the maximum amount we could pay for a piece of property in order to earn a rate of return equal to the interest rate in the formula.
    d. how much a piece of property will be worth at the time we wish to sell it.

14. What is the capitalized value of a piece of property that yields $100 per year into perpetuity if the interest rate is 10 percent?
    a. $10   c. $1,000
    b. $100   d. $10,000

15. The higher the rate of interest, the _____ the _____ .
    a. higher; capitalized value
    b. lower; capitalized value
    c. higher; rate of return
    d. lower; rate of return

16. During inflation the demand for loan funds _____ , their supply _____ and the nominal rate of interest _____ .
    a. increases; decreases; increases
    b. decreases; increases; increases
    c. increases; decreases; decreases
    d. decreases; increases; decreases

17. Interest rates tend to be lowest for, _____ , _____ -risk loans.
    a. small; high
    b. small; low
    c. large; high
    d. large; low

18. If the rate of inflation is 5 percent, and the nominal rate of interest is 8 percent, the real rate of interest is _____ percent.
   a. 13
   b. -3
   c. 3
   d. -13

19. Capital purchased with money raised by the sale of stocks is called _____ capital while that purchased by the sale of bonds is _____ capital.
   a. debt; equity
   b. equity; debt
   c. monetary; nonmonetary
   d. nonmonetary; monetary

20. If a stock selling for $100 pays a $5 dividend, its price-earnings ratio is _____and rate of return is _____ percent.
   a. 5; 20
   b. 20; 5
   c. 95; 5
   d. 100; 20

21. Stock prices decline when the demand for stocks _____ and/or their supply _____ .
   a. increases; increases
   b. decreases; decreases
   c. increases; decreases
   d. decreases; increases

Chapter 24

Project Evaluation

Key Concepts

Cash-flow analysis

Cash-flow table

Discounted present value

Benefit-cost ratio

Internal rate of return

Effect of Inflation

Ranking of investment opportunities

The main objective of this chapter is to show how to evaluate an investment project. It applies the technique of cash-flow analysis to an example of investing in an apartment house. Three ways of evaluating the expected profitability of an investment are presented.

CASH-FLOW ANALYSIS

An important decision made by managers of firms and government agencies is whether to invest in a capital item. Since these decisions run into millions of dollars, it is important to have a way to determine if the investment will be profitable, that is, whether the rate of return on the investment is at least as great as the interest paid on borrowed funds or the opportunity cost of the firm's funds.

A technique in widespread use for evaluating the profitability of an investment is cash-flow analysis. It compares the outflow of funds (cost) with the inflow of funds (returns). The information bearing on these figures is contained in a cash-flow table.

CASH-FLOW TABLE

A cash-flow table contains four pieces of information:
1. Gross cash outflow—this is the cost of the capital item. The sum includes the money from both equity and debt financing.
2. Gross cash inflow—the additional gross income received by owning the asset. The figure is approximated by the difference between the estimated income with the asset and the estimated income without the asset.
3. Added expense—these are the additional expenses such as repairs, fuel, taxes, and labor incurred by owning the asset. It does not include an interest or depreciation charge. This information is implicitly taken into account in calculating the rate of return.
4. Net cash flow—gross cash inflow minus added expense—the bottom line.

Use of this information in evaluating an investment is best explained in a specific example. Suppose you have an opportunity to purchase an apartment house for $200,000. The necessary information for constructing the cash-flow table follows:

Purchase price:	$200,000
Rental income:	$32,400 per year
Added expenses:	$12,400 per year
Expected selling price in four years:	$200,000

To simplify the example, assume the money used to purchase the house is laid out at the beginning of the first year of ownership, but the rental income and expenses are not forthcoming until the end of each year. The cash-flow table contains this information:

	Year 0	Year 1	Year 2	Year 3	Year 4
Cash outflow	−$200,000				
Gross cash inflow		+$32,4000	+$32,400	+$32,400	+$232,400
Added expense		−12,400	−12,400	−12,400	−12,400
Net cash inflow	−$200,000	+$20,000	+$20,000	+$20,000	+$220,000

The reason for the large cash inflow figures in the last year of ownership is that this year's figures include the expected selling price of the house; it is a cash inflow when sold.

The four positive net cash inflow figures total $280,000. This looks like a profitable investment; $200,000 is spent and $280,000 is taken in. The problem is that money forthcoming in the future is not worth as much as money in hand at the present; it is necessary to compute discounted present value.

DISCOUNTED PRESENT VALUE

One dollar forthcoming in the future is worth less than one dollar in hand today. If one wished to have the dollar now, a loan could be taken out that requires the payment of interest. This interest would reduce the net value of the dollar once it was obtained. The net value of the dollar obtained in the future after paying the interest on the dollar loan to obtain current use of the dollar is called discounted present value.

The formula for computing the discounted present value (DPV) is:

$$DPV = 1/(1 + r)^n$$

In this formula r is the rate of interest and n is the number of years one dollar is forthcoming in the future. To compute DPV of a sum different than one dollar, this formula is multiplied by that sum. The usual case is for an investment to yield a stream of returns over time. In such a case the above formula is multiplied by the various annual returns and then summed over the entire period. The general formula for computing DPV over a number of years is:

$$DPV = \sum_{i=1}^{n} R_i/(1 + r)^n$$

where $\sum_{i=1}^{n}$ is a summation sign telling us to sum the results of the computations from year 1 to year n. R_i is the expected returns forthcoming in year i, r is the interest rate, and n is the number of years in the future the returns are expected to be forthcoming.

We can now calculate the DPV of future returns from the apartment house.

$$DPV = \frac{20{,}000}{(1 + r)^1} + \frac{20{,}000}{(1 + r)^2} + \frac{20{,}000}{(1 + r)^3} + \frac{220{,}000}{(1 + r)^4}$$

Choosing an interest rate of 12 percent yields a $188,168 DPV of the apartment house return at the point where the $200,000 was spent. Notice that the DPV of the future returns is less than the purchase price; the house doesn't look like a good investment now.

If the DPV of the return is greater than the cost, buy it. The interest rate used in the formula should be the interest paid on borrowed money or the opportunity cost of one's own funds.

BENEFIT-COST RATIO

A second way of comparing the cost of a capital item with the discounted present value of its returns is by the benefit-cost (B/C) ratio. The benefit of an investment is defined as the discounted present value of its net cash inflows. Dividing the value of this benefit by the cost of the investment yields the B/C ratio. In the apartment house example, its B/C ratio is $188,168/$200,000 = 0.941 with a 12 percent interest rate. An investment is deemed acceptable if its B/C ratio is 1 or greater, preferably greater. Of course, the interest rate used to discount the returns influences the size of the B/C ratio. A 10 percent interest rate increases the discounted present value of the apartment house to $200,434, yielding a B/C ratio of 1.00. In this case, the apartment house investment becomes marginally acceptable. This example illustrates the importance of the interest rate. The higher the interest rate used to discount future returns, the lower is the discounted present value of future returns and the lower is the B/C ratio.

INTERNAL RATE OF RETURN

Because the interest rate that is used to discount future returns has such an important bearing on the discounted present value and B/C ratio, it is important to inquire what interest rate is used to compute these figures. An unusually low interest rate can make an otherwise unacceptable investment look good. For this reason, another criterion called the internal rate of return (IRR) is commonly used to evaluate investments. The internal rate of return is defined as that rate of interest which makes the discounted present value of the net cash inflows of an investment equal to its cost. The internal rate of return has a meaning that is comparable to the rate of return received on one's savings account or money market fund. For example, a 10 percent internal rate of return on an investment is comparable to a 10 percent rate of return received from money market funds.

An important advantage of using the internal rate of return to evaluate an investment is that the outcome of the evaluation does not depend on the rate of interest chosen, as is the case for obtaining the discounted present value, or the B/C ratio. With the internal rate of return measure, the decision to invest or not to invest depends on the computed rate of return. The investment will be profitable if the internal rate of return is at least as much as the rate of interest paid on borrowed funds, or what could be earned in the next best alternative use of one's own funds.

The internal rate of return is computed by a trial and error process. You start out by picking a rate of interest that you think makes the discounted present value equal to the cost of the investment. If the discounted present value you obtain is greater than the cost of the investment, the internal rate of return is greater than the interest rate you have chosen. Thus you have to repeat the calculations using a higher rate of interest. If this time the discounted present value is smaller than the cost of the investment, the internal rate is smaller than the interest rate you have tried. At some point the discounted present value will be exactly equal to the cost of the investment. When this occurs you have found the internal rate of return.[1]

THE EFFECT OF INFLATION

In the apartment house example, it was assumed that the price level remained constant over the course of the returns. In reality, one might expect some inflation, although no one knows what future inflation will be. Inflation increases the gross cash inflow, added expense, and net cash inflow figures over time. Even though gross cash inflow and added expense grow at the same percentage rate, in absolute terms the former grows more than the latter because they are larger figures. Hence, net cash inflow becomes larger. The apartment house example showing a 6 percent inflation rate is:

	Year 0	Year 1	Year 2	Year 3	Year 4
Cash outflow	−$200,000				
Gross cash inflow		+34,344	+36,288	+38,556	+292,824
Added expense		−13,144	−13,888	−14,756	−15,624
Net cash inflow	− 200,000	+21,200	+22,400	+23,800	+277,200

Since the net cash inflow figures in this example exceed those figures when no inflation was assumed, the internal rate of return for a given investment increase with inflation. This result does not imply that investments will always be more profitable during a period of inflation. As explained in the preceding

---

1 From a mathematical standpoint, a unique solution for the internal rate of return is possible only if the stream of returns stays positive over the life of the investment.

chapter, the nominal rate of interest also increases during inflation. This also requires that the IRR is higher for the investment to be profitable.

RANKING OF INVESTMENT OPPORTUNITIES

Most businesses and public agencies have a variety of investment opportunities that they might undertake in a given period. Which ones? A convenient way to answer this question is to list all investment opportunities that exist, perform a cash-flow analysis on each, and then rank them by IRR. A cumulative ranking, illustrated by the figures below, shows the IRR of the marginal dollar invested. If $11,000 is invested, a 21 percent IRR is obtained. As more money is invested, lower-return projects are done. Investing a total of $24,000 drives the IRR of the marginal dollar down to 12 percent, and so on.

With this information, the firm can decide how much to invest. If the interest rate is 12 percent, for example, $24,000 should be invested to maximize profits. Stopping short of this point causes the firm to unnecessarily forgo profits because the returns would exceed the costs. If the interest rate declines to 10 percent, then $34,000 should be invested to maximize profits, and so on.

Project	IRR	Project Investment	Cumulative Investment
A	21%	$11,000	$11,000
B	12	13,000	24,000
C	10	10,000	34,000
D	7	15,000	49,000

Although the procedure for evaluating an investment is straightforward, the hard part is finding accurate figures, especially the future costs and returns. The technique does not help much if erroneous figures are used. Although no one has a crystal ball to foresee the future, the accuracy of expected future costs and returns depends on the competence and sound judgment of the evaluator.

QUESTIONS

1. In the context of a cash-flow table define these terms:
   a. Cash outflow
   b. Gross cash inflow.
   c. Added expense.
   d. Net cash inflow.
2. a. Why is a dollar forthcoming some time in the future worth less than a dollar in hand today?
   b. What is the discounted present value of $100 forthcoming in two years if the interest rate is 10 percent?
3. a. Using the information given in the cash-flow table below, calculate the internal rate of return to the $200,000 investment. (This is the apartment house example assuming a 6 percent inflation rate.)
   b. Why is the internal rate of return higher if inflation occurs than with stable prices?
   c. If the internal rate of return increases during inflation, does it follow that more investment will occur during inflationary times than during times of stable prices? Explain.
   d. What is the net present value of this apartment house with a 10 percent rate of interest?
   e. What is its benefit-cost ratio with a 10 percent rate of interest?

4. How would you use the following to evaluate the profitability of an investment:
   a. The discounted present value?
   b. The benefit-cost ratio?
   c. The internal rate of return?
5. Consider the opportunity of investing in land that you expect will double in value in five years. What is its internal rate of return? Assume the land costs $100,000 now and that there is no added expense of ownership.
6. a. How do changes in the rate of interest affect investment spending?
   b. How do changes in expectations of future economic conditions affect investment spending?
7. If a firm wishes to maximize profits, how much should it invest in new capital each year?

SELF-TEST

1. A profitable investment is one that yields a:
   a. positive rate of return.
   b. rate of return at least as large as the interest paid on borrowed funds.
   c. rate of return at least as large as the opportunity cost of the investor's own funds.
   d. b or c.

Cash-Flow Table

	Year 0	Year 1	Year 2	Year 3	Year 4
Cash outflow	−$200,000				
Gross cash inflow		+$34,344	+$36,288	+$38,556	+$292,824
Added expense	_____	−13,144	−13,888	−14,756	−15,624
Net cash inflow	−$200,000	+$21,200	+$22,400	+$23,800	+$277,200

2. The cash outflow in a cash-flow table represents:
   a. the income generated by the capital.
   b. the depreciation plus interest charge.
   c. money repaid on the loan.
   d. the purchase price of the capital item.

3. Gross cash inflow in a cash-flow table is:
   a. the gross income stream generated by the capital item.
   b. the depreciation and interest charge.
   c. funds borrowed to purchase the capital.
   d. the gross income stream generated by the capital item minus interest and depreciation.

4. The added-expense figures in a cash-flow table include:
   a. interest and depreciation plus miscellaneous expenses such as insurance and repairs.
   b. interest and depreciation only.
   c. the expenses incurred by owning the capital item excluding interest and depreciation.
   d. the purchase price of the capital item less interest and depreciation.

5. The net cash inflow in a cash-flow table equals gross cash inflow minus:
   a. the purchase price of the capital item.
   b. total interest plus depreciation.
   c. interest on borrowed funds plus depreciation.
   d. added expenses.

6. One dollar forthcoming one year from now is worth _____ now.
   a. one dollar.
   b. one dollar plus an interest charge.
   c. less than one dollar.
   d. nothing.

7. The discounted present value of one dollar forthcoming two years from now is $_____ if the interest rate is 10 percent.
   a. .90   c. 1.10
   b. .83   d. 1.21

8. An investment is expected to be profitable if the discounted present value of its future net income stream is greater than:
   a. one.
   b. the rate of interest.
   c. its purchase price.
   d. zero.

9. A benefit-cost ratio is the _____ divided by _____ .
   a. discounted sum of future returns; the interest cost
   b. sum of future returns; the interest rate
   c. discounted sum of future returns; the purchase price
   d. sum of future returns; the purchase price

10. An investment will be profitable if the benefit-cost ratio is:
    a. greater than one.
    b. less than one.
    c. greater than zero.
    d. less than zero.

11. The internal rate of return is that rate of interest that makes the sum of the discounted future returns equal to:
    a. one.
    b. the interest rate.
    c. purchase price of the capital item.
    d. zero.

12. In calculating the internal rate of return, if the sum of the discounted future returns is greater than the purchase price of the capital item, it is an indication that the internal rate of return is _____ the rate of discount used.
    a. greater than
    b. less than
    c. equal to

13. An investment is expected to be profitable is the computed internal rate of return is:
    a. between zero and one.
    b. greater than the rate of interest
    c. equal to one.
    d. any positive value.

14. Inflation _____ the internal rate of return on an investment because the absolute difference between the gross cash inflow and the added-expense figures _____ .
    a. increases; decreases
    b. decreases; decreases
    c. increases; increases
    d. decreases; increases

15. To maximize profits a firm should undertake those investments where the expected internal rate of return is at least as large as:
    a. one.
    b. the rate of interest.
    c. the purchase price of the investments.
    d. zero.

Part VIII

Human Capital

Chapters 25-27

Chapter 25

Cost and Returns of a College Education

Key Concepts

Human capital defined

Personal cost of education

Public cost

Personal returns to education

Social returns

Financing education

Monetary costs

Monetary returns

Internal rates of return

A college education is an investment with a cost and returns. Estimates of these figures for a typical student are presented along with expected rates of return for various students.

HUMAN CAPITAL DEFINED

We defined capital as durable or long-lasting inputs, such as buildings and equipment, that contribute to the production of goods and services. We noted that capital inputs are expensive and that the present value of their stream of returns must be greater than their purchase price for them to yield a net positive contribution to total output. In recent years, there has been growing awareness that the acquisition of knowledge and skills by human beings also results in the creation of capital—human capital. While the special characteristics of human beings are recognized, there are similarities between human capital, the skills and knowledge acquired through education or training, and nonhuman capital.

First, both kinds of capital, human and nonhuman, enhance the productive capacity of society. Human beings without tools and without knowledge are unproductive creatures. Moreover, even a cursory study of history reveals that human capital must exist before nonhuman capital can be produced. For example, the wheel was invented when humans learned that a round object rolling along the ground encountered less friction and took less power to move than a flat object being dragged. There are innumerable examples of new knowledge that have led to the production of new nonhuman capital.

A second similarity between the two kinds of capital is that they both pay off over a long time. The stream of returns to education for most people covers 30 or more years. There are a couple of important consequences of this long payoff period. First, it precipitates much uncertainty. Students are faced with the nagging question of whether the job they prepare for will be available when they graduate, to say nothing of l0 to 20 years in the future. At the high school and undergraduate level of training, it is impossible to predict what kind of employment will be forth coming. Since a person's job can be expected to change several times during a lifetime, it is important that training, particularly at the college level, facilitates learning new jobs and adjusting to new environments. A second consequence of the long payoff is the need to discount future returns. For instance, $1 forth coming 40 years from now discounted back at a l0 percent interest rate is worth less than 2 cents today. With the present demand on a young person s resources, such as car, clothes, and travel, the decision to invest now for a payoff far into the future is difficult.

Third, human capital, like some nonhuman capital, requires a lengthy building period. With human capital, the period is longer. Ten years is the least amount of time that can be devoted to the process, and it may run up to 18 or 20 years for people who obtain a Ph.D. or professional degree. This long gestation or building period, coupled with the long payoff period, makes the discounting factor especially important in the case of human capital.

A fourth similarity between the two kinds of capital is that both tend to depreciate. The ultimate depreciation for human capital is growing old and passing from the scene. But there is a more immediate depreciation that begins the minute we learn something new—forgetting. Educators tell us that a large part of what we learn is forgotten in a short time. How much do you recall of a book you read or a course you took last year, or even last term? Depreciation of human capital also occurs because of obsolescence. Each year, new knowledge is produced that reduces the value of existing knowledge. Skills such as the ability to repair a steam locomotive or fly a propeller-driven air-craft are no longer in demand because of new knowledge and technology. Because of obsolescence, most people must continue learning throughout their careers. This is particularly true for persons in the professions or skilled trades. College professors who want to keep abreast of new knowledge in their field, for example, probably should spend about 20 to 25 percent of their time learning.

The major part of all human capital is the result of formal schooling provided by elementary schools, high schools, trade and vocational schools, and colleges and universities. Not all learning, of course, needs to be of this type. Much learning takes place on the job, either through apprenticeship programs or through learning by doing.

In addition, some learning occurs through individual study, although the truly self-made person, such as Abraham Lincoln, always has been rare. Most of us require someone who can tell us what is important or what to study.

PERSONAL COST OF EDUCATION

Education is not a free good. Indeed, it is more expensive each year, as every student and parent knows. It is useful to itemize the major costs that students or parents bear for education. These include: (1) forgone earnings, (2) tuition, and (3)books and supplies.

It is tempting to exclude forgone earnings (the money you could earn if you were not in school) as part of the cost of an education because this cost is not paid by check or cash. However, a person who decides to go to work after high school gives up a college or technical school education. It is logical to argue that a person who decides to go to school gives up full-time employment earnings during the college years.

In the more developed countries of the world, forgone earnings are negligible for the elementary and junior high school student but are a factor as the student finishes high school and enters college or other advanced training. In developing countries, where educational attainment is low and children enter the labor force at a young age, forgone earnings are important even in the lower grades.

Although the average student may not feel the pinch of forgone earnings as much as the out-of-pocket costs of tuition, books, and so forth, it is necessary to account for this money when deciding how far to go in school. Considering the modest salary that a high school graduate can obtain the first few years out of school, say $12,000 to $14,000 per year, it is clear that even a modest amount of income forgone is large when viewed as a cost.

The other two components—tuition, and books and supplies-are obvious, although tuition generally does not cover the full educational costs of colleges and universities. We will consider this part of the cost in the next section.

One cost item that is conspicuous by its absence is board and room. Surely, a student who pays $5,000 during the school year for a room and meals at the college residence hall should include this amount as a logical part of college costs. But remember that everyone has to be somewhere, so if the student did not pay the $5,000 for living on or near campus, as much or more would have to be paid to live wherever the individual worked. Thus, the cost items that are included are only the extra costs involved in attending college, as opposed to doing something else. Costs are measured in this manner so they can be compared with the extra income obtained by furthering an education.

PUBLIC COST

From the viewpoint of society, all private costs considered in the previous section are a part of the total educational cost that society must bear. The operation of schools and colleges financed in part by tuition, the production of books and supplies, and the loss of earnings during school years, all involve using real resources that could have been used to produce something else—had they not been used to produce education.

In most educational institutions, however, tuition does not come close to covering the cost of operating the schools. In the public elementary and high schools, tuition is zero, so the entire cost is borne by taxpayers. In colleges and universities, tuition varies; some city or community colleges set tuition close to zero, while the more exclusive private schools try to cover a larger share of operating costs by tuition. Most of the high-tuition private schools, however, must rely on endowments to make ends meet. The total cost of education for most students is greater than the cost borne by the individual student or parent.

PERSONAL RETURNS TO EDUCATION

What does an individual obtain from education? There are two components: monetary and nonmonetary. The monetary component is the increased earning power that can be obtained with additional years of schooling. This increased earning power comes from two factors: (1) an increase in the productive capacity of the individual, and (2) the ability to conceive of and produce new goods or services that are more valued by society.

The contribution of education to increased productivity appears to stem, in part, from an increased ability to organize and use resources efficiently, including the scarce resource of time. No one appreciates the importance of time more than the student. With two or three exams coming up and a term paper to finish, the student is forced to make each minute count. The experience gained in allocating time efficiently is one of the most important advantages of a college education, at least from the standpoint of individual productivity. Education also enhances productivity by enabling the individual to accept new technology more readily and use it effectively. Education is particularly important with regard to technology that requires new or different skills. The more educated person seems to possess a greater capacity for self-teaching and adapting to new situations.

The effect of education on the kinds of goods and services produced is demonstrated clearly by comparing the output of a modern industrialized society that has a high proportion of educated people with a traditional society. The traditional society's choice of goods and services is limited to a narrow array of low-quality items, most of which are necessities. The output of the more educated society is of a higher quality and more diverse. The world would be dull for the educated person if education resulted in only greater output of the traditional necessities such as food, clothing, and shelter. Thus, the monetary rewards of additional education stem at least in part from an increased ability to conceive of and produce new and different goods and services that are demanded by a more affluent society.

When considering the monetary rewards of increased education, it is always possible to find exceptions: self-made people with eighth-grade educations who have built up fortunes in the business world, or high school dropouts who made it big in show business. But, if we look at large numbers of people, we find that high school graduates, on the average, earn more than people with an eighth-grade education, and people with college training earn more than high school graduates. Thus, an individual who does not achieve a high school or college education is not necessarily doomed to a life of poverty, but the chances that the person will remain poor are substantially higher than if he or she had received the schooling.

For most people, the returns to additional education exceed the monetary value of increased earnings over a lifetime. The nonmonetary returns to education include: (1) the immediate utility or satisfaction that a person receives during the time of schooling, and (2) the long-run stream of increased satisfaction that accrues during his or her lifetime because of the educational experience.

Although few students think fondly of exams or assignments, most derive some satisfaction from being in an educational environment. The friends that are made, the dances and parties, the dates, the sporting events, the good books that are read, even the pleasure of learning, all provide immediate satisfaction that is not measured in monetary terms.

But the nonmonetary rewards to schooling are not limited to the immediate time spent in school. Many friendships that begin in school endure over a lifetime. Many people meet their spouses in college. Also, education enhances the quality of life by facilitating an awareness and greater understanding of the world around us. The lives of educated people are ruled less by superstition and fear and more by rational thought and deliberate choice. Although we do not have adequate quantitative measures of happiness, psychological studies indicate that people with more education are happier and find greater fulfillment in life than persons with less education. Perhaps education is even more important than money in finding that elusive and nebulous good called happiness.

SOCIAL RETURNS

The returns to education are not limited to the individual. Society also gains. Economists call these gains social returns or externalities, that is, the benefits that are external to the individual receiving the education.

At the family level, the education of the parents should benefit the children. For one thing, it broadens the children's cultural background and opportunities. Children of college-educated parents are more likely to attend college than the children of parents who stopped at the high-school level, although this is less important now because of the accessibility of community colleges. There is also a tendency for at least part of the knowledge gained by parents during their school years to be transmitted to their children. Children who gain an appreciation for the importance of knowledge have gained a great deal.

At the community level, the education of individuals makes the community a better place to live for all. For example, one's chances of getting mugged are greater in neighborhoods where people are poorly educated and have low incomes than in places where the majority is highly educated and affluent. Granted, the income level may be the important factor in this difference, but education has an important bearing on income. An increase in the educational level of people also reduces the amount of fear and suspicion that people have of one another. Because education usually acquaints us with people of different backgrounds and ideas, it helps us become more tolerant of persons who are different than ourselves.

Different kinds of education provide different degrees of social returns. Education that imparts purely technical skills, such as programming a computer, repairing an automobile, or setting a broken bone, primarily benefits the person receiving the education because of the larger income that can be earned by selling these skills.[1] Social returns may be greatest from an education that provides a better understanding of people and society, such as the liberal arts and social sciences.

---

1 The people who purchase the goods and services made possible by education also benefit.

The amount of social return derived from the education of individuals is important because it bears on the financing of education. If social returns are important, then society ought to pay part of the cost of educating the individual. If society receives some benefit from education above what is received by the individual, it should pay part of the individual's educational expense for the person to be willing to invest in education. On the other hand, if the individual receives all the benefits of the education, should the individual be willing to buy the amount that provides a return equal to other investments the person could make?

FINANCING EDUCATION

The relative increase in the cost of providing educational services in recent year has prompted considerable discussion on the optimum methods of paying for these services. In the United States and most other countries, a substantial share of the cost of operating educational institutions has been provided by public funds. The popularity of this method stems from a special characteristic of education. People who buy this service, students, have had little or no opportunity to earn and save enough to pay for it. Of course, many other goods and services, such as baby food and the services of pediatricians, also exhibit this characteristic. However, their benefits are more certain and immediate than the returns to education. By using public tax funds to finance a part of the cost of education, we spread its current cost over several generations, as opposed to concentrating it on one or two generations, that is, the students or their parents.

One alternative to public tuition payment is for families to pay for the education of their children. Among upper-middle- and high-income people, this is frequently done. However, for a large segment of our population the cost of purchasing 12 to 16 years of quality schooling for their children is prohibitive. Children of poor parents would continue to be doomed to poverty because of an inability to buy a means of escape through education. If society desires its young people to continue to achieve 12 to 16 years of quality schooling, then it will have to continue to use public funds to finance part of the education cost. Whether such funding leads to a so-called optimum amount of education is a debatable question. Such funding provides an incentive to over-invest in education because the full cost is not borne by the individual. That is, when the cost of something is subsidized, there is an incentive to buy more of it than if the buyer had to bear the full cost.

On the other hand, the uncertainty faced by the individual who must pay the entire educational cost leads to the purchase of less education than is desirable from the standpoint of society. The argument is that the individual faces more uncertainty regarding the payoff to education than a large group of individuals, that is, society. Thus, each individual is inclined to invest less in education than if the person faced the same uncertainty as the whole society. Therefore, society will have to bear a part of the individual's education cost to make the individual willing to purchase as much education as he or she would if faced with the same uncertainty as society. The existence of any so called social returns, as mentioned previously, also implies the use of public tax funds for education. However, this argument has lost some appeal in recent years because of the inability to quantify the magnitude of such returns or even demonstrate their existence.

An argument for using public funds to support education also can be made on the basis of achieving a more equal distribution of income. If only the rich could afford to buy education for their children, the children of poor parents would remain poor. The use of public funds to finance part of the cost of education has become a widely accepted means of achieving a somewhat more equal distribution of income. Education provides a means of giving people more equality of opportunity to make something out of their lives. Other income-redistributive devices such as welfare programs or a negative income tax scheme are less accepted. In these cases, some taxpayers feel that low-income people do not pull their weight in society and live off of persons who work. Education provides a means of escaping poverty, but it requires considerable work. It is a way for society to help persons who are willing to help themselves. Remember, though, that students at the high school and college level will continue to bear a substantial share of the cost of schooling, regardless of how tuition is financed, because of their forgone earnings. Forgone earnings probably loom larger in the minds of poor students than students from high-income families.

The common method of using public funds to finance education is by allocating the funds directly to the educational institutions. An alternative to this procedure is to provide grants in the form of vouchers directly to the students or parents, allowing them to spend the vouchers at the school of their choice. The school then turns in the vouchers and receives money from the government. Major advantages of this approach are that it gives people more freedom of choice and promotes competition among schools. Public schools now enjoy substantial freedom from competitive forces and have little incentive to innovate and improve the quality of their services or strive for greater efficiency.

Although the returns to education are reflected in more than just monetary rewards, it is helpful to obtain measures of both the costs and returns to investment in human capital or education. If education is an acceptable investment from a strictly monetary point of view, then it is an even better investment when nonmonetary returns are considered.

MONETARY COSTS

As mentioned, the monetary cost of higher education to the student contains three main components: (1) forgone earnings of the student, (2) tuition and fees, and (3) books and supplies. The first component, forgone earnings, is easy to overlook but for most students it represents the largest single item in the total cost of higher education. As the label implies, forgone earnings represent the amount the student could earn if he or she were not going to school. Even the relatively modest wage that a high school graduate is able to earn the first few years out of school becomes quite large when viewed as a cost. It is logical to view forgone earnings as a cost of going to school because they would not have to be given up if the decision were made to take a job rather than take more schooling. Similarly, those young people who decide to go to work right after high school give up the opportunity of a college or technical school education. For them the cost of earning their immediate income is the education or training they did not obtain.

Most students are able to reduce their forgone earnings somewhat by taking summer employment. Thus the forgone earnings expense of one year of school for these students is closer to forty weeks of forgone earnings than fifty-two weeks. Students also work part-time during the school year. These earnings reduce the forgone earnings expense. However, the practice of working part-time involves an opportunity cost. Less time is available for studying, extra-curricular activities, or leisure.

The other two cost components of higher education, tuition and fees and books and supplies, are obvious to the student and therefore require little explanation. It should be noted, however, that the tuition paid by students (or their families) does not cover the full instructional cost in publicly supported institutions and in many if not most private colleges. In most community colleges tuition is kept very low. Even in publicly supported universities where tuition is not a trivial sum, it generally covers only about one-third of the cost of providing the educational services for undergraduates. The remaining two-thirds comes from tax funds. People still pay the full tuition, but this part of the tuition cost is borne by taxpayers rather than by students or their families. The main rationale for this funding procedure is to provide educational opportunities for students from low as well as from high-income families. It seems reasonable to believe that without publicly supported education the distribution of income in the country would be even less equal than it now is.

MONETARY RETURNS

Probably the largest component of the returns to education, and probably the main reason most people attend colleges and technical schools, is the monetary component of the returns to education: the additional earnings that a person may expect over a lifetime. On the average, people with more education tend to earn higher incomes than people with less. There are exceptions, of course, and stopping at the eighth or twelfth year of school doesn't mean a person is doomed to a life of poverty. But the chances of remaining poor are much greater for people who obtain relatively little education.

The figures in Table 25-1 provide an indication of the differences in annual earnings of people with various levels of schooling. In all age categories, people with one to three years of college earn more than those who terminate their schooling at the high school level, and people with four years of college earn more than those with one to three years. This is true of both men and women. Moreover the difference is substantial. Men in the 25-34 age group with a Bachelor's degree earn over $12,000 more per year than men with a high school education. For women of this age group, the difference is nearly $10,000 per year.

Table 25-1. Average Earnings by Age and Education, Year-Around Full time Workers, 1991.

Age	Years of Schooling		
	4 yrs. H.S.	1-3 yrs. College	4 yrs. College
Men			
18-24	$16,559	$16,749	—
25-34	24,045	28,135	$36,198
35-44	28,984	34,377	46,238
45-54	32,468	41,121	50,715
55-64	32,484	35,291	53,008
Women			
18-24	$13,558	$14,850	—
25-34	18,269	20,993	$28,021
35-44	19,824	24,100	32,192
45-54	20,342	23,369	31,586
55-64	18,914	24,049	29,684

Source: U.S. Department of Commerce, Current Population Reports, "Consumer Income," Series P-60, No. 180, Table 30, August, 1992.

A measure of the monetary returns to a college education can be obtained by computing the differences between the earnings of people with a high school education and those with college training. About one-half of all students who begin college drop out before graduating. Therefore the returns to both one to three years of college and a completed four year degree program are computed.

In calculating the forgone earnings cost of attending college, it is assumed that 1600 hours (40 weeks) of full time work are given up. Census figures reveal that women in the 18 to 24 age group earn about 18 percent less than men. Therefore the following hourly wages are assumed for men and women in their

Freshman and Sophomore, and Junior and Senior years.

Men: $6 per hour—Freshman and Sophomore
          $8 per hour—Junior and Senior
Women: $5 per hour —Freshman and Sophomore
          $7 per hour—Junior and Senior

Both forgone earnings and gross earnings of people with college training are reduced 25 percent to take into account payroll taxes. Tuition and fees are from a large public university. Miscellaneous expenses include books and supplies as well as extra expenses associated with college life. These costs will vary from person to person but they provide a starting point from which to figure the expenses. A summary of these costs is presented in Table 25-2.

Table 25–2. Costs of a College Education by Years in School.

	Men		Women	
	1st and 2nd	3rd and 4th	1st and 2nd	3rd and 4th
Forgone Earnings	$9,600	$12,800	$8,000	$11,200
Less: payroll taxes	-2,400	-3,200	-2,000	-2,800
Net	7,200	9,600	6,000	8,400
Tuition and fees	3,300	3,600	3,300	3,600
Miscellaneous	700	900	700	900
Total per year	$11,200	$14,100	$10,000	$12,900

DISCOUNTING THE RETURNS

In assessing the costs and returns to higher education it is important to bear in mind that the returns are forthcoming over a long period of time after the schooling is complete. For most people this period is over forty years in length. We know from a previous chapter that the returns which are not forthcoming until some time in the future are not worth as much as the same number of dollars in hand at the present. And the more distant the returns, the more they are reduced in value. Recall that one dollar forthcoming n years in the future is worth $1/(1 + r)^n$ at the present. As you can see, a dollar forthcoming thirty to forty years from now will not be worth very much at the present. The main point is that we just cannot add up the expected returns in all future years and compare them with the cost. Rather, we have to obtain the discounted present value of these returns, as was done in the apartment house example.

ACCUMULATING THE COSTS

In assessing the cost of education it is necessary to take account of the fact that the costs also are incurred over a period of years, as opposed to a point in time, as occurred in the apartment house example. If it takes a number of years to produce a capital good such as it does for education, then it is necessary to "accumulate" the costs forward in time. This has to be done in order to take account of the interest that could have been earned on the money invested. For example, one dollar of cost incurred one year ago is equivalent to $1.06 expenditure today (if the interest is 6 percent), because during the year the dollar could have earned 6 cents in interest. The general formula for accumulating one dollar of costs forward in time is $(1 + r)^n$ where r is the interest rate, and n is the number of years in the past the cost was incurred. For example, the accumulated cost of one dollar spent four years ago is equal to $(1.06)^4$, or $1.26. In other words, one dollar spent four years ago is equivalent to $1.26 in present expenditure. Of course, this number would have to be multiplied by the number of dollars actually spent four years ago to obtain the total cost. For example, if $1,000 is spent in each of four preceding years, then the total accumulated cost is equal to: $1,000 $(1.06)^4$ + 1,000 $(1.06)^3$ + 1,000 $(1.06)^2$ +1,000 (1.06) = $4,637.10. Notice that the accumulated cost is substantially more than just adding up the four $1,000 figures.

Using this accumulating procedure in conjunction with the discounting technique, we can determine whether or not investment in education is a good buy. Just as for any other investment, education will be profitable if the discounted present value of the returns is at least as great as the accumulated costs.

ACCUMULATED COSTS AND DISCOUNTED RETURNS

The accumulated costs and discounted returns for men and women with one to three years of college (denoted as 2-year individuals) and four years of college using a 10 percent rate of interest are presented in Table 25–3. In calculating the returns, a modest three percent rate of inflation is assumed to prevail over a person's 40 year working life. This assumption increases the absolute difference between the earnings of high school and college trained people. For example, the difference in annual earnings for women with a college degree, age 64, and women with a high school education is $27,084 with a three percent inflation assumption. It is $8,077, assuming constant prices over the 40 years.

Table 25–3. Accumulated Costs and Discounted Returns of a College Education. Ten percent Rate of Interest.

	Accumulated Costs	Discounted Returns
4-year men	$63,819	$152,696
2-year men	25,872	54,541
4-year women	57,699	107,513
2-year women	23,100	33,887

INTERNAL RATES OF RETURN

Recall that the internal rate of return is that rate of interest which makes the accumulated costs of an investment equal to the discounted returns. As shown in Table 25–3, the discounted returns exceed the accumulated costs using a 10 percent rate of interest. Therefore the internal rate of return is larger than 10 percent. The calculated internal rates of return for the four groups of people are presented in Table 25–4. Men with a four year degree have the highest rate of return (17 percent) followed by two-year men and four year women at 15 percent, and two-year women at 13 percent. While these rates of return are not spectacular, they are competitive with returns to investment in nonhuman capital which tend to be in the neighborhood of 15 percent. Also, for most people, education has a nonmonetary return as well.

Table 25–4. Internal Rates of Return to a College Education

	Men	Women
4-year degree	17%	15%
2-years of college	15%	13%

Because of the earnings differentials of large numbers of people are relatively stable from year to year, these rates can be expected to prevail for people leaving college in the mid-to-late 1990s. It is encouraging to observe that over the long run, there has been an upward trend in the rates of return to investment in a college education, especially for women. In the 1960s and 1970s, the estimated rates of return for women were about half as large as the figures presented in Table 25–4.[2]

---

2 See Willis Peterson, *Principles of Economics*: Micro, 3rd ed. 1977, p. 383.

QUESTIONS

1. a. What is human capital?

    b. What are the similarities between human and nonhuman capital?

2. What are the personal and public costs of education?

3. What are personal and social returns to education?

4. In recent years, there has been discussion about the voucher plan for funding part of the educational cost of students. Under this plan, students (or their parents) would receive vouchers that they could use to pay tuition at the school of their choice.

    a. Who would benefit from this plan?

    b. Who would be against it? Why?

5. In contrast to most other things that people buy, such as food, clothing, and shelter, a substantial part of the cost of education is paid for by public tax funds. Why should education be different than other goods?

6. If inflation turns out to be greater than 3 percent per year over the next 40 years, will the estimated internal rate of return figures presented in Table 25–4 increase or decrease? Explain.

7. a. Estimate the cost of your schooling this year. What is the cost of this course for each hour the class meets?

    b. What is the accumulated cost of four years of schooling at this institution with the prevailing rate of interest?

    c. How much additional income per year do you expect to earn because of your college training? Using these figures compute the expected internal rate of return to your investment in a college education.

SELF-TEST

1. Human capital represents _____ people.
    a. wealth owned by
    b. natural abilities of
    c. skills or knowledge possessed by
    d. the labor contributed by

2. Both human and nonhuman capital:
    a. increase the output of society.
    b. pay off over a long period of time.
    c. require real resources to produce.
    d. all of the above.

3. Human capital:
    a. does not depreciate.
    b. depreciates due to obsolescence.
    c. depreciates due to people growing old.
    d. b and c.

4. The monetary returns to education:
    a. cannot be measured.
    b. come from the increased earning power made possible by education.
    c. are measured by the cost of operating schools.
    d. are especially attractive because they are not subject to income taxes.

5. The social returns to education accrue to:
    a. teachers.
    b. people obtaining the education.
    c. others than those obtaining the education.
    d. the government in the form of higher tax receipts.

6. Which of the following does not represent an added cost of attending college?
    a. tuition and fees
    b. books
    c. board and room
    d. forgone earnings

7. Which of the following represents the largest single component of the cost of a college education for most students?
    a. tuition and fees
    b. books

c. board and room

d. forgone earnings

8. The cost of operating public universities _____ the tuition paid by students.

   a. exceeds

   b. is less than

   c. is equal to

9. Education differs from most other services in that the consumers:

   a. pay less than the full cost.

   b. pay more than the full cost.

   c. receive no utility from the service.

   d. are not able to assess the utility from the service.

10. The use of public tax funds to finance part of the cost of education can be justified by the desire of society to:

    a. provide employment for teachers.

    b. keep students off the streets.

    c. achieve a more equal distribution of income.

    d. increase the demand for goods and services, thereby decreasing the unemployment rate.

11. The annual monetary returns to a college education can be measured by:

    a. the annual earnings of college graduates.

    b. the annual earnings of high school graduates.

    c. the difference between the annual earnings of high school and college graduates.

    d. the sum of the annual earnings of high school and college graduates.

12. If inflation should occur over the next 30 to 40 years, the absolute difference between the earnings of high school graduates and the earnings of college graduates should:

    a. increase.   c. disappear.

    b. decrease.   d. remain the same.

13. Because the cost of attending college is incurred over a period of several years before a return is forthcoming, annual costs must be _____ to the end of the senior year. This is accomplished by _____ each cost figure by _____

    a. accumulated; dividing; $(1 + r)^n$

    b. accumulated; multiplying; $(1 + r)^n$

    c. discounted; dividing; $(1 + r)^n$

    d. discounted; multiplying; $(1 + r)^n$

14. The accumulated cost of obtaining a four-year college education at a public university is about:

    a. $10,000   c. $25,000.

    b. $20,000   d. $60,000.

15. The internal rate of return to a college education is equal to that rate of interest which makes the_____equal to_____

    a. accumulated cost; one

    b. discounted returns; the accumulated cost.

    c. accumulated cost; 100

    d. discounted returns; 100

16. The internal rate of return to investment in a college education is in the range of _____ to_____percent.

    a. 5; 10   c. 18; 20

    b. 13; 17   d. 20; 25

17. Because the total cost to society of a college education is _____ than the cost borne by the student, society's internal rate of return of a college education will be _____ than the return realized by the individual.

    a. greater: greater

    b. less; greater

    c. greater; less

    d. less; less

Chapter 26

Time Management

Key Concepts

The student as a firm
Human capital production
Intermediate goods production
Household production
Utility maximization
Behavioral differences
Value of time management

Time is a scarce resource. This chapter provides a framework for allocating time to its most productive uses. Emphasis is given to part-time employment by college students and how it influences time allocation and grades. The experience gained in managing time is one of the most valuable experiences obtained from a college education.

ThE STUDENT AS A SMALL, MULTIPRODUCT FIRM

In the study of time management it is helpful to cast the student in the role of a small, multiproduct firm engaged in producing three categories of output: (1) human capital, (2) intermediate goods via the labor market (for students who work part-time), and (3) final goods for current consumption. Because of the output diversity we will use utility as a measure or common denominator of output. Our main interest is the allocation of time to each of the categories of activities. Hence, the marginal physical product (MPP) of time is the extra utility resulting from the input of one more hour of time to any of the three activities.

A. Human Capital

In the production of human capital, the student combines time with other purchased inputs such as faculty services, instructional facilities, and books. The marginal product of time in the production of human capital depends on the inherent capability of the student and the quantity and quality of complementary inputs such as the teacher and instructional materials. The marginal productivity of study time (for a given quantity) is greater for more capable and highly motivated students than for unmotivated students. Similarly, the marginal product of time is higher for students who have good teachers and effective instructional materials, or for students enrolled in high-payoff programs.

Remember that the MPP of study time depends on the quality and quantity of other inputs used in the production of human capital. If the prices of these inputs become more expensive, less will be purchased, which will reduce the MPP of study time.[1] In other words, if it becomes more expensive to attend college, fewer educational services will be purchased by young people, which will reduce the amount of time allocated to study. For persons who decide not to attend college, little time is allocated to study.

The utility (returns) derived from human capital production includes both monetary and nonmonetary components. Also, the utility forthcoming in the future, from either monetary or nonmonetary sources, should be discounted back to the present to be comparable with the utility produced through part-time employment or household production. No student knows how much income will be increased by education or how much education will enrich life in the future. In spite of the difficulties of assessing the utility forthcoming from edu-

---

1 This assumes that study time and educational services are net complements.

cation, each student must make allocative decisions about time and other inputs within school activities, and between this category and other activities.

B. Intermediate Goods

Students who work part-time participate in a second kind of production activity. Although work may not result in utility, the income received yields utility through the goods and services it can buy. In addition, some earnings may be used to purchase inputs for the production of human capital, such as in paying tuition or the purchase of books and supplies. For a given input of time to part-time employment, the higher the real wage, the greater the MPP of this time because the extra hour of work allows for the purchase of more goods and services.

Some jobs are less agreeable than others. Therefore, the utility received by the goods and services purchased through earnings from work should be adjusted by differences in the kind of work performed. For example, higher wages earned by cleaning the sewer or collecting garbage do not necessarily increase utility in proportion to the higher earnings from these jobs.

C. Household Production

The third type of activity is household production. Here, the student combines time with conventional goods, such as food, clothing, housing, transportation, and entertainment services, to produce utility. The MPP of time in household production depends on individual tastes. For example, the student who loves to ski will spend more time on the slopes than a person who receives more utility from an automobile purchased from the earnings of part-time employment. The second person will spend more time working on a part-time job.

Similar to the production of human capital, the prices of other inputs, such as the car or skiing activities, determine the MPP of time devoted to each activity. For example, if cars become relatively expensive compared to skiing, the MPP of work time devoted to buying the car will decline because the extra hour of work time will buy less car than if cars were cheaper. Most of the discussion in this chapter will focus on how differences in the price of time influence the allocation of time, but remember that changes in the prices of other inputs used with time also influence its allocation.

UTILITY MAXIMIZATION

Recall from Chapter 4 that a person maximizes utility from a given level of income by equalizing the MU/P ratios. The same is used to maximize the utility from a given value of time. The MPP of time is measured in utils, so MU and

MPP are the same. The price of time in an activity is its value in the next best alternative activity—its opportunity cost.

The rule for maximizing utility for a given value of time is:

$$MPP_1/P_1 = MPP_2/P_2 = MPP_3/P_3$$

This rule says that the marginal utility (MPP) per dollar of time should be the same in all three production activities. If one ratio is higher than another, a person's total utility can be increased by allocating more time to the high-ratio activity and less time to other activities. For example, if the MPP per dollar of time is 10 in household production and 15 in the production of human capital, 5 additional units of satisfaction are obtained by transferring $1 of time from household to human capital production.

Because the opportunity cost of time differs between different people and different times of day, the price of time varies accordingly. During the normal daytime or early evening working hours, the price of time devoted to study will be wages forgone (net of taxes) from a full-time job. Similarly, the price of time devoted to employment during these hours is the implicit value of time devoted to study or household activities, whichever is higher. During normal rest or sleep hours, the price of time devoted to study is the implicit value placed on sleep. Conversely, the price of time devoted to sleep or rest is the implicit value of either study or employment, whichever is higher. The price of time to employment or household activities also varies according to the proximity of examinations, increasing just before examinations, when an extra hour of study may have a high payoff in terms of obtaining better grades.

One unique characteristic of time, as opposed to other purchased inputs, is that the individual must utilize 24 hours per day regardless of price. The allocation of time to various activities will vary as price changes, but as long as a person is alive, time is utilized in one of the three production activities. (Leisure and sleep are included in household production of utility.)

PART-TIME EMPLOYMENT AND TIME ALLOCATION

In measuring the cost of a college education, it was assumed that students receive no earnings during the school year. Yet, more than half of all college students work part-time during the school year. Part-time earnings reduce the total forgone earnings, which represent the largest cost of a college education for most students. Hence, if we accounted for part-time earnings, the total cost of a college education should decrease, and the estimated rate of return should increase.

On the other hand, students who participate in part-time employment during the school year must give up something. The time spent working must be taken away either from school or leisure activities. Since these activities also have value, it is incorrect to subtract part-time earnings from the cost of education without subtracting the value of the utility lost by devoting less time to other activities. The fact that many students decide to work part-time means that they believe they gain more from the part-time employment earnings than what they give up. It is useful, therefore, to look at the effect of part-time employment on time allocation.

We can use the utility-maximizing rule to predict what happens when a student engages in part-time employment. Let us consider a student who is engaged only in the production of utility through school and household activities, that is, a full-time student. Assume that the student maximizes utility by equalizing the MPP/P ratios of time for these two activities. Suppose an attractive job opportunity occurs so that the MU per dollar of time becomes larger in the production of intermediate goods purchased from earnings than in the other two activities. The opportunity of earning higher wages also increases the price of time devoted to school activities. Recall that the price of time is its value in the next best alternative. This throws the student out of equilibrium further by reducing the MPP/P of time in school activities.

The price of time devoted to household production may initially increase because of the superior job opportunity. If the job is available only during daytime work hours on weekdays, the opportunity cost of time to household production may still be the wages that could be earned on less desirable jobs or the implicit value of study time, whichever is higher. If the job entails night or weekend work, the opportunity cost of time devoted to household production of utility will increase initially. However, we will see that it ultimately makes no difference whether the job entails day, night, or weekend work; the price of time to household production will still increase as the student adjusts to the new situation.

Assuming that the job requires daytime work, say 20 hours per week, the initial consequence of the job, taking the adjustment in steps, is to reduce study time. If study time is subject to diminishing returns, the reduction in study time will increase the implicit price of time to household activities (entertainment, sleep, and so forth) because the MU obtained from the last hour of study time will increase. This reduces the MPP/time price ratio of time devoted to household production, and consequently the student will utilize some time originally allocated to household production for study. In reality, the adjustment in study and household time will occur simultaneously.

As the student approaches a new equilibrium, the amount of time devoted to study and household production must decrease a total of 20 hours per week in this example. How much each is reduced depends on the slope of the MPP curves of time in the production of human capital and household goods. If the MPP curve of study time is steeply sloped relative to the MPP curve of household time, the largest reduction in time will come from the latter. This depends on the individual. The main point is that the decision to work part-time results in a reduction in time allocated to study and to household activities because both of their MPP/time price ratios are reduced when a job is accepted.

We might also expect the allocation to change between different terms. If the MPP of study time shifts to the right because of stimulating teachers or courses, for example, a greater proportion of work time will be taken away from household activities. Also, the student may quit the job if the MPP of study time shifts to the right enough so that the MPP/time price ratio for study exceeds what is experienced in part-time employment.

We also would expect different students to react differently to the same job opportunity. If the MPP/time price ratios for study and household activities are high because the student is highly motivated, extremely capable, attending a high-quality school, or enrolled in a high-payoff program such as medical school, the job opportunity may be declined. The production of utility from part-time-work may also decline after a period of work if the student has saved enough to pay for goods such as room and board in the immediate future. This can explain why students tend to be in and out of the job market.

PART-TIME EMPLOYMENT AND GRADES

One should not conclude, however, that a reduction in study time necessarily reduces the time allocated to each course. When working on a part-time job, the student has the option of reducing his or her credit load while maintaining the time devoted to each course. Which option the student chooses depends on the value of grades and knowledge given up by working and maintaining a full-credit load versus the cost of extending the degree program. Students who place a high value on good grades because of personal satisfaction, a belief that good grades will increase future income, or because of an intention to pursue graduate or professional study, will reduce their credit loads and extend the length of their programs if they decide to work part-time. Of course, as the hours worked per week approaches the equivalent of a full-time job, both grades and credit hours will be reduced. Although our theory tells us that student participation in part-time employment should reduce the amount of time devoted to school and household activities, it does not reveal the magnitude of these reductions. Nor does it tell us whether part-time employment reduces grades, credit load, or both.

Preliminary evidence from a sample of students at the University of Minnesota suggests that students both reduce grades and credit load, although as shown by the figures in Table 26–1, the relative effects are not the same for all students. As indicated in Table 26–1A, freshmen and sophomores who work part-time experience significant grade reductions, while juniors and seniors do not. The numbers in Table 26–1 indicate the reduction in GPA out of a maximum 4.0 for students who work the respective hours per week compared to students who do not work—holding constant a number of student characteristics.[2]

---

2 Characteristics held constant include hours spent on extracurricular activities, classes cut per week, high school rank, number of math, chemistry, and biology courses, and a qualitative measure of the importance of grades to the student. The latter, along with classes cut per week, attempts to account for differences in motivation among students.

On the other hand, the numbers in Table 26–1B suggest that juniors and seniors are more likely to reduce their credit load when working part-time. These figures indicate the reduction in credits taken per quarter by students who work the respective hours in comparison with students who do not work, again holding constant student characteristics such as GPA and class absences. The tendency for juniors and seniors to reduce their credit loads when working probably explains why they do not suffer grade reductions. Why juniors and seniors appear to behave differently in these respects is open to speculation. Perhaps students who survive the first two years receive the greatest utility from good grades and therefore do not jeopardize grades by attempting to maintain a full-credit load when working, or do not work as many hours per week.

TABLE 26–1 Reductions in Grade Point Averages and Credits Taken by Students Who Work Compared with Students Who Are Not Employed Part-Time*

	(A) Grade-Point Average Reductions		(B) Credit Reductions per Quarter	
Hours Worked per Week	Freshman-Sophomore	Junior-Senior	Freshman-Sophomore	Junior-Senior
1-12	0.22	NS	NS	NS
13-25	0.31	NS	NS	1.44
More than 25	0.39	NS	1.48	2.50

NS = Not Statistically Significant from Zero.

*From Sample of 133 Students at the University of Minnesota Covering Fall Quarter 1973 and winter 1974. A = 4.0.

Source: Willis Peterson, "The Effect of Part.Time Employment on Student Allocation of Time and Academic performance," University of Minnesota Staff Paper /P73-11, June 1973, p. 12.

STUDENT BEHAVIOR

Although there is much variation among students in terms of ability, courses taken, major, career objectives, part-time employment opportunities, extracurricular activities, etc., we can reasonably assume that all try to maximize utility, given their resources. The desire to maximize utility results in substantial variability in how students allocate their time. Some examples follow.

A. Highly Motivated, Capable Student

For a given amount of study time this student will exhibit a relatively high MPP of study, compared to one not so highly endowed or motivated. As a result this student will enjoy a relatively high MPP/P ratio of study time, given the price of time. In order to equalize the MPP/P ratios the good student will allocate an above average amount of time to study, driving down MPP of study time to the point where the MPP/P of study time is equal to the other two ratios. The same is true of a student who values good grades highly, or desires a high GPA to get into a postgraduate professional program or graduate school.

B. High-Payoff Major

Bear in mind that a sizable part of the MPP of study time is the discounted present value of expected earnings obtained in one's career. If the career being prepared for offers a high income potential, such as engineering or medicine, the expected MPP of study time will be relatively high. Therefore students enrolled in such programs will allocate more time to study than their counterparts in low payoff programs, other things equal. As for the highly motivated student above, this behavior drives the MPP of study time down, such that the MPP/P ratio is again equal to the other two ratios, thus maximizing utility.

C. High Opportunity Cost of Study Time

Students experiencing good part-time job opportunities, such as those in large metropolitan areas, will have a relatively high price of study time. This causes the MPP/P ratio for study to be relatively low, other things equal. To raise the MPP of study time, less time is allocated to study. Also high wages in part-time employment increases the MPP of time in this endeavor, making for a high MPP/P ratio. As more time is allocated to part-time employment, the MPP of time in this activity declines, which in turn decreases the ratio. Eventually the ratios come into balance.

D. Talented Athlete

This student has a high price of study time and a high MPP of time in practicing his or her sport. This makes the MPP/P ratio for study relatively low and the ratio for practice relatively high. To equalize the ratios, the student will allocate more time to practice and less to study. The pressure on student athletes to perform well in the classroom forces them into a time allocation that does not maximize their utility, particularly those who have the ability to enter the professional ranks. It should not be surprising, therefore, that athletes are reluctant to allocate as much time to study as the rest of the student body.

VALUE OF TIME MANAGEMENT

By now it is evident that the management of time by college students is a complex endeavor. Students have to assess the MPP (utility) of time not only among various activities but also within activities. For example, should the student allocate slightly more time to economics and less to some other subject, or vice versa? It is like juggling 10 balls at once. In addition, the optimum allocation of time will change from one term to the next, depending on teachers, courses, the opportunities for part-time employment, recreational and social activities, and so forth. How well a student manages time largely determines the individual's success in college.[3] In fact, the experience gained in managing time may be one of the most important things gained from college. This may surprise students who think that the knowledge gained from courses taken represents the main value of a college education. Certainly this knowledge is important, but learning how to manage time, a valuable and scarce resource, is equally important.

Although the discussion in this chapter has focused on student allocation of time, the principles apply to any individual or family. For nonstudents, there are two broad categories of production: the production of intermediate goods via the labor market and the production of final goods in the context of the household activities during nonworking hours. In this case, the individual should allocate time such that the MPP/time price ratios are equalized within each broad category and among the categories. Again, the MPP of time is the utility produced by an extra hour of time, while the price of time is the value of this hour in the next-best alternative activity. Whenever there is a change in MPP or in the price of time, the individual should reallocate away from the low MPP/time price ratio activities toward activities with high ratios.

---

3 You might have heard the story of a college student who brought home a grade report showing three Fs and a D. The student's parents were concerned and inquired about the problem. After some thought, the student replied, "I spent too much time on one subject."

QUESTIONS

1. A college student can be viewed as a small multiproduct firm. What is produced and what are the inputs?

2. a. How should time be allocated so a given value of time yields the greatest utility?

   b. What is the MPP of time? What is the price of time?

   c. What is the meaning of the MPP/time price ratio?

3. A large proportion of college students hold part-time jobs.

   a. According to the theory of time allocation, will part-time work reduce the time allocated to study? Explain.

   b. Does the theory of time allocation tell us that part-time work reduces grades? Explain.

4. College students study hardest just before examinations. Does this behavior represent an efficient allocation of time? Explain.

5. Would the attainment of a straight-A academic record represent an efficient allocation of time for most students? Explain.

6. State whether each of the following college students should allocate an "above-average" or a "below-average `amount of time to study, and explain why.

   a. A bright and highly motivated student.

   b. A student enrolled in a school where the payoff to the training is high.

   c. A talented basketball player who has a chance of signing a million-dollar contract if he makes All-American..

   d. A student working as a high-paid salesperson.

   e. A student who receives little utility from good grades.

SELF-TEST

1. College students who work part-time produce:

   a. human capital.

   b. intermediate goods via the labor market.

   c. final goods for current consumption.

   d. all of the above.

2. Output of the three production activities can be represented by the common denominator:

   a. money.   c. knowledge.

   b. utility.   d. grade points.

3. In the production of human capital the MPP of time for a given amount of study will be highest:

   a. in economics.

   b. for a bright, highly motivated student.

   c. for a student of average ability.

   d. in poorly taught courses.

4. The price of time devoted to human capital production equals:

   a. the wage rate in part-time work.

   b. the value of time in household production.

   c. a or b, whichever is smallest.

   d. a or b, whichever is largest.

5. Time is unique among the various inputs in the three types of production in that:

   a. the maximum amount is always employed.

   b. it has no value.

   c. it cannot be varied among the various activities.

   d. it is not subject to the law of diminishing returns.

6. The maximum utility can be obtained from a given value of time only if:

   a. the MPPs of time are equal in all activities.

   b. the price of time is equal in all activities.

   c. the marginal utility (MPP) per dollar

of time is equal in all activities.

   d. all of the above.

7. Part-time employment by college students _____ forgone earnings during a specific time period but involves:

   a. increases; a monetary cost.

   b. decreases; a monetary cost.

   c. increases; an opportunity cost.

   d. decreases; an opportunity cost.

8. The appearance of an attractive part-time job _____ the _____ of time utilized for human capital and household production.

   a. increases; price

   b. decreases; price

   c. increases; MPP

   d. decreases; MPP

9. The greater the number of hours devoted to part-time employment and study the _____ the MPP of time in _____ production.

   a. greater; intermediate goods

   b. greater; human capital

   c. greater; household

   d. less; household

10. In the production of utility through part-time employment, the MPP of work time for a given amount of work will be highest for:

   a. bright, highly motivated students.

   b. student of average ability.

   c. high-wage employment.

   d. low-wage employment.

11. The theory of time allocation suggests that a college student who works 20 hours per week on a part-time job will allocate 20 hours less per week to:

   a. study.

   b. household activities.

   c. sleep.

   d. a and b.

12. The evidence suggests that Freshmen and Sophomores who work part-time experience a decrease in _____ , whereas Juniors and Seniors:

   a. credit loads; are not affected by part-time work.

   b. grades; carry a lighter course load.

   c. credit loads; experience lower grades.

   d. grades; are not affect by part-time work.

13. Of the following students, those who can be expected to hold a part-time job are:

   a. enrolled in a high-payoff program.

   b. bright and highly motivated.

   c. talented athletes.

   d. located in a high wage area.

14. Of the following students, those who can be expected to allocate the least amount of time to study are:

   a. enrolled in a high-payoff program.

   b. talented athletes who have a chance of signing a million dollar contract after four years of schooling.

   c. bright and highly motivated.

   d. have few opportunities for part-time work.

15. Which of the following students can be expected to allocate the most amount of time to study?

   a. an average student located in a high wage area

   b. a bright student located in a high wage area

   c. a bright student enrolled in a high-payoff program

   d. a talented athlete

16. Students can be observed studying hardest just before examinations. This behavior is _____ because the _____ of study is high just before exams.

   a. rational; MPP

   b. irrational; MPP

   c. rational; price

   d. irrational; price

17. For most college students a straight-A academic grade average would be:

   a. the best of all possible worlds.

   b. physically impossible.

   c. irrational because the price would be too high.

   d. the ideal attainment.

Chapter 27

Science and Technology

Key Concepts

The book concludes with an economic analysis of investment in science and technology. Without advances in science, higher education would not exist in its present form. After exploring the nature of research, the discussion focuses on the main contributions of new knowledge in modern society.

THE PRODUCTION OF NEW KNOWLEDGE

In Chapter 25, education, the transfer of knowledge from books and teachers into the minds of students, was treated as an investment involving a cost and a return. In this chapter, we will probe deeper into this process, seeking an understanding of the production of knowledge itself.

At the beginning of history, the stock of knowledge was small as measured by today's standards. Hunting and fishing skills and the ability to transform nature's bounty into food, clothing, and shelter constituted knowledge. Somewhere along the way, humans acquired the ability to communicate by sound. Although we take this skill for granted, reflection suggests the tremendous advance in knowledge that the introduction of verbal skills represented. Every object, action, or thought became associated with a sound. Moreover, there was a common agreement, at least within an area or tribe, about the meaning of sounds produced by vocal cords. Anyone who has studied a foreign language can appreciate the difficulty of learning correct sounds and the advanced knowledge it represents.

As verbal skills were mastered, it became possible to pass on to the next generation important information that otherwise would have been relearned by each individual through trial and error. Equally important was the introduction of written language, which is more efficient as a permanent means of communication and more efficient for the transfer and acquisition of knowledge.

A common characteristic of knowledge produced during the dawn of history is that it occurred by accident. In sustaining themselves, people learned new things about plants, animals, and the environment. In Greek and Roman civilizations, scholars and philosophers began to pursue knowledge as a full-time occupation. In the Middle Ages, the early church emerged as a center of learning. Mendel, one of the church's best-known monks, discovered the principle of hybridization while experimenting with peas. Although the pursuit of knowledge by gifted individuals had important consequences, the knowledge industry, that is, the employment of people solely for advancing knowledge, was unknown. During the Dark Ages, the overall stock of knowledge appeared to decrease.

RESEARCH AS A PRODUCTION ACTIVITY

In history, it became apparent that if certain people could devote themselves to the full-time pursuit of knowledge, a much greater intellectual output per unit of effort was possible than when knowledge was a by-product of daily activities. People with special talents in developing new knowledge could accomplish more if they were freed from other tasks. Galileo, Newton, Edison, Franklin, and Einstein could not have accomplished their achievements if they had to toil as full-time farmers or shopkeepers.

Thus, the production of new knowledge through research began as a by-product of daily activities and gradually emerged as the domain of a select few. Now, it is a full-fledged industry. In the United States during the immediate post-World War II years, research was one of the nation's most rapidly growing industries. We refer to research as an industry because it has much in common with traditional types of production. Research is a production activity. Inputs consist mainly of scientists and engineers, laboratories and testing facilities: output consists of new knowledge. The same concepts we used in our discussion of producer choice and product supply—such as marginal and average product, marginal and average costs, diminishing returns, and economies of scale—also apply to the production of new knowledge.

At the same time, there are unique characteristics of research. First, there is the difficulty of measuring output. Knowledge does not come in easy-to-measure units like kilograms, or dollars. Economists have found ways of measuring knowledge indirectly, however.

A second unique characteristic of research is that there is a possibility that in the aggregate it may not be subject to the law of diminishing returns. Recall that the law of diminishing returns refers to a situation where the addition of a variable input to one or more fixed inputs results in a diminished marginal physical product to the variable input. Scientists and their supporting personnel and facilities are the variable input and nature's secrets or the potential stock of knowledge are the fixed input in the production of new knowledge (research). Will the addition of more scientists result in a diminishing and eventually zero marginal product of scientific research? If nature's secrets or the potential stock of knowledge is finite, we would expect diminishing returns at some point. But if all knowledge, known and unknown, is infinite, then research need not be subject to the law of diminishing returns.

A third unique characteristic of research is that its outcome is uncertain. In most other production activities, quantity and nature of the outcome are predicted with a high degree of certainty. For example, if the blueprint is followed, the construction of a building will result in the expected outcome. Most other production is routine in nature—it has been done many times before. But research is something that has not been done before. Thus, it is impossible to predict with any certainty the outcome of an individual research project. If we could predict its outcome, the research would not be worth the effort. The implication of the uncertain outcome of research is that some research will add to the stock of knowledge and other research will not. Research is like drilling for oil. Out of every 10 holes drilled, there may be nine dry holes for every gusher. But, the successful projects more than pay for the failures. The uncertainty of the payoff to research makes it impossible to predict the rate of return to individual projects. When large numbers of projects are grouped together, however, the proportion of successful ventures will remain relatively constant from year to year, which enables one to predict their overall average payoff with some accuracy.

It is useful to probe more deeply into research. It encompasses a wide array of endeavors, ranging from basic research to more applied and developmental activity.

BASIC RESEARCH

Basic research is activity concerned with unlocking the secrets of nature without solving a particular problem. This does not imply that the output of basic research is of little use. Some of the most important research results have come from basic research.

A small proportion of research and development funds is spent on basic research. In recent years, expenditures for basic research amounted to only 10 to 12 percent of all research and development expenditures. It is easy to understand why basic research has remained small. An industrial firm invests in research to increase profits. If the firm has no guarantee that the research results can be applied to the firm's operation, such as for basic research, it has little incentive to pay for it. Some large firms give their scientists a small amount of free time for basic research, but this is mainly a fringe benefit.

Consequently, most basic research is done by colleges and universities or the federal government. Even here, there is reluctance to turn scientists loose; this might be due to a public fear that the funds would be squandered on scientists' pet projects with little chance for any payoff to society. Basic research is risky business. Perhaps one or two projects out of 10 add something significant to knowledge.

APPLIED RESEARCH

Applied research is concerned with solving a particular problem or finding out an unknown. For example, the problem might be finding a way to reduce air pollution caused by automobiles or to curb the noise of jet engines.

Both industry and public institutions are more willing to finance applied research than basic research. Understandably, a business is more certain that a return will occur if the research is centered on a problem concerning the firm. The same is true for publicly sponsored research. Society feels more certain that it receives its money's worth from research if scientists work on a recognized problem.

DEVELOPMENT

Development is the almost exclusive domain of large industrial firms and the federal government. Development activities include building prototypes of new products and testing them before their market introduction. However, it is difficult to separate development from applied research. Development is a kind of applied research because it seeks the unknown of a product or production technique. Most industrial research is lumped into one category and called *research and development* (R&D).

It is not easy to even distinguish between basic and applied research. An applied research project can bring unexpected knowledge totally unrelated to the problem at hand. In this sense, applied research has the same characteristics as basic research. It is best, therefore, to view these three research categories as a continuum ranging from pure basic research, to applied research, to development activity on the other end of the scale.

RESEARCH BY INDUSTRIAL FIRMS (R&D)

Research by industrial firms is concentrated in applied and development activity. The overall motivation for a firm to do R&D is to improve its profit position. Research and development can increase profits for the firm by: (1) the development of new or improved products, which increases demand for the firm's products, or (2) the development of new cost-reducing techniques of production, which reduces average and marginal costs for the firm. The production of new or improved products resulting from R&D is illustrated in Figure 27–1.

Figure 27–1A illustrates the situation for an imperfectly competitive firm before it undertakes the development of a new or improved product. If the R&D program is successful and a new product is developed, the demand facing the firm shifts to the right, as shown by D_1 in Figure 27–1B. This might depict an auto manufacturer that has developed an engine with better gas mileage. The demand for the company's product will shift to the right as customers switch from companies that do not offer the improved engine. Remember, however, that R&D is costly. Hence, the R&D program increases the firm's average total cost (ATC) and marginal cost (MC). Thus, ATC_1 and MC_1 in Figure 27–1B are drawn in slightly higher than their original position in Figure 27–1A. In this example, total profits, depicted by the shaded areas, are higher after R&D than before, which indicates that the additional revenue from increased product demand offsets the additional cost of R&D.

The second possibility for increasing profits through R&D is to reduce production costs through the discovery and adoption of new cost-reducing techniques. For example, a firm might develop a new, more efficient method of assembling its product with robots. This would shift ATC and MC down and to the right, as illustrated in Figure 27–2. Here, assume that the product remains

FIGURE 27–1 The Effect of New and Improved Products Resulting from R&D

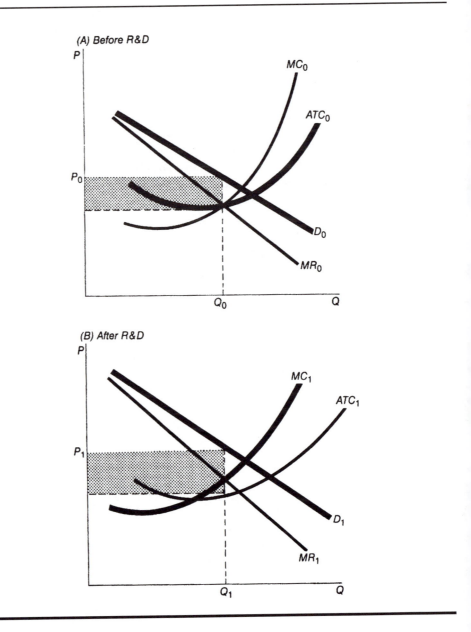

the same so that the demand and marginal revenue curves are the same in both diagrams.

In this example, we also have assumed that the cost saving obtained through the new technique more than offset the increased costs brought on by R&D. Total profits, denoted by the shaded areas in Figure 27–2, increase as a result of the increased R&D expenditure.

FIGURE 27-2 Effect of New Cost-Reducing Techniques Resulting from R&D

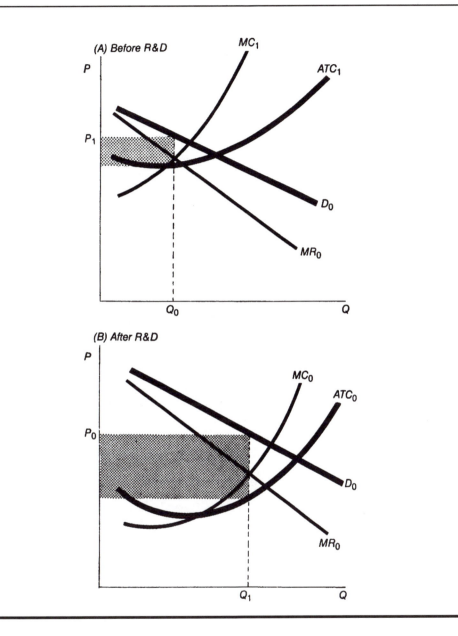

RETURNS TO INDUSTRIAL R&D

The decision about doing R&D is straightforward; it should be done as long as expected revenue increases more than expected costs. But, in an actual decision-making situation, the main problem is assessing the returns to R&D. The firm has no guarantee that demand will shift to the right or that costs will shift down.

The usual procedure for a firm is to begin with a modest R&D program, perhaps hiring an engineer to think of new or improved products. If total revenue increases more than salary and expenses, the firm may add another R&D person, and so on. In other words, decisions about doing R&D are marginal. Because of the substantial increase in R&D recently, we can infer that most firms have found it profitable; hence they are doing it more.

The decision to engage in R&D may also be motivated by the desire to maintain a profit position. If other firms in the industry are investing in R&D to create new or improved products or to lower production costs, the firm that does not keep up will have few customers or excessively high costs and eventually will fail. Even in this context, the effects of R&D are illustrated by Figures 27–1 and 27–2. Profits after R&D are higher than otherwise.

In deciding whether or not to engage in R&D, the overriding consideration by the firm must be whether or not it will be possible to capture a return on its investment. If the knowledge produced by R&D is available to competing firms, the firm that originally produced the knowledge will not gain any special advantage. For example, a pharmaceutical firm that develops a new ingredient that makes a drug more effective will guard its secret closely. If other firms duplicated the ingredient, they could gain all of its advantages without paying the cost. This explains why some firms and governments find it profitable to employ industrial spies. One alternative for the firm or individual who develops something new is to takeout a patent with the government patent office. Patent laws forbid duplication of the patented item or process by other firms or individuals for a period of 17 years.Without these laws or protection, there is little incentive to invest in R&D.

In reality, however, patent laws have not offered perfect protection. Although a patented item cannot be duplicated exactly, in many cases, a close substitute can be developed by making a few minor changes. Patenting certain products or processes actually may hasten their discovery and adoption by competing firms. For this reason, firms sometimes do not patent something they have developed; they try to keep it a secret. The decision whether to take out a patent depends mainly on the product or process. If it is something easy to keep secret, such as an additive or minute ingredient as in Coca-Cola or Tootsie Rolls, it might be best not to patent. But, if it is a machine or a gadget that will be widely used, patenting provides some protection, although rarely complete protection, against copying by other firms.

Another important factor that affects whether or not a firm will invest in R&D is the absolute size of the firm. It will not pay for a small firm to engage in sizable R&D effort. Consider a small farm. Even if no one copied its research results, it would not pay for it to spend several million dollars attempting to increase yields. The expected return would be small compared with the probable cost.

On the other hand, a large firm like General Motors can find it profitable to spend a great deal on something that may improve quality or decrease costs only a small amount per vehicle. A small unit gain multiplied by a large volume will yield a handsome return to a sizable R&D expenditure. In general, the larger the firm, the more profitable it is to invest in R&D to achieve a given percentage increase in demand or decrease in costs.

Thus far, we have considered only the private returns, that is, extra profits of industrial R&D. But R&D can still be a good investment for society even if it does not provide higher profits for the firm doing the R&D. Generally, the extra profits from a new product or production technique are eventually eroded away as more firms copy the product or technique. But, the fact that the individual firm's extra profits from R&D eventually disappear does not mean that society's benefits from R&D also disappear. Society continues to enjoy a return from R&D long after its profits are eroded away because of the resulting new or improved products that continue to be consumed and/or the reduced costs brought about by new technology. In other words, R&D allows society to obtain a greater value of output from its limited resources. Economists refer to this benefit as a social return.

PUBLICLY SPONSORED RESEARCH

An industrial firm will not choose to invest in research unless it has reasonable assurance that it will add to profits, and the small firm will not engage in research because the expense is too great to be borne by small output. However, society benefits from research that may not be profitable for an individual firm or that affects the output of industries made up of firms too small to do their own research, such as agriculture. For this reason, federal and state governments either sponsor research or do it in their own laboratories or institutions.

Most publicly sponsored research is done in colleges and universities. Because of the risk involved and the small chance of capturing a profit on the knowledge produced, much of the country's basic research is done in these institutions. Most economic research (with the exception of market research on individual products)is done in institutions of higher learning. This is also true for research in the humanities and other social sciences.

The decisions on what kind of and how much public research should be done are more difficult than for industrial research. The decision-making process is slow, cumbersome, and often based on inadequate information. But someone must make these decisions, regardless of the information available. The basic decisions are made by society's elected representatives in state and federal governments. They must decide how much of the taxpayers' money will be devoted to research. Usually the amount allocated to research for a current year is based on what was allocated the year before, plus a little extra for increasing prices and new problems or programs.

Once funds reach research institutions, more decisions are required to further allocate the money. How much goes to physics, chemistry, economics, agriculture, child development, and so forth? Again, the current allocation is usually based on past allocation. Marginal changes occur with changes in personnel or with the emergence or recognition of new and pressing problems such as the environment or health.

Ideally, public research allocation should be made based on the highest payoff to research, but the problem is identifying the returns to public research.

RETURNS TO PUBLIC RESEARCH

The returns to public research, like education, are classified into monetary and nonmonetary components. In the nonmonetary area, society will pay to gain information about itself or about the universe, even though this knowledge may not lead to an increase in the value of real output in society. For example, society has been willing to pay to develop a means of getting to the moon and back. Society also considers it worthwhile to find out more about man's origin. Even though this knowledge may not add to the monetary value of real output, it adds something to the utility of society.

Aside from the space program, most public research is aimed at increasing the value of output for society, that is, a dollar or monetary return. People value good health or the avoidance of the grim reaper before their time; hence, they will pay for medical research. Society places a value on a clean environment, so it supports research on ways of achieving this goal without giving up the goods and services that contribute to pollution. Most basic research, such as the work in physics, chemistry, biology, and mathematics, may not be aimed at a specific problem, but it is anticipated that the knowledge produced will somehow have a monetary value.

Measuring the monetary value of public research is a difficult problem, and much work remains to be done in this area. Unless quantitative measures are available, decisions to allocate public research will have to be made from purely subjective criteria or historical precedence, neither of which guarantees that society gets the most for its money.

AGRICULTURAL RESEARCH

We include a separate discussion of agricultural research for two reasons: (1) it is an area where some progress has been made in estimating social returns, and (2) there is widespread misunderstanding about who benefits from this research.

The nation's agricultural research is done about equally by farm supply firms-including seed, chemical, and machinery companies and by agricultural experiment stations. The latter are funded by taxes. Private firms conduct research that can be incorporated into a product. A firm must capture a return on its investment, or else it would not pay to invest. Agricultural experiment stations conduct the agricultural research that private firms do not find profitable but, nevertheless, provides a return to society.

The overall objective of agricultural research, whether private or public, is to increase the productive capacity of farmers. The output of such research includes new, higher-yielding crop varieties; breeding and disease-control advances to make livestock and poultry more efficient converters of feed; new inputs such as herbicides and pesticides; new and improved machines; and better management practices for farmers.

As pointed out in Chapter 12, new technology increases, or shifts to the right, the supply curve of individual producers and the industry, as shown in Figure 27–3. For a given price, producers will put more on the market or will sell a given amount for a lower price because their unit costs are lower.

The increase in productive efficiency and hence the increase in product supply, brought about by agricultural research, increases the total value of agricultural output for a given amount of traditional resources such as land, labor, and capital. In other words, by producing knowledge and new, more productive inputs, society obtains more output from its scarce resources. The annual value of this additional output to society is illustrated in Figure 27–3 by the shaded area lying between S_0 and S_1, bounded on the top by the demand for agricultural products.

Supply curve S_0 in Figure 27–3 represents what the supply of agricultural output would be without new technology. By measuring the increase in the productive efficiency of agriculture, economists have determined the location of S_1 for a given year. The difference between these two curves, therefore, represents the annual value of output attributable to agricultural research.

By comparing the annual expenditure on research with the value of extra output attributable to research, economists have obtained estimates of its internal rate of return. The procedure is the same as computing the rate of return to education. In this case, the cash outflows are expenditures on agricultural research (industrial and public). The cash inflows are the value of additional output obtained from agricultural research—the value of the shaded area in Figure 27–3.

Estimates of the *marginal* internal rate of return to additional investment in agriculture research in the United States are 40 to 50 percent.[2] It is though the nation places over $2 billion per year (the recent annual investment in agricultural research and extension services) in a savings account and reaps a 40 to 50 percent return. This is a high-payoff investment.

---

2 George Norton and Jeffrey Davis, "Evaluating the Returns to Agricultural Research: A Review," *American Journal of Agricultural Economics* 63, no. 4 (November, 1981) pp. 685-99.

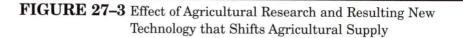

FIGURE 27–3 Effect of Agricultural Research and Resulting New Technology that Shifts Agricultural Supply

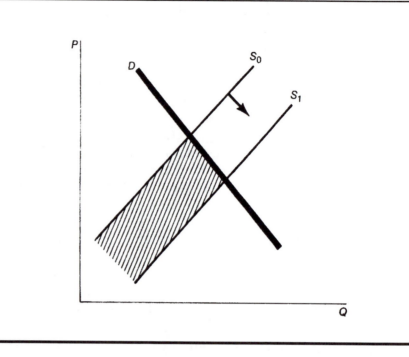

This leads to a second major point. The long-run beneficiaries of agricultural research are mainly consumers of farm products, rather than farmers. Of course, farmers benefit as consumers along with everyone else. Consumers benefit from agricultural research because the increase in productive efficiency shifts the supply of agricultural products to the right, which increases food output and reduces food prices below what they would otherwise be. The reduction in food prices benefits low-income people more than high-income individuals because the former spend a larger share of their income on food. Also, the major portion of agricultural research conducted in the public sector is paid for by taxes from middle- and high-income people. Thus, agricultural research reduces the inequality of living standards between income levels. It is equivalent to achieving more equality of incomes.

Many people argue, however, that food prices are not cheap, judging from current supermarket prices. But, one must look at the real cost of food—the proportion of a country's resources devoted to food production. Currently, Americans spend less than 15 percent of their income on food. Contrast this to most less-developed countries, where food often accounts for 70 to 80 percent of a family's budget.

At the turn of the century, U.S. citizens spent almost 40 percent of their income on food. A nation with an unproductive agricultural sector must devote many resources to food production. As agricultural productivity increases, more people leave agriculture to produce other things that make life more interesting and enjoyable. If two-thirds of a nation's population is required to produce food, modern conveniences such as reasonably priced automobiles, adequate medical care, and labor-saving appliances cannot be produced. Life might have been simpler when most people were farmers, but few people today would trade their current standard of living for the past.

The substantial decline in the proportion of incomes devoted to food in the United States understates the decline in the real price of food if we remember the quality improvement that has occurred over the years and the increased amount of services purchased with food nowadays. There are two dimensions to the increase in quality: (1) the increase in the wholesomeness of food, meaning the reduction in disease and insect damage, and (2) the greater share of the nation's food derived from animal sources. Both aspects of quality improvement require more resources and increase the cost of food. Similarly, the purchase of services such as those embodied in bakery bread, cake mixes, and dressed, cut, and frozen meats cost money and add to food bills. If U.S. consumers were willing to buy food of the same quality and with the same amount of services as in years past, or as exists in less-developed countries, they would spend even less of their income on food. Of course, there is nothing wrong with people wanting to spend some of their increased purchasing power on higher-quality food and more services.

This is not to say that agricultural research can take sole credit for economic development. Other knowledge also is required to produce the variety of modern goods and services that raise the standard of living. But as developing nations are learning, little progress can be made without technological advances in agriculture.

SOCIAL COSTS OF NEW TECHNOLOGY

There is a growing concern in the United States and other highly developed nations that the true cost of research to produce new knowledge and technology may exceed expenditures for research. One concern is the movement of people between occupations and areas. If new technology makes a job obsolete, what is the social cost of having the person who held the job move to another occupation in another location?

It is fairly easy to measure moving costs, but there are other considerations. People who move must leave family, friends, and familiar ways of living for the unknown. Some find moving an exciting experience; others dread it. The largest case is the huge rural-to-urban migration that has occurred in the United States. The increased concentration of population in urban areas has contributed to many problems: air and water pollution and congestion of transportation systems and housing.

Without new technology would these problems disappear? Perhaps. But, problems have always plagued mankind. Consider the disease, isolation, and long hours of drudgery both in the home and on the job with which our ancestors had to contend. Even pollution existed in those days. Imagine the smell in the cities when vehicles were horse-drawn, or the smoke and soot that spewed out when coal was the main source of heat and power. Some of the worst pollution in the world exists in countries that have experienced little advance in technology. When dealing with present-day problems, we tend to visualize things as we want to see them without regard for their historical background.

QUESTIONS

1. How is research similar to and how is it different from conventional types of investment?

2. a. Differentiate between basic and applied research.

   b. Who does basic research? Who does applied research?

3. How does research benefit society?

4. How does R&D increase profits of private firms?

5. It is sometimes argued that private firms deliberately suppress technological innovations resulting from R&D to maintain the value of assets that utilize older technology. Evaluate this argument.

6. a. Would you expect the social return to private R&D to be equal to the private return? Explain.

   b. Would your answer to question 6a imply anything about whether private firms will invest the optimal amount of funds in R&D each year? Explain.

7. a. How does agricultural research affect the food supply?

   b. If the demand for agricultural products is inelastic, how does agricultural research affect the total revenue received by farmers from the sale of their products?

SELF-TEST

1. A basic prerequisite for the accumulation of knowledge is:
   a. verbal and written communication.
   b. full time research people.
   c. the concept of hybridization.
   d. population growth.

2. In the early stages of civilization, the production of knowledge:
   a. did not exist.
   b. proved to be of little practical value.
   c. came as a by-product of daily activities.
   d. was the exclusive domain of the Greeks and Romans.

3. During the 20th century most new knowledge came into existence as a result of:
   a. happy accident.
   b. organized research.
   c. the daily activities of farmers, workers, and managers.
   d. skilled artisans.

4. The production of new knowledge:
   a. is not possible because knowledge exists, it cannot be produced.
   b. is characterized by inputs and an output.
   c. is subject to a certain outcome.
   d. is a free gift of nature.

5. As more and more new knowledge is produced, the MPP of scientific effort:
   a. will increase.
   b. will decrease.
   c. will remain constant.
   d. may increase, decrease, or remain constant, no one knows.

6. Which of the following characteristics distinguishes research from more conventional production activities?
   a. is costless
   b. there is no blueprint to follow
   c. is routine
   d. utilizes both labor and capital

7. Basic research:
   a. is of little use or practical value.
   b. must always precede applied research.
   c. is concerned with unlocking the secrets of nature.
   d. is carried on primarily by business firms.

8. Applied research:
   a. attempts to solve a problem or discover a specific unknown.
   b. is concerned with building prototypes.
   c. is the exclusive domain of public institutions.
   d. cannot yield basic knowledge.

9. Business firms conduct R&D to:

a. fulfill their social obligation.

b. increase employment.

c. increase unemployment.

d. increase profits.

10. R&D increases a firm's profits by _____ demand and/or _____ costs.

a. decreasing; decreasing

b. increasing; increasing

c. increasing; decreasing

d. decreasing; increasing

11. Patent laws exist to:

a. protect consumers.

b. encourage R&D.

c. discourage R&D.

d. encourage litigation.

12. Other things equal, large firms:

a. will produce an innovation at a smaller cost than small firms.

b. are less likely to conduct R&D than small firms.

c. can expect to reap a larger return to an innovation than can a small firm.

d. will produce an innovation at a higher cost than small firms.

13. Publicly sponsored research attempts to produce knowledge that:

a. has a low social but high private return.

b. has a better chance of yielding a payoff than privately funded research.

c. has a low private but a high social return.

d. is primarily for military uses.

14. Agricultural research has the effect of _____ the _____ of (for) food.

a. increasing; demand

b. increasing; supply

c. decreasing; demand

d. decreasing; supply

15. Estimates reveal that the rate of return to investment in agricultural research is in the range of:

a. 5 to 10 percent.

b. 10 to 15 percent.

c. 20 to 30 percent.

d. 40 to 50 percent.

16. If the demand for food is inelastic, agricultural research _____ the total revenue received by farmers.

a. increases

b. decreases

c. has no effect on

Glossary

A

annual cost of capital Interest plus depreciation.

applied research Research aimed at solving a specific problem.

average-cost pricing Product price is set equal to average total cost plus a markup for profit.

average fixed cost Total fixed cost divided by output.

average physical product Output divided by the input.

average total cost Total cost divided by output.

average variable cost Total variable cost divided by output.

B

basic research Unlocking the secrets of nature without having a specific use in mind.

benefit/cost ratio The ratio of discounted present value (DPV) over the investment cost.

budget line A line showing various combinations of two goods that cost a given amount of money. Always a straight downward-sloping line regardless of the degree of substitution between the two goods.

C

capital Durable or long-lasting inputs such as buildings or machines that yield a stream of services over time.

capitalized The increase in the price of an asset such as land due to expected pure profits in the future.

capitalized value The amount a piece of property is worth based on its annual net returns which are assumed to continue indefinitely.

cartel When two or more firms collude and act as if they are a single firm—a monopoly. In the United States, this is illegal.

cash-flow table Contains expected costs and returns of an investment.

ceiling prices Maintaining the price of a good below the market equilibrium level. Sometimes called price controls; they cause shortages.

centrally planned economy Another name of a Communist or socialist society whose resources are owned and controlled by the central government. The resources are allocated by a central planning committee.

collective bargaining Contractual negotiations between a union and an employer specifying wages and working conditions. The objective is to set wages higher than would exist in a free-market equilibrium.

complementary input It increases the MPP of another input when more of the complement is used.

complements in consumption Demand decreases when the price of a complement increases They exhibit a negative cross elasticity of demand.

complements in production The quantity supplied of one good increases when the price of the other good increases. They exhibit a positive cross elasticity of supply.

concave to the origin A line that bends out from the origin and decreases at an increasing rate.

conglomerate A large firm that owns or controls other firms that may be in different industries.

constant-cost industry Long-run average total cost curve of the average firm does not shift as industry expands. Exhibits a perfectly elastic long-run supply.

constant opportunity cost The amount of one good that is given up to obtain an additional unit of another good remains the same as the maximum output of the good being increased is approached.

constant returns to scale Long-run average total cost remains constant as the firm's size increases; corresponds to horizontal portion of the LRATC curve.

consumer sovereignty Where the aim of production is to satisfy the wants of consumers.

convex to the origin A line that bends in toward the origin and decreases at a decreasing rate.

cost-minimizing rule All P/MPP ratios are equal.

craft union A union representing workers in a specific craft such as plumbers, electricians, and bricklayers; usually skilled workers.

cross elasticity of demand Percent change in quantity demanded of one good resulting from a one-percent change in the price of a related good.

cross elasticity of supply Percentage change in the quantity supplied of one product resulting from a one-percent change in the price of another product.

curvilinear negative relationship A curved, downward-sloping line that decreases at either an increasing or a decreasing rate.

curvilinear positive relationship A curved, upward-sloping line that increases at either an increasing or decreasing rate.

D

dead weight loss or social cost The reduction in the value of output to society resulting from the movement of resources to lower-value uses.

debt capital Capital obtained from borrowing.

decreasing cost industry Long-run average total cost curve of the average firm shifts down as industry expands. Can occur because of a decrease in the prices of inputs as suppliers are able to capture scale economies. Long-run supply slopes down.

demand A negative relationship between price and quantity.

demand facing a monopoly It shows the quantities its customers will buy at various prices; it is the same as the market demand curve for the product sold by the monopoly.

demand facing the perfectly competitive firms A horizontal line corresponding to the market price of the product.

depreciation A decrease in the value of an asset over time.

development Experimentation with new knowledge to construct a product or accomplish a task.

discounted present value (DPV) The present value of a sum of money forthcoming in the future, calculated by dividing the amount forthcoming by $(1 + r)^n$ where r is the rate of interest and n is the number of years in the future the money will be obtained.

diseconomies of scale Long-run average total cost increases as the firm increases in size; corresponds to upward-sloping portion of the LRATC curve.

E

economic decisions Choosing among alternatives. Must be made at every level of society because of scarcity.

economic efficiency Maximization of the value of output to society for a given amount of resources. Requires: (1) maximum technical efficiency, (2) minimum costs, and (3) output of each firm corresponds to the point where product price equals marginal cost.

economic growth Sustained increase in the real output of society.

economies of scale A reduction in long-run average total cost as the firm expands in size; corresponds to the downward-sloping portion of the LRATC curve.

elasticity of supply Percentage change in quantity supplied resulting from a one-percent change in price of the product.

Engel curve Shows the relationship between expenditures on food and family income.

equilibrium price The price where sellers place on the market the exact quantity that buyers will take off the market. Corresponds to the intersection of the demand and supply curves.

equity capital Capital provided by the owners of the firm.

explicit costs Out-of-pocket expenses.

external economies A reduction in the LRATC of the individual firm as the industry expands.

F

fixed costs They remain constant at all levels of output.

fixed proportions No substitution is possible. They are represented by L-shaped isoquants.

G

gestation period The time interval between the expenditure on an asset and when it begins to pay off.

H

high rate of time preference A strong desire to consume now rather than later.

hostile takeover The acquisition of one firm by another firm or person against the wishes of the acquired firm's management.

household production Production of utility from any activity not included in human capital or intermediate goods production.

human capital Knowledge and skills possessed by human beings.

human capital production Activities such as attending classes and studying.

I

imperfect competition Each firm has some control over the price it charges and faces a downward-sloping demand curve.

imperfect substitutes in consumption More of the abundant good must be used to compensate for each unit reduction in the scarce good to maintain a given level of utility. They are represented by indifference curves that are convex to the origin.

imperfect substitutes in production More of the abundant input must be obtained to give up successive units of the scarce input to maintain a given level of output. Illustrated by isoquants that are convex to the origin.

implicit costs The charge to the firm for the resources provided by the owner(s) of the firm.

income effect The change in purchasing power of a given amount of money income when the price of a product changes. Also pertains to the supply of labor. When wage increases, workers have more income to buy leisure and, therefore, may work less.

income elasticity of demand Percent change in demand resulting from a one-percent change in money income.

increase (decrease) in demand Shift to the right (left) of the demand curve.

increase (decrease) in supply Shift to the right (left) of the supply curve.

increasing-cost industry Long-run average total cost curve of the average firm shifts upward as the industry expands. Long-run supply slopes upward.

increasing opportunity cost The amount of one good that is given up to obtain an additional unit of another good becomes larger and larger as the maximum output of the good being increased is approached.

indifference curve A line showing various combinations of two goods that yield a constant level of satisfaction or utility.

indifference map A collection of indifference curves. Curves up and to the right show higher levels of satisfaction than those closer to the origin.

industrial union A union representing all workers in an industry such as the steelworkers or the auto workers.

inferior goods Goods that people buy less of when their incomes increase; they exhibit a negative income elasticity.

intermediate goods production Part-time employment.

internal rate of return (IRR) The rate of interest that makes the DPV of future returns equal to the investment cost.

isocost A straight, downward-sloping line that shows various combinations of two inputs that can be purchased with a given sum of money.

isoquant A line showing various combinations of two inputs that produce a given level of output.

L

law of diminishing marginal utility Beyond some point the additional satisfaction received from consuming an additional unit of a good will become less and less holding constant the amounts of all other items consumed.

law of diminishing returns Diminishing marginal physical product.

linear negative relationship A straight, downward-sloping line.

linear positive relationship A straight, upward-sloping line.

long run Period of time long enough to change the level of fixed inputs or number of firms.

long-run adjustment The entry (exit) of new firms or resources in response to pure profits (losses).

long-run average total cost (LRATC) curve An envelope of all possible short-run ATC curves that shows the lowest cost of producing a given level of output.

long-run supply Consists of minimum points of the average firm's LRATC curve. Slopes up for an increasing-cost industry, is horizontal for a constant-cost industry, and slopes down for a decreasing-cost industry.

low rate of time preference A willingness to postpone consumption—to save.

M

macroeconomics Concerned mainly with the problems of unemployment and inflation, and what can be done to avoid or alleviate these problems.

marginal cost The additional cost incurred by producing one more unit of output.

marginal physical product The additional output obtained from one additional unit of the input.

marginal revenue The additional revenue earned by selling one more unit of output; less than price for a firm facing a downward-sloping demand curve.

marginal revenue product (MRP) The same as VMP; a label designating the demand for labor by an imperfectly competitive seller of products.

marginal unit The unit added to or subtracted from the top of whatever is being considered.

marginal utility The additional satisfaction received by consuming one more unit of a good or service.

market demand Summation at each price of the quantities demanded by all buyers in the market.

market economy Decentralized economic decision making by consumers and producers. Market price plays a key role in answering the three economic questions.

market failure The discharge of pollutants into the environment without accounting for the cost to society. Also occurs in the public sector and non-market economies.

market supply The summation, at each price, of the quantities supplied by all the producers or suppliers in the market.

microeconomics Deals primarily with the economic decisions of households and businesses and with the pricing of goods and services as well as resources.

minimum wage laws State and federal laws stipulating the minimum wage that an employer must pay.

monetary returns Additional earnings due to added schooling.

monopolistic competition An industry consisting of small or medium-size firms each selling a small share of the market and differentiated products.

monopsony One buyer of an input.

N

negative relationship The variables change in opposite directions; when one increases the other decreases.

nominal rate of interest The interest rate quoted on loans or savings accounts.

nonhuman capital Resources such as machines, tools, computers, and buildings.

nonmonetary returns Additional utility obtained from schooling above what is obtained by higher earnings.

O

oligopoly A market where a few large firms supply a major share of the market. Oligopolies can sell either homogeneous or heterogeneous products.

oligopsony Few buyers of an input.

opportunity cost That which is given up to obtain more of something else.

other things equal Allows the impact of events to be considered one at a time.

P

perfect complements Goods that are used together in a fixed ratio. No substitution is possible. Illustrated by L-shaped indifference curves.

perfect substitutes in consumption The amount of one good required to compensate for giving up successive units of another good remains constant at all combinations of the two. Illustrated by indifference curves that are straight, downward-sloping lines.

perfect substitutes in production The amount of one input required to compensate for a unit reduction in another input remains constant at all combinations of the two inputs. They are represented by isoquants that are straight downward-sloping lines.

perfectly competitive firm A firm that takes the price of its product as given. Such a firm sells a small share of the market and sells a product undifferentiated from the product of other firms in the industry.

perfectly competitive industry An industry made up of perfectly competitive firms. Agriculture.

personal costs of education Includes forgone earnings. tuition, and books and supplies.

personal returns to education Monetary plus nonmonetary returns.

positive relationship Both variables change in the same direction; both either increase or decrease.

price-determined costs The revaluation of assets due to pure profits or losses.

price-determining costs Changes in product price due to shift in the MC and ATC curves.

price elasticity of demand Percent change in quantity resulting from a one-percent change in price.

price leadership Market price is set by the dominant firm.

price of present consumption The amount of future consumption given up to consume one more dollar today.

price theory A name given to microeconomics in more advanced courses.

prime rate Interest rate paid by large, low-risk borrowers.

product differentiation Products that have different characteristics, different services attached, or are sold in different locations.

production Any activity that creates present and/or future utility.

production function A physical relationship between inputs and output.

production possibilities curve A line showing various combinations of two goods that can be produced with a given amount of resources.

production possibilities schedule A table showing various possible combinations of two goods that can be produced from a given amount of resources.

profit-maximizing price The point on the demand curve that corresponds to the profit-maximizing quantity.

profit-maximizing quantity It corresponds to the point where MR = MC.

profit-maximizing rule Produce that level of output where MR = MC.

profits The excess of total sales over total costs.

public costs of education Personal costs plus the tax money that pays for part of students' education.

public goods Produced and/or distributed by governments for society's use.

public sector Comprises federal, state, and local governments.

public utilities Firms given exclusive right to supply a good or service to avoid duplication of facilities. They are regulated by government rather than by competition.

pure monopoly A single firm sells the entire output of the industry.

Q

quantity demanded Refers to a particular quantity on a specific demand curve

quantity supplied Refers to a particular quantity on a specific supply curve.

R

rate of return The number of cents each dollar earns per year.

real rate of interest The nominal rate of interest minus the rate of inflation.

research A production activity having inputs and an output. Produces knowledge.

S

scarcity Exists because resources are limited in supply and human wants exceed our ability to produce goods and services.

short run Period of time too short to change the level of fixed inputs such as land and buildings or the number of firms.

shortage Quantity supplied is less than quantity demanded at that price; occurs if price is below equilibrium.

slope of a line Change in the vertical axis divided by change in the horizontal axis, or rise over run.

social cost The cost to society of producing a product over and above the cost borne by the firm; it is associated with pollution.

social cost of monopoly The loss in value of output to society because the value of the marginal unit sold by a monopoly exceeds its opportunity cost at its profit-maximizing quantity.

social returns to education Benefits received by people who do not receive the education.

social returns to research The increase in value of output to society because of research.

stage I MPP exceeds APP, and APP is pulled up.

stage II MPP less than APP, and APP is pulled down.

stage III MPP is negative.

substitute input It decreases the MPP of another input when more of the substitute is used.

substitutes in consumption Demand increases when the price of a substitute increases.

substitutes in production Supply decreases when the price of a substitute increases.

substitution effect The change in the amount of a good purchase due to a change in relative prices. Also pertains to labor supply. When wage increases, the opportunity cost of leisure increases. Thus, workers have an incentive to substitute work for leisure, that is, to work more.

superior goods Goods that people buy more of when their incomes increase; they exhibit a positive income elasticity.

supply A positive relationship between price and quantity.

support prices Maintaining the price of a good above its market equilibrium; they cause surpluses.

surplus Quantity supplied is greater than quantity demanded at that price; occurs if price is above equilibrium.

T

technical diseconomies An increase in the LRATC of the individual firm as the industry expands due to increased technical difficulties such as disposing of waste material.

the three economic questions (1) What and how much of each good to produce, (2) How to produce each good, and (3) For whom?

theory Simplification or abstraction of the real world. Contains the important information bearing on a decision or problem.

total physical product (TPP) Physical units of output.

transformation curve Another name for a production possibilities curve.

U

util A unit of satisfaction.

utility Another name for satisfaction.

utility-maximizing rule Equalized MU/P ratios (marginal utility per dollar) for all goods and services available for purchase.

V

variable costs They vary with the level of output.

value of the marginal product (VMP) The value of the additional output obtained by adding one more unit of an input. It corresponds to the demand for labor for a perfectly competitive seller of products.

Index